CATHOLIC AND REFORMED
SELECTED THEOLOGICAL WRITINGS
OF JOHN WILLIAMSON NEVIN

Edited by

Charles Yrigoyen, Jr.

and

George H. Bricker

THE PICKWICK PRESS

Pittsburgh, Pennsylvania

1978

Library of Congress Cataloging in Publication Data

Nevin, John Williamson, 1803-1886.
  Catholic and Reformed.

  (Pittsburgh original texts & translations series ; 3)
  Includes bibliographical references.
  1.   Reformed Church in the United States--Doctrinal
and controversial works--Collected works. 2.   Theology--
Collected works--19th century. 3.   Mercersburg theology
--Collected works. I.   Yrigoyen, Charles, 1937-
II.   Bricker, George H.   III.   Title.
BX9559.N48   1978   230'.5'733   78-2567
ISBN 0-915138-37-9

J. W. Nevin

CONTENTS

FOREWORD

Others have assisted us in bringing together this collection of materials. We would be remiss if we did not acknowledge their contributions. Above all, we are grateful to Dikran Y. Hadidian, General Editor, who encouraged us to begin and to complete the volume. Mrs. Jane Vandevort graciously accepted the typing assignment and has devoted her patient and expert care to it. Albright College through its Academic Dean, Dr. Robert E. McBride, provided financial assistance for the typescript. We are also profoundly aware of teachers, scholars, and colleagues, too many to mention by name, who have enriched our understanding of the Mercersburg Theology and John Williamson Nevin. They have helped us to appreciate this important chapter in American religious history. Perhaps more than anyone else they deserve our deepest gratitude.

Charles Yrigoyen, Jr.
Albright College

George H. Bricker
Lancaster Theological Seminary

INTRODUCTION

The place of the Mercersburg Theology in American religious history has been widely recognized. Some mention of it
is found in almost every major historical survey of the religious development of the nation published in the last two or
three decades. It is usually viewed as one of the unique
movements in 19th century American Protestantism, principally
because it challenged many of the prevailing theological ideas
and practices of the time. Two recent surveys of American
religious history have described it as a "theologically and
liturgically creative high church movement"[1] and as the "most
creative manifestation of the Catholic tendency" among 19th
century American Protestants.[2]

In addition to general references in the survey literature
there have been several specialized studies which have examined
the origins and development of the Mercersburg Theology as well
as its contribution to American Christianity in general and the
German Reformed Church in particular. Some of these have been
published as volumes or articles.[3] Others have remained in unpublished form.[4] The secondary sources fulfill their function
by describing, contextualizing, and analyzing the movement as a
whole or one particular facet of its evolution. They establish
a framework within which we may critically and appreciatively
read the original documents which transmit the germinal ideas
of the Mercersburg Theology. In a variety of books, pamphlets,
denominational publications, correspondence, and their own
quarterly journal, the *Mercersburg Review,* the progenitors of
the movement, John Williamson Nevin and Philip Schaff, and
their followers circulated their views. The primary source
material is voluminous. Some of it has been made available in

1

such collections as the uncompleted "Lancaster Series on the Mercersburg Theology"[5] and James H. Nichols' *The Mercersburg Theology*.[6]

There is a continuing need to publish more of the essential primary materials. There are at least two reasons why this is so. First, there is no substitute for examining the original documents themselves. They illuminate the various themes and the logic of Mercersburg thought in a manner which the secondary works can only summarize at best. They help us to tune in to the movement in a more comprehensive fashion. Second, many of the issues with which the Mercersburg men dealt are still disputed in our day and will be for some time to come. Ecclesiology, liturgy, Christology, evangelism and revivalism are hardly insignificant concerns for our age or any other! While the Mercersburg scholars may not have intentionally anticipated the theological problems of our day and while their views are surely not a panacea, nevertheless, they shed important light on our way. For these reasons we are pleased to bring to your attention this volume which contains some of the notable writings of John Williamson Nevin which are no longer accessible to many. A second volume containing selections from the writings of Philip Schaff is expected to follow.

John Williamson Nevin (1803-1886) was one of the most influential and controversial figures in the German Reformed Church in America in the 19th century. To a limited extent his views also circulated among a wider body of American Protestants usually stirring mixed and vigorous responses. These were occasioned because Nevin criticized many of the most popular forms of American Protestant religion of his era, especially from 1843 until 1860, the years when the Mercersburg Theology was being formulated. His ideas were usually issued in a style which clearly divided sympathizers from opponents. He rarely, if ever, avoided conflict and argument. He seemed always ready to attack defective religion and just as prepared to defend his own beliefs. With rare exception his views originated in keen analysis and careful thought.

Nevin was born into and raised by a Scotch-Irish Presbyterian family in the Cumberland Valley of Pennsylvania. He was a graduate of Union College near Schenectady, New York, and Princeton Theological Seminary from which he received a degree in 1826. In addition to his general academic excellence at Princeton, Nevin displayed unusual competence in his mastery of the Hebrew language. When one of his Princeton professors, Charles Hodge, temporarily left the seminary to study in Europe for two years, Nevin was invited to teach his biblical courses. He gladly accepted.

The Carlisle Presbytery granted Nevin his license to preach in 1828. In the same year he accepted an invitation to teach in the infant Western Theological Seminary (Presbyterian) at Allegheny near Pittsburgh, Pennsylvania. He arrived at his new post in 1829 and spent the next decade there in continued study and teaching. He described his tenure at Western as a period of personal assessment in which he recognized certain theological and historical deficiencies and took measures to correct them. His study of several prominent German theologians, e.g. Isaac Dorner and J. A. W. Neander, begun at Princeton and continued at Western, was beneficial to that task. Serious internal financial difficulties at Western and growing theological tension within Presbyterianism resulted in Nevin's resignation in 1839.

While Nevin was still a student at Princeton the German Reformed Church had begun a small seminary. It was founded in 1825 at Carlisle, Pennsylvania. In 1829 it was moved to York and then to Mercersburg in 1837. In 1839 the seminary had two professors, Lewis Mayer (1783-1849) and Frederick Augustus Rauch (1806-1841). Mayer's failing health and his theological

incompatibility with Rauch led to his resignation in the fall
of 1839. With the strong recommendation of two prominent
clergymen in the German Reformed Church, S. R. Fisher and
B. S. Schneck, its Synod elected John Williamson Nevin to succeed Mayer as Professor of Theology. At the time Nevin was
known for his extraordinary competence as a theologian and
biblical scholar, well versed in German thought, and sympa-
thetic to the tradition of the German Reformed Church. He
later wrote that he considered himself kin to the German people
because he had been raised among them and was familiar with
their modes of life and thought.

Nevin arrived in Mercersburg in the spring of 1840 and
began his teaching duties. He soon discovered major areas of
common interest and agreement between himself and Rauch. He
had a profound regard for Rauch's Christian commitment and
theological acumen. Rauch's sudden death in March, 1841
created a serious void in the lives of both the seminary and
John Williamson Nevin. Until Philip Schaff joined the faculty
in 1844 Nevin was almost solely responsible for the educational
program of the seminary. The heavy demands of the seminary's
life, its financial instability, and his own theological struggles resulted in Nevin's resignation from the seminary faculty
in 1851. He remained active in the German Reformed Church,
however, especially on the committee to prepare a liturgy for
the denomination which began its work in 1856.

In 1861 Nevin was appointed Professor of Philosophy, History and Aesthetics at Franklin and Marshall College in Lancaster, Pennsylvania. Five years later he became President of the
college, a post he held until his retirement in 1876. Nevin's
life stretched another decade during which both his mind and
pen remained active with regard to theological matters. He
died on June 6, 1886.

The scope of Nevin's theological insights cannot be easily

summarized. We can, however, mention a few of his concerns
which bear on the selections to follow.

When Nevin began his work at Mercersburg he became alarmed
at the drift of the German Reformed Church and American Protestantism away from biblical faith, the spirit of the early
church, and the insights of the Reformation. In his estimation
the German Reformed Church partook of the general malaise of
American Protestantism. It was unchurchly, unhistorical, and
unsacramental. It was based on a faulty Christology.

The Anxious Bench marked the beginning of Nevin's quarrel
with many of his brethren. In it he fired a broadside at the
most popular form of American religion in the second decade of
the 19th century, "New Measures" revivalism, developed by
Charles Grandison Finney (1792-1875). Nevin later wrote:

> Finneyism, as it used to be called, was not to my
> taste; although I was slow and cautious in my judg-
> ment with regard to its exhibitions; because I
> made large account in fact of experimental piety,
> and also of religious awakenings in what I conceived
> to be their proper character. It was not the earnest-
> ness of this system that I disliked; but what seemed
> to me to be too generally the mechanical and super-
> ficial character of its earnestness. Its professional
> machinery, its stage dramatic way, its business-like
> way of doing up religion in whole and short order, and
> then being done with it - - all made me feel that it
> was at best a most unreliable mode of carrying forward
> the work and kingdom of God.[7]

Not only was revivalistic religion of the New Measures
type superficial and spiritually inferior, it was also responsible for the growing sectarianism among American Protestants
in the first half of the 19th century. The German Reformed
Church had experienced the "sect spirit" in such unpleasant
ways as John Winebrenner's (1797-1860) exodus to found the
Church of God in 1830, an event deeply lamented by Nevin.[8]

Revivalism was unchurchly. It was divisive. It did not acknowledge the importance and value of liturgy as itself a vehicle for God's grace. It fostered an anemic interpretation of the sacraments. It had strayed far from the genius of the apostolic and post-apostolic church. It led to an inadequate understanding of the historical evolution of the Christian church. The indictment was intense and unceasing! Much of the problem was ultimately located in a wrong Christology. American Protestants did not appreciate the real meaning of the Incarnation and its implications for ecclesiology, soteriology, liturgy, the sacraments, etc. Nevin's treatment of these areas was not merely critical. He also sought to recover what he felt were the best doctrinal formulations of these ideas based upon biblical evidence and historical tradition. He found in Philip Schaff a willing ally in his criticism and proposals. The fruit of their labors was the Mercersburg Theology.

NOTES TO THE INTRODUCTION

1. Robert T. Handy, *A History of the Churches in the United States and Canada* (New York: Oxford University Press, 1977), p. 206.

2. Sydney E. Ahlstrom, *A Religious History of the American People* (New Haven: Yale University Press, 1972), 615.

3. James H. Nichols, *Romanticism in American Theology* (Chicago: The University of Chicago Press, 1961), remains the best general volume on the Mercersburg Theology. Jack Martin Maxwell, *Worship and Reformed Theology: The Liturgical Lessons of Mercersburg* (Pittsburgh: The Pickwick Press, 1976), is the most recent volume and has made a unique and valuable contribution to this literature.

4. E. g. John Charles Meyer, "Philip Schaff's Concept of Organic Historiography as Related to the Development of Doctrine: A Catholic Appraisal" (unpublished Ph.D. dissertation, The Catholic University of America, 1968) and John T. Cordoue, "The Ecclesiology of John Williamson Nevin: A Catholic Appraisal" (unpublished Ph.D. dissertation, The Catholic University of America, 1968).

5. Two volumes of the projected series of six were published. They included: Philip Schaff, *The Principle of Protestantism,* edited by Bard Thompson and George H. Bricker (Philadelphia: United Church Press, 1964) and John W. Nevin, *The Mystical Presence and Other Writings on the Eucharist,* edited by Bard Thompson and George H. Bricker (Philadelphia: United Church Press, 1966).

6. (New York: Oxford University Press, 1966).

7. John Williamson Nevin, *My Own Life: the Earlier Years* (Lancaster: Papers of the Eastern Chapter, Historical Society of the Evangelical and Reformed Church, 1964), p. 125.

8. Richard Kern, *John Winebrenner: Nineteenth Century Reformer* (Harrisburg: Central Publishing House, 1974), especially Chapter 5, is helpful for understanding the Nevin-Winebrenner controversy.

EDITORIAL INTRODUCTION TO *THE ANXIOUS BENCH*

The Anxious Bench, published in 1843, was Nevin's opening
volley against the revivalistic techniques developed by Charles
G. Finney popularly known as the "New Measures." It disturbed
Nevin that some of the congregations of the German Reformed
Church had incorporated these methods into their ministry. John
Winebrenner, who later founded the Church of God, was one of
the earliest German Reformed pastors to do so. The Race Street
congregation, Philadelphia, actually invited Finney to lead a
revival for them in 1828-1829 in which the New Measures played
an important role. Denominational periodicals reveal that this
type of revivalism spread within the denomination in the 1830's.

Nevin was incensed that German Reformed clergy and laity
would abandon a sound approach to Christianity for one so
totally inadequate for the times and so false to the essential
nature of Christian Faith. He referred to the former as the
"system of the catechism" and to the latter as the "system of
the bench."

Nevin's tract, an expansion of lectures on pastoral theology delivered to his seminary students, met with considerable
opposition both within and outside the denomination. For
several years many of the German Reformed clergy and congregation engaged in bitter diatribe concerning the issues raised by
Nevin. A record of the debate has been preserved in the denominational publications.

In 1844 Nevin issued a second edition of *The Anxious
Bench*. It was revised, enlarged, and carried Nevin's answers
to some of his critics. The text that follows reproduces the
material found in the second edition published in Chambersburg,
Pennsylvania, by the Publication Office of the German Reformed
Church.

A TRACT FOR THE TIMES.

THE
ANXIOUS BENCH

by

JOHN W. NEVIN, D.D.,

Professor of Theology in the Seminary of the Ger. Ref. Church

Second Edition,
Revised and Enlarged

Tekel. — *Daniel* v. 27.

Chambersburg, Pa.

Printed at the Publication Office of the German Ref. Church

. . . . .

1844

PREFACE TO THE SECOND EDITION

In coming before the public with a second edition of *The Anxious Bench,* it seems proper to introduce it with a short preface.

The publication, as was to be expected, has produced considerable excitement. At least half a dozen of replies to it, shorter or longer, have been announced in different quarters, proceeding from no less than five different religious denominations. Various assaults, in addition to this, have been made upon it from the pulpit; to say nothing of the innumerable reproaches it has been required to suffer in a more private way.

All this, however, calls for no very special notice in return. I am sorry to say that of all the published replies to the tract, which have come under my observation, not one is entitled to any respect, as an honest and intelligent argument on the other side. In no case has the question at issue been fairly accepted and candidly met. I do not feel myself required at all, then, to enter into a formal vindication of the tract, as assailed in those publications. I consider it to be in itself a full and triumphant answer to all they contain against it, in the way of objection or reproach. If permitted to speak for itself, by being seriously and attentively read, it may safely be left to plead its own cause. In such circumstances it would be idle to enter into a controversial review of the manifold misrepresentations, to which it has been subjected. The only proper reply to them is a republication of the tract itself.

With the reproaches that have been showered upon me personally, in different quarters, I have not allowed myself to be

9

much disturbed. I had looked for it all beforehand; knowing
well the spirit of the system with which I was called to deal.
I knew of course that I should be calumniated as an enemy to
revivals, and as an opposer of vital godliness. But I felt
satisfied at the same time that the calumny would, in due
season, correct itself, and recoil with disgrace on the heads
of those from whom it might proceed. It has begun to do so
already, and will continue to do so, no doubt, more and more.

Some have wondered that I did not take more pains to define my position with regard to revivals, by writing a chapter
on the subject, so as to cut off occasion for the reproach now
mentioned. But this would have been, in some measure, to justify and invite the wrong, which it was proposed to prevent.
There is gross insolence in the assumption that a man should
at all *need* to vindicate himself in this way, in venturing to
speak against the system of New Measures. And then, it is not
by formal protestations, when all is done, that the point, in
any such case, can be fully settled. A chapter on revivals
would be of little account in my tract if my own character,
and the whole spirit of the tract itself, were not such as to
show an honest zeal in favor of serious religion. The publications which have come out in reply to it, all affect an extraordinary interest in the subject of revivals, exhibited often
with a very blustering air; but in the case of some of them,
this pretension is utterly belied, to all who have the least
amount of spiritual discernment, by the tone of feeling with
which they are characterized throughout. They carry in them no
savor at all of the wisdom that cometh from above, no sympathy
whatever with the mind of Jesus Christ. The remark is made of
some of these publications, not of the whole of them indiscriminately.

Nor would any special protestation in favor of revivals be
of much account to guard the tract from being perversely used

by those who are in fact opposed to this precious interest.
The only true and proper provision against such abuse must be
found, if it exists at all, in the general spirit of the tract
itself. Let this be right, and it must be considered enough.
It may be perverted still; but men can pervert the Bible, too,
if they please.

Fears have been expressed that in the present position of
the German Churches particularly, the publication may operate
disastrously upon the interests of vital godliness. But in my
own view there is no good reason for any such fears. I believe
its operation has been salutary already, and trust it will be
found more salutary still in time to come. It has engaged
attention extensively to the subject of which it treats, and
is likely to go farther than anything that has appeared before,
in correcting the confusion and mystification in which it has
been so unhappily involved, in certain parts of the country, to
the great prejudice of religion. It may be hoped now that the
subject of New Measures will be so examined and understood,
that all shall come to make a proper distinction between the
system of the Anxious Bench and the power of evangelical godliness, working in its true forms. In the case of the German
Churches, this would be a result of the very highest consequence. If the present tract may open the way for its accomplishment, its mission will be one in which all the friends of
true religion in these Churches will have occasion to rejoice.

But instead of lending their help to secure this most
desirable object, the friends of the Anxious Bench seem concerned to maintain as long as possible the very mystification
that stands in its way. They tell us we must not speak against
New Measures, because this term is made to include, in some
parts of the country, revivals and other kindred interests; and
then, when we propose to correct this gross mistake, by proper
instruction, they set themselves with all their might to coun-

teract the attempt, and insist that the people shall be suffered to confound these different forms of religion as before.
Those who act thus are themselves enemies in fact to the cause
of revivals. From no other quarter has it been made to suffer
so seriously. Its greatest misfortune is, that it should lie
at the mercy of such hands.

It is with a very bad grace that reference is made occasionally by some to the idea of a *foreign* spirit in the tract,
as related to the German Churches. It is in full sympathy with
the true life of these Churches, as it stood in the beginning.
The charge of seeking to force a foreign spirit on them, lies
with clear right against the other side. The system of New
Measures has no affinity whatever with the life of the Reformation, as embodied in the *Augsburgh Confession* and the *Heidel-
bergh Catechism*. It could not have found any favor in the eyes
of Zwingli or Calvin. Luther would have denounced it in the
most unmerciful terms. His soul was too large, too deep, too
free, to hold communion with a style of religion so mechanical
and shallow. Those who are actively laboring to bring the
Church of Luther, in this country, into subjection to the system, cannot be said to be true to his memory or name. The
challenge, *Why are you a Lutheran?* is one which they would do
well seriously to consider. It is most certain that the interest they are pushing forward, in this view, is not Lutheranism
in any sense that agrees with the true historical life of the
Church, or of its most evangelical representatives in modern
Germany. It is another element altogether that surrounds us in
the writings of such men as Olshausen, Tholuck, Sartorious and
Neander. The system in question is in its principle and soul
neither Calvinism nor Lutheranism, but Wesleyan *Methodism*.
Those who are urging it upon the old German Churches, are in
fact doing as much as they can to turn them over into the arms
of Methodism. This may be done without any change of denomi-

national name. Already the *life* of Methodism, in this country,
is actively at work among other sects, which owe no fellowship
with it in form. So in the present case, names may continue to
stand as before; but they will be only as the garnished sepul-
chres of a glory that belonged to other days.

But is not Methodism Christianity? And is it not better
that the German Churches should rise in this form than not rise
at all? Most certainly so, I reply, if that be the only alternative. But that is *not* the only alternative. Their resurrection may just as well take place, in the type of their own
true, original, glorious life, as it is still to be found enshrined in their symbolical books. And whatever there may be
that is good in Methodism, this life of the Reformation I affirm to be immeasurably more excellent and sound. Wesley was a
small man as compared with Melancthon. Olshausen, with all his
mysticism, is a commentator of the inmost sanctuary in comparison with Adam Clark. If the original, distinctive life of the
Churches of the Reformation be not the object to be reached
after, in the efforts that are made to build up the interests
of German Christianity in this country, it were better to say
so at once openly and plainly. If we *must* have Methodism, let
us have it under its own proper title, and in its own proper
shape. Why keep up the walls of denominational partition in
such a case, with no distinctive spiritual being to uphold or
protect? A sect without a soul has no right to live. Zeal for
a separate denominational name that utters no separate religious *idea,* is the very essence of sectarian bigotry and
schism.

In opposing the Anxious Bench, I mean no disrespect, of
course, to the many excellent men, in different Churches, who
have given it their countenance. This has been done by some of
the best ministers in the land, for whom I entertain the very
highest regard. Not a few are to be found who themselves con-

demn their own former judgment in so doing; which does not imply surely any want of proper *self*-respect. The *system* of the
Anxious Bench, in its full development, is one which these persons have always disapproved; only they have not considered
this particular measure to be a part of the system. That this
should be the case need not seem strange; for in the view of
the measure here taken, it is supposed to be in its simple
form, on the bright side of this system, and close upon the
boundary that separates it from the territory of the truth.
The tract exhibits the measure in this view, not as the origin
of the system historically, not as necessarily conducting in
all cases to worse things that lie beyond; but as constitutionally involving the principle of those worse things, under the
least startling form, and legitimately opening the way for
their introduction, if circumstances should permit. It would
seem to show the correctness of this view, that while the answers to the tract protest against it, as a false and arbitrary classification, they all conform to it notwithstanding,
in spite of themselves, in a practical way. They defend the
use of the bench as the Thermopylae of New Measures; and their
argument, such as it is, has just as much force to justify the
system in full, as it has to justify this measure in particular.
An effort is made, indeed, to mystify the subject, by dragging
into connection with it interests of a different order altogether; but still it is plain enough that this is done with
violence, and the controversy falls back always in the end to
its proper limits.

The abuse of a thing, it is said, is no argument against
its proper use; and therefore the object, in the present case,
should be to reform and regulate rather than to abolish. To
this I reply, the whole system contemplated in the tract is an
abuse, from which it is of the utmost importance that the worship of the sanctuary, and the cause of revivals, should be

rescued. Belonging as it does to this system, then, and con-
tributing to its support, the Anxious Bench is a nuisance that
can never be fully abated except by its entire removal. Its
tendencies, as shown in the tract, are decidedly bad, without
any compensation of a solid kind. It may be used with moderation; but it will stand still in the same relation to the system it represents, that moderate drinking holds to intemperance
in its more advanced forms. Popery started, in the beginning,
under forms apparently the most innocent and safe. What might
seem to be, for instance, more rational and becoming than the
sign of the cross, as used by Christians, on all occasions in
the early Church? And yet, when the corruptions of Rome were
thrown off by the Protestant world, in the sixteenth century,
this and other similar forms were required to pass away with
the general mass. And why is it that the sign of the cross, as
once used, is now counted a dangerous superstition, not to be
permitted among Protestants? Simply because it falls naturally
over to that vast system of abuses, of which it forms a part in
the Romish Church. Thus it *represents* that system, and furnishes a specimen of it constitutionally, under the most plausible shape. Such is the position of the Anxious Bench, as a
particular measure, in the general case now under consideration. It is just as easy to conceive of a judicious and salutary use of the Anxious Bench; and I have no doubt at all but
that the first has been owned and blessed of God full as extensively, to say the least, as this has ever been the case with
the last.

J. W. N.

Mercersburg, Pa., January, 1844

CHAPTER I

*Design of the Tract.--Occasion for Inquiry.--Importance and
Solemnity of the Subject*

It is proposed to institute a free inquiry into the merits
of the *Anxious Bench*, as it has been enlisted extensively of
late years in the service of religion. My object will be to
show that the measure is adapted to obstruct rather than to
promote the progress of true godliness, and that it deserves to
be discouraged on this account.

No one needs to be informed what is meant by the *Anxious
Bench*. Its nature and design have come to be as familiar to
most people as the nature and design of the pulpit itself.
Even among those who dislike it there are few perhaps who have
not had the opportunity at one time or another of witnessing
its operation, while all are well acquainted with it at least
in the way of description and report.

It will be understood that the Anxious Bench is made to
stand, in this case, as the type and representative of the entire system of what are technically denominated in our day *"New
Measures."* It is not meant by this, of course, that it is so
bound to the system as never to be separated from other parts
of it in actual practice. It may be in use where no new measures besides are tolerated; and it is possible, on the other
hand, that it may not be employed by some who in other respects
are wholly in this interest. But still it may very fairly be
exhibited as a type of the system at large. These measures
form properly a *system*; and it is only in this view that it is
possible to estimate rightly their nature and character. It is
not uncommon to class with them things of a different nature
altogether; and then advantage is taken of the confusion thus

produced to evade the point of objections urged against new
measures in the proper sense. This, however, is sophistry of a
very shallow order. The idea of *New Measures* is just as well
defined in itself and as generally intelligible in the American
Church as the idea of popery, Methodism, Presbyterianism, or
almost anything else of the same general character that might
be named. It is only by a gross and palpable abuse that some
wish to make it include the best things in the Church. New
measures, in the technical modern sense, form a particular system, involving a certain theory of religious action, and characterized by a distinctive life, which is by no means difficult
to understand. Of this system the Anxious Bench is a proper
representative. It opens the way naturally to other forms of
aberration in the same direction, and may be regarded in this
view as the threshold of all that is found to follow, quite out
to the extreme verge of fanaticism and rant. The measure belongs to the system, not in the name simply, but in its life
and spirit. At the same time, it is the most favorable aspect
in which the cause of New Measures can be presented to our
view. The simple Anxious Bench, as it is often used in a sober
way, is the most moderate and plausible shape the system can
well take. If this then be found unworthy of confidence, the
whole system will be shorn of its title to confidence at the
same time. If the Anxious Bench can claim no indulgence, it
must be idle to put in a plea for its kindred measures. All
beyond this is only something worse.

It is well too that we can thus deal with our subject. If
there be no room, as some pretend, for treating it in a clear
and satisfactory way under the title of New Measures, by reason
of the confusion with which that term is used, it is so much
the more important that we should substitute the particular for
the general; and we have reason to congratulate ourselves on
finding a single, well known form of action that can be taken

fairly as the representative of the whole system. In this way
our argument will not be abstract and vague, but pointed and
clear. Whatever dust it might be contrived to raise with regard to the proper sense of the term *New Measures,* all know at
least the meaning of the *Anxious Bench.* Here then we have a
tangible, concrete subject with which to deal. Let it serve as
a specimen of the system to which it belongs. In this way the
system is characterized and distinguished. It includes things
of the same general constitution and spirit with the Anxious
Bench. In trying the merits of this, we try at the same time
all these kindred practices and nothing more.* If any choose
to incorporate with *their* idea of New Measures, things of a
different constitution and spirit entirely, it cannot be helped.
But they can have no right to force any view of this sort upon
the present argument. Our business is with New Measures in the
proper sense; and that we may not seem to run uncertainly, or
beat the air, we characterize the system by one of its most
familiar exhibition. It stands before us in the type of the
Anxious Bench.

Here too is the proper point for grappling with the heresy
of New Measures. It can answer no purpose to discountenance
the system in general, if we lend our influence theoretically or
practically to uphold a measure forming like this a legitimate
stepping stone to all the system is found to embrace. No satisfactory line can be drawn between this and the more advanced

---

* "How can the import of this measure exhibit the character of protracted meetings, both which in many German churches
are well known to be included in their idea of New Measures?"
--*Luth. Obs., Nov. 17, 1843.* Of a truth, it may be replied,
not very well; and for this reason precisely it is made to
stand here as the representative of the system to which it of
right belongs, that every body may be able at once to see and
understand that prayer meetings, protracted meetings, and other
interests of the same complexion come not in any sense within
the scope of the present inquiry.

forms of extravagance for which it prepares the way. They will be found to involve in the end the same principle. That is a false position, therefore, by which some excellent men allow themselves to speak freely against noise and disorder and bodily exercises in public worship under other forms, while at the same time the Anxious Bench is not only spared, but treated with honor and confidence, as though it had come to form part of the accredited and regular service of God's house. Men who occupy this position may preach or write an abundance of wholesome advice on the subject of false excitement in religion; but their advice is not likely to carry much weight with it in the end, as not going after all to the ground of the error against which it is directed. If we would utter an intelligible and consistent testimony against New Measures, we must make no exception, openly or tacitly, in favor of the Anxious Bench. Here precisely is the proper point at which to grapple with the whole system.

There is occasion for the inquiry here proposed. It is true, indeed, that throughout a large portion of the country the Anxious Bench, after having enjoyed a brief reputation, has fallen into discredit. It has been tried, and found wanting; and it might have been trusted that this experiment would be sufficient to drive it completely out of use. But unfortunately this has not been the case. Over a wide section of the land we find it still holding its ground, without any regard to the disgrace with which it has been overtaken in the north and east. Peculiar circumstances have conspired to promote its credit on this field.

It is within the range particularly of the German Churches that a new life may be said to have been communicated latterly to the system of New Measures. No field is more interesting at this time than that which is comprehended within these limits. A vast moral change is going forward upon it, involving conse-

quences that no man can properly calculate. From various causes
a new feeling is at work everywhere on the subject of religion.
As usual, the old struggles to maintain itself in opposition to
the new, and a strong tendency to become extreme is created on
both sides. The general mind unhappily has not been furnished
thus far with proper protection and guidance in the way of full
religious teaching; and the result is that in these interesting
circumstances it has become exposed more or less at almost
every point to those wild fanatical influences which in this
country are sure to come in like a desolating flood wherever
they can find room. Upstart sects have set themselves to take
possession, if possible, of the entire field in this way, on
the principle that the old organizations are corrupt and deserve to be destroyed. Their reliance, of course, in this work
of reformation, is placed largely on New Measures! Thus a whole
Babel of extravagance has been let loose upon the community far
and wide in the name of religion, one sect vieing with another
in the measure of its irregularities. In these circumstances
it has not been easy for the friends of earnest piety always in
the regular churches to abide by the ancient landmarks of truth
and order. The temptation has been strong to fall in, at least
to some extent, with the tide of fanaticism as the only way of
making war successfully on the dead formality that stared them
in the face in one direction, and the only way of counteracting
the proselyting zeal of these noisy sects in the other.

This and other considerations have had the effect of opening the way for the use of New Measures to some extent in the
German Reformed Church, and to a much greater in the Lutheran.
It is well known that a large division of this last denomination has identified itself openly and zealously with the system,
both in doctrine and practice. The *Lutheran Observer*, which
has a wide circulation and great influence, has lent all its
authority to recommend and support the Anxious Bench with its

accompaniments, taking every occasion to speak in its favor and making continually the most of its results. The "revivals" of the Church latterly have been very generally carried forward with the use of New Measures, as may be perceived from the reports of them published from time to time in the "Observer." The great awakening of last winter, pronounced by the editor of that paper to have been probably the greatest since the days of the Apostles, seems almost everywhere to have involved the free use of this method. Thus ministers and congregations have become extensively committed in its favor; so that with many the use of the Anxious Bench, and a zeal for evangelical godliness, are considered to be very much the same thing. It might seem indeed as though all the interests of religion, in the case of the German community, were to the view of a large class suspended on the triumphant progress of New Measures.* These are with them emphatically the "great power of God," which may be expected to turn and overturn, till old things shall fairly pass away and all things become new. And it must be acknowledged that the system bids fair at present to go on conquering and to conquer in its own style within the limits at least of this widely extended and venerable denomination. It seems to bear down more and more all opposition. It has become an in-

---

*"And let me tell you, Sir, that whatever Prof. Nevin may (in the abstraction of his study) have written to the contrary, I am nevertheless strongly convinced, as a pastor, that the so-called *'Anxious bench'* is the lever of Archimedes, which by the blessing of God can raise our German churches to that degree of respectability and prosperity in the religious world which they ought to enjoy."--*Correspondence of the Luth. Obs., Nov. 17, 1843.*

"Such measures are usually inseparable from great revivals, and if the great luminaries in the Church set themselves up against them, why they must be content to abide the consequences. By the judicious use of such measures, the millennium must be accelerated and introduced; &c."--*Luth. Obs., Jan. 26, 1844.*

terest too strong to be resisted or controlled. What are to be its ultimate issues and results, time only can reveal.

All this is within the reach of the most common observation. And no one reflecting on the actual state of things at this time on the field occupied by the German Churches can well fail to perceive that there is full occasion for calling attention to the subject which it is here proposed to consider. An inquiry into the merits of the Anxious Bench and the system to which it belongs is not only seasonable and fit in the circumstances of the time, but loudly called for on every side. It is no small question that is involved in the case. The bearing of it upon the interests of religion in the German Churches is of fundamental and vital importance. A crisis has evidently been reached in the history of these Churches; and one of the most serious points involved in it is precisely this question of New Measures. Let this system prevail and rule with permanent sway, and the result of the religious movement which is now in progress will be something widely different from what it would have been under other auspices. The old regular organizations, if they continue to exist at all, will not be the same Churches. Their entire complexion and history in time to come will be shaped by the course of things with regard to this point. In this view the march of New Measures at the present time may well challenge our anxious and solemn regard. It is an interest of no common magnitude, portentous in its aspect, and pregnant with consequences of vast account. The system is moving forward in full strength, and putting forth its pretensions in the boldest style on all sides. Surely we have a right, and may well feel it a duty, in such a case, to institute an examination into its merits.

Nor is it any reason for silence in the case that we may have suffered as yet comparatively little in our own denomination from the use of New Measures. We may congratulate our-

24

selves that we have been thus favored, and that the impression
seems to be steadily growing that they ought not be be encouraged in our communion. Still, linked together as the German
Churches are throughout the land, we have reason to be jealous
here of influences that must in the nature of the case act upon
us from without. In such circumstances there is occasion, and
at the same time room for consideration. It might answer little purpose to interpose remonstrance or inquiry if the rage
for New Measures were fairly let loose, as a sweeping wind,
within our borders. It were idle to bespeak attention from the
rolling whirlwind. But with the whirlwind in full view, we may
be exhorted reasonably to consider and stand back from its destructive path. We are not yet committed to the cause of New
Measures in any respect. We are still free to reject or embrace them as the interests of the Church, on calm reflection,
may be found to require. In such circumstances precisely may
it be counted in all respects proper to subject the system to
a serious examination.

It has been sometimes intimated that it is not safe to oppose and condemn the use of New Measures, because of their connections and purpose. Their relation to the cause of revivals
is supposed to invest them with a sort of sacred character
which the friends of religion should at least respect, even if
they may not be able in all cases to approve. The system has
taken hold of the "horns of the altar," and it seems to some
like sacrilege to fall upon it there, or to force it away for
the purposes of justice to any other place. It is a serious
thing, we are told, to find fault with any movement that claims
to be animated by the Spirit of God. By so doing we render it
questionable whether we have ourselves any proper sympathy with
revivals, and furnish occasion to the world also to blaspheme
and oppose everything of the kind. But this is tyrannical
enough to take for granted the main point in dispute, and then

employ it as a consideration to repress inquiry or to silence
objection. If New Measures can be shown to proceed from the
Holy Ghost, or be identified in any view with the cause of revivals, they may well demand our reverence and respect. If
they can be shown even to be of *adiaphorous* character with regard to religion, harmless at least if not positively helpful
to the Spirit's work, they may then put in a reasonable plea
to be tolerated in silence, if not absolutely approved. But
neither the one nor the other of these positions can be successfully maintained. It is a mere trick unworthy of the gospel for any one to confound with the sacred idea of a revival
things that do not belong to it in truth at all for the purpose
of compelling a judgment in their favor. The very design of
the inquiry now proposed is to show that the Anxious Bench, and
the system to which it belongs, have no claim to be considered
either salutary or safe in the service of religion. It is believed that instead of promoting the cause of true vital godliness, they are adapted to hinder its progress. The whole system is considered to be full of peril for the most precious
interests of the Church. And why then should there be any reserve in treating the subject with such freedom as it may seem
to require? We may well feel indeed that the subject is solemn.
All that relates to the interests of revivals, and the welfare
of souls, is solemn; and it becomes us to approach it in a
serious way. But this is no reason why we should close our
eyes against the truth, or refuse to call things by their
proper names. This would be to trifle with sacred things truly.

And it should be born in mind that the danger against
which we need to be warned in this case is not confined by any
means to one side. It is a serious thing to profane the worship of God by offering upon His altar strange fire. Those who
recommend and practice New Measures should see well to it that
they be not themselves chargeable with the very sin which they

are too prone to charge upon such as withstand their views. It
is surely not a case in which men can be justified in taking up
a judgment lightly and with little or no reflection. Mighty
interests are concerned in the question whether such means
should be employed in the service of God's sanctuary or not. A
great responsibility is involved in urging the system upon a
congregation, or in trying to give it currency and authority in
a religious community. If it should be found after all to be
not the wisdom and power of God unto salvation, but the fruitful source of error and confusion in religion, an occasion of
reproach to the gospel and of ruin to the souls of men, it
would be a heavy account surely to answer for any part taken in
its favor.

It is truly strange how one-sided the patrons of this system show themselves, as a general thing, in their views and
feelings with regard to the point now presented. They affect
an extraordinary interest in the cause of revivals, and seem to
have a pious dread of sinning against it in any way. But the
danger of doing so is all, to their view, in one direction.
The idea of opposing the work of God is terrible. Whatever
claims to be His work then, must be respected and reverenced.
No matter what irregularities are attached to it, so long as it
stands before us in the holy garb of a revival, it is counted
unsafe to call it to account. The maxim *Prove all things,* must
be discarded, as well as the caution, *Believe not every spirit.*
No room must be allowed to criticism where the object proposed
is to rescue souls from hell. To stand upon points of order in
such a case is to clog the chariot wheels of salvation. Meanwhile the disastrous consequences of false excitement, in the
name of religion, are entirely overlooked. No account is made
comparatively of the danger of bringing both the truth and
power of God into discredit by countenancing pretentions to the
name of a revival where the thing itself is not present. The

danger itself is by no means imaginary. Spurious excitements are natural and common. Gross irregularity and extravagance, carried often to the point of downright profanity, are actually at work in connection with such excitements on all sides. The whole interest of revivals is endangered by the assumption impudently put forward that these revolting excesses belong to the system. False and ruinous views of religion are widely disseminated. Thousands of souls are deceived into a false hope. Vast obstructions are thrown in the way of true godliness. But of all this no account is made by those who are so sensitively jealous of danger on the other side. The only alternative they seem to see is *Action* or *No action*. But the difference between *right* action and *wrong* action one would think is fully as important, to say the least, as the difference between action and no action.

We are told however that the term *"New Measures"* is vague, covering in the view of some more than it covers in the view of others; so that there is danger of encouraging prejudice and opposition against the best things as well as the worst in venturing to criticize and censure the general system. In the German community in particular it is well known that great confusion prevails with regard to the subject in this view. With many all active efforts in favor of serious evangelical piety are branded with the reproach of new measures. Protracted meetings, prayer meetings, the doctrine of the new birth, special efforts for the salvation of sinners, revivals in the true and proper sense, tract societies, missionary societies, and benevolent operations generally, all are regarded with suspicion, or it may be actually opposed as belonging to the same system of extravagance that includes the Anxious Bench and its natural connections. To oppose the latter then we are told is virtually to oppose the former. People will not distinguish. By exposing the nakedness of the Anxious Bench, we must expect to strengthen the hands of those who cry out against all active religion. Better to be silent than to incur so heavy a responsibility. Especially at this juncture should we observe such sacred caution, it is intimated, when the German Churches are waking from the sleep of years and passing the crisis of a great spiritual revolution whose consequences no one can measure.

Most certainly in such circumstances caution does become us all. We should tremble to touch the ark of God with unhallowed hand. It were only to be wished that this might be seriously laid to heart by the champions of the Anxious Bench themselves, as well as by others.

It has been already stated that the Anxious Bench is made the direct object of regard in this tract rather than New Measures in general for the very purpose of cutting off occasion, as much as may be from those who seek occasion, for confounding in this way things that are entirely distinct. The particular is made to stand for the general in the way of specimen or type, so as to exclude all that is not of the same complexion and spirit. If any choose notwithstanding to take the idea of New Measures in a wider sense, they have a right to please themselves in so doing if they see proper; but they can have no right surely to obtrude their own arbitrary view on the present discussion. There is a broad difference between New Measures in the one sense, and the New Measures in the other sense. It is overbearing impudence to pretend that a protracted meeting or a meeting for social prayer is of the same character with the anxious bench, or the various devices for theatrical effect with which this is so frequently linked. Such meetings lie in the very conception of Christian worship and are as old as the Church. The assertion sometimes heard that the idea of protracted meetings now so familiar and so generally approved is one of recent origin for which we are indebted to the system of

New Measures, serves only to expose the ignorance of those by
whom it is made. It is no less an abuse of terms as well as of
common sense to include in this system tract societies, the
cause of missions, and the benevolent agencies in general, by
which the Church is endeavoring to diffuse the knowledge of the
truth throughout the world. All these things are natural, direct utterances of the spirit of Christianity itself, and have
no affinity whatever with the order of action represented by
the Anxious Bench. The same thing may be said of revivals.
They are as old as the gospel itself. Special effusions of the
Spirit the Church has a right to expect in every age, in proportion as she is found faithful to God's covenant; and where
such effusions take place, an extraordinary use of the ordinary
means of grace will appear, as a matter of course. But still
a revival is one thing, and a Phrygian dance another; even
though the Phrygian dance should be baptized into Christian
Montanism. Life implies action, but all action is not life.
It is sheer impudence to say the new measures and revival measures are the same thing.

And there is good reason to believe that the confusion
which is said to prevail with regard to the whole subject is
much less in fact than is sometimes represented. As a general
thing, people know very well that there is no affinity or connection between the system represented by the Anxious Bench and
such evangelical interests as have now been mentioned. Even in
those sections where it has been found convenient to stretch
the idea of New Measures over this hallowed territory, there is
a better knowledge of the true state of the case probably than
is often supposed.

But allowing the confusion to be as complete among the
German Churches as it is represented, shall no effort be made
to correct it and put things in their proper light? Admit that
the best practices and most important interests are in the eyes

of many identified with the system of New Measures in the proper sense, so that to assault the latter is considered an assault at the same time upon the former; still, is that a reason
for sparing and sheltering the system under its own bad form?
Is there no help for the German Churches in this predicament?
Must they have revivals in the way of the Anxious Bench, or no
revivals at all? Must it be with them Finneyism, Methodism,
Winebrennerism, or open war with serious religion, and the
spirit of missions under every form? Is the necessary alternative in their case quackery or death? Rather, in these circumstances, it becomes a solemn duty to take the difficulty by the
horns, and reduce it to its proper posture. We owe it to the
German Churches not to suffer things so different in a case of
such vast moment to be so deplorably confounded. The case is
one that calls loudly for light, and it is high time that light
should be extended to it without reserve. If it be a reigning
error to involve light and darkness in this way, under a common
term, in the same sweeping censure, that is not a reason surely
why we should try to uphold the darkness for the sake of the
light, but a sacred requisition upon us rather to insist on a
clear, full discrimination of the one element from the other.
If Finneyism and Winebrennerism, the anxious bench, revival
machinery, solemn tricks for effect, decision displays at the
bidding of the preacher, genuflections and prostrations in the
aisle or around the altar, noise and disorder, extravagance and
rant, mechanical conversions, justification by feeling rather
than faith, and encouragement ministered to all fanatical impressions; if these things, and things in the same line indef-
inately, have no connection in fact with true serious religion
and the cause of revivals, but tend only to bring them into
discredit, let the fact be openly proclaimed. Only in this way
may it be hoped that the reproach put upon revivals and other
evangelical interests by some, under cover of their pretended

connection with this system of New Measures in the true sense, will be in due time fairly rolled away.

The fact that a crisis has come in the history of the German Churches, and that they are waking to the consciousness of a new life with regard to religion, only makes it the more important that this subject should *not* be suffered to rest in vague confusion. It is a popish maxim by which ignorance is made to be the mother of devotion. We say rather, Let there be light. The cause of the Reformation was more endangered by its own caricature, in the wild fanaticism of the Ababaptists, than by the opposition of Rome. Luther saved it, not by truckling compromise, but by boldly facing and unmasking the false spirit, so that all the world might see that *Lutheran* Christianity was one thing, and wild Phrygian Montanism, with its pretended inspiration, quite another. So in the present crisis, the salvation of the old German Churches in this country is to be accomplished, not by encouraging them to "believe every spirit," but by engaging them, if possible, to "try the spirits, whether they be of God." Let things that are wrong be called by their right names, and separated from things that are right.

A heavy responsibility, in this case, rests upon the friends of New Measures. The circulation of spurious coin, in the name of money, brings the genuine currency into discredit. So also the surest way to create and cherish prejudice against true piety is to identify it with counterfeit pretences to its name. Popery, in popish countries, is the fruitful source of infidelity. So in the case before us it is sufficiently clear that the zeal which the sticklers for the system of the Anxious Bench display, in pressing their irregularities on the Church as a necessary part of the life and power of Christianity, is doing more at present than any other cause to promote the unhappy prejudice that is found to prevail in certain quarters against this interest in its true form. Many are led honestly

to confound the one order of things with the other; and still
more, no doubt, willingly accept the opportunity thus furnished
to strengthen themselves in their opposition to evangelical interests, under a plausible plea, against their own better knowledge. In either case we see the mischievous force of the false
issue which the question of New Measures has been made to involve. The Anxious Bench and its kindred extravagances may be
held justly responsible for a vast amount of evil in this view.
As a caricature always wrongs the original it is made falsely
to represent, so has this spurious system, officiously usurping
a name and place not properly its own, contributed in no small
degree to bring serious religion itself into discredit, obscur-
ing its true form, and inviting towards it prejudices that
might otherwise have had no place. It has much to answer for,
in the occasion it has given, and is giving still, for the name
of God to be blasphemed, and the sacred cause of revivals to be
vilified and opposed.

CHAPTER II

*The Merits of the Anxious Bench not to be Measured by its
Popularity; nor by its Seeming Success.--Circumstances
in Which it is Found to Prevail.--No Spiritual Force
Required to Give it Effect*

The *popularity* of the Anxious Bench proves nothing in its
favor.* We find it, to be sure, extensively in vogue, and with
a large portion of the community in high honor. There are
whole sects that seem to have no conception of any thing like a
vigorous life in the Church without its presence. And beyond
the range of these, scores of ministers and congregations are
found who glory in it as the very "gate of heaven," and consider it no less essential than the pulpit itself to the progress
of any considerable revival. During the last winter, as already mentioned, there were places where the spirit of the
Anxious Bench might be said to carry all before it, and it is
likely that it will be so again during the winter that is to

---

* "It proves nothing *against* it," we are told from the
other side. The remark is most true; but most foreign at the
same time from the point, so far as the position of the tract
is concerned. The object of this chapter is, not to present
any positive argument against the Bench, but simply to undermine certain presumptions in its favor, which are known to
stand in the way of a calm and dispassionate consideration of
its merits, as afterwards examined. The argument here is *negative,* not positive. The patrons of the system, it is plain,
make much account of its popularity, of the success with which
it seems to be attended, and of the power it is supposed to
manifest on the part of those who can use it with effect. In
the present chapter it is attempted to show simply that opportunity and apparent success prove nothing, and that the measure
is of such a character as to call for no particular moral force
to give it effect. In the following chapter the argument becomes *positive,* showing that there is actual weakness and quackery at the bottom of the whole system.

come.

But all who are at all acquainted with the world know that the worst things *may* thus run for a season and be glorified in the popular mind. And especially is this the case where they hold their existence in the element of excitement, and connect themselves with religion, the deepest and most universal of all human interests. No weight of fashion enlisted in favor of the Anxious Bench can deserve to be much respected in such a trial of its merits as we are here called to make.

It should be remembered, however, that this popularity, such as it is, is in a certain sense but the echo of a sound which has already ceased to be heard. Whatever may be the pretensions of the Anxious Bench, on the field we are now contemplating, it is after all a stale interest, so far as the Church at large is concerned. Not many years since it stood in very considerable credit in different parts of the Presbyterian Church and over a large portion of New England. But on this ground the thing has fairly exploded. It has been tried and found wanting. Here and there it may still be held in honor. But in a general view even those who were formerly its friends have come to look upon it with distrust, and are no longer willing to give it their countenance. As with general consent throughout New England and New York the Congregational and Presbyterian Churches have abandoned the use of the Anxious Bench for "a more excellent way."* With all its popularity

---

* This has been contradicted; with more courage, however, than wisdom. It is notorious to all who know anything about the subject that the system of New Measures, in the sense of the present tract, as represented some years since in the north by such men as Burchard and Finney, has latterly fallen into discredit and general disuse throughout the Congregational and Presbyterian Churches. They still cherish of course prayer meetings, protracted meetings, and revivals; and it is quite possible that a number of ministers may still have recourse to the anxious bench as a particular measure at certain times;

then where it now prevails it is after all a stale interest, worn threadbare and flung aside in a different quarter of the religious world. In these circumstances no great account is to be made of its present credit in any view.

Nothing can be argued again in favor of the Anxious Bench, from the *Success* with which it may appear to be employed in the service of religion. This is often appealed to for this purpose. We are referred triumphantly to the actual results of the system as tried in different places. We are told of hundreds awakened and converted in connection with its use. God, it is said, has owned it, and impressed His seal upon it by working through it mightily as a means of salvation; and if He choose to honor it in this way, who are we that we should find fault or condemn?* We should rejoice to see souls brought into the kingdom in any way. We should be willing to make room in such a case for the manifold grace of God, allowing it to have free course in any channel through which it is found to flow,

---

but the *system*, to which this measure of right belongs, is no longer in vogue. By general consent the churches have fallen back upon the evangelical method to which the use of the anxious bench can adhere only as an accident, if it adhere at all. The revivals of last winter in the north, according to the testimony furnished concerning them in the *New York Observer*, were of a wholly different stamp from those of Mr. Finney's school in former years. These last had strength; but it was such as a lasting fever imparts to a sick man, opening the way for a long prostration afterwards. The revivals of the past winter, it may be trusted, have been the first fruits only of the quiet and enduring vigor that springs from repentance and faith.

* "Who can behold a congregation of Christians wrestling for an altar full of penitent, anxious sinners, and witness the success of such instrumentality, and say, this is ignorance or fanaticism? God blesses only one way, which is the right way; He has blessed this way, therefore it is the right way"--*Correspondence of the Lutheran Observer*, Feb. 17, 1843.

and not seeking to force it into conformity with our own narrow
views. All this carries with it a plausible sound. But after
all the representation is entitled to no respect.

In the first place, to draw an argument for the Anxious
Bench from its immediate visible effects, is to take for granted that these are worth all they claim to be worth. We are
pointed to powerful awakenings, of which it is considered to
be the very soul. We are referred to scores and hundreds of
conversions effected directly or indirectly by its means. But
who shall assure us that all this deserves to be regarded with
confidence as the genuine fruit of religion? It is marvellous
credulity to take every excitement in the name of religion for
the work of God's Spirit. It is an enormous demand on our
charity when we are asked to accept in mass, as true and solid,
the wholesale conversions that are made in this way. It will
soon be made to appear that there is the greatest reason for
caution and distrust with regard to this point. No doubt the
use of the Anxious Bench may be found associated, in certain
cases, with revivals, the fruits of which are worthy of all
confidence. But this character they will have, through the
force of a different system, that would have been just as complete without any such accompaniment. In such cases the revival may be said to prevail *in spite* of the new measures with
which it is encumbered. On the other hand, in proportion as
the spirit of such measures is found to animate and rule the
occasion, there will be reason to regard the whole course of
things with doubt. One thing is most certain. Spurious revivals are common, and as the fruit of them false conversions
lamentably abound. An Anxious Bench may be crowded where no
divine influence whatever is felt. A whole congregation may be
moved with excitement, and yet be losing at the very time more
than is gained in a religious point of view. Hundreds may be
carried *through* the process of anxious bench conversion, and

yet their last state may be worse than the first. It will not
do to point us to immediate visible effects, to appearances on
the spot, or to glowing reports struck off from some heated
imagination immediately after. Piles of copper, fresh from the
mint, are after all something very different from piles of gold.

Again, it does not follow by any means that a thing is
right and good because it may be made subservient occasionally
in the hands of God to a good end. Allow that the system represented by the Anxious Bench has often had the effect of
bringing souls by a true and saving change to Christ, and still
it may deserve to be opposed and banished from the Church. God
can cause the wrath and folly of man both to praise Him in such
ways as to Himself may seem best. And so, under the influence
of His Spirit, He can make almost any occasion subservient to
the awakening and conversion of a soul. But it would be wretched logic to infer from this the propriety of employing every
such occasion, with preparation and design, as a part of the
regular work of the gospel. It is sometimes said indeed that
if only *some* souls are saved by the use of new measures, we
ought thankfully to own their power, and give them our countenance; since even one soul is worth more than a world. But it
should be remembered that the salvation of a sinner may notwithstanding cost *too much!* If truth and righteousness are
made to suffer for the purpose, more is lost than won by the
result. We must not do *wrong*, even to gain a soul for heaven.
And if for one thus gained, ten should be virtually destroyed
by the very process employed to reach the point, who will say
that such a method of promoting Christianity would deserve to
be approved? There may be movements in the name of religion,
and under the form of religion, and yielding to some extent the
fruits of religion, which after all come from beneath and not
from above. The history of the Church is full of instances
illustrating the truth of this remark.

Simeon, the Stylite, distinguished himself, in the fifth century, by taking his station on the top of a pillar, for the glory of God and the benefit of his own soul. This whimsical discipline he continued to observe for thirty-seven years. Meanwhile he became an object of wide-spread veneration. Vast crowds came from a distance to gaze upon him, and hear him preach. The *measure* took with the people wonderfully. Thousands of heathen were converted, and baptized by his hand. Among these, it may be charitably trusted, were some whose conversion was inward and solid. God made use of Simeon's Pillar to bring them to Himself. The seal of His approbation might seem to have rested upon it to an extraordinary extent. No wonder the device became popular. The quackery of the Pillar took possession of the Eastern world, and stood for centuries a monument of the folly that gave it birth. We laugh at it now; and yet it seemed a good thing in its time, and carried with it a weight of popularity such as no New Measure can boast of in the present day.

But why speak of Stylitism in particular? The whole system of monkery may be taken as an example, of the same force, on a larger scale. What a world of abominations has it not been found to embrace? And yet, under what plausible pretences, it sought the confidence of the Church in the beginning! There were not wanting powerful reasons to give it recommendation. The whole Christian world in fact fell into the snare. The interest became a torrent, before which no man was found able to stand. Most assuredly, too, there was the life and power of religion, to some extent, at work in the movement. Monkery was to many in fact the means of conversion and salvation. And to this hour an argument might be framed in its favor, under this view, not less plausible, to say the least, than any that can be presented for the use of the Anxious Bench.

The Romish Church has always delighted in arrangements and

services animated with the same false spirit. In her penitential system all pains have been taken to produce *effect* by
means of outward postures and dress, till in the end, amid the
solemn mummery, no room has been left for genuine penitence at
all. Yet not a ceremony was ever introduced into the system
that did not seem to be recommended by some sound religious
reason at the time. The same thing may be said for the services of that Church generally.

In another sphere, look at *Millerism*. The error, as it
has been zealously preached within the past year (1843), has no
doubt had an awakening effect on the minds of many; and some,
it may be trusted, have been actually conducted by means of it
into the kingdom of God. But will any pretend to say that it
deserves to be encouraged on this account? It is said, indeed,
that such an idea has been occasionally thrown out. Only, however, where the judgment had been in some measure corrupted by
the spirit of quackery previously at work. No morally sane man
could be willing for a moment to patronize such a lie, on
account of any apparently salutary effects it might be found to
have in particular cases.

Let us not be told, then, that the Anxious Bench is a godly
interest, because many *seem* to be convicted by its means, and
some are converted in fact. All this may be, and the general
operation of the system remain notwithstanding intrinsically
and permanently bad.

As a general thing, the movement of coming to the Anxious
Bench gives no proper representation of the religious feeling
that may be actually at work in the congregation at the time.
It is always more or less theatrical, and often has no other
character whatever. A sermon usually goes before. But frequently this has no felt relation at all to the subsequent
excitement, so far as its actual contents are concerned. The
writer was present, not a great while ago, as a stranger in a

church, where a preacher of some little note in connection with
the subject of revivals had been introduced under the expectation and hope that something of the kind might be secured at
the time by his instrumentality. The congregation had but little appearance of life at the beginning, and still less as the
sermon drew towards a close. The truth is, it was a very dull
discourse at the best. The preacher was not well, and altogether he failed to make the least impression on the great body
of his audience. A number were fairly asleep, and others were
bordering on the same state. The preacher saw and felt that he
had preached without effect; and took occasion, after the sermon was properly ended, to express his regret in view of the
fact, and to add a few valedictory remarks in the prospect of
his leaving the place the next day, without any thought evidently of calling out the anxious, where not a trace of feeling
had been discerned. But the new strain adopted at the close,
served to rouse attention and create interest. The congregation put on a more wakeful aspect, and something like emotion
could be perceived in the countenances of a few. The preacher
took courage, and after a few minutes dared to try the Anxious
Bench. As usual, the hymn was started, "Come, humble sinner,"
etc., and carried through, with pauses, in which sinners present were urged and pressed to seek their salvation by coming
forward. Soon a female was seen going to the place, then another, and another--till at last a whole seat was filled. One
old lady rose and moved around, trying to induce others to go
forward. At the close of the meeting I retired, wondering
within myself that educated men, as were both the preacher in
this case and the pastor at his side, could so impose upon
themselves as to attach any importance to such a demonstration
in such circumstances. It was attempted to carry forward the
work by an appointment for the next evening. But on coming together at the time, it was found that it *would* not go forward,

and so it was dropped altogether.

Commonly indeed those who deal in the anxious seat rely far less upon the presentation of truth to the understanding than they do upon other influences to bring persons forward. Pains are taken rather to raise the imagination, and confound the judgment. Exciting appeals are made to the principle of fear. Advantage is taken in every way of the senses and nerves. Especially the mysterious force of sympathy is enlisted in support of the measure, and made to tell in many cases with immense effect.

As might be expected accordingly, the most favorable subjects for the operation of the system are persons in whom feelings prevail over judgment, and who are swayed by impulse more than reflection. In an enlightened, well instructed congregation the anxious bench can never be generally popular. Where it is in full favor, a large proportion of those who are brought out by it are females and persons who are quite young.* It often happens that the "bench" is filled altogether with such cases, the greater part of them perhaps mere girls and boys. So, where a community is characterized by a general ig-

---

* "Females and persons who are quite young have souls to be saved, as well as males and persons who are advanced in life; nay 'mere girls and boys' have an eternal interest pending." --*Luth. Observer,* Dec. 29, 1843.
"And was not woman last at the cross, and first at the tomb, of the Son of God?"--*Davis' Plea,* p. 45.
"Low and jejune indeed must be the conception of a religion which can allow a *divine* to attempt to destroy a 'measure,' through which *'females, girls and boys,'* run to as a means to enable them to flee the wrath to come."--*Denig's Strictures,* p. 26.
What a coincidence of judgment, among the critics of the tract, at this point! And what shall we say of the relevancy and honesty of the criticism itself, in view of the passage thus censured, as it actually stands, and taken in its plain sense? This is a fair specimen, however, of a large part of all that has been *argued* against the tract in these publications.

norance with regard to the nature of true religion, the measure
is frequently applied with great effect; and those precisely
who are the most rude and uncultivated, are the most likely in
such circumstances to come under its power.

It requires then no spiritual power to use the Anxious
Bench with effect. To preach the truth effectually, a man must
have a certain spiritual force in himself which others are made
to feel. But nothing of this sort is needed to secure success
here. The object sought is a mere outward demonstration on the
subject of religion, which may be gained by other forms of influence just as well. It shows no inward power whatever to be
able to move a congregation in this way. It can be done without eloquence, and calls for no particular earnestness or depth
of thought. It is truly wonderful, indeed, with how little
qualification of intellect and soul a man may be fitted to carry
all before him at certain times, and to show himself off to
the eyes of a bewitched multitude as "the great power of God,"
by having recourse to new measures. He may be vulgar, coarse
and dull, and so pointless and sapless in his ordinary pulpit
services that it will be a weariness to hear him; and yet you
shall find him, from time to time, throwing a whole community
into excitement, gathering around him crowded houses night
after night, and exercising as it might seem, for the space of
three or four weeks, an irresistible sway in favor of religion.
Such cases are by no means uncommon. Some of the most successful practitioners in the art of the Anxious Bench show themselves lamentably defective in the power of serious godliness,
as well as in mental cultivation generally. The general habit
of their lives is worldly and vain, and their religion, apart
from the occasional whirlwinds of excitement in which they are
allowed to figure in their favorite way, may be said to be
characteristically superficial and cold. Nay, the evidence may
be palpable that religion has nothing at all to do with the

system in cases where it is employed with the greatest apparent
effect. Nothing is more common than for those even who glory
in the power of the Anxious Bench, as employed within their own
communion, to look with entire distrust on its results as exhibited in the practice of other sects. What is trumpeted in
the one case as a glorious revival, is allowed to pass in the
other without notice as at best a questionable excitement. In
this way it is practically acknowledged that the system does
not necessarily involve spiritual power. It can be made to
work as well in connection with truth. It is as fully at the
service of quackery and imposture, as it can be available in
the cause of genuine religion. It is well adapted, indeed, to
become the sport of quacks under every name. All wild and
fanatical sects employ it with equal success. Campbellites,
Winebrennerians and Universalists show the same power, when
necessary, in producing revivals under this form. Millerism
and Mormonism, it may be added, are just as capable of doing
wonders in the same way; though the last has declared itself
not favorable to the Anxious Bench as interfering with regular
and rational worship. Nothing can be more precarious, then,
than the argument for this system, as drawn from its apparent
effects and results. In the sphere of religion, as indeed in
the world of life generally, the outward can have no value, except as it stands continually in the power of the inward. To
estimate the force of appearances, we must try their moral constitution; and this always involves a reference to the source
from which they spring. A miracle, in the true sense, is not
simply a prodigy, nakedly and separately considered. It must
include a certain moral character. Especially there must be
inward freedom and divine strength in the person from whom it
proceeds. No wonder-works could authenticate the mission of a
man pretending to come from God who should display in all his
movements an inward habit at war with the idea of religion.

And just as little are we bound to respect, in the present case,
the mere show of force, without regard to the agency by which
it is exhibited. Those who deal in the Anxious Bench are accustomed to please themselves with the idea that it is an argument of power on the part of their ministry, to be able in this
way to produce a great outward effect.* This is considered
sufficient, it might seem, apart from the personality of the
preacher altogether, to authenticate his strength. But no
judgment can be more superficial. The personality of the
preacher must ever condition and determine the character of his
work. It were easy to give a score of living examples in which
the semblance of success on a large scale, in the use of this
system at the present time, is at once belied by palpable defect here. The men are of such a spirit that it is not possible to confide intelligently in any results it may seem to
reach by their ministry. We are authorized before all examination to pronounce them valueless and vain. So utterly weak, in
this argument, is the appeal to *facts*, as managed frequently by
superficial thinkers. In every view of the case, the fruits of
the Anxious Bench must be received with great caution, while to
a great extent they are entitled to no confidence whatever.

———

    * "Who ever dreamed that a single invitation to penitents
to come forward, and a personal conversation with them on their
spiritual condition and duties, demanded uncommon inward spiritual force?" Thus the editor of the *Luth. Observer*, November
17, 1843, mystifying the point as usual. His colleague of
Pittsburgh, however, comes up boldly to the mark, "A quack may
preach a sermon and make a long prayer," he tells us; "but it
takes something more than a quack *so* to preach the truth that
sinners will *immediately* come forward to the anxious bench."--
Davis' Plea, p. 32. Right bravely spoken; but the very dialect of quackdom itself.

CHAPTER III

Nature of Quackery.--To Rely on Forms or Measures Shows Inward Weakness.--"New Measures" a Substitute for True Strength,-- Where They are in Honor, Ample Space is Found for Novices and Quacks

It has been shown that the successful use of the Anxious Bench calls for no spiritual power. It is within the reach of fanaticism and error to be employed in their service, with as much facility as it may be enlisted in the service of truth. It is no argument of strength, as is often imagined, that a preacher is able to use such an agency with effect. I now go to a step farther and pronounce it an argument of *spiritual weakness* that he should find it either necessary or desirable to call in such help. There is a measure of quackery in the expedient, which always implies the want of strength, so far as it may be relied on at all, as being of material account in carrying on the work of God.*

---

* It has been found convenient with some, it would seem, to misunderstand what is said of spiritual weakness and spiritual strength in this part of the tract. They affect to take it as having respect to intellect, learning, eloquence, &c.; as though it implied that men of ordinary or small abilities are entitled to no respect in the Church; and so we are referred to Paul's *Not many wise men after the flesh, not many mighty, &c.* 1 Cor. i. 26-28, as a Scriptural rebuke upon every such judgment. Thus also the editor of the *Lutheran Observer*, Jan. 5, 1844, lugs in by the neck a passage to the same purpose by President Edwards to show that this "great master-spirit did not look upon the *inward weakness* of his co-workers as a matter of reproach." At the close of it he gravely adds; "This quotation needs no comment from us; it speaks for itself. All we ask is to compare it with Dr. N.'s labored effort about the oft-repeated 'inward weakness' of revival preachers in the present day." Now if there be anything plain in the whole tract, it is that the inward weakness attributed by it, not to *revival* preachers, but to such as glory in the system of the Bench, is

46

Quackery consists in pretension to an inward virtue or power, which is not possessed in fact, on the ground of a mere show of the strength which such power or virtue is supposed to include. The self-styled physician who, without any knowledge of the human frame, undertakes to cure diseases by a sovereign panacea in the shape of fluid, powder or pill, is a quack; and there is no doubt abundance of quackery in the medical profession, under more professional forms, where practice is conducted without any true professional insight and power. Such practice may at times seem eminently successful, and yet it is quackery notwithstanding. The same false show of power may, of course, come into view in every department of life. It makes up in fact a large part of the action and business of the world. Quack lawyers, quack statesmen, quack scholars, quack teachers, quack *gentlemen*, quacks in a word of every name and shape, meet us plentifully in every direction. We need not be surprised, then, to find the evil fully at home also in the sphere of religion. Indeed it might seem to be more at home here than any where else. Here especially the heart of man, "deceitful above all things and desperately wicked," has shown itself most ingenious in all ages in substituting the shadow for the reality, the form for the substance, the outward for the inward. The religion of the world has always been, for the most part, arrant quackery. Paganism can exist under no other form. The mummery of Rome, as aping powers of a higher order, is the most stupendous system of quackery the world has ever witnessed. But quackery in the Church is not confined of course to Rome. Christianity, in its very nature, must ever act on the corrupt

---

that of the "flesh" mainly as opposed to the strength which is from God's Spirit. When I am weak, says Paul, then am I strong. Quackery affects to be strong, but is weak in fact. Its weakness does not stand in the measure of its own resources so much as in its separation from the ground of all strength in God.

nature of man as a powerful stimulus to the evil. No system
embraces such powers, inward, deep and everlasting. These man
would fain appropriate and make his own, in an external way,
without relinquishing himself, and entering soul and body that
sphere of the Spirit in which alone they can be understood and
felt. So Simon Magus dreamed of purchasing the gift of God,
and clothing himself with it in the way of outward possession.
He was a quack; the prototype and prince of evangelical quacks.
The second century shows us the whole Christian world bril-
liantly illuminated with rival systems of quackery under the
name of Gnosticism, which for a time seemed to darken the sun
of truth itself by their false but powerful glare. Afterwards,
under a less idealistic garb, the veil fairly enthroned itself
in the Church. The Reformation was the resurrection of the
Truth once more, in its genuine and original life. Luther was
no quack. But Protestantism itself soon had its quacks again
in plentiful profusion, and has them all the world over at the
present day. Christianity, as of old, serves to call the false
spirit continually into action. Some whole sects stand only in
the element of quackery. And among all sects it is easy to
find the same element to some extent actively at work; sometimes under one form, and sometimes under another; but always
exalting the outward at the cost of the inward and promising in
the power of the flesh what can never be accomplished except in
the power of the spirit.

Wherever *forms* in religion are taken to be--we will not
say the spiritual realities themselves with which the soul is
concerned, for the error in that shape would be too gross--but
the power and force at least by which these realities are to be
apprehended, without regard to their own invisible virtue,
there we have quackery in the full sense of the term. Religion
must have forms, as well as an inward living force. But these
can have no value, no proper reality, except as they spring per-

petually from the presence of that living force itself. The
inward must be the bearer of the outward. Quackery, however,
reverses the case. The outward is made to bear the inward.
The shrine, consecrated with the proper ceremonies, *must* become
a shechinah. Forms have a virtue in them to bind and rule the
force of things. Such forms may be exhibited in a ritual, or
in a creed, or in a scheme of a religious experience mechanically apprehended; but in the end the case is substantially the
same. It is quackery in the garb of religion without its inward life and power.

That *old* forms are liable to be abused, and have been extensively thus abused in fact, is easily admitted. But it is
not always recollected that *new* forms furnish precisely the
same opportunity for the same error. It is marvellous indeed
how far this seems to be overlooked by the zealous advocates
of the system of New Measures in our own day. They propose to
rouse the Church from its dead formalism. And to do this effectually, they strike off from the old ways of worship, and
bring in new and strange practices that are adapted to excite
attention. These naturally produce a theatrical effect, and
this is taken at once for an evidence of waking life in the
congregation. One measure, losing its power in proportion as
it becomes familiar, leads to the introduction of another. A
few years since a sermon was preached and published by a somewhat distinguished revivalist, in which the ground was openly
taken that there must be a constant succession of new measures
in the Church, to keep it alive and awake; since only in this
way could we hope to counteract permanently the force of that
spiritual gravitation, by which the minds of men are so prone
continually to sink towards the earth in the sphere of religion.
The philosophy this precisely by which the Church of Rome, from
the fourth century downward, was actuated in all her innovations. Her worship was designed to make up through the flesh

what was wanting in the spirit. The friends of new measures affect to be more free than others from the authority of mere forms. They wish not to be fettered and cramped by ordinary methods. And yet none make more account in fact of forms. They discard old forms, only to trust the more blindly in such as are new. Their methods are held to be all-sufficient for awakening sinners and effecting their conversion! They have no faith in ordinary pastoral ministrations, comparatively speaking; no faith in the Catechism. Converts made in this way are regarded with suspicion. But they have great faith in the Anxious Bench and its accompaniments. Old measures they hold to be in their very nature unfriendly to the spirit of revivals; they are the "letter that killeth." But new measures "make alive." And yet they are *measures* when all is done; and it is only by losing sight of the inward power of truth that any can be led to attach to them any such importance.

To rely upon the Anxious Bench, to be under the necessity of having recourse to new measures of any sort to enlist attention or produce effect in the work of the gospel, shows a want of inward spiritual force. If it be true that old forms are dead and powerless in the minister's hands, the fault is not in the forms, but in the minister himself; and it is the very impotence of quackery to think of mending the case essentially by the introduction of new forms. The man who had no power to make himself felt in the catechetical class is deceived most assuredly and deceives others when he seems to be strong in the use of the anxious bench. Let the power of religion be present in the soul of him who is called to serve at the altar, and no strange fire will be needed to kindle the sacrifice. He will require no new measures. His strength will appear rather in resuscitating, and clothing with their ancient force the institutions and services already established for his use. The freshness of a divine life, always young and always new, will

stand forth to view in forms that before seemed sapless and
dead. Attention will be engaged; interest excited; souls drawn
to the sanctuary. Sinners will be awakened and born into the
family of God. Christians will be builded up in faith, and
made meet for the inheritance of the saints in light. Religion
will grow and prosper. This is the true idea of evangelical
power. But let a preacher be inwardly weak, though ambitious
at the same time of making an impression in the name of religion, and he will find it necessary to go to work in a different way. Old forms must needs be dull and spiritless in his
hands. His sermons have neither edge nor point. The services
of the sanctuary are lean and barren. He can throw no interest
into the catechism. He has no heart for family visitation and
no skill to make it of any account. Still he desires to be
doing something in his spiritual vocation, to convince others
and to satisfy himself that he is not without strength. What
then is to be done? He must resort to quackery; not with clear
consciousness, of course; but instinctively, as it were, by the
pressure of inward want. He will seek to do by the flesh what
he finds himself too weak to effect by the spirit. Thus it becomes possible for him to make himself felt. New measures fall
in exactly with his taste, and are turned to fruitful account
by his zeal. He becomes theatrical; has recourse to solemn
tricks; cries aloud; takes strange attitudes; tells exciting
stories; calls out the anxious, &c. In this way possibly he
comes to be known as a revivalist, and is counted among those
who preach the Gospel "with the demonstration of the Spirit and
with power." And yet when all is done he remains as before
without true spiritual strength. New measures are the refuge
of weakness.

There may be cases indeed in which genuine power will express itself in new forms. But when this occurs it will always

be without ostentation or effort. Miracles are ever natural as
distinguished from mere wonder-works and feats of legerdemain.
The form is the simple product of the power it represents, growing forth from it, and filled with it at every point. Where
this is the case, what is new is at the same time free and entitled to our respect. But such instances can never authorize
imitation where the same inward power is not present. Such imitation is quackery and an argument of weakness. Paul had
power to wield the name of Jesus with effect for the expulsion
of demons: but when the sons of Sceva, the Jew, undertook to
exorcise in the same way, the demoniac fell upon them, and
drove them naked and wounded from the house. They were quacks.
Ezekiel prophesied in the valley of dry bones, and there was a
noise and bodily action, as though *this* must certainly include
the breath of life, the whole business sinks into a solemn
farce. The Spirit of God, on the day of Pentecost, came like
a mighty rushing wind on the disciples in Jerusalem, causing
them to speak with tongues; but when a religious meeting is
turned into a babel, to make it pentecostal, it deserves to be
reprobated as savoring more of hell than heaven. Life is always beautiful in its place; but hideous and ghastly are the
muscular actings of a galvanized corpse. An apostrophe from
the lips of Whitefield might thrill, like an electric shock,
through a whole congregation, and yet be no better than a vulgar mountebank trick, as imitated by an ordinary revivalist,
affecting to walk in his steps. An Edwards might so preach the
truth as to force his hearers from their seats, and yet be no
pattern whatever for those who with design and calculation call
in the device of "decision acts," as they are termed, to create
a similar show of power. Whitefield and Edwards needed no new
measures to make themselves felt.* They were genuine men of

_____

* Whitefield and Edwards! exclaim the champions of the

God, who had strength from heaven in themselves. They were no quacks.

The system of New Measures then is to be deprecated, as furnishing a refuge for weakness and sloth in the work of the ministry, and in this way holding out a temptation, which, so far as it prevails, leads ministers to undervalue and neglect the cultivation of that true inward strength without which no measures can be at last of much account. This is a great evil.

It is a vastly more easy thing to carry forward the work of religion in this way than it is to be steadily and diligently true to the details of ministerial duty as prescribed by the apostle Paul. To be "vigilant, sober and of good behaviour"-- not "self-willed, not soon angry"--"just, holy, temperate"-- "one that ruleth well his own house, having his children in subjection with all gravity"--holding fast the faithful word in such sort "that he may be able by sound doctrine both to exhort and convince the gainsayers;" to "follow after righteousness,

-----

Bench; they were both thorough going New Measure men, and it is a slander upon their names to speak of them as belonging to the opposite interest. Now it is not said here that they tolerated no new things in the worship of God; but only that they *needed* nothing of this sort to make themselves felt. What was new, in their case, was not sought; it came of itself, the free natural result of the power it represented. Whitefield had recourse to new methods himself to some extent, and Edwards carried his toleration of such things far in favor of others; but in neither instance could it be said that any value was attached to what was thus out of the common way, for its own sake, or as something to be aimed at with care and design beforehand. The judgment of Edwards in this case moreover, it should be remembered, as given in his *Thoughts on the Revival in New England,* had respect to the particular things it sanctions, not in a general way, but as related to an extraordinary work of God, of great extent and long continuance, most amply authenticated on *other* grounds. It is a widely different case when we are required to accept such things on their *own* credit as the evidence of a revival, or as the power of which it is to be secured.

godliness, faith, love, patience, meekness," so as to be "an
example of the believers in word, in conversation, in charity,
in spirit, in faith, in purity;" to be "gentle unto all men,
apt to teach, patient, in meekness instructing those that oppose themselves;" to meditate on divine things, and to be
wholly given to them, so as to be continually profiting in the
view of all; to "endure hardness as a good soldier of Jesus
Christ;" to be a scribe well instructed in the law, a workman
that need not to be ashamed, able to bring forth from the
treasury of God's word things new and old, as they may be
wanted; to preach week after week, so as to instruct and edify
the souls of men, to be earnest, faithful, pungent in the lec-
ture room and catechetical class; to be known in the family
visitation, in the sick chamber, in the dwelling places of poverty and sorrow, as the faithful pastor, "watching for souls,"
whose very presence serves to remind men of holiness and heaven,
not at certain seasons only, but from month to month, from one
year always to another; all this is something great and difficult, and not to be compassed without a large amount of inward
spiritual strength. But it calls for comparatively little
power for a man to distinguish himself as a leader in period-
ical religious excitements, where zeal has room for outward
display, and wholesale action is employed to discharge within a
month the claims of a year. It is not asserted that a minister
must be destitute of the qualifications that are required to
make a regularly faithful and efficient pastor in order that he
may be fitted to make himself conspicuous in this way; but most
assuredly such *may* be the case. A man may be mighty in the use
of new measures, preaching every day if need be for three weeks
to crowded congregations, excited all the time; he may have the
anxious bench filled at the close of each service and the whole
house thrown into disorder; he may have groaning, shouting,
clapping, screaming, a very bedlam of passion, all around the

altar; and as the result of all, he may be able to report a
hundred converts or more, translated by the process, according
to his own account, from darkness into God's marvellous light.
He may be able to act the same part in similar scenes, at different places, in the course of a winter; and, for the time
being, his name may be familiar to the lips of men as a *revivalist,* whose citizenship might be supposed to hold in the third
heavens. All this *may* be, where to an attentive observer it
shall soon be painfully evident, at the same time, that the
true and proper strength of a man of God is wholly wanting. A
man may so distinguish himself and yet have no power to study,
think or teach. He may be crude, chaotic, without cultivation
or discipline. He may to too lazy to read or write. There may
be no power whatever in his ordinary walk or conversation to
enforce the claims of religion. Meet him in common secular
connections, and you will find him in a great measure unfelt in
the stream of worldliness with which he is surrounded. Often
he is covetous, often vain; often without a particle of humility or meekness. His zeal, too, seems to exhaust itself in
each spasmodic "awakening" through which it is called to pass.
The man who appeared to be all on fire for the salvation of
souls, and ready to storm even the common proprieties of life
for the sake of the gospel, shows himself now marvellously
apathetic towards the whole interest. He has no heart to seize
common opportunities, in the house or by the way, to say a word
in favor of religion. It is well indeed if he be not found re-
laxing altogether his ministerial activity, both in the pulpit
and from house to house. The truth is, he has no capacity, no
inward sufficiency, for the ordinary processes of evangelical
labor. Much is required to be a faithful minister of the New
Testament; whilst small resources in comparison are needed for
that semblance of power to which a man may attain by the successful use of the system now in view.

Here, then, is a strong temptation presented to ministers. They are in danger of being seduced by the appeals which this system makes to their selfishness and sloth. It offers to their view a "short method of doing God's great work," and a sort of "royal road," at the same time, to ministerial reputation. How easy, in these circumstances, for even a good man to have his judgment warped and his practice disturbed. And how natural that weakness, under every form, should rejoice to take refuge in the shelter thus brought within his reach.

It should be considered a calamity in any community, or in any religious denomination, to have this system in fashionable and popular use. Let the idea prevail that those who employ new measures in the gospel work are the friends pre-eminently of serious heart religion, and of all evangelical interests; whilst such as frown upon them are to be regarded with suspicion, as at best but half awake in the service of Christ. Let it be counted enough to authenticate the power of a pastor's ministrations that he shall be able to furnish, from winter to winter, a flaming *report* of some three week's awakening in his charge, in the course of which scores of sinners have been drawn to the anxious bench, and immediately afterwards hurried to the Lord's table. Let some religious paper, known as the organ of the Church, herald these *reports,* from week to week, without inquiry or discrimination, as revival intelligence, proclaiming them worthy of all confidence, and glorifying both the measures and the men concerned in the triumphs they record. Let those who are counted "pillars in the church" give their sanction to the same judgment, openly honoring the new system, or quietly conniving at what they may not entirely approve, so as by their very cautions and exceptions to forward the whole interest in fact. Let the sentiment be industriously cherished that with this interest is identified in truth the cause of revivals itself, and that lukewarmness, and dead orthodoxy, and indifference, if not absolute hostility, towards prayermeetings, missionary efforts, and all good things, characterize as a matter of course all who refuse to do it homage. Let this state of things hold with respect to the subject, and it needs no great discernment to see that it is likely to work disastrously upon the character and fortunes of the Church so circumstanced. The attention of ministers will be turned away from more important, but less ostentatious methods of promoting religion. Preaching will become shallow. The catechism may be possibly still treated with professed respect, but practically it will be shorn of its honor and force. Education may be considered to some extent necessary for the work of the ministry, but in fact no great care will be felt to have it either thorough or complete. Ignorance, sciolism and quackery will lift up the head on all sides and show themselves off as the "great power of God." Novices will abound, "puffed up with pride," each wiser in his own conceit than seven men that can render a reason. Young men, candidates for the sacred office, will be encouraged to try their hand at the new system before they have well commenced their studies, and finding that they have power to make themselves felt in this way, will yield their unfledged judgment captive to its charms, so as to make no account afterwards of any higher form of strength. Study and the retired cultivation of personal holiness will seem to their zeal an irksome restraint; and making their lazy, heartless course of preparation as short as possible, they will go out with the reputation of educated ministers, blind leaders of the blind, to bring the ministry into contempt, and fall themselves into the condemnation of the devil. Whatever arrangements may exist in favor of a sound and solid of religion, their operation will be to a great extent frustrated and defeated by the predominant influence of a sentiment, practically adverse to the very object they are designed to reach.

Thus will the ministry be put, more or less, out of joint by the force of the wrong judgment involved in the system of New Measures, where it has come to be fashionable and popular. The Church must suffer corresponding harm, of course, in all her interests. The old landmarks grow dim. Latitudinarian views gain ground. Fanatical tendencies gather strength. The ecclesiastical body is swelled with heterogenous elements loosely brought together and actuated by no common life, except sectarian bigotry may be entitled to such name. False views of religion abound. Conversion is everything, sanctification nothing. Religion is not regarded as the life of God in the soul that must be cultivated in order that it may grow, but rather as a transient excitement to be renewed from time to time by suitable stimulants presented to the imagination. A taste for noise and rant supersedes all desire for solid knowledge. The susceptibility of the people for religious instruction is lost on the one side, along with the capacity of the ministry to impart religious instruction on the other. The details of Christian duty are but little understood or regarded. Apart from its seasons of excitement, no particular church is expected to have much power. Family piety and the religious training of the young are apt to be neglected.

It is a calamity, then, in the general view of the case now taken, for a community to be drawn into the vortex of this system as a reigning fashion. The occasional use of it might be comparatively safe; in some hands, *perhaps*, without harm altogether. But let it be in credit and reputation for a short time on a given field, and its action will be found to be just as mischievous as has now been described. It will prove the refuge of weakness and the resort of quacks. It will be a "wide and effectual door" to let in fanaticism and error. It will be as a worm at the root of the ministry, silently consuming its strength; and as a mildew on the face of congregations

and churches, beneath whose blighting presence no fruit can be
brought to perfection.

CHAPTER IV

*Action of the Bench.--It Creates a False Issue for the
Conscience.--Unsettles True Seriousness.--Usurps
the Place of the Cross.--Results in Widespread,
Lasting Spiritual Mischief*

Let us now fix our attention on the action of the new system, directly and immediately considered. Without regard to
its more remote connections and consequences, let us inquire
what its merits may be in fact, as it respects the interest it
proposes to promote, namely, the conversion of souls. Is it
the wisdom of God and the power of God, as its friends would
fain have us believe, for convincing careless sinners and
bringing them to the foot of the Cross? Let the Anxious Bench,
in this case, be taken as the representative of the entire system. No part of it carries a more plausible aspect. If it be
found wanting and unworthy of confidence here, we may safely
pronounce it to be unworthy of confidence at every other point.

As usually applied in seasons of religious excitement, I
hold the measure to be spiritually dangerous; requiring great
skill and much caution to be used without harm in any case, and
as managed by quacks and novices (who are most ready to be
taken with it) more suited to ruin souls than to bring them to
heaven. This view is established by the following positions.

1. *The Anxious Bench, in the case of an awakened sinner,
creates a false issue for the conscience.* God has a controversy with the impenitent. He calls upon them to acknowledge
their guilt and misery with true repentance, and to submit
themselves by faith to the righteousness of the gospel. It is
their condemnation that they refuse to do this. When any sinner begins to be sensible in any measure of his actual position
in this view, he is so far awakened and under conviction. Now

in these circumstances what does his case mainly require?
Clearly, that he should be made to see more and more the true
nature of the controversy in which he is involved, till he
finds himself inwardly engaged to lay down the weapons of his
rebellion and cast himself upon the mercy of God in Jesus
Christ. He needs to have his eyes fastened and fixed on his
own relations spiritually considered, to the High and Holy One
with whom he is called to make his peace. The question is,
will he repent and yield his heart to God or not? This is the
true issue to be met and settled; and it is all-important that
he should be so shut up to this in his thoughts that he may
have no power to escape the force of the challenge which it involves. That spiritual treatment must be considered best in
his case which serves most fully to bring this issue into view,
and holds him most effectually confronted with it in his conscience, beneath the clear light of the Bible. But let the
sinner in this state be called to come forward to a particular
seat in token of his anxiety. He finds himself at once under
the force of a different challenge. The question is not, will
he repent and yield his heart to God, but will he go to the
anxious bench; which is something different altogether. Thus a
new issue is raised, by which the other is obscured or thrust
out of sight. It is a false issue too; because it seems to
present the real point in controversy, when in fact it does not
do so at all, but only distracts and bewilders the judgment so
far concerned. While the awakened person is balancing the
question of going to the anxious bench, his mind is turned away
from the contemplation of the immediate matter of quarrel between himself and God. The higher question is merged, for the
time, in one that is lower. A new case is created for the conscience of artificial, arbitrary form and ambiguous authority.
Can it be wise thus to shift the ground of debate, exchanging a
strong position with regard to the sinner for one that is weak?

Suppose it were made a point with awakened persons that they should rise up and confess before the congregation all their leading sins, in detail and by name, to break their pride, show their desire to be saved, excite prayer in their behalf, &c.; would not this requirement, interposed as a preliminary to the main point of conversion itself, and enforced by no proper sanction for the conscience, serve only to turn away the attention of such persons from the object with which it should be employed, thwarting the very interest it might affect to promote? And is there not room for objection to the Anxious Bench on the very same ground? It is certainly a little strange that the class of persons precisely who claim to be the most strenuous in insisting upon unconditional, immediate submission to God, scarcely tolerating that a sinner should be urged to pray or read the Bible, lest his attention should be diverted from that one point, are as a general thing nevertheless quite ready to interpose *this* measure in his way to the foot of the cross, as though it included in fact the very thing itself. And yet a pilgrimage to the Anxious Bench is in its own nature as much collateral to the duty of coming to Christ as a pilgrimage to Jerusalem. In either case a false issue is presented to the anxious soul by which for the time a true sight of circumstances is hindered rather than promoted.

It may be thought, indeed, that the movement of going to the Anxious Bench is so easily performed as not to be properly open to this exception. It may be considered a mere *circumstance* that can have no weight practically in the view now presented. But we shall see that this is not the case. However small the point involved may seem, it is not only of account, as producing for the moment a factitious case of conscience, open to "doubtful disputation," but it includes also actual difficulty that cannot fail to be felt. Whether the challenge be refused or accepted, it becomes in most cases more than a cir-

cumstance, and is of no small force in fact in the way of em-
barrassing the proper exercises of an awakened soul.

2. *The Anxious Bench, in the case of those who come to it,
is adapted by its circumstances to disturb and distract the
thoughts of the truly serious, and thus to obstruct the action
of truth in their minds.* It is no doubt quite a common thing
for persons to be carried into this movement who have little or
no seriousness at the time, urged forward by sympathy, or
superstition, or a mere taste for distinction. There is much
reason in the remark of the Rev. Dr. Miller when he tells us
that he should expect, in calling out the anxious, to find the
persons rising and presenting themselves to be, for the most
part, the forward, the sanguine, the rash, the self-confident
and the self-righteous, while many who keep their seats would
prove to be the modest, the humble, the brokenhearted, the very
depth of whose seriousness had restrained them from coming forward in this way.* And yet the measure may be expected to prevail of course with many persons also who are truly under conviction, and whom nothing but the fear of losing their souls
could engage to thrust themselves thus into view. In any case,
however, the genuine religious feeling that may exist is likely
to be in a great measure overwhelmed by the excitement that
must be involved in the very act of coming to such a resolution, and subsequently in carrying it into effect. The truth
of this remark will be more clear when we remember that young
persons, and females especially, form the main body commonly of
those who are drawn to the anxious bench. Their susceptibility
fits them to be wrought upon more readily than others to the
extent that is necessary to secure this point. But the same
susceptibility renders it certain that in circumstances so

---

* Appendix to Sprague on Revivals, p. 38.

exciting it will be impossible for them to hold their thoughts
or feelings in any such balance as the interest of religion requires. They of all others would *need* to be sheltered from
stimulating impressions in this form at such a time instead of
being forced to face them in their weakness.

Take a single case in illustration of the way in which the
system may be expected to work. Here is a gentle girl, sixteen
or seventeen years of age. She finds herself in the midst of a
large congregation where at the close of the sermon the minister, encouraged by the general seriousness of the house,
invites all who are concerned for the salvation of their souls
to come forward and place themselves on the anxious seat. She
has been perhaps a long time under some concern, or it may be
that God's truth has been felt for the first time on this occasion; not with *great* force perhaps, but so at least as to bring
her spirit to a solemn stand in the presence of her Maker. She
hears the invitation, but shrinks from the thought of doing
what the minister demands. The call however is reiterated, and
enforced by the most exciting appeals to the imagination.
After a few moments there is a stir; one is going forward to
the bench, and then another, and another. She is struck, moved,
agitated. A struggle has commenced in her bosom which she
herself is not prepared to understand. May she not be fighting
against God, she asks herself, in refusing to go forward with
the rest? All this is crowded on her alarmed conscience by the
character of the occasion in the way in which it is managed by
the minister. Already her soul has passed from the element of
conviction to that of excitement. The "still small voice" of
the Spirit is drowned amid the tumult of her own conflicting
thoughts. But see, she yields. With a desperate struggle, she
has thrown herself forth into the aisle. Trembling and agitated in every nerve, poor victim of quackery, she makes her way,
consciously in the eye of that large watching assembly, from

one end of the house to the other, and sinks half fainting with the effort, into a corner of the magic seat. And now where is she, in spiritual position? Are her tears the measure of her sorrow for sin? Alas, she is farther off from God than she was before this struggle commenced in her father's pew. Calm reflection is departed. Her hold upon the inward has been lost. Could any intelligent Christian parent, truly anxious for the salvation of his daughter, deliberately advise her in circumstances which have been supposed, to seek religion in this way? Can the pastor be wise who is willing to subject the lambs of his flock to such a process, with the view of bringing the good seed of the word to take root and vegetate in their hearts?

3. *The Anxious Bench is adapted to create and foster the ruinous imagination that there is involved in the act of coming to it a real decision in favor of religion.* It is well known in the Church of Rome certain observances are held to carry with them a sort of inward merit in this way, as though by themselves they had power to secure a spiritual blessing. There is a constant tendency with men, indeed, to invest the outward under *some* form with the virtue that belongs only to the inward, so as if possible to "get religion," and hold it as property or means for some other end, instead of entering into it as the proper home of their own being. It is not strange then that the Anxious Bench should be liable to be so abused. It is only strange that sensible persons should make so little account of this danger as is sometimes done. We are gravely told, it is true, that coming to the anxious bench is not considered to be the same thing as coming to Christ.* The

---

* "Who ever pretended that going to the anxious bench is *conversion?*"--*Luth. Observer*, Dec. 15, 1843. And yet, in the same article, it is said again of one who yields to the measure: "Does he not *resolve* no longer to resist the influences of divine grace, and wage war against God, and the efforts of his

measure is represented to be important on other grounds, and
for other purposes. Certainly it is not imagined for a moment
that any one in his senses will be found ready to *say* that coming to the bench is itself religion. But still that some such
impression is liable to be created by the measure, and is extensively created by it in fact as it is commonly used, admits of
no dispute. It is not uncommon indeed for those who make use
of it to throw in occasionally something like a word of caution
with regard to this point; and in some few instances, possibly,
such prudence may be observed as fully to guard against the
danger. But this is not common. As a general thing, even the
cautions that are interposed are in such a form as to be almost
immediately neutralized and absorbed by representations of an
opposite character. The whole matter is so managed as practically to encourage the idea that a veritable step towards Christ
at least, if not actually into His arms, is accomplished in the
act of coming to the anxious seat. I have had an opportunity
of witnessing the use of the measure in different hands and on
different occasions; but in every case it has seemed to me that
room was given for this censure.* Indeed I do not see well how

faithful minister?" Such submission is commonly taken to be
conversion.--In another place the editor finds the *principle* of
the Bench in John vii., 37, *If any man thirst, let him come unto me and drink,* and in Matt. xi., 28, *Come unto me all ye that
labor and are heavy laden, &c.* The parallel is monstrous, and
has a rank smell of pelagianism. In like strain Mr. Davis, of
Pittsburgh, calls the bench a "test," and compares it with the
"anxious river" in which Naaman, the Syrian, was required to
wash, 2 Kings v., 10-12, that he might be cured of his leprosy.
"If no *test-questions* are presented, how can men ever *act,* or
determine whether they will serve God or not?" "Viewed as a
means of bringing sinners to an *immediate decision* on the subject of religion, no reasonable objection can be brought against
it."--*Plea for New Measures,* p. 23-3?. Right bravely spoken
again; but, I repeat it, the very dialect of QUACKDOM!

* "He exhorted them to repent of their sins, and go to

66

the measure could be employed in any case with much effect without the help of some such representation. We find accordingly that the whole process, as it were in spite of itself, runs ordinarily into this form. Sinners are exhorted to come to the anxious bench as for their life by the same considerations precisely that should have force to bring them to Christ, and that could have no force at all in this case if it were not confounded more or less to their perception with the other idea. The burden of all is presented in the beautiful but much prostituted hymn usually sung on such occasions, *Come humble sinner.* The whole of this is made to bear with all the weight the preacher can put into it on the question of coming to the anxious seat. Every effort is employed to shut up the conscience of the sinner to this issue; to make him feel that he *must* come or run the hazard of losing his soul. Advantage is taken of his hopes and fears in every form of awakening and stimulating appeal to draw him from his seat. The call is so represented as to make this the test of penitence. Those who come are welcomed as returning prodigals who have decided to come out from the world and be on the Lord's side; while all who refuse to come are treated as showing just the opposite temper; and it often happens that the preacher, in the warmth of his zeal, charges upon their refusal in this view the same guilt and mad-

---

their forsaken God. To aid them in their return, an anxious seat was prepared on Sabbath evening, &c."--*Corresp. Luth. Obs.,* Dec. 16, 1842. "The anxious seat was introduced through some opposition--and at it the high and the low, the rich and the poor, the old and young, the male and female bowed. They were not ashamed of the despised seat, but presented themselves there with as much avidity as if they were certain of getting a fortune there. And so they did. There they received a title to mansions in the skies, &c."--Jan. 6, 1843. "On Sunday night the anxious were invited to occupy the front seats, for the usual purposes, and O what a crowding was there to the foot of the cross!"--June 8, 1843.

ness and peril precisely that lie upon the deliberate rejection
of Christ himself. Now it is an easy thing to say, in these
circumstances, that after all the Anxious Bench is not substituted for Christ. So the Puseyite and Papist disclaim the idea
of putting into His place the Baptismal Font. But in both cases
it is perfectly plain that Christ is seriously wronged notwithstanding. In both cases the error is practically countenanced
and encouraged that coming to Christ and the use of an outward
form are in whole, or at least to some considerable extent, one
and the same thing; with the difference only that the form in
one case is of divine prescription, while in the other it is
wholly of man's device.

It is true indeed that the "mourners," as they are sometimes termed, are still treated after coming to the bench or
altar as persons yet unconverted. This should neutralize, it
might seem, the idea of any such saving virtue in the measure
as is here supposed to be encouraged in the usual style of
calling out the anxious. But this is not the case. The coming
is not accepted at once as conversion, though exhibited apparently as the same thing immediately before; but still it is
taken practically for something closely bordering on conversion. The mourners are counted nearer to the kingdom of heaven
than they were before. They are exhorted now to "go on," as
having actually begun a divine life. The process of conversion
is commenced. They have come to the birth; and all that is
wanted to bring them fully into the new world of grace is the
vigorous prosecution of the system of deliverance to which they
have now happily committed their souls. The Anxious Bench is
made still to be the laver of regeneration, the gate of paradise, the womb of the New Jerusalem. Conversion is represented
to be far easier here than elsewhere. We find accordingly that
this idea fairly carried out leads certain sects of the full
New Measure stamp to profess a peculiar tact and power in

carrying the process of spiritual delivery regularly out at
once to its proper issue. It is only for want of proper treatment they say, and because "there is not strength to bring
forth," in other cases, that souls are brought thus far without
being born at once into the kingdom. *Their* Anxious Bench, or
the altar where their mourners kneel and roll, is commended to
the world as a more perfect organ of conversion. Once fairly
within its grasp, the soul as a general thing is quickly set
free; often in the course of a few minutes, and very commonly
before the close of the meeting. They know how to "get the
anxious *through*." All this is sufficiently extravagant; but
still it is only a gross expression of the feeling commonly encouraged by the use of the Anxious Bench with regard to its
virtue as a help to conversion. The whole measure is so ordered as to promote the delusion that the use of it serves *some*
purpose in the regeneration of the soul.

4. *Harm and loss to the souls of men flow largely from the
use of the Anxious Bench.* It is an injury in the case of an
awakened sinner to have his attention diverted, in the first
place, from the real issue before him to one that is false. It
is an injury farther to have reflection arrested, and the working of true conviction in part or altogether overwhelmed, by
the excitement of obeying a call to come out in this way. It
is an injury again to be induced to lean upon such a movement;
as though it could have any efficacy at all to bring the soul
near to God. But the harm and loss occasioned by the system
reach much farther than this.

The inward tumult resulting from the occasion is in a high
degree unfavorable to genuine seriousness while it lasts, and
is sure to be followed by a reaction still more hurtful to the
spirit when the occasion is over.

"All means and measures," says the Rev. Dr. Alexander

in his letter to Dr. Sprague, "which produce a high
degree of excitement, or a great commotion of the
passions, should be avoided; because religion does
not consist in these violent emotions, nor is it
promoted by them; and when they subside, a wretched
state of deadness is sure to succeed."

A most unhappy influence is often exerted on those who are
drawn to the anxious bench, and afterwards fall back again
openly to their former careless state. They may have had but
very little conviction, perhaps none at all. But their feelings have been excited, and without knowledge or reflection
they have gone forward among the professed mourners, vaguely
expecting to gain religion in this way. Afterwards they find
themselves completely stripped of all feeling. They have too
much understanding to set any value on their experience, and
too much conscience to be willing that it should pass for more
than they know it to be worth in fact; or possibly they have
swung clear over to the opposite quarter, and have no wish at
all to be, or to be considered religious. And yet they have
been on the anxious bench, and in great distress apparently for
their sins. They have publicly committed themselves in the
case in a way that is not likely soon to be forgotten. All
this works injuriously on their minds now. Rash vows are always hurtful. The posture with regard to religion is altogether worse than it was before. Often disgust and irritation
towards the whole subject are the unfortunate consequence.

But in a vast multitude of instances the operation of the
measure is worse still. The slightly convicted are full as
likely to go forward in the way of profession as they are to go
back. Powerful considerations are at hand besides the interest
of their own salvation to hold them to the course on which they
have entered. They are committed, and have no prospect of coming honorably or comfortably out of their present posture, except by *getting through* on the side towards the Church, and not

70

towards the world. There is room too for the workings of ambition and emulation; a desire to be noticed, and an impatience of being left behind by others in the career of spiritual experience.

> "It ought not to be forgotten," says Dr. Alexander, "that the heart is deceitful above all things, and that strong excitement does not prevent the risings of pride and vain glory. Many become hypocrites when they find themselves the objects of much attention, and affect feelings which are not real."*

And if all such impure motives might be supposed to be out of the way, there is still enough to render the danger of spurious conversion in such circumstances alarmingly great. The mourner strives of course to *feel* faith. The spiritual helpers standing round are actively concerned to see him brought triumphantly through. Excitement rules the hour. No room is found either for instruction or reflection. A sea of feeling, blind, dark and tempestuous, rolls on all sides. Is it strange that souls thus conditioned and surrounded should become the victims of spiritual delusion? All high wrought excitement must in its very nature break when it reaches a certain point. How natural that this relaxation, carrying with it the sense of relief as compared with the tension that had place before, should be mistaken on such an occasion for the peace of religion, that mysterious something which it is the object of all this process to fetch into the mind. And how natural that the wearied subject of such experience should be hurried into a wild fit of joy by this imagination, and stand prepared, if need be, to clap his hands and shout hallelujah over his fancied deliverance. Or even without this mimic sensation, how natural that

---

* Sprague on Revivals. Appendix, p. 7.

the mourner at a certain point should allow himself to be persuaded by his own wishes, or by the authority of the minister perhaps, and other friends telling him how easy it is to believe and urging him at last to consider the thing done; so as to take to himself the comfort of the new birth as it were in spite of his own experience, and be counted among the converted. Altogether the danger of delusion and mistake where this style of advancing the cause of religion prevails must be acknowledged to be very great. The measure of the danger will vary of course with the extent to which the characteristic spirit of the system is allowed to work. A Winebrennerian camp-meeting, surrendering itself to the full sway of this spirit, will carry with it a more disastrous operation than the simple Anxious Bench in a respectable and orderly church. But in any form the system is full of peril as opening the way to spurious conversions and encouraging sinners to rest in hopes that are vain and false.

There need be no reserve in speaking or writing on this subject. Neither charity nor delicacy require us to be silent where the truth of religion is itself so seriously concerned. To countenance the supposition that the souls which are so plentifully "carried through" what is called the process of conversion under this system are generally converted in fact, would be to wrong the Gospel. "Let God be true, though every man should be a liar." Of all the hundreds that are reported from year to year as brought into the kingdom among the Methodists, United Brethren, Winebrennerians, and others who work in the same style, under the pressure of artificial excitement, how small a proportion give evidence subsequently that they have been truly regenerated. The Church at large does not feel bound at all to accept as genuine and worthy of confidence the many cases of conversion they are able to number as wrought with noise and tumult at camp-meetings and on other occasions.

It is taken for granted that a large part of them will not
stand. And so it turns out, in fact. In many cases the fruits
of a great revival are reduced almost to nothing before the end
of a single year. So the system unfolds its own nakedness in a
practical way. And this nakedness comes to view in some measure wherever much account is made of the Anxious Bench. There
may be no methodistical extravagance, no falling down or rolling in the dust, no shouting, jumping or clapping; only the excitement and disorder necessarily belonging to the measure itself; still it is found that conversions made in this way do
not as a general thing wear well. No one whose judgment has
been taught by proper observation will allow himself to confide
in the results of a revival, however loudly trumpeted, in which
the Anxious Bench is known to have played a prominent part. He
may trust charitably that out of the fifty or a hundred converts thus hurried into the Church some will be found "holding
fast the beginning of their confidence firm unto the end;" but
he will stand prepared to hear of a great falling away in the
case of the accession as a whole in the course of no considerable time. Of some such revivals scarce a monument is to be
found at the end of a few months, unless it be in the spiritual
atrophy they have left behind. And it often happens that
churches instead of growing and gathering strength by these triumphs of grace as they are called, seem actually to lose ground
in proportion to their frequency and power. If any weight is
to be attached to observations which are on all sides within
the reach of those who choose to inquire, it must be evident
that this system is in all respects *suited* to produce spurious conversions, so it is continually producing them in fact
to a terrible extent. For the evil is not to be measured of
course simply by the actual amount of open defection that may
take place among those who are thus brought to "embrace religion." So many and so strong are the considerations that must

operate upon a supposed convert to hold fast at least the form
of godliness after it has been once assumed, though wholly ignorant of its power, that we may well be surprised to find the
actual falling away in the case of such ingatherings so very
considerable as now represented. As it is, it becomes certain
in the very nature of the case that this apostacy forms only a
part of the false profession from which it springs. While some
fall back openly to the world, others remain in the Church with
a name to live while they are dead. This presumption is abundantly confirmed by observation. Very many thus introduced into the Church show too plainly by their unhallowed tempers and
the general worldliness of their walk and conversation, that
they have never known what religion means. They have had their
"experience" centering in the Anxious Bench, on which they continue to build their profession and its hopes; but farther than
this they give no signs of life. They have no part nor lot in
the Christian salvation.

Notoriously, no conversions are more precarious and inse-
cure than those of the Anxious Bench. They take place under
such circumstances precisely as should make them the object of
earnest jealousy and distrust. The most ample evidence of
their vanity is presented on every side. And yet the patrons
of the system are generally ready to endorse them, as though
they carried the broad seal of heaven on their face. Of conversions in any other form, they can be sufficiently jealous.
They think it well for the Church to use great caution in the
case of those who have been led quietly under the ordinary
means of grace to indulge the Christian hope. They shrink perhaps from the use of the Catechism altogether, lest they might
seem to aim at a religion of merely human manufacture. But let
the power of the Anxious Bench appear, and, strange to tell,
their caution is at once given to the winds. *This* they proclaim to be the finger of God. Here the work of religion is

presumed at once to authenticate itself. With very little instruction, and almost no examination, all who can persuade
themselves that they are converted, are at once hailed as
brethren and sisters in Christ Jesus, and with as little delay
as possible gathered into the full communion of the Church.
And this is held to be building on the true foundation gold,
silver and precious stones, while such as try to make Christians in a different way are regarded as working mainly, almost
as a matter of course, with wood, hay and stubble. Wonderful
infatuation! Stupendous inconsistency!

CHAPTER V

The Bench Vindicated on Insufficient Grounds:—1. *As Bringing The Sinner to a* Decision; —2. *As Involving Him in a* Committal; —3. *As Giving* Force to His Purpose; —4. *As a Penitential* Discipline;—5. *As Necessary for the Purposes of* Instruction; —6. *As Opening the Way for* Prayer

In view of such disastrous action as we have now been called to contemplate, we ask on what grounds the use of the Anxious Bench is vindicated. These should be of great force to counterbalance the weight of mischief with which it is attended. No divine appointment is pleaded in its favor.* We could not suppose for a moment indeed that any appointment of God could be associated with such bad influences and tendencies as are found to hold in connection with this invention. But it is not pretended to make it of Scriptural authority. It is

---

* A good deal has been said indeed of the *principle* of the Old and New Testaments. But Mr. Denig has just been as successful in vindicating woman preaching, shouting, rolling, &c., in this way, as the editor of the *Lutheran Observer* has been in justifying the anxious bench. All fanatical sects are able to muster something from the Bible which seems to cover, in sound at least, the principle of their peculiarities. So every abuse in the Church of Rome came in, under the shadow of pretended Scriptural precedent. Her fasts, her vigils, her relics, her penances, &c., all found a show of support in the word of God. The angelic institute of *monkery* was abundantly commended by the same authority. Was not John the Baptist a monk, and Elijah the Tishbite; and Elisha the son of Shaphat; and the sons of the prophets of Jordan; and the Rechabites; were they not examples in point so far at least as the *principle* of the system was concerned? So argued the fathers of the fourth century; and it must be confessed with full as much reason on their side as the friends of New Measures have when they appeal to the Bible in like strain for the support of their favorite system.

vindicated on other grounds with variable argument to suit the
occasion. These, however, are by no means satisfactory.

1. It serves, we are told, to bring awakened sinners to a
decision. They are disposed to avoid this. They halt between
two opinions. They should not be allowed to leave the sanctuary in this state. The Gospel calls for a present determination. It is well, therefore, to shut them up to that point.
This is done by the Anxious Bench.*

This sounds well, But what is it that the sinner decides
when he rises and goes forward to the anxious seat? He is encouraged to come, singing,

> "I'll go to Jesus, though my sin
>   Hath like a mountain rose;
> I know His courts, I'll enter in,
>   Whatever may oppose."

Is *this* the decision which the movement really involves?
Then it is the same thing with conversion; the resolution of
the prodigal carried into effect when out of a deep sense of
his poverty and misery he *arose and went to his father*. And so
much as this the considerations by which he is urged to come
forward would seem to imply. But when the point is pressed, we
learn that no such extravagant supposition is entertained.
Coming to the anxious bench is *not* coming to Christ. The
sinner seated upon it is unconverted still; hangs still between
Christ and the world; and may still go away halting between two

---

*"It presents the conscience with the *true* issue, and invites the sinner, without delay, to manifest his choice of God
by coming forward. The 'anxious bench' does not suffer the
sinner to go away simply meditating upon what he has heard; to
go away in a state of rebellion, &c. But it calls upon him at
once to submit to God." "Coming to the 'anxious bench' is a
token of submission, and is used as a means wholly to that end."
--*Davis' Plea*, p. 56.

opinions, as fully as if he had not come out in this way at all.
What shall we say of such a *decision*? A decision that decides
nothing? The apostles, we are told, insisted on men's coming
to the point at once in the business of religion, and we should
do the same thing. So certainly we should. But is this such
a point as the apostles were accustomed to press? When Peter
found the multitude awakened on the day of Pentecost, he called
them to an immediate decision. But what was the form in which
this was done? "Repent, and be baptized every one of you in
the name of Jesus Christ, for the remission of sins," cried the
preacher. "Come," roars the modern revival-monger, pleasing
himself with the thought of being like Peter, on the day of
Pentecost, "Come humble sinner, in whose heart a thousand
thoughts revolve, come, come without delay this night, this
moment, come--to the altar or to the anxious bench." Alas for
the parallel!* If it *be* conversion to come out in this way,
let the thing be openly affirmed at once; but if not, why mock
us by calling it a decision, and pretending to find precedents
for it in the Acts of the Apostles?

2. But the ground now is shifted; sinners are not brought
exactly to a decision by the Anxious Bench, but they are
brought at least to a *committal*; and this is considered to be
of great account. Let them go away from the house of God without this, and there will be a reason to fear that their seriousness may evaporate before the next meeting. We should take ad-

---

* "We do not disparage baptism by comparing it to the
anxious bench. By no means; we regard it as a sacrament, and
intended for high purposes; but it also involved the precise
principle in that day that the anxious bench does not. It afforded an opportunity for a public manifestation on the part of
those who submitted to it, of their determination to be Christians. So also does the anxious bench."--*Luth. Obs.*, Dec. 1,
1843. Alas, one may well be pardoned for whispering, *"Why are
you a* LUTHERAN?"

vantage of their feelings when they are excited, and engage them, if possible, to take a step by which they shall feel themselves committed to the world, as well as to their own consciences, in favor of religion. This is done when we get them out to the anxious bench. They bind themselves by this act to seek the Lord. The thing is known and talked about. They *feel* themselves bound, and their shame and pride come in to fortify the higher influences, by which they are urged to go forward and not "draw back unto perdition."

Low and jejune must be the conception of religion which can allow such a view as this to be entertained. It is well indeed that sinners should bind themselves by an inward resolution to seek the Lord while He is to be found; and it is right that they should be urged to do this on all suitable occasions. But such a resolution, to be of any account, must proceed from intelligent reflection and inward self-possession; and it can have no salutary force, except as entertained in the consciousness of God's presence and God's authority, to the exclusion comparatively of all inferior references. Nothing can be more irrational than to think of making the sinner's feelings in this case a trap for his judgment, and then holding him fast by the force of an outward bond. The circumstances in which he is urged to put his soul thus under pledge are the very worst that could well be imagined for the purpose. Volney, in the storm at sea, was not more fully at the mercy of an element beyond himself. Death-bed resolution, notoriously hollow as they are, embrace just as much rational freedom. The vows of a drunkard, in ordinary cases, are but little respected. But here, where excitement, sympathy and passion combine to wrap all spirits in a moral tornado till the brain is found to reel with the bewildering, intoxicating element that surrounds it, the greatest account is made of such engagements, and every art is employed to secure them even from hysterical girls if need be,* that they may feel themselves bound subsequently to "follow on to know the Lord." A large proportion of such resolutions must necessarily be without inward force; and now the sense of the *committal* is indeed required to sustain the solemn step which has been taken. But what is this, in such circumstances, but the substitution of low worldly references, as far as it prevails, for that consciousness of the soul's relations to God, in which alone, as we have already seen, any resolution of this sort can truly stand. So far exactly as the anxious person may be swayed by the thought of consistency, credit, or any similar interest, in continuing to seek religion, the true posture of conviction is wanting altogether. "How *can* ye believe," said Christ, "which receive honor one of another, and seek not the honor that cometh from God only." A reigning respect to the authority of the world under any form disqualifies the soul for transacting honestly in the great interest of religion.

In a multitude of instances these committals are followed by a reaction in the minds of those who are drawn into them of the most unhappy kind. They fall back openly to the world, but not without a feeling of humiliation and spite in the recollection of their own weakness; and their state subsequently is worse than it was before. In the case of many others, the committal has its force no doubt in carrying them forward till they get fully into the Church; and their profession possibly may have the same power to hold them to the forms of religion afterwards, even to the end of life. But it is for the most part a false hope to which they are thus conducted. The Church, in this way, is filled with hypocrites, and not with true

------

* "Have not *hysterical girls* souls to be saved?"--*Luth. Obs.*, Dec. 15, 1843. After due reflection, it seems necessary to answer this searching interrogation in the *affirmative*.

converts.

3. But the ground may be slightly shifted again so as to
present the measure, not in the light exactly of a bond upon
the sinner's soul, but as a *prop* and *support* rather to his weakness. A first step often costs more than a hundred that follow.
A world of hesitation, in certain circumstances, is surmounted
by a single effort to move. The sinner, when first awakened,
shrinks from making his case known, and his concern, pent up in
his own bosom, it not likely to be as strong and active as it
would be if it could appear in an outward form. Let him come
then to the altar or the anxious bench. The man who signs a
temperance pledge finds his resolution to be sober supported by
the act. Hundreds of drunkards have been enabled in this way
to reform completely, who without this help would have had no
power to rise.

This is plausible; but it will not bear examination. A
first step is of great account in religion; but only where it
springs freely from the will; which it cannot do without reflection and self-command. An outward engagement to seek the
Lord can be of no use without a certain measure of intelligent
conviction at work within; and where this is present, it will
not be difficult to secure whatever may be proper or desirable
in the other form without having recourse to an expedient so
full of danger. It is a part of the spiritual policy of the
Romish Church to entice those who are serious by means of vows
into positions from which they cannot draw back, with the view
of thus establishing them in the purpose of a religious life.
But we all know how little is gained in the Romish Church by
this policy. It is true indeed that a drunkard may sign the
temperance pledge even when he is drunk and afterwards keep it.
But there is a vast difference between the object of the temperance pledge and that which it is proposed to reach by means
of the Anxious Bench. The one is fully within the compass of

human will and human strength; the other is beyond it entirely.*
The one may be mastered in the flesh; the other cannot be ap-
proached or understood except in the spirit. In any case however, vows and pledges that spring from excitement rather than
reflection are to be considered fanatical, and as such neither
rational nor free; and though in certain cases men may seem to
be strengthened and supported by them in the prosecution of
good ends belonging to a lower sphere, they are ever to be
deprecated in the sphere of religion as tending only to delusion and sin.

4. The measure is sometimes recommended on the ground
that it is well suited to humble and break the sinner's pride.
The carnal mind is not willing to stoop to the shame of the
cross in the view of a sinful world. It is difficult at the
same time to bring it to a clear sight of this fact in its own
case. But the anxious bench reduces the question to a present
point. If unwilling to stoop to the self-denial involved in
coming to this, how can the awakened person be willing to do
anything that religion requires. Thus the pride and wickedness
of the heart, in relation to the gospel, are forced home upon
the individual's consciousness; and when at length, under
the pressure of this conviction, he goes forward and joins himself openly with the anxious, his pride is prostrated, and he

----

* Mr. *Finney* holds the pledge in the one case, a fair
exemplification of the advantage gained by bringing a sinner to
the bench in the other. The idea is quoted also with approbation by the *Lutheran Observer*, Dec. 1, 1843. Mr. *Davis* finds
gross heresy, antinomianism, fatalism, &c., in the statement of
the tract just at this point, *Plea*, p. 50-54. He speaks forth
boldly the error that lies wrapped up in the very heart and
core of the system he represents. "Does the sinner submit to
God," it is asked with an air of triumph, "or does the Holy
Ghost?" The only proper answer to such a question is, The Holy
Ghost *in the sinner,* or the sinner as born of the Spirit of
Christ submits to God. Any view that stops short of this is
rotten as Pelagianism itself.

is no longer ashamed to appear earnestly concerned for the salvation of his soul.

But it is easy to see that on the same principle any *test*
which might be imagined, for the same purpose, could be justified with equal ease. The sinner might be required to sit at
the church door, clothed in sackcloth and ashes, begging an
interest in the prayers of all the entering worshippers; or to
travel through all the aisles of the church on his knees in
token of his humiliation. If unwilling to bend to such a requirement, how should he be counted truly in earnest with respect to the main point? In this way the whole system of
Romish penance might challenge our respect. In truth, however,
no account is to be made of any such outward demonstration as a
test or token of the sinner's feelings in the particular view
now considered! Popish penances involve commonly no spiritual
mortification, and have no tendency whatever to reconcile men
to the reproach of Christ. The sinner may be brought to lick
the dust, if need be, under the pressure of an alarmed conscience, without a particle of that inward humiliation before
God which the idea of religion demands. So it is possible, and
no doubt exceedingly common, for persons to take their seat on
the anxious bench with very little if any feeling at all of
this sort. Where the idea prevails that there is religion to
some extent in the very act itself of coming out in this way,
hundreds may easily be engaged to do so, just as under parallel
circumstances they might be engaged to flagellate themselves
publicly through the streets, without the least benefit in the
way of a conquest over their carnal pride. In some cases the
occupancy of the bench may indeed be attended with the wholesome discipline of humiliation in the way supposed, preparing
the spirit to follow Jesus "without the camp, bearing his reproach;" but it is just as certain that the same result has
been secured in *some* cases by the penitential castigations of

the Church of Rome, or the wilful self-inflictions of fanaticism in its worst forms. Where the soul is already prepared
for spiritual humiliation, either the scourge or the bench, if
duly accredited to the mourner's conscience as the power of God
for the purpose, may serve as an occasion to promote this end.
This is no reason however why we should have recourse to one or
the other in seeking to advance the interests of religion.
There is no direct adaptation in either to produce evangelical
humiliation. They are suited rather, as has been shown already
in the case of the bench, to blind the soul to the true nature
of such humiliation by fixing its attention unduly on outward
references and outward acts, and challenging it to a *wilful*
more than to a *willing* service. It is well to remember here
what the apostle says most profoundly on the subject of all
such "will-worship," with its "show of wisdom," at the close of
the second chapter of his epistle to the Colossians.

5. But again the use of the Anxious Bench is vindicated,
as affording an opportunity for meeting the case of awakened
sinners with suitable *instruction*. When they are called out in
this way they become known. They can be addressed collectively,
and conversed with individually. What they need is particular
instruction suited to their particular states. It is not by
dashing water in a large way over a congregation of empty bot-
tles that a minister can expect to get even a few of them
filled; if he would labor to any purpose he must come down and
take each bottle separately by the neck, and pour the water in
according to the capacity of its mouth.

But when we look a little into the matter we shall find
this object of instruction reduced to a perfect farce. There
are two ways in which the occupants of an Anxious Bench may be
addressed. What is said may be spoken to all at once, or they
may be taken one by one in succession. If there are too many
for the minister to manage himself in this way, he may engage

others to take part with him in the work. This must be considered the method most congenial with the idea of the system.
For the object, we are told, is to make instruction particular
and specific; and how can this be accomplished so well as by
taking each case separately? It is customary accordingly, when
the anxious are fairly in their place, for the process of
instruction to commence in this way. The minister comes to one,
the first on the bench, and bending forward proceeds in a low
voice to ask a question or two with regard to the person's
spiritual condition. These are answered commonly in the most
general and confused way. Then follows a short exhortation,
for the most part in the same general strain. The whole conference may not last more than some three or four minutes; for
there are a number to be conversed with; and regard must be had
at the same time to the patience of the congregation. So the
ceremony passes forward to a second, and then to a third, and
so on, till all have their turn. And this is called spiritual
instruction! If a physician were seen handling a dozen of
patients in the same style the spectacle might well call for
derision. But after all it would be no such mummery as we have
here. One of the most difficult and delicate functions a minister is called to perform, is that of giving counsel to awakened sinners. None calls for more caution and discrimination.
It is hard to ascertain correctly the state of the spiritual
patient, and hard to suit the prescription wisely to his particular wants. It is so where there may be the fullest opportunity for free, calm investigation in the family visit or a
private interview. But here, where all surrounding influences
conspire to complicate the difficulty to the greatest extent,
in the midst of commotion without and commotion within, it is
pretended to dispose of a dozen such cases perhaps in the
course of half an hour. And to make the matter worse, if the
number of the anxious be considerable, this, that, and the

other helper is called in, some crude exhorter perhaps, some
strippling student just starting on his way *towards* the ministry, or some forward novice, himself still in the swaddling
clothes of the new birth, to take part in the solemn ghostly
work under the same form. And is it possible that sensible men
in the fair use of their senses can fail to be struck with the
absurdity of such a process? The only fair parallel to it in
the medical sphere would be the mockery of three or four raw
practitioners going the rounds of a hospital and administering
to fifty cases of diversified diseases, within the same time,
as many doses of Thompson's mixture, *Number Six*. In the latter
case the thing would be counted and called *quackery* of the
first degree; and it is hard to see why it should go under any
softer appellation in the former. The only difference might
seem to be in the solemnity of the interests involved in the
two different circles of action. The Thomsponian tampers only
with the life of the body, while the spiritual practitioner
plays blindly with the precious life of the soul. If "profitable for instruction" at all then, the Anxious Bench must be
made subservient to this end in a different way. Considering
the circumstances of the case, the only rational course with a
company thus brought forward is to spend the few minutes that
can be devoted to them in counsels and exhortations addressed
to them collectively. Let it not be said that such instructions must needs lack point. The cases of the truly awakened
are always sufficiently near alike to admit of a large amount
of most pointed and pertinent direction in the same form for
all; and one who is truly a well instructed scribe in the Gospel will be able to address an Anxious Bench to much more purpose in this way than if he were to pass round directing a few
remarks to each one separately. But is it necessary to call
them out from the congregation for this purpose? The same
truths may just as well be presented to inquirers, as included

in the general audience, and it might reasonably be expected, in the case of the truly serious, with much better effect. But is it not desirable, we are asked, to have inquirers together by themselves? No doubt, there may be an advantage in this. But let it be with fitting time and place; not under circumstances which can hardly fail to obstruct and defeat all the purposes that should be aimed at the case.*

The Anxious Bench is of no account in any view as a help to instruction; and it is not hard to perceive that as a general thing where it is used this does not form in reality its main recommendation in the eyes of its friends. It may be convenient to advocate the use of the measure on this ground, and consistency will require always some show of improving it accordingly. The anxious, in one way or another, must be instructed and directed after they have come out. But just at this point there is apt to appear a sort of giving way in the general pressure of the occasion as though the main object of it had been already reached in the coming out itself. It often happens that a very short exhortation is allowed to wind up the whole scene; or it becomes evident that the conversation with the anxious is protracted amid the flagging interest of the congregation with mechanical rather than with living force. This where order and sobriety still continue to assert their proper rights in the

---

* "Let it not be said that inviting to "anxious seats" is the only effectual method of ascertaining who are under serious impressions and who are not. Why is not quite as effectual to give a public invitation to all who are in any degree seriously impressed or anxious to remain after the congregation is dismissed or to meet for the purpose of disclosing their feelings, and of being made the subject of instruction and prayer? Nay, why is not the latter method very much preferable to the former? It surely gives quite as good an opportunity to ascertain numbers and to distinguish persons and cases. It affords a far better opportunity to give distinct and appropriate instruction to particular individuals."
—*Dr. Miller. Letter to Dr. Sprague.*

feelings of the people. Where that is not the case it will be
contrived to keep up the excitement still, in connection with
the show of instruction, in such way that this shall come but
little into view, while all stress is laid upon the first. The
anxious then are encouraged to weep aloud, cry out and wring
their hands. Now they are enveloped in the loud tones of some
stimulating spiritual song. Then there is prayer which soon
becomes as loud; commencing perhaps with a single voice, but
flowing quickly into a sea of tumultuating sounds from which no
sense can be extracted even by the keenest ear. The mourners
besiege the "altar" pell-mell, kneeling, or it may be flounder-
ing flat upon the floor, and all joining in the general noise.
Then may be heard perhaps the voice of the preacher shouting
some commonplace word of exhortation which nobody hears or regards; while at different points vague, crude expostulations
and directions are poured into the ears of the struggling sup-
pliants by "brethren," now suddenly transformed into spiritual
counsellors, who might be at a loss themselves to explain at
any other time a single point in religion. In due time one and
another are *brought through*; and thus new forms of disorder,
shouting, clapping, &c., are brought into play. In this way
the interest of the occasion, such as it is, may be kept up
till a late hour. But who will pretend to say that *instruction*
has been regarded or intended as a leading object in any part
of the process?

  6. Lastly it is said that the anxious should be called
out in order that thay may be made the subjects of *prayer*.
They need the prayers of the Church; and the Church, it may be
supposed, has a heart to plead with God in their behalf. But
how shall this be if they are not known? By the Anxious Bench
they are brought into view, piteously seeking an interest in
the prayers of God's people; whose bowels of compassion cannot
fail to be stirred by the spectacle.

This might seem to be the great object in the case of such
methodistical displays as we have just had under observation.
But scenes of this sort have no tendency to stimulate the
spirit of prayer. They form an element, unfriendly, if not
absolutely fatal to the true idea of devotion. This is evident
generally from a certain character of irreverence, often grossly profane. That is sure to put itself forward in such circumstances in proportion exactly to the strength of the reigning
excitement. And in any case there is reason to believe that
more is lost than gained for the anxious as it regards this
interest by the commotion necessarily connected with their
movement to the anxious bench. It is a suspicious kind of
prayer at best that can be engaged in such circumstances only
by the *sight* of its objects, theatrically paraded to produce
effect without the power of a more general interest. But it is
not necessary that the awakened should be unknown in the church
to which they belong. They can be discovered without the aid
of the Anxious Bench, and can be carried so upon the hearts of
God's people, in the sanctuary and in the closet, with an interest far more deep and active than any that is produced in
the other way.

I know of no other ground than those which have now been
considered on which the use of the Anxious Bench can be vindicated with any plausible defence. And as these separately
taken have no force, so neither can they be allowed to weigh
any thing collectively against the condemnation in which the
system is properly involved.

CHAPTER VI

*The System of the Bench Tends to Disorder.--Connects Itself
Readily with a Vulgar and Irreverent Style in Religion.--
Women Praying in Public.--Influence Unfavorable to
Deep, Earnest Piety.--Relation of the System
to that of the* Catechism.

The Anxious Bench tends naturally to disorder. Where any
considerable excitement prevails it is almost impossible for
the measure to be applied without confusion and commotion. It
is common indeed to have it said in the accounts given afterwards of such occasions that they were conducted in a quiet and
orderly way. But the true idea of quiet and order is apt not
to be understood; for it not frequently happens that these accounts themselves, in close connection with such a statement,
present evidence sufficient to show it not strictly correct.*

---

* "In giving accounts of similar visitations of mercy in
other places our correspondents sometimes take especial care to
let us know that all things were done 'decently and in order.'
If by this is meant that all was quiet and conducted with measured propriety and entire regard to the prejudice of those who
are opposed to religious excitements, then we cannot say so
much of the revival in---church. For there was *noise* there not
a little, *measured propriety* not much, &c."--*Luth. Obs.*, Nov.
11, 1842.--"We had no confusion, but considerable noise--and,
dear brother, how could it be otherwise? Fifty and sixty souls
crying to God for mercy, some finding peace and praising God,
Christians conversing with, and praying for mourners, &c."--
Luth. Obs., Apr. 14, 1843.--The following would seem to be
quite orderly. "On one occasion the whole church, that is the
mass of professors of religion who were present, came forward
in a body, including men and women, old and young, married and
unmarried, and prostrating themselves around the altar and in
the aisles, renewed their covenant with God and solemnly pledged themselves to increased efforts for the conversion of the
impenitent." Dec. 2, 1842. Also the following as reported
April 7, 1843, by one who has written a book on revivals. Mr.
S., a very moral and worthy man, "became awakened and converted

Some appear to think that there is no disorder at such times
unless it comes to loud noise and gross confusion, in the style
of the Methodists. But the proper order of the sanctuary may
be seriously unsettled long before it has gone so far as this.
The measure involves irregularity to some extent in its very
nature, and opens the way for extravagance. It is always ready
accordingly to run into disorder. It leads naturally, if encouraged, to more striking deviations from the line of Christian sobriety. It forms the threshhold properly to the whole
system of New Measures. We may pretend to draw a line between
it and other more noisy and disorderly forms of action, but the
line will be an arbitrary one, separating things that after all
are inwardly related. The general principle of the Anxious
Bench and its proper soul are substantially the principle and
soul of the entire system to which it belongs. Let it be considered orderly and edifying to call out the anxious in this
way, and why should they not be encouraged as well to surround
the altar on their knees or to lay themselves down in token of
their humiliation in the dust?* If one measure of irregularity

---

in his own house just the night before our meeting commenced."
The next evening when the call was given for the anxious to
come forward he passed up to the altar and asked leave to speak.
This granted, he cried out, 'O my old companions and friends,
who of you will now come and take me by the hand, and go to
heaven with me! Last night at midnight God blessed my soul,
and I must now tell you what He has done for me!' The effect
was electric. 'Where are you, my brethren, who have covenanted with God?' he asked again. Instantly there was a general
rush from all parts of the house, and I suppose every male member in the church came up to the altar to grasp our dear brother by the hand, and covenanted to go to heaven together. O
what a scene! We all wept together. It happened the first
night of our meeting, and a most glorious revival followed."

* "If I were to place myself on what is called an *anxious
seat*, or should kneel down before a whole congregation to be
prayed for, I know that I should be strangely agitated, but I
do not believe that it would be of permanent utility. But if

and noise may be allowed on the principle that we should give
room to the Spirit, why should not a larger amount of the same
be tolerated on the same plea? "Should *man* enforce 'decent'
silence"--asks the editor of the *Lutheran Observer*, in view of
a scene where "crushed sinners," it is said, "prostrate upon
their knees, lay scattered around the altar, the females in one
group and the males in another," and the united tones of all
together reminded him of the noise of many waters--"Should *man*
enforce 'decent' silence when *God's power* had produced 'strong
crying and tears?' Should we prescribe limits to the workings
of divine grace, and say to the swelling waves of overwhelming
contrition, thus far shall ye come and no further?" The apology was intended to cover only a certain measure of noise and
confusion. But it is of sufficient breadth plainly for any
extent of extravagance we may be pleased to imagine. The most
frantic disciple of Winebrenner could ask no more to his greatest outrages on common decency and common sense. Screaming,
shouting, jumping, tumbling, and in one word the whole wildfire
of fanaticism, including the "holy laugh," and the "holy grin,"
might be vindicated in the same way. Only let persons persuade
themselves that the "power of God" within them *must* reveal itself in this style, and all becomes at once rational and right.
For there are *diversities of operations;* and it should be re-

------

it should produce some good effect, am I at liberty to resort
to anything in the worship of God which I think will be useful?
If such things are useful and lawful, why not add other circumstances to increase the effect? Why not require the penitent
to appear in a white sheet or to be clothed in sackcloth with
ashes on his head? and these, remember, are Scriptural signs
of humiliation. And on these principles who can reasonably object to holy water, to incense, and the use of pictures or
images in the worship of God? All these things came into the
Church upon the same principle, of devising *new measures* to do
good.'--*Thoughts on Religious Experience*, by Dr. Alexander,
page 72.

membered that "rules of propriety are conventional and often
very arbitrary things, and so is taste; what is thought decent
in one community may be deemed very disorderly in another."
Even Mr. Winebrenner himself, when interrogated on the subject
of noise, only answers, "What is from heaven I approve of, but
what is from men I disapprove of;" though he goes on immediately to sanction "loud groaning, crying, shouting, clapping of
hands, jumping, falling down, &c." as forms in which a divine
influence may be expected at times to work. Still he "has no
inclination to justify all sorts of noise and bodily exercises."
The truth is, as already said, that no satisfactory stopping
place can be found in the system of New Measures. It has a
life and spirit of its own, that begin to be developed in the
simple Anxious Bench, and naturally flow onward from that point
to the very worst excesses. Good men may try to hold the
stream in check, some at one point and some at another; but it
will not consent to be held within the limits imposed upon it
by *their* sense of propriety. it claims to have its origin in
heaven, and who in such case shall presume to say to it, "Thus
far shalt thou come, but no farther, and here shall thy proud
waves be stayed?"

As the spirit of the Anxious Bench tends to disorder, so
it connects itself also naturally and readily with a certain
vulgarism of feeling in religion that is always injurious to
the worship of God, and often shows itself absolutely irreverent and profane. True religious feeling is inward and deep;
shrinks from show; forms the mind to a subdued humble habit.
"The language of experience is," says one whose word should
have weight, "that it is unsafe and unwise to bring persons,
who are under religious impressions, too much into public view.
The seed of the word, like the natural seed, does not vegetate
well in the sun." We may say then that there is a measure of
rudeness connected with this particular style of action in the

Church from the very nature of the case. It is a wrong feeling in this respect that makes it seem desirable at all that awakened persons should be dragged thus theatrically into public view; and the process is well suited to generate wrong feelings, under the same form, in those who are subjected to its rough operation. The circumstances of such an occasion are by no means favorable to true inward solemnity, such as causes the heart to exclaim, "How awful is this place!" High excitement always tends to destroy men's reverence for God and sacred things. And so this "high pressure" system, as it is sometimes called, in proportion as it prevails, is always found to work. It gives rise to a style of preaching which is often rude and coarse, as well as uncommonly vapid; and creates an appetite for such false aliment, with a corresponding want of taste for true and solid instruction. All is made to tell upon the one single object of *effect*. The pulpit is transformed, more or less, into a stage. Divine things are so *popularized* as to be at last shorn of their dignity as well as their mystery. Anecdotes and stories are plentifully retailed, often in low, familiar, flippant style. Roughness is substituted for strength, and paradox for point. The preacher feels *himself*, and is bent on making himself felt also by the congregation; but God is not felt in the same proportion. In many cases self-will and mere human passion, far more than faith or true zeal for the conversion of souls, preside over the whole occasion. Coarse personalities and harsh denunciations, and changes rung rudely on terms the most sacred and things the most solemn, all betray the wrong spirit that prevails. But to see the character of the system in the aspect now considered fully disclosed, we must look at it again in its more advanced positions where the genius that animates it is permitted to work with full scope. Here the so-called awakening, on the camp ground or at the quarterly meeting, is often presented under a form that is ab-

94

solutely shocking to a truly serious mind. Noise and confusion
unite to overwhelm every right sentiment in the soul. Decency
and order are given to the winds. A dozen perhaps are heard
praying at once in all unseemly postures and with the most
violent gestures. And then the form and spirit of these prayers, as far as they can be heard! What rude familiarity with
the High and Holy One; what low belittling and caricaturing of
all that is grand in the Gospel; what gross profanity in the
style of many of the petitions with which it is pretended to
storm the citadel of God's favors! The atmosphere of such a
meeting may be exciting, intoxicating, bewildering; but it has
no power whatever to dispose the mind to devotion. There is
nothing in the scene to impress those who are present with the
sense of God's awful, heart-searching presence. Very frequently while such a chaos of prayer is going forward in full
strength at one end of the house, the lookers-on at the other
show themselves as much at their ease and betray as little emotion as though they were sitting in a bar-room. They have
grown obtuse to the stirring show, and feel themselves in no
connection with what is going forward, except as they find an
opportunity from time to time to fall in with the catch of some
familiar revival-song, which they shout forth as boisterously
as any body else. Fanaticism has no power to make God's presence felt. It is wild, presumptuous and profane where it
affects to partake more largely of the power of heaven. No
wonder that the religion which is commenced and carried forward
under such auspices should show itself to be characteristically
coarse and gross. Wanting true reverence for God, it will be
without true charity also towards men. It is likely to be narrow, intolerant, sinister, and rabidly sectarian. All that is
high will become low, and all that is beautiful be turned into
vulgarity in its hands.*

---

* "Fanaticism often blazes with a glaring flame, and

One striking illustration of the coarseness of this spirit is found in the disposition it has shown in all ages to set aside the rule which forbids women to speak publicly in religious assemblies. Nature itself may be said to teach us that woman cannot quit her sphere of relative subordination with regard to man without dishonoring herself and losing her proper strength. And it is no small argument for the divine origin or the gospel that while it teaches the absolute personal equality of the sexes as it had never been understood before, it still echoes, while it rightly interprets, the voice of nature with regard to this point. "I suffer not a woman to teach," says the apostle, "nor to usurp authority over the man, but to be in silence." And again, "Let your women keep silence in the churches; for it is not permitted unto them to speak.--It is a shame for a woman to speak in the church." True religion this judgment. No female with the Gospel in her heart can wish to have it reversed. She would feel her nature wronged rather in being required to appear in the way here forbidden before the public. But of *such* delicacy no account is made by the fanatical temper now under consideration. It is coarse and vulgar, and would fain show itself wiser at this point than Paul himself. It encourages women to pray in public, and to address promiscuous meetings, and by the spirit it infuses makes them willing to unsex themselves in this way. There can be no surer sign of grossness and coarseness in religion than a disposition

---

agitates assemblies as with a hurricane or earthquake; but God is not in the fire, or the wind, or the earthquake. His presence is more commonly with the still, small voice. There is no sounder characteristic of genuine devotion than reverence. Where this is banished, the fire may burn fiercely, but it is unhallowed fire. Fanaticism, however much it may assume the garb and language of piety, is its opposite; for while the latter is mild, and sweet, and disinterested, and respectful, and affectionate, the former is proud, arrogant, censorious, selfish, carnal, and when opposed, malignant."--*Dr. Alexander's Letter to Dr. Sprague.*

to tolerate this monstrous perversion under any form.

The general system to which the Anxious Bench belongs, it
may be remarked again, is unfavorable to deep, thorough and
intelligent piety. This must be the case of course if there be
any truth in the observations already made with regard to its
character. A system that leads to such a multitude of spurious
conversions, and that makes room so largely for that low, gross,
fanatical habit which has just been described, cannot possibly
be associated to any extent with the power of godliness in its
deeper and more earnest forms. The religion which it may produce so far as it can be counted genuine, will be for the most
part of a dwarfish size and sickly complexion. The "experience"
of the Anxious Bench is commonly shallow. The friends of the
new method often please themselves, it is true, with the idea
that *their* awakenings include a vast amount of power in this
way; and they are not backward to insinuate that those who oppose their measures are ignorant of what pertains to the
"depths" of experimental piety. Were such persons themselves
experimentally acquainted with the pangs of the new birth, it
is intimated, they would not be so easily offended with the
noise and disorder of poor souls *agonizing* at the altar; and if
they had ever themselves tasted the joys of pardoned sins they
might be expected to have other ears than they now have for the
shouts and hallelujahs of the redeemed, suddenly translated in
these circumstances from the power of Satan into the glorious
liberty of the family of God. But in fact no "experiences" are
more superficial commonly than those which belong to this
whirlwind process. The foundations of the inward life are not
reached and moved by it at all. All that would be wanted often
to hush an "altar-full" of chaotic cries to solemn stillness,
would be that the hearts of the "agonizing" mourners should be
suddenly touched with some real sense of the presence of God
and their own sins. "I have heard of Thee," says Job, "with

the hearing of the ear; but *now mine eye seeth Thee*: wherefore
I abhor myself, and repent in dust and ashes." Alas, it is not
the *depth* of these anxious bench and camp-meeting conversions,
but their utter want of depth that exposes them to complaint.
They involve little or nothing of what the old divines call
heart work. They bring with them no self-knowledge. They fill
the Church with lean professors who show subsequently but
little concern to *grow* in grace, little capacity indeed to
understand at all the free, deep, full life of the "new man" in
Christ Jesus. Such converts, if they do not altogether "fall
from grace," are apt to continue at least babes in the Gospel
as long as they live. The natural fruit of the system is a
sickly Christianity that is sure to be defective or one-sided,
both in doctrine and practice. It proceeds upon a wrong conception of religion from the start, and error and heresy in the
nature of the case are wrought plentifully into the very texture of all that is reached by its operations. There is involved in it a spirit of delusion which cannot fail to show its
power disastrously after a short time in any community in which
it is suffered to prevail.

Here is another most serious charge demanding our special
attention. I have denominated the system a *heresy*, not incon-
siderately or for rhetorical effect simply, but with sober calculation and design. In religion, as in life universally,
theory and practice are always inseparably intertwined in the
ground of the soul. Every error is felt practically; and wherever obliquity in conduct comes into view, it must be referred
to some corresponding obliquity in principle. It is not by
accident then that the system of New Measures if found producing so largely the evil consequences which have been thus far
described. Error and heresy, I repeat it, are involved in the
system itself, and cannot fail sooner or later, where it is
encouraged, to evolve themselves in the most mischievous re-

sults. Finneyism is only Taylorism reduced to practice, the
speculative heresy of New-Haven actualized in common life. A
low, shallow, pelagianizing theory of religion runs through it
from beginning to end. The fact of sin is acknowledged, but
not in its true extent. The idea of a new spiritual creation
is admitted, but not in its proper radical and comprehensive
form. The ground of the sinner's salvation is made to lie at
last in his own separate person. The deep import of the declaration, *That which is born of the flesh is flesh,* is not
fully apprehended; and it is vainly imagined accordingly that
the flesh as such may be so stimulated and exalted notwithstanding as to prove the mother of that spiritual nature which
we are solemnly assured can be born only of the Spirit. Hence
all stress is laid upon the energy of the individual will (the
self-will of the flesh) for the accomplishment of the great
change in which regeneration is supposed to consist. The case
is not remedied at all by the consideration that due account is
made at the same time *professedly* of the aids of God's Spirit
as indispensable in the work of conversion. The heresy lies
involved in the system. This is so constructed as naturally,
and in time inevitably, to engender false views of religion.
Sometimes the mere purpose to serve God in the same form with a
resolution to sign a temperance pledge is considered to be the
ground of regeneration. At other times it is made to stand in
a certain state of feeling, supposed to be of supernatural origin, but apprehended notwithstanding mechanically as the result
of a spiritual process which begins and ends with the sinner
himself. The experience of the supposed supernatural in this
case stands in the same relation to the actual power of the new
birth that magic bears to the true idea of a miracle. The
higher force does not strictly and properly take possession of
the lower, but is presumed rather to have been reduced to the
possession and service of this last, to be used by it for its

own convenience. Religion does not get the sinner, but it is the sinner who "gets religion." Justification is taken to be in fact by *feeling*, not by faith; and in this way falls back as fully into the sphere of self-righteousness as though it were expected from works under any other form. In both the views which have been mentioned, as grounded either in a change of purpose or a change of feeling, religion is found to be in the end the product properly of the sinner himself. It is wholly subjective, and therefore visionary and false. The life of the soul must stand in something beyond itself. Religion involves the will; but not as self-will, affecting to be its own ground and centre. Religion involves feeling; but it is not comprehended in this as its principle. Religion is subjective also, fills and rules the individual in whom it appears; but it is not created in any sense by its subject or from its subject. The life of the branch is in the trunk. The theory we have been contemplating then, as included practically in the system of New Measures, is a great and terrible heresy; which it is to be feared is operating in this connection to deceive and destroy a vast multitute of souls.

The proper fruits of Pelagianism follow the system invariably in proportion exactly to the extent in which it may be suffered in any case to prevail. A most ample field for instruction with regard to this point, for all who care to receive instruction, is presented in the history of the great religious movement over which Mr. Finney presided some years ago in certain parts of this country. Years of faithful pastoral service on the part of a different order of ministers working in a wholly different style have hardly yet sufficed in the northern section of the state of New York to restore to something like spiritual fruitfulness and beauty the field over which this system then passed as a wasting fire in the fulness of its strength. The perfectionism of Oberlin with its low conceptions of the law of God is but a natural development of the false life with which it is animated. The wide West abounds in every direction with illustrations of its mischievous action under all imaginable forms. In many places a morbid thirst for excitement may be said to exhaust the whole interest that is felt in religion. The worst errors stand in close juxtaposition with the most bold pretensions to the highest order of Christian experience. All might seem to begin in the Spirit, and yet all is perpetually ending in the flesh. It were an easy thing, too, to gather exemplifications supporting the same lesson from the past history of the Church. For the system, properly speaking, is not new. The same theory of religion has led, in all ages, to substantially the same bad fruits.

The question of "New Measures" then, as it claims at this time particularly the attention of the German Churches, is one of much greater importance than some might be disposed to imagine. The truth is, this system, as we have said, has a life and spirit of its own. It may be associated to some extent, in certain hands, with the power of a more vigorous life derived from a different quarter so as to seem comparatively sound and safe. But it ought not to be thought on this account that it may be incorporated practically with one order of thinking on the subject of religion as easily as with another. It is not by accident only that it is found connecting itself with the faults and defects that have now been mentioned. A false theory of religion is involved in it which cannot fail to work itself out and make itself felt in many hurtful results wherever it gains footing in the Church. No religious community can grow and prosper in a solid way where it is allowed to have any considerable authority; because it will always stand in the way of those deeper and more silent forms of action by which alone it is possible for this end to be accomplished. It is a different system altogether that is required to build up the

interests of Christianity in a firm and sure way. A ministry
apt to teach; sermons full of unction and light; faithful, systematic instruction; zeal for the interests of holiness; pastoral visitation; catechetical training; due attention to order
and discipline; patient perseverance in the details of the ministerial work; these are the agencies by which alone the kingdom of God may be expected to go steadily forward among any
people. Where these are fully employed, there will be revivals;
but they will be only as it were the natural fruit of the general culture going before, without that spasmodic, meteoric
character which too often distinguishes excitements under this
name; while the life of religion will show itself abidingly at
work in the reigning temper of the Church at all other times.
Happy the congregation that may be placed under such spiritual
auspices! Happy for our German Zion if such might be the system that should prevail to the exclusion of every other within
her borders! We may style it, for distinction sake, the system
of the *Catechism*. It is another system wholly from that which
we have been contemplating in this tract. We find the attempt
made in some cases, it is true, to incorporate the power of the
Catechism with the use of new measures But the union is unnatural, and can never be inward and complete. The two systems
involve at the bottom two different theories of religion. The
spirit of the Anxious Bench is at war with the spirit of the
Catechism. Where it comes decidedly to prevail, catechetical
instruction and the religious training of the young generally
are not likely to be maintained with much effect; and it will
not be strange if they should be openly slighted even, and
thrust out of the way as an incumbrance to the Gospel rather
than a help.* What is wrought in the way of the Catechism is

------

* A graphic illustration of this point was furnished
lately, it is said, by a minister of the New Measure school in

considered to be of man, what is wrought by the Bench is taken
readily for the work of God. And the reason of this is near at
hand. The Catechism is indeed weak in the hands of those who
have this judgment. They have no inward power to make themselves felt in this way. But they *seem* to have power in the
use of the Bench; and it is no wonder they should magnify it
accordingly. The systems are antagonistic. Particular men
standing under one standard may be to some extent entangled in
views and practices properly belonging to the other; but so far
they must be inconsistent with themselves. Each system as such
has its own life and soul, in virtue of which it cannot truly
coalesce with the other. They cannot flourish and be in vigorous force together. The Bench is against the Catechism, and
the Catechism against the Bench. I mean of course not the Catechism as a mere dead form in the way in which the original
order of the Church has been too often abused; and it is silly,
if not something worse, to insist upon *this* view of it when the
two systems are drawn into contrast as though there could be no
other alternative to the Bench than the Catechism without life.
It is the living Catechism, the Catechism awakened and active,
that is intended in this opposition. As such it stands as the

---

this neighborhood. On the morning of a sacramental Sabbath his
catechetical class was admitted by profession of faith to the
Lord's table and the full communion of the Church. On the very
same evening they were drawn forward to the anxious bench for
the purpose of conversion! Towards the close of the year 1842
we find in the *Lutheran Observer* a glowing report from this
same workman of splendid results effected by his ministry on a
different field which he was obliged soon after to leave. In a
single protracted meeting in one case he was able to muster
"about one hundred and fifty" converts. Since that time he has
reported another revival which came and went so rapidly that
the community generally had no knowledge of it till it was all
over. No wonder such a man should put honor on the Bench and
scorn on the Catechism, and rail out from the pulpit against
the present tract as though it were the "abomination of desolation" itself.

representative and symbol of a system, embracing its own theory of religion, and including a wide circle of agencies peculiar itself for carrying this theory into effect. These agencies, in the pulpit and out of it, will be understood, and honored, and actively applied in proportion exactly as the spirit of the system may prevail; and in the same proportion the Christianity of the Church may be expected to show itself large, deep, full, vigorous and free. Between such a Christianity and that which is the product of the Bench, there can be no comparison; and it must be counted an immense misfortune in the case of any religious denomination when the views, feelings, and forms of action that are represented by this through the force of a perverse judgment gain such ground as to push the other system aside. It must be ever a wretched choice when the *Bench* is perferred to the *Catechism*.

CHAPTER VII

*System of the Catechism.---Its Theological Ground and
Constitution.---Its General Methods and Forms
of Action.---Historical Exemplification.*

It seems to be due to the whole subject that the system of
the **Catechism**, as here opposed to the system of the *Bench,*
should be a little more fully described. This might well form
the theme of a separate tract. As a closing chapter to the
present publication it can claim our attention only in a very
general way.

The Anxious Bench has stood before us as the representative and type of a certain religious system, having its own
theory and its own practice, both replete with dangerous error.
In the same way we exhibit the Catechism as the representative
and type of another system including in like manner both theory
and practice of an opposite character. It is not meant of
course that the whole system originated in the Catechism or
that it must stand or fall in every instance with the use of
the Catechism; but simply that this belongs to it in principle
and constitution, and is well fitted at the same time to stand
as a specimen of its general meaning and force.

The theory of religion in which the system of the Catechism stands is vastly more deep and comprehensive, and of
course vastly more earnest also than that which lies at the
foundation of the other system. This last we have seen to be
characteristically pelagian with narrow views of the nature of
sin, and confused apprehensions of the difference between flesh
and spirit; involving in the end the gross and radical error
that conversion is to be considered in one shape or another
the product of the sinner's own will, and not truly and strict-

ly a new creation in Christ Jesus by the power of God. This is
an old heresy of which notice is taken by the apostle Paul in
the second chapter of his epistle to the Church at Colossae,
and which has been actively at work in the Christian world
under various forms and disguises from that time to the present.
It has often put on the fairest appearances, seeming even to go
beyond the general life of the Church in the measure of its
zeal and spirituality. It can easily affect also, deceiving
itself as much as others to honor the grace of God, and to derive all its life from a source beyond itself. But still the
imagination remains that this life is something that stands in
the individual separately taken, the property of a particular
self, rather than a more general power in which every such
particular self is required to lose itself that "old things may
pass away and all things become new." The man *gets* religion,
and so stands over it and above it in his own fancy as the
owner of property in any other case. From such monstrous perversion the worst consequences may be expected to flow. The
system may generate action; but it will be morbid action, one-
sided, spasmodic, ever leaning towards fanaticism. In opposition to this the true theory of religion carries us continually
beyond the individual to the view of a far deeper and more
general form of existence in which his particular life is represented to stand. Thus sin is not simply the offspring of a
particular will, putting itself forth in the form of actual
transgressions, but a wrong habit of humanity itself, a general
and universal force which includes and rules the entire existence of the individual man from the very start.* The disease

------

* This point is well maintained in a Defence of the Sec-
ond Article of the Augsburg Confession, ("gegen alte und neue
Gegener,") by *Dr. Sartorius*, one of the most distinguished
Lutheran divines of the present age. Had the treatise been

is organic, rooted in the race, and not to be overcome in any
case by a force less deep and general than itself. As well
might we look for the acorn to forsake in growing the type of
its proper species, and put forth the form of a mountain ash
or stately elm. "That which is born of the flesh is flesh."
So deep and broad is the ruin from which man is to be delivered
by the Gospel. And here again the same depth and breadth are
presented to us also in the Christian salvation itself. Man is
the subject of it, but not the author of it in any sense. His
nature is restorable, but it can never restore itself. The
restoration to be real, must begin *beyond* the individual. In
this case as in the other the general must go before the particular, and support it as its proper ground. Thus humanity
fallen in Adam, is made to undergo a resurrection in Christ,
and so restored flows over organically as in the other case to
all in whom its life appears. The sinner is saved then by an
inward living union with Christ as real as the bond by which he
has been joined in the first instance to Adam. This union is
reached and maintained through the medium of the Church by the
power of the Holy Ghost. It constitutes a new life, the ground
of which is not in the particular subject of it at all, but in
Christ, the organic root of the Church. The particular subject
lives, not properly speaking in the acts of his own will separately considered, but in the power of a vast generic life that
lies wholly beyond his will, and has now begun to manifest itself through him as the law and type of his will itself as well

---

written expressly against the theory of sin brought forward
some time since in this country by Dr. Taylor of New Haven, of
whom probably the German theologian had never heard, it could
hardly have furnished a refutation of it more thorough and complete. It is directed against the Rationalism of modern Germany which only reiterates here the Pelagianism of the Romish
Church as we find it withstood in the ever memorable Confession
of Augsburg. This shallow theory, as exhibited by Dr. Taylor,
constitutes as we have seen the very soul of Finneyism, which
is simply another name for the system of the Anxious Bench.

as of his whole being. As born of the Spirit in contradistinc-
tion from the flesh he is himself spiritual, and capable of
true righteousness. Thus his salvation begins, and thus it is
carried forward till it becomes complete in the resurrection of
the great day. From first to last it is a power which he does
not so much apprehend as he is apprehended by it, and comprehended in it, and carried along with it as something infinitely
more deep and vast than himself.

Now as one or the other of the two opposite theories of
religion thus briefly described may be found to reign, not in
the written or oral creed of those who take an interest in the
subject, but in the inmost core of their life, the result will
appear with characteristic difference in the whole tenor and
bearing of their religion, practically considered. And this
difference will be substantially that of the two systems now
compared, the religion of the Catechism and the religion of the
Bench.

It might seem indeed at first view that the theory which
sets the particular before the general in this case would be
found more favorable than its opposite to earnest and vigorous
religious action in every direction. And so it is often taken
to be, in fact. The other scheme, involving as it seems to do
a helpless dependence of the individual upon a generality deeper and more comprehensive than himself, first as it regards
sin, and then again as it regards righteousness, is held up to
reproach, as a view that cuts the sinews of moral action, and
may be expected where it prevails to lie like a paralysing incubus on all the energies of the Church. But this idea is contradicted by universal experience as well as by the true philosophy of life. To be moved deeply and strongly in any case,
man *must* be wrought upon by a force deeper and more comprehensive than his separate self. Great purposes and great efforts
appear only when the sense of the general overpowers the sense

of the particular, and the last is constrained to become tribu-
tary to the tendencies and purposes of the first. There may be
a great show of strength where the man acts simply from and for
himself; noise, agitation, passion, reaching even to violence;
but it will be only a display of imbecility when all is done.
The will acting in this way is very weakness itself; and all
the blustering and violence it may put on serves but to expose
the deficiency of strength that prevails within. To acquire in
any case true force it must fall back on a power more general
than itself. And so it is found that in the sphere of religion
particularly the pelagian theory is always vastly more impotent
for practical purposes than that to which it stands opposed.
The action which it produces may be noisy, fitful, violent; but
it can never carry with it the depth, the force, the fullness
that are found to characterize the life of the soul when set in
motion by the other view.

Conviction of sin is never deep and thorough till it comes
to a clear consciousness with the sinner that his sinful life
is rooted in a sinful nature, older and broader than himself,
which he has no power to renovate or control. Nor is the
Christian salvation rightly understood till it is felt that it
must be something more deep and comprehensive than the will of
the individual subject himself in whom it is to appear. Such
experience carrying the man beyond himself, and merging the
consciousness of the particular in the consciousness of the
general, may be much less ostentatious and much more quiet than
the experience generated by the other view; but it will be so
only because it is far less superficial and far more full of
truth. Religion in this form becomes strictly a life, the life
of God in the soul. So far as this life prevails it is tran-
quil, profound and free. It overcomes the world; "not by might
and by power," the unequal, restless, fitful and spasmodic
efforts of the flesh, "but by the Spirit of the Lord." The

believer can do all things standing in Christ.

And as this theory of religion is the ground of all deep
experience in the case of the individual Christian, so it gives
rise to the more vigorous and comprehensive action on the part
of the Church for carrying into effect the provisions of the
gospel for the salvation of men. In proportion exactly as it
is understood and felt, will such action display itself in all
its proper forms; and under no other circumstances can any
agency be employed for the same end that will be entitled at
all to take its place.

From first to last the action now mentioned will go forward under a due practical recognition of the truth that both
the ruin of man and his recovery rest in a ground which is beyond himself as an individual. If saved at all, he is to be
saved by the force of a spiritual constitution established by
God for the purpose, the provisions of which go far beyond the
resources of his own will, and are expected to reach him, not
so much through the measure of his own particular life, as by
the medium of a more general life with which he has to be filled and animated from without. This spiritual constitution is
brought to bear upon him in the *Church* by means of institutions
and agencies which God has appointed, and clothed with power
expressly for this end. Hence where the system of the Catechism prevails great account is made of the Church, and all
reliance placed upon the means of grace comprehended in its
constitution as all-sufficient under God for the accomplishment
of its own purposes. The means are felt to be something more
than mere devices of human ingenuity, and are honored and diligently used accordingly as the "wisdom of God and the power of
God" unto salvation. Due regard is had to the idea of the
Church as something more than a bare abstraction, the conception of an aggregate of parts mechanically brought together.
It is apprehended rather as an organic life springing perpet-

ually from the same ground, and identical with itself at every point. In this view the Church is truly the *mother* of all her children. They do not impart life to her, but she imparts life to them. Here again the general is left to go before the particular, and to condition all its manifestations. The Church is in no sense the product of individual Christianity as though a number of persons should first receive the heavenly fire in separate streams, and then come into such a spiritual connection comprising the whole; but individual Christianity is the product, always and entirely, of the Church as existing previously and only revealing its life in this way. Christ lives in the Church, and *through* the Church in its particular members; just as Adam lives in the human race generically considered, and through the race in every individual man. This view of the relation of the Church to the salvation of the individual exerts an important influence in the case before us on the whole system of action by which it is sought to reach this object.

Where it prevails, a serious interest will be taken in the case of children as proper subjects for the Christian salvation from the earliest age. Infants born in the Church are regarded and treated as members of it from the beginning, and this privilege is felt to be something more than an empty shadow. The idea of infant conversion is held in practical honor; and it is counted not only possible, but altogether natural that children growing up in the bosom of the Church under the faithful application of the means of grace should be quickened into spiritual life in a comparatively quiet way, and spring up numerously "as willows by the water-courses" to adorn the Christian profession, without being able at all to trace the process by which the glorious change has been effected.* Where the Church

---

* To cut off occasion from such as *seek* occasion for mis-

has lost all faith in this method of conversion, either not
looking for it at all or looking for it only in rare and extraordinary instances, it is an evidence that she is under the
force of a wrong religious theory, and practically subjected,
at least in some measure, to the false system whose symbol is
the Bench. If conversion is not expected nor sought in this
way among infants and children, it is not likely often to occur.
All is made to hang methodistically on sudden and violent experiences belonging to the individual separately taken, and
holding little or no connection with his relations to the
Church previously. Then as a matter of course baptism becomes
a barren sign, and the children of the Church are left to grow
up like the children of the world under general most heartless,
most disastrous neglect. The exemplifications of such a connection between wrong theory and wrong practice in this case
are within the reach of the most common observation. Only
where the system of the Catechism is in honor and vigorous

------

representation, it may be well enough to remark here (though in
ordinary circumstances the remark might seem to be wholly superfluous) that the idea of such a comparatively silent process of
conversion, as something to be desired and sought in the case
of infants and children, does not imply at all that regeneration
in any case is a *gradual* change. Nor is it intended to throw
discredit by any means on all sudden conversions in later life,
attended with experience more or less violent and marked in the
case of those who have grown up to some age in an impenitent
state. Conversions of this sort under proper circumstances are
entitled to entire confidence, and may be expected to occur frequently under faithful ministrations on the part of the Church.
But the error is in making this the exclusive conception of the
process. It is of immense account to hold fast with Luther and
the other Reformers to the other conception at the same time.
Regeneration is instantaneous, but as such not to be perceived
directly in any case by the subject. It can be perceived only
in its effects. But these belong to *conversion*, the change that
flows from regeneration. Regeneration may take place in the
womb, or in infancy, or in early childhood, or in adult age. In
every case its symbol is the *wind;* "thou hearest the sound thereof, but canst not tell whence it cometh, nor whither it goeth."

force do we ever find a properly earnest and comprehensive regard exhibited for the salvation of the young; a regard that
operates not partially and occasionally only, but follows its
subjects with all-compassing interest like the air and light of
heaven from the first breath of infancy onwards; a regard that
cannot be satisfied in their behalf with the spasmodic experience of the anxious bench, but travails in birth for them continually till Christ be formed in their hearts the hope of
glory.

Thus due regard is had to the *family,* the domestic constitution, as a vital and fundamental force in the general organization of the Church; and all proper pains are taken to promote religion in families as the indispensable condition of its
prosperity under all other forms. Parents are engaged to pray
for their children, and to watch over them with true spiritual
solicitude, continually endeavoring to draw them to Christ.
With such feelings they will have of course a family altar, and
daily sacrifices of praise and prayer in the midst of their
house. They will be careful, too, to instill into the minds of
their children the great truths of religion "in the house and
by the way." Catechetical instruction in particular will be
faithfully employed from the beginning. And to crown all the
power of a pious and holy example will be sought as necessary
to impart life to all other forms of influence. All this belongs properly to the system of the Catechism.

In close connection with this domestic training the ministrations of the Church come in under a more public form to
carry forward the same work. The Church feels herself bound to
watch over the children born in her bosom, and to follow them
with counsel and instruction and prayer from one year always on
to another. They are required to attend upon the services of
the sanctuary. Especially the process of Catechetical instruction is employed with constancy and patience to cast if possible

both the understanding and the heart into the mould of evangelical doctrine.

The regular administration of the word and sacraments forms of course an essential part of the same system. The ordinances of the sanctuary being of divine institution, are regarded as channels of a power higher than themselves; and are administered accordingly with such earnestness and diligence as bespeak a proper confidence in their virtue under this view.

Then again the system includes the wide range of the proper pastoral work as distinguished from that of the pulpit. The faithful minister is found preaching the gospel from house to house as well as in more public way; visiting the families that are under his care expressly for this purpose; conversing with old and young on the great subject of personal religion; mingling with the poor in their humble dwellings as well as with those in better circumstances; ministering the instructions of religion or its consolations at the bed side of the sick or dying; and in one word laying himself out in continual labors of love towards all as the servant of all for Jesus' sake. The holiness of his own life particularly becomes in these circumstances an agency powerful beyond all others to recommend and enforce the gospel he is called to preach. To all who know him, his very presence carries with it the weight of an impressive testimony in favor of the truth.

The object in all these efforts is not simply to bring sinners in the first instance to repentance and faith, but to build them up through the knowledge of the truth in all righteousness unto everlasting life. The ministry with all the resources of the sanctuary is made to look to "the perfecting of the saints," and "edifying of the body of Christ," as its main end. Individual Christians, and each congregation of believers as a whole, are to be established, strengthened and carried forward with regular and symmetrical growth to the "measure of the stature of

the fulness of Christ." It is characteristic of the opposite
system that it makes conversion in its own sense to be the all
in all of the gospel economy, and the development of the Christian life subsequently a mere secondary interest; as though by
bending all efforts immediately towards the accomplishment of
the first object separately taken, the last might be safely
left in a great measure to take care of itself. All this on
the false principle again that the Church is to be enlarged by
additions mechanically brought into connection with it from
without rather than by the extension of its own organic life
from within. But in the gospel all is made to hang on the
growth of the Church itself in grace and living power. This is
the great object to be reached after in the ministerial and
pastoral work; and it is only as this is in some good measure
secured that this work can be brought to bear with proper effi-
ciency on the world beyond. Where the Church is in a living
and growing state, "fitly joined together and compacted by that
which every joint supplieth, and according to the effectual
working in the measure of every part making increase of the
body unto the edifying of herself in love," she becomes by this
very process of growth itself the fountain of spiritual life to
the dead mass with which she is surrounded; taking up the element of humanity as "flesh," and by the assimilating force of
her own vitality, changing it into humanity as "spirit and
life." In such circumstances all the functions of the mystical
body, and that of the ministry of course among the rest, will
be carried forward through their proper organs with full power
and effect. Where this order is not maintained, there may be
exhibited often in the work of the gospel vast excitement and
great show of strength, and what for the moment shall seem to
be immense effect; but it will be a manifestation of comparative weakness in fact, by which only the surface of life's
broad stream has been tossed into waves, while its interior

depths roll quietly forward as before. "Not by might, nor by
power, but by my Spirit, saith the Lord." It is in the kingdom
of grace as in the kingdom of nature; the greatest, deepest,
most comprehensive and lasting changes are effected constantly,
not by special, sudden, vast explosions of power, but by processes that are gentle, and silent, and so minute and common as
hardly to attract the notice of the world which is so deeply
affected by their action. God is not with so much effect in
the whirlwind, earthquake and tempest as in the "still small
voice" of the falling dew or growing grass. And so in the
Church the common and the constant are of vastly more account
than the special and transient; the noiseless and the unseen of
immensely greater force than that "which cometh with observation," and fills the world with the sound of its presence.

Such in a general view is the action generated by the system of the Catechism for the great purposes of the gospel, as
compared with that which flows legitimately from the system of
the Bench.

This system then gives no encouragement to religious tor-
por or sloth. That some take shelter under its name who are
opposed to all that is serious or earnest in religion, while
they affect to magnify the Catechism and the common ministrations of the sanctuary, only shows that they have no communion
in fact with the Jews of old, who trusted in the outward temple
while they showed themselves false to all that made the temple
sacred. Dead churches and dead ministers that turn catechetical instruction into an empty form, and make no account of
inward living piety as a necessary qualification for membership
in the Church of Jesus Christ, have no right most assuredly to
identify themselves with the system of the Catechism; and it is
a gross wrong inflicted upon it by such as seek to bring it
into discredit, when such instances of orthodox formality and
deadness are taken to be proper exemplifications of its charac-

ter and power as though it had a natural tendency to beget
death in this way rather than life. It produces action and
calls for strength to a far greater extent than the system of
the Bench. It is the greatest and most difficult work in the
world to be a faithful minister of Jesus Christ in the spirit
of this system; which might well constrain even an apostle to
exclaim, *Who is sufficient for these things?* God forbid that
we should countenance for a moment the dreadful supposition
that the work of the ministry calls for no special zeal, no
missionary devotion, no full and entire consecration to Christ,
no earnest concern for the salvation of the immortal souls; or
that a church may be considered in a right state where the
voice of prayer is silent, the tear of penitence unknown, the
hand of benevolence palsied, the language of Canaan despised,
and the power of godliness treated as an idle dream. A church
without life is an abomination in the sight of God. The ministry is horribly profaned when it is made a retreat for world-
lings, drones, hirelings that care not for the flock, but only
for the fleece. *"Instant in season and out of season,"* is its
proper watchword, the motto that floats on its heaven-descended
banner; and it is under the system of the Catechism precisely
that the power of this is fully understood and felt, and may be
expected to come in a practical way broadly into view.

In this system room is found naturally and easily of course
for all evangelical interests. It is a prodigious abuse of
terms when some of the most vital and prominent of these are
crowded out of their proper place and made to stand in another
connection entirely; when social prayer-meetings, for instance,
and the various missionary and benevolent operations of the
Church are divorced in imagination from the regular life of
Christianity, and ranked in the same bad category with such
tricks of human device as the anxious bench. Family prayer and
social prayer belong as much as private prayer itself to the

very nature of the Church. The spirit of missions is identical
with the spirit of Christianity. For a church or a minister to
oppose prayer-meetings or efforts to send the gospel to the
heathen, or efforts to raise up faithful ministers, or to circulate Bibles and tracts, for the promotion of genuine godliness at home, is to oppose Christ. We hear, it is true, of
churches and ministers that look upon all these things as fanaticism, while they pretend to honor the good old way of the
Catechism; but such ministers and churches in the emphatic
language of the apostle "lie and do not the truth." They honor
neither the Catechism, nor the Bible, or Christ. And the evidence of this appears invariably in the fact that the same ministers and churches hate all serious, earnest godliness, are
perfectly worldly in their temper, make no account of the new
birth, and show no sense of religion whatever any farther than
as it may be supposed to consist in a decent morality, and an
outward use to some extent of its standing ordinances.

It is a most unfair view again of the system of the Catechism to think of it or speak of it as unfriendly to all special
and extraordinary forms of action in the work of the gospel.
The system, it is true, makes more account of the regular, the
ordinary, and the general than it does of the occasional and the
special; more account of rills and the perpetually flowing
breezes of heaven than of mountain torrents, water-spouts and
storms. But it does not by any means preclude the presence of
what is out of the usual way, or refuse to suit itself to its
requirements when it comes. The extraordinary in this case however is found to stand *in* the ordinary, and grows forth from it
without violence so as to bear the same character of natural and
free power. It is not the water-spout, but the fruitful, plentiful shower, causing the fields to sing, and the trees of the
wood to clap their hands for joy. Such is the true conception
of a *Revival*. For such special showers of grace it is the

privilege of the Church to hope, and her duty to pray, at all times. To call in question either the reality or the desirableness of them is a monstrous scepticism that may be said to border on the sin of open infidelity itself. They are the natural product of the proper life of the Church. Wherever the system of the Catechism is rightly understood and faithfully applied, it may be expected to generate revivals in this form; though in proportion to the measure of this faithful use it may be said the ordinary and the extraordinary as here distinguished will be found continually coming closer and closer together till in the end they may appear almost identical, and the church shall seem to bask, as on the "Delectable Mountains," in the perpetual sunlight of heaven itself. This may be denominated of a truth her "best state," and we may add her most true, proper and natural state. Churches that hate revivals may be said emphatically to "love death." Every faithful pastor will be concerned to see his ministrations crowned with such special effusions of God's Spirit; and will stand prepared at the same time to hail with joy the first indications of their approach, and to put forth special efforts for the purpose of turning them to the largest account. These efforts, however, will be in the general form of ordinary ministrations and services. If need be, however, they may be allowed to involve to some extent modes of action entirely *new*; it is not the mere circumstances of novelty of course that forms the true ground of objection to "New Measures," technically so called, but the spirit, life, principle of a certain system rather, as old as Christianity itself, which the measures thus designated are found to embody and represent. A revival in the very nature of the case, so far as it may be a special visitation, transcending the ordinary life of a particular church, must call forth special action on the part of both minister and people. Meetings for prayer will naturally be multiplied. The call for preaching will be increased. Protracted meetings, as they are styled, may be required. Visiting from house to house, and direct personal conversation with sinners on the state of their souls, are carried forward of course with more diligence and vigor than before. Sermons and exhortations may be expected to become more earnest and pungent. A greater amount of feeling will prevail in meetings. It will become necessary to have special conferences with the awakened. All this is a simple extension of the processes by which the ordinary life of the Church is to be maintained, made necessary by the special outpouring of God's Spirit, and fairly comprehended from first to last in the system of the Catechism as distinguished from the system of the Bench.

It is true indeed that the spirit of the Bench may take possession of these measures, and infuse into them its own life and complexion. It is not by merely mechanical and formal distinctions that we can hold ourselves always to the territory of one of these systems as distinguished from the other. What we are most concerned to understand is the spirit or soul by which each is animated. Thus it often happens that all the processes by which a revival is carried forward show themselves to be in fact pervaded with the false spirit of the Bench at every point. But so far as this is the case, the revival itself ceases to be such in the true sense of the term. It becomes a mere mock revival, a bastard imitation of the truth, the mushroom product of feeling and fancy wrought into a compost of fanaticism from which it shoots forth as it were in the course of a single night, without substance or strength. In such case the various forms of action which have been mentioned may be so exhibited as to breathe throughout the spirit of the system represented by the Bench; and there may be good reason for condemning the whole as quackery and wildfire. And no doubt it is owing to the frequent caricaturing to which revival measures have been thus subjected more than to any other cause that so strong a prejudice is found to prevail sometimes against everything of the sort. But still such measures as have been mentioned are not in their own nature of the same complexion with the Anxious Bench. They spring from the very conception of a revival; and no abuse to which they may happen to be subjected in the hands of revival-manufacturers should be suffered to bring them into discredit under their legitimate form. They belong constitutionally to the system of the Catechism.

It was on this system emphatically the Reformers of the 16th century relied in carrying forward the great work for which they were raised up by the Spirit of God. It might be denominated indeed with great propriety the system of the Reformation. Luther, Zwingli, Calvin, were all in the fullest sense men of the Catechism; and it was in this character preeminently they showed themselves so mighty and so successful in laying foundations, and rearing the superstructure of that vast spiritual work which has since been associated with their names. They had ample opportunity, if they had seen proper to use it, for going to work by the other method. The age was ripe for agitation and commotion in the name of religion to any extent. Luther could have created a revival in this form that would have made all Europe rock with whirlwind excitement. But he left such work to the Anabaptists; or rather his giant strength was successfully opposed to it in their hands. The Anabaptists were the men of the Bench in that day. Luther belonged wholly to another school.

I cannot perhaps close the subject better than by exhibiting a most interesting and instructive exemplification of the true character and force of the system now explained and recommended, as furnished from the history of the century following the Reformation in England by the celebrated *Richard Baxter* and his parish of *Kidderminster*. Switzerland, Germany, Holland,

and most of all, Scotland, present in their history innumerable attestations to the same point. But it is well to fix our attention for a moment on a single case peculiarly striking in its character, and more than commonly prominent through the world-wide reputation of the pastor.

Baxter, it is well known, lived in the most stormy period of English history, during which for more than half a century both Church and State might be said to rock perpetually as with the earthquake throes of revolution. He was intimately connected at the same time with public affairs and public men, and deeply concerned in the political changes which were going forward. He was moreover a scholar and a writer with such attachment to his books, and such a zeal in the use of his pen, as have characterized but few ministers in any age. Add to all this, he labored under such a complication of bodily infirmities and ailments that one can hardly help wondering how he was able to do anything at all. It is distressing only to think over the catalogue of his disagreeable maladies as they are presented in his life.

Kidderminster, when he began to preach there, was a most neglected, unpromising charge, like many others in England at that time. His predecessor had been a common tippler and drunkard, without any fitness whatever for his work. The congregation was large, but composed for the most part of ignorant, careless, rough-mannered people. At the end of two years the excitement produced by the civil wars compelled him to withdraw. After the lapse of some time however he was permitted to resume his labors in the same place, and continued in them about fourteen years, till separated from his charge by the new order of things, brought in with the restoration of the Second Charles. His ministry at the first was by no means generally palatable. It seemed to be altogether too serious and strict for the views that reigned commonly among the people, and called forth in fact no small amount of opposition. But he was not a man to be discouraged with difficulties of this sort. He went forward patiently and faithfully with his work, and in the end saw it crowned with complete success.

The parish of Kidderminster would seem to have been one precisely of that sort which those who glorify "New Measures" in our day are accustomed to consider specially in need of being wrought upon in this way. Were one of this school planted down in the midst of such a congregation, rude, ignorant, immoral, and having no sense whatever of the power of godliness as distinguished from its forms, his very first thought would be probably that nothing could be done to purpose till the whole community should be roused and stimulated into violent action in some sudden wholesale way. So perhaps he would appoint a protracted meeting, call in the aid of some professional revivalist, bear down with the whole apparatus of his favorite system upon the people, drive excitement to the uttermost; and then when the field should seem to be carried in this style, it might be trumpeted, with due flourish, in some religious paper that the parish had become morally regenerated. A most summary and convenient method of turning a dry, barren Kidderminster into a fruitful field, and causing it to put forth blossoms as the rose. But after all it did not suit the views of Richard Baxter. Mere excitement was of little account in his eyes, except as it might spring from the truth; and he had no conception or expectation of any general good to be accomplished by his ministry, except in the way of a patient, constant attendance upon the work itself, in its most minute details, kept up with prayer and faith from one end of the year to the other. Besides his Sabbath work and occasional sermons at other times, he preached once every Thursday. On Thursday evening he held a religious conference at his own house, calling sometimes on one, and sometimes on another, to lead in prayer. The young people held besides a weekly prayer-meeting. On Saturday evenings the people were encouraged to meet together at some of their houses to repeat the sermon of the preceding Sabbath, and to prepare themselves by prayer for the following day. "Two days every week," he tells us, "my assistant and myself took fourteen families between us for private catechising and conference; he going through the parish, and the town coming to me. I first heard them recite the words of the Catechism, and then examined them about the sense; and lastly urged them with all possible engaging reason and vehemency to answerable affection and practice. I spent about an hour with each family, and admitted no others to be present; lest bashfulness should make it burthensome, or any should talk of the weakness of others. All the afternoons on Mondays and Tuesdays I spent in this way."

Such was the general method of Baxter's ministry. It was constant, regular, earnest; not marked with noise and parade; but like the common processes of nature, silent rather, deep, and full of invisible power. He was a man of prayer, and his whole soul was in his work. Thus his ministrations were clothed with uncommon interest and force. Prejudice and opposition gradually gave way. The pastor became the centre of all hearts. In the end the change was complete. We hear of no sudden general excitement, no pains taken to secure anything of that sort; no *revival*, in the ordinary acceptation of the term, as denoting an occasional and transient awakening in the history of a church. But the life of religion in the place was constantly progressive, and the power of a quiet revival might be said to reign at Kidderminster all the time The result was wonderful. "The congregation," he says, "was usually full, so that we were fain to build about five galleries after my coming thither; the church itself being very capacious, and the most commodious and convenient that ever I was in. Our private

meetings also were full. On the Lord's days there was no disorder to be seen in the streets; but you might hear a hundred
families singing psalms and repeating sermons, as you passed
through them. In a word, when I came thither first there was
about one family in a street that worshipped God and called on
His name; and when I came away there were some streets where
there was not one poor family in the side that did not so; and
that did not by professing serious godliness give us hopes of
their sincerity. And in those families which were the worst,
being inns and ale-houses, usually some persons in each house
did seem to be religious." The church numbered six hundred
communicants; "of whom there were not twelve," says Baxter,
"that I had not good hopes of as to their sincerity."

Most happy would it be for our Reformed German Church if
all her pastors could be engaged to lay to heart the weight of
this great example. Let no one think within himself that his
circumstances make it impossible for him to work and prevail
in the same style. It would be hard to find among all our
charges a field so rough and unpromising as was the parish of
Kidderminster, when first subjected to the labors of Baxter.
And it is only the zeal and faithfulness of Baxter that are
needed to transform the worst among them in the course of a few
years into the image, at least in part, of what Kidderminster
was when his ministry in the place was brought to a close. He
has himself drawn a most stirring picture of what the pastor
should be in his small work entitled, **"Gildas Salvianus:**
*The Reformed Pastor; showing the nature of the pastoral work,
especially in private instruction and catechising."* I consider
it a privilege to close the present work with a pointed reference to this most excellent publication. If any wish to see
the **System of the Catechism** explained and enforced, as
with a pencil dipped in heavenly light, let them read Baxter's
"Gildas Salvianus." One sentence of his own with regard to it

should never be forgotten. "If God would but reform the ministry, and set them on their duties zealously and faithfully, the
people would certainly be reformed: all churches either rise
or fall, as the ministry doth rise or fall; not in riches and
worldly grandeur, but in knowledge, zeal and ability for the
work."

"The *Reformed Pastor*," says the distinguished Dr. Dodd-
ridge, "is a most extraordinary performance, and should be read
by every young minister before he takes a people under his
stated care; and, I think, the practical part of it reviewed
every three or four years. For nothing would have a greater
tendency to awaken the spirit of a minister to that zeal in his
work, for want of which many good men are but shadows of what,
by the blessing of God, they might be, if the maxims and measures laid down in this incomparable treatise were strenuously
pursued."

EDITORIAL INTRODUCTION TO "THE SECT SYSTEM"

The *Mercersburg Review* was established in 1849 to circulate the ideas of what came to be known as the Mercersburg Theology. John Williamson Nevin had a major role in the journal's birth and served as its first editor. During the earlier years of its publication Nevin contributed a large number of articles to it. For the opening volume he wrote a two-part article titled "The Sect System." That article is reproduced here in its entirety as it originally appeared in the *Mercersburg Review*.

The occasion for the article was the publication in 1848 of John Winebrenner's *History of All the Religious Denominations in the United States*. Winebrenner's book offered Nevin the opportunity to denounce the growing number of Christian groups in the nation. He referred to that phenomenon as "the sect plague." It was a serious ailment which afflicted American Protestantism. Summoning his sharpest rhetoric Nevin attempted to show the "sect system's" most severe weaknesses and its departure from an authentically catholic Christianity. In his estimation there were few more dangerous developments in the history of the church. The "sects" had no appreciation for the catholicity or the historical development of the "body of Christ." They were full of misunderstanding, subjectivity, and contradiction. In this and other writings Nevin revealed his abhorrence of this feature of American religious life.

ART. XXXIV.—THE SECT SYSTEM.

*History of all the Religious Denominations in the United
States: containing authentic accounts of the rise, progress,
faith and practice, localities and statistics, of the different
persuasions: written expressly for the work, by fifty-three eminent authors belonging to the respective denominations. Second Improved and Portrait Edition.* Harrisburg, Pa: Published by John Winebrenner, V. D. M. 1848. 8vo. pp. 598.

THE idea of this work is ingenious.   Our ordinary Histories of Religions, it is well known, besides being in general seriously defective in other respects, have never been able to satisfy completely the different sects of which they give an account.   However impartial the compiler may have supposed himself to be, he had his own standpoint, as the Germans say, which affected more or less all his observations, his own theological spectacles that gave both shape and color somewhat to every object which came within the range of his vision.   How could a rigid Calvinist do justice to a body of Arminians, or be content to sit for his own picture under the hands of a limner belonging to any such blear-eyed tribe?   How could an Episcopalian be expected to speak of Presbyterianism with becoming reverence and respect; or how could a Presbyterian be trusted to set forth, without distorting prejudice or passion, the claims and doings of Episcopacy?   Even Buck's Theological Dictionary, with all its popularity, was found to be greatly defective in this view; while the rapid march of sectarianism, besides, especially on this side of the Atlantic, called loudly for additions and improvements, which it became always more difficult and delicate to make with due satisfaction to the parties concerned.   In these circumstances, it occurred to our worthy and respected friend, *I. D. Rupp*, Esq., of Lancaster, Penna., to project and publish an entirely new work in this line, in which every denomination, instead of taking its picture from abroad, should be permitted to paint itself according to its own pleasure and liking; the whole to be constructed, as the almanac-makers say, for the horizon of the United States, as distinguished from that of all the world besides.   " A work thus prepared," it was supposed, " must be entirely free from the faults of misrepresentation, so generally brought against books of this character."   The thought was certainly felicitous, so far as that particular desideratum went; it met approbation and favor on all sides; the requisite number of pens, each pledged to do honor to its own sect, were soon set in motion; and in the course of two years, April, 1844, the *He Pasa Ecclesia*, as it was called, or Church Universal, made its appearance, with all befitting order and solemnity, in the literary world.   Its success was such as to do full credit to the originality and ingenuity of its plan.   Each sect was content to let all others glorify themselves, while it was allowed the privilege of glorifying itself before the public in the same way. None found occasion to quarrel with a mirror, which so faithfully gave them back their own image according to their own mind. The book became thus the joint product and property of the sects represented in it, and gained, at the same time, a clear passport to circulate among them indiscriminately as it best could. This circulation proved to be both large and profitable, which is a great object, we all know, in every enterprise of this sort. A very considerable part of the first heavy edition, as we are informed, made its way to England. As a business interest, at all events, the importance of the work is fully established. We have it, accordingly, stereotyped now, and done up in holiday style, as a second improved edition, under the auspices of Mr. Winebrenner, V. D. M., (by interpretation, *Minister of the Word of God*); who himself figures conspicuously in the book, both as the founder and historiographer of one of its sects, (one among the " fifty-three eminent authors" mentioned on its title-page,) with the honor of a portrait to sigalize such double distinction. How the work got into his hands, and out of the hands of its original projector and proprietor, we are unable to say. We know only that Mr. Rupp has felt himself in some way wronged in the case, and that he proposed, not long since, to re-occupy the field with another publication, on the same general plan, but of more complete and thorough execution. The list of sects, which stood as before given, between forty and fifty, was to be considerably enlarged; to do full justice to the fruitful history of our country, the new work was to contain " authentic accounts of upwards of *seventy* religious denominations," that have belonged to it thus far. This design, we presume, has fallen to the ground; the other enterprise being too fully master of the field, to allow under any similar form, a safe and successful competition. So this " History of Denominations," as it now stands, with Mr. Rupp's name extinguished and Mr. Winebrenner's made to flourish in its stead, would seem to be fairly seated upon the saddle as a sort of popular text book and standard for reference, in the department it pretends to fill. It is in the way of being most extensively disseminated. Agents are called for in every part of the United States, to promote its sale. Printed on good paper, "embellished with 24 splendid portraits," handsomely bound "with gilt backs and embossed sides," it is retailed at the rate of $2 50 per copy, allowing, no doubt, a fair profit all round to those who take the trouble of placing it thus widely in the hands of the public.

We are willing to acknowledge, that we made very small account of this book when it first came in our way. It was not to be imagined, of course, that a work got up in such *omnibus* style could be trusted at all, as a faithful and competent survey of the general field it proposed to represent. However unsatisfactory a history of sects might be, from the standpoint of any one of them affecting to be the centre, the case was not likely to be materially improved by allowing every sect to play in turn the same central part in its own favor. Such a course might, indeed, promote the popularity of the work, by enabling it to tickle the vanity of all parties; but it could not insure at all its truthfulness as to any part, nor its scientific worth as a whole. The idea of a history requires it to be as much as possible objective, and independent of all personal references and interests; whereas, in this case, full rein was given to the principle of subjectivity, to shape and fashion everything, at each turn of the kaleidoscope, according to its own accidental pleasure. The original editor, accordingly, seems not to have expected a true and complete history of sects in this way, but only a more successful *approximation* to something of the sort than had been reached on the old plan. It is admitted that each writer "may have been influenced by a bias, natural to many, to present the *beauties of his own faith* in glowing colors;" but for all this due allowance must be made by the intelligent; and out of the data, here outwardly brought together, the unprejudiced reader, it is hoped, may have it in his power to draw his own conclusions, as to the whole, in some safe and sufficient way. This has some force. It goes, however, to confirm what we have just said of the worthlessness of any such literary *salmagundi*, viewed as a veritable History of Religious Denominations; and it was in this view that we were disposed to look upon it in the beginning, as now said, with rather more contempt than heartfelt respect. We had no ambition to have it in our library; and, to speak the plain truth, when called upon by a strenuous agent, not long since, who insisted on making us buy a copy of this second improved edition, with pictures, gilt backs and embossed sides, we took it finally, more to get rid of the application, (the book is reasonably cheap,) than for the sake of any comfort or satisfaction we expected to find in its ownership.

But we were wrong. That first judgment was quite too hasty and sweeping; and we have been brought to entertain since, a much more favorable feeling towards the work thus forced into our hands. Allowing it to be as valueless as now represented, for the purposes of a scientific text-book, or dictionary, of the widely extended sphere it proposes to fill, are there not other sides and aspects under which it may still deserve to challenge our careful regard; and this too, in the most close connection, indirectly, at least, with the highest interests of religion and science? We had no right to take it for a veritable and proper History of Sects, in the true sense of any such title; and then to hold it responsible for flaws and defects, offences and shortcomings, that might be found to attach to it under this high view. In the nature of the case, it could be no such history. How could the "fifty three *eminent* authors belonging to the respective denominations," described in it, (Mr. Winebrenner himself, Shem Zook, Joe Smith, and others,) be expected all to conspire in any such idea and scheme, as would be necessary to impart to it the philosophical unity, rotundity and wholeness, which a complete work of this sort must be felt to require? But aside from any such high character as this, there are other very important uses plainly enough to be derived from a work so constructed, which should be taken, in truth, as its proper end and meaning, and on the ground of which it has a full right to circulate at large in the republic of letters. These uses have come to seem so considerable in our eyes, the claims of the book to our respect, on this ground, have so diverted our attention from the wrong relations in which we were disposed to look at in the beginning, that we may be in danger now, possibly, of being carried too far, by natural reaction, in our estimate of its merits. Our prejudice is fairly converted into a sort of fond partiality. We positively like the book, and would not consent to part with it easily. Though no

History of Religious Denominations, exactly, in the sense of an
Ullmann or a Neander, it is, in its own way, a most interesting and
valuable Commentary on the Sect System, which both Ullmann
and Neander would read, no doubt, with no small amount of instruction and profit.   In this view, the conception of the work is
such as to do credit to the mind from which it sprang. It was well,
aside from all bibliopolistical ends, to give this moral Babel an opportunity of speaking for itself; and now that it has thus spoken, it
is well to lend an ear to the cataract of discordant sounds that is
poured forth from its tongue. There is much to be learned from
it for a seriously thoughtful mind ; something directly ; and a
good deal more in the way of suggestion and silent circuitous
meditation.   What a world of pensive reflection is furnished by
Catlin's Indian museum?   This exhibition of American sects is
not quite as complete ; but as each tribe paints *itself*, the whole
gallery of portraits wins, in the same general view, a monumen-
tal interest which it could not well have in any other way, and is
likely to be gazed upon with curious admiration hereafter, when
the sects themselves, in most cases, (it is to be trusted,) shall
have passed away, with the Pottawottamies, into mere memory
and song.

It was a happy thought, to add in this second edition the twenty
four lithographed pictures of " distinguished men in the different denominations." This is a decided improvement, worth
itself almost the price of the book ; for the pictures are good in
their kind, and may be taken we believe, as very fair and truth-
ful images of the men they represent. They have in this way
a double value ; they make the book *pictorial*, which is a great
point nowadays in the art of popular literature ; and, they serve
to shed, at the same time, a true *historical* light on its contents,
which is not the case with the " splendid illustrations" that enter
commonly into the texture of these pictorial publications. We
have no taste, we confess, for such fancy prigments, redolent of
trade far more than of divine art ; however well suited they may
be to capture the eye of children, young or old. The " Pictorial
Bible" especially we hold in absolute dislike as something worse
than a money-making humbug, and would not be willing to
make use of it even if it were given to us in the way of a free

present. But the case is very different, where pictures exhibit to us the actual forms of history itself, and bring us thus into contact with its true original spirit and life. In the case before us particularly, a good likeness may be of itself a window to let in light on a whole world of facts, which finds its significance mainly in the man whose personality is thus presented to our view. The face of a sect hero, in some instances, may be of itself a key, to unlock the interior sense of the sect. At all events, after reading the account of a new religious movement in this form, we like to have it in our power to turn to the picture of its leading representative, whether living or dead ; we seem to catch, by means of it, a more vivid impression of the history ; the face of the man becomes a type, to explain and illustrate the genius of the denomination. Altogether then we are pleased with these portraits. They have already fixed themselves in our mind, and we frequently revert to them, in the view now mentioned, as subjects for profitable contemplation. With some of them, we were familiar before ; but the greater part of them have been introduced to us, for the first time, by this book. Here is the smooth quiet face of Pope Pius IX., well worthy of being considered in connection with the outward troubles of his pontificate. Here are the well known images of Luther and Zuingli, and Calvin, all strikingly significant of the high and solemn mission they came to fulfil, in the work of the Reformation. Here are Menno Simon, and Emanuel Swedenborg, and Count Zinzendorf, and George Fox, (a rich face to study,) and the Rev. John Wesley. Then we have a number of more modern heads; of American growth; some of which happily "remain unto this present," though others are fallen asleep. Interesting among these are the portraits of the Rev. Richard Allen, " Bishop of the First African M. E. Church of the U. S.," (Bethelites,) and the Rev. Christopher Rush, who represents another African M. E. Church of like independent organization. Elias Hicks again is a face to study — a psychological gem, worthy to stand close by the side of the original founder of Quakerism. You seem to read there the very sense of his system, the inward light run out into the most outward rationalism, the flesh ironically parading its own powers and pretensions as the highest law of the spirit.

We love also to gaze upon the features of Jacob Albright. The man's face is a voucher in full for the simple honesty of his character. It is serious, humble, and wholly without guile. We doubt not his well-meaning zeal. But, alas, what a countenance for a Moses of God's Israel, as compared with the face of Luther! David Marks, the Free Will Baptist, and William Miller, of *Millerite* fame, are also worth inspection. Last, though of course not least, deserves to be mentioned the full bust, and particularly speaking face of John Winebrenner, V. D. M., the present publisher of this book himself; to whom we are indebted for the idea of these "splendid portraits of distinguished men," and who has the honor besides, as we here learn, of being the originator of a sect styling itself the "Church of God," (about the year 1825,) one of the heroes thus of his own book; to say nothing of the distinction which belongs to him as the historiographer of his sect, one of the "fifty-three eminent authors," as before noticed, to whose united paternity the book before us refers itself on the title page. Mr. Winebrenner's portrait may be said to go beyond all the rest, in a certain self-consciousness of its own historical significance and interest. It has an attitude, studied for dramatic effect; an air of independence; an open Bible in the hands; in token, we presume, that Winebrennerism makes more of this blessed volume than any other sect, and that it was never much understood till Mr. Winebrenner was raised up at Harrisburg, in these last days, to set all right, and give the "Church of God" a fresh start, by means of it, out of his own mind.

This professed regard for the Bible, however, is by no means peculiar to Mr. Winebrenner. It distinguishes the sects in general; and just here is one important lesson offered for contemplation, by the pages of this work. The Adventists or Millerites (p. 41,) own "no other creed or form of discipline than the written word of God, which they believe is a sufficient rule both of faith and duty." The Baptists, (p. 49,) "adhere rigidly to the New Testament as the sole standard of Christianity," and take the Holy Scripture for "the only sufficient, certain and infallible rule of saving knowledge, faith and obedience, the supreme judge by which all controversies of religion are to be determined, &c." So the Freewill Baptists, p. 78; the Free Communion

Baptists, p. 85; the Old School Baptists, (p. 87,) who oppose " modern missionism and its kindred institutions" as unscriptural; the Six Principle Baptists, p. 90; the German Baptists, p. 92; the Seventh Day Baptists, " who have no authentic records by which they can ascertain their origin other than the New Testament," p. 95, and who tell us that the church can never contend successfully " with catholicism, even in our own country," till the lesson is fairly learned, that the " Bible *alone* is the religion of Protestants," p. 103; the German Seventh Day Baptists, who (p. 110,) " do not admit the least license with the letter and spirit of the Scriptures, and especially of the New Testament—do not allow one jot or tittle to be added or rejected in the administration of the ordinances, but practice them precisely as they are instituted and made an example by Jesus Christ in his word." The Sect of the Bible Christians, as their name imports, " believe it to be the duty of every one, in matters of faith, (p. 124,) to turn from the erring notions, and raise traditions that are to be found in most of the denominations of professing Christians, and to draw their principles directly from the bible." The " Christians," constituted about the beginning of this century by the confluence of three different streams of independency, reject all party names to follow Christ, take the Bible for their guide, (p. 166,) and carry the principle of shaping their faith by it so far, that a doctrine which cannot be expressed in the language of inspiration they do not hold themselves obligated to believe;" and a strange *system*, it must be allowed, they make of it in their way. The " Church of God," as called into being by Mr. Winebrenner, (p. 176,) " has no authoritative constitution, ritual creed, catechism, book of discipline or church standard, but the Bible"—with a short manifesto or declaration simply, showing what the Bible, according to Mr. Winebrenner's mind, must be taken clearly to mean. The Congregationalists, of course, appeal to the Scriptures (p. 281,) "as their only guide in all matters both of faith and polity;" though they do but speak in the name of all the sects, when they say, somewhat curiously in such company, speaking of creeds and confessions : " By the Bible they are to be measured, and no doctrine which cannot be found in it is to be received, however endeared to us by its associations, or venerable by its antiquity. This strict adherence to the Scriptures, as the only rule of faith and practice, must necessarily prevent many of those erroneous opinions, and that credulous reliance upon tradition, which are too apt to characterize those who follow the Bible only at second hand." In the enterprise of Alexander Campbell to reconstruct the church, a. 1810, which has given rise to the Disciples of Christ, (or Campbellite Baptists,) it was laid down as a fundamental maxim, (p. 224,) " that the revelations of God should be made to displace from their position all human creeds, confessions of faith, and formalities of doctrine and church government, as being not only unnecessary, but really a means of perpetuating division." The Albright Sect, a. 1803, "unanimously chose the sacred Scriptures for their guide in faith and action, (p. 275,) and formed their church discipline accordingly, as any one may see who will take the pains to investigate and examine the same." So in other cases. However they may differ among themselves in regard to what it teaches, sects all agree in proclaiming the Bible the only guide of their faith ; and the more sectarian they are, as a general thing, the more loud and strong do they show themselves in reiterating this profession.

All this is instructive. It sounds well, to lay so much stress on the authority of the Bible, as the only text-book and guide of Christianity. But what are we to think of it, when we find such a motley mass of protesting systems, all laying claim so vigorously here to one and the same watchword? If the Bible be at once so clear and full as a formulary of Christian doctrine and practice, how does it come to pass that where men are left most free to use it in this way, and have the greatest mind to do so, according to their own profession, they are flung asunder so perpetually in their religious faith, instead of being brought together, by its influence apparently, and, at all events, certainly in its name? It will not do to reply, in the case, that the differences which divide the parties are small, while the things in which they agree are great, and such as to show a general unity after all in the main substance of the Christian life. Differences that lead to the breaking of church communion, and that bind men's consciences to go into sects, can never be small for the actual life of

Christianity, however insignificant they may be in their own nature. Will it be pretended, that the Bible is friendly to sects; that it is designed and adapted to bring them to pass; that they constitute, in short, the normal and healthy condition of Christ's Church? It is especially worthy of notice, that one great object proposed by all sects, in betaking themselves, as they say, to the exclusive authority of the Scriptures, is to get clear of human dogmas and opinions, and so come the more certainly to one faith and one baptism. They acknowledge the obligation of such unity, and just for this reason call upon the Christian world to come with them to the pure fountain of God's word, as having, no doubt, that it is to be secured in this way. Winebrennerism, Campbellism, Christianism, &c., are all based, (we doubt not, honestly,) on a design to "restore the original unity of the Church;" and for the accomplishment of this object, they hold it, most of all, necessary, "that the Bible alone should be taken as the authorized bond of union and the infallible rule of faith and practice," to the full exclusion of every creed or formulary besides. This however, as we have seen, is just what all our sects are eternally admitting and proclaiming as their own principle. There is not one of them, that is not disposed to take the lead, according to its own fancy, in such wholesome submission to the Holy Scriptures; and the great quarrel of each with all the rest is just this, that they are not willing like itself, to sacrifice to this rule all rules and tradition besides. How does it happen then that the sect distraction has not been prevented or healed by this method, but is found to extend itself perpetually in proportion to its free and untrammelled use? When Congregationalism tells us, (p. 201,) that its principle of strict adhesion to the Bible, in the sense now noticed, serves to shut out divisions, it tells us what is palpably contradicted by the whole history of the sect system from beginning to end. However plausible it may be in theory, to magnify in such style the unbound use solely of the Bible for the adjustment of Christian faith and practice, the simple truth is, that the operation of it in fact is, not to unite the church into one, but to divide it always more and more into sects. The thing is too plain to admit any sort of dispute. The work before us is a commentary in proof of it throughout. Clearly, then, the principle in question requires some qualification.   No one can intelligently study this book of sects, without finding occasion in it to distrust the soundness in full of a maxim, which all sects proclaim, with equal apparent sincerity, as lying at the foundation of their theology, and which is so plainly at the same time the main prop and pillar of their conflicting systems.   We must either admit a limitation in some form to the principle, *No creed but the Bible*, or else make up our minds at once to the hard requirement of accepting this array of sects as the true and legitimate form of the Christian life, equally entitled to respect and confidence in all its parts.

The full misery of the case becomes more evident, when we connect with it the idea of *private judgment*, in the full sense, as the necessary accompaniment and complement of the exclusive authority thus attributed to the Scriptures.   This, we may say, is always involved in the maxim, under its usual sectarian form ; since the admission of any controlling influence whatever from beyond the individual mind, must serve of itself materially to qualify the maxim, changing it indeed into quite a new sense.   It is easy enough to see, accordingly, throughout this book, that the supreme authority of the Bible, as it is made to underlie professedly the religion of all sects, is tacitly, if not openly, conditioned always by the assumption that every man is authorized and bound to get at this authority in a direct way for himself, through the medium simply of his own single mind.   We have a somewhat rampant enunciation of the whole maxim, on page 512, in behalf of the Cumberland Presbyterians, in which, no doubt, however, the sects generally would without any hesitation concur. " The supremacy of the Holy Scriptures," it is there said, " and the right of private judgment, have long been the great governing principle of all evangelical Christians.   These abandoned, and there is no excess, extravagance, or superstition, too monstrous for adoption.   The Bible must be the supreme rule of faith and practice, or else it will be converted into fables and genealogies, unless we grant to the many the privilege of thinking for themselves, we must grant to the few, or one, the power of infallibility." An open Bible and private judgment, the only help against excess, extravagance and superstition, in the name of re-

ligion! So say the Cumberland Presbyterians. So say the Baptists, through all the tribes of all their variegated Israel, from
Maine to California. So the followers of Winebrenner, the Albright Brethren, and, in one word, every wild sect in the land.
And why then are they not joined together as one? Why is
Winebrenner's " Church of God" a different communion from
Campbell's " Disciples of Christ;" and why are not both merged
in the broad fellowship of the " Christians," as the proper ocean
or universe of one and the same Bible faith? Theory and fact
here, do not move, by any means, in the same line. The theory,
however, still requires, in these circumstances, that the fact, such
as it is, should be acknowledged to be right and good. Private
judgment in religion is a sacred thing, which we are not at liberty to limit or restrain in any direction, but are bound to honor as
the great palladium of piety, in every shape it may happen to
assume. The Congregationalist, then, has no right to quarrel
with the results to which it conducts the honest Baptist; and
the honest Baptist again has just as little right to find fault with
the use made of it, by the Albright Brethren, or the African sect
of the Bethelites. This principle of private judgment, the hobby
of all sects, places all plainly on the same level, and unless men
choose to play fast and loose with their own word, opens the
door indefinitely for the lawful introduction of as many more, as
religious ingenuity or stupidity may have power to invent.

The principle, in truth, is absurd and impracticable, and such
as always necessarily overthrows itself. We find, accordingly,
that the glorification of it in the sect world, is very soon resolved
into mere smoke. Just here we encounter first, on a broad scale,
the spirit of hypocrisy and sham, which enters so extensively
into the whole constitution of sectarian christianity. Every sect
is ready to magnify the freedom of the individual judgment and
the right of all men to read and interpret the Bible for themselves;
and yet there is not one among them, that allows in reality anything of the sort. It is amusing to glance through the pages of
this auto-biography of Religious Denominations, and notice the
easy simplicity with which so many of them lay down the broad
maxim of liberty and toleration to start with, and then at once go
on to limit and circumscribe it by the rule of their own narrow

horizon; proving themselves generally, to be at once unfree and illiberal, in proportion precisely to the noise they make about their freedom. The " Church of God," according to her V. D. M., at Harrisburg, has no constitution, ritual creed, catechism, book of discipline, or church standard, but the Bible. This she believes to be the only creed or text book, which God ever intended her to have. " *Nevertheless*, it may not be inexpedient," we are told (p. 176,) "*pro bono publico*, to exhibit a short manifesto, or declaration, showing her views, as to what may be called leading matters of faith, experience and practice ;" and so we have a regular confession of 27 articles, (p. 176–181,) all ostensibly supported by proof from the Bible as understood by Mr. Winebrenner, fencing in thus her " scriptural and apostolical" communion, and of course fencing out all who, in the exercise of their private judgment, may be so unfortunate as not to see things in precisely the same way. This is only a specimen of the inconsistency and contradiction which characterize sects in general. Their common watchword is: The Bible and Private Judgment! But in no case do they show themselves true to its demands. It is always, on their lips, an outrageous lie, of which all good men should feel themselves ashamed. What sect in reality, allows the Bible and Private Judgment to rule its faith? Is it not notorious that every one of them has a scheme of notions already at hand, a certain system of opinion and practice, which is made to underlie all this boasted freedom in the use of the Bible, leading private judgment along by the nose, and forcing the divine text always to speak in its own way? It is of no account, as to the point here in hand, that sects agree to tolerate one another politically; the want of religious toleration is enough of itself to falsify their pretended maxim of following simply the Bible and private judgment. It shows plainly that this maxim is *not*, at least, the measure of their religious life, but that some other rule is required to keep it to its particular form and shape.

But there is a vast chasm also, in the political or outward toleration itself, as it may be called, to which the sect system affects in general to be so favorable. It is full of zeal, apparently for human freedom in every shape, the rights of man, liberty of conscience, and the privilege of every man to worship God in his own way. The Independents claim the merit of opening, in regard to all these great interests, a new era in the history of the human race; but they had no toleration originally, for the Quakers and Baptists; and both these bodies, accordingly, carry away the palm from them on this ground, as having by their patient testimony done far more signal service to the cause of religious freedom. Roger Williams is taken by his sect to be the father emphatically of our American Independence (p. 57,); and it is of the first Baptists in particular, we are told, that these words of Hume in favor of the Puritans stand good : " By these alone the precious spark of liberty was kindled, and to these America owes the whole freedom of her constitution." But, alas, the regular Baptists, themselves have been found continually prone to assert, in one shape or another, the old tyranny over conscience; on which account it has been necessary for one new sect after the other to take a fresh start in the race of independence, so that one is left quite at a loss in the end to know, to which of all the number, the modern world should consider itself most deeply indebted for its full democratic emancipation in the affairs of religion. In Rhode Island itself, under the free charter of Roger Williams, the Seventh Day Baptists, (p. 97,) had to endure much for the right of differing from their more othodox neighbors ; " a hostile spirit was soon raised against the little band and laws were enacted severe and criminal in their nature ; John Rogers, a member of the church, was sentenced to sit a certain time upon a gallows with a rope about his neck, to which he submitted." So the German Seventh Day sect in Pennsylvania, protests loudly against all legislation, that would force it in any way to keep a different sabbath than its own, and claims the honor of standing with this question, in the very Thermopylæ of American freedom. " The great principle, we are told, (p. 122,) for which the Seventh Day People are contending—*unfettered religious liberty*—is alike dear to all the churches of the land ; it belongs equally to all denominations, however large or however small." The " Christians" sprang from the same idea of independence. One portion of them styled themselves at first characteristically " Republican Methodists," p. 165 ; another grew out of " a peculiar travel of mind in relation to sectarian names and human creeds," on the part of one Dr. Abner Jones, a Baptist of Vermont; a third broke away from the Presbyterian Synod of Kentucky, at the time of the great revival, to escape "the scourge of a human creed." As a general thing, sects are loud for liberty, in the more outward sense, and seem to be raised up in their own imagination for the express purpose of asserting in some new way what they call liberty of conscience. But all history shows that they are bold for this liberty only in their own favor, and not at all in favor of others. It is not enough in their case that they acquiesce in the independence of other sects as already established; their maxim of private judgment, if they were honest, should lead them to throw no obstruction whatever in the way of new sects, starting out of their own bosom. Even if they might not feel bound to retain such divergent tendencies in their communion, they ought, at least, to recognize the perfect right they have to make their appearance, as legitimately flowing from the proper life of Christianity, and, instead of laying a straw in their way, should assist them rather to develope their force, and stand out as new phases of religion in the generrl sect system to which they belong. Nothing short of this deserves to be considered true toleration, on the ground professedly occupied by private judgment sects. Where, however, do we meet with any such sect, whose practice is governed by any such rule?

The truth is, as any one may see who has any familiarity at all with the character and history of sects, that no more unpropitious atmosphere for liberty and independence can well be conceived, than that which they everywhere tend to create. Those precisely which make the greatest boast of their liberty, are as a general thing, the least prepared either to exercise it themselves or to allow its exercise in others. The sect habit, as such, is constitutionally unfree. All true emancipation in religion begins only where the power of this habit has begun to be broken, and the sense of a true catholic Christianity is brought to reign in its place. Each sect has its tradition; in most cases, a very poor and narrow tradition; the fruit of accident or caprice in the history of its founder, conditioned more or less by the outward relations in which he was called to his apostolic mission; a certain scheme of notions and words, passing over always more and more to the character of dead mechanical gibberish and cant ; to whose authority all are required to swear, within its communion, and whose little circle or ring none may transgress without losing cast. Take, for instance, the small community of the Albright Brethren. Is it not just as much bound in this respect, full as servile and full as intolerant, to say the least, as the Church of Rome ? Is it not, in its way and measure, a papacy, a would-be ecclesiastical domination, which seeks as far as possible to nullify and kill all independent thought and all free life ? It is full indeed of professed zeal for Protestant liberty, free inquiry, an open Bible, universal toleration, the right of all men to think for themselves, and all such high-sounding phrases ; but we must be simple enough, if we can be led for a moment to take such professions for anything *more* than so much sound. The liberty of the sect consists at last, in thinking its particular notions, shouting its shibboleths and passwords, dancing its religious horn-pipes, and reading the Bible only through its theological goggles. These restrictions, at the same time, are so many wires, that lead back at last into the hands of a few leading spirits, enabling them to wield a true hierarchical despotism over all who are thus brought within their power. All tends to crush thought, and turn the solemn business of religion into a sham. True spiritual independence must ever be an object of jealousy in such a communion, as much so fully as in any popish convent. Let a generous minded man begin really to think for himself, by rising above the life of the mere sect, and it matters not how much he may have of the Spirit of Christ, or how truly he may reverence God's word, he will fall into suspicion and condemnation ; and if true to himself, must find it necessary in the end to quit the association altogether, the victim of reproach and persecution, for those very rights of conscience, whose special guardianship the little brotherhood has been affecting to take almost exclusively into its own hands. This is only an instance, to exemplify a general fact. All sects, in proportion as they deserve the name, are narrow, bigoted and intolerant. They know not what liberty means. They put out men's eyes, gag their mouths, and manacle their hands and feet. They are intrinsically, constitutionally, incurably popish, enslaved by tradition and prone to persecution. The worst of all schools for the formation of a true manly character, is the communion of such a sect. The influence of sects is always illiberal; and it should be counted in this view a great moral calamity, in the case of all young persons, especially, to be thrown upon it, in any way, for educational training.

The book before us illustrates instructively the *unhistorical* character of the sect system. The independence which it affects, in pretending to reduce all Christianity to private judgment and the Bible, involves, of necessity, a protest against the authority of all previous history, except so far as it may seem to agree with what is thus found to be true; in which case, of course, the only real measure of truth is taken to be, not this authority of history at all, but the mind, simply, of the particular sect itself. The idea of anything like a divine substance in the life of Christianity, through past ages, which may be expected of right to pass forward into the constitution of Christianity as it now stands, is one that finds no room whatever in this system. A genuine sect will not suffer itself to be embarrassed for a moment, either at its start or afterwards, by the consideration that it has no proper root in past history. I s ambition is rather to appear in this respect *autochthonic*, aboriginal, self-sprung from the Bible, or through the Bible from the skies. "A Six Principle Baptist," we are told, p. 88, "who understands the true principles of his profession, does not esteem it necessary to have his tenets through the several ages of the church. He is fully persuaded, however early or generally other opinions may have prevailed, that those principles which distinguish him from other professions of Christianity, are clearly taught and enjoined by the great head of the Church, in the grand commission to his apostles." This language suits all sects. If the past be with them, here and there, it is all very well; but if not, it can only be, of course, because they are right, and the universal past wrong; for they follow (multifariously) the Bible, which is the only infallible rule of faith and practice. The Baptists glory in having no succession before the Reformation, except by occasional gleams and flashes athwart the darkness of the middle ages, here and there, in out-of-the-way crevices and corners, produced by sects and fragments of sects, of whom almost nothing is known, and concerning whom, accordingly, all things may be the more easily *guessed*. But what of that? Every congregation has power to originate a new christianity for its own use, and so may well afford to let that of all other ages pass for a grand apostacy, if need be, to keep itself in countenance. In the same spirit, one Baptist sect is continually rising after another, and setting in motion a new church, without the least regard to the "want of fellowship" proclaimed against it by the body it leaves behind. "It makes no difference to me who disowns me," cries Mr. Randall, in the face of such an exclusion, p. 75, "so long as I know that the Lord owns me; and now let that God be God who answers by fire, and that people be God's people, whom he owneth and blesseth." This, in his own words, "is the beginning of the now large and extensive connection called *Freewill Baptists.*" Hear another tribe: "Every denomination (p. 95,) is proud of tracing its origin back to its founder. But not so with the Seventh Day Baptists. They have no authentic records by which they can ascertain their origin, other than the New Testament." Hear again the "Christians," self-started in Kentucky, A. D. 1803. "As they had taken the Scriptures for their guide, pedobaptism was renounced, and believers baptism by immersion substituted in its room. On a certain occasion, one minister baptized another minister, and then he who had been baptized, immersed the others." So Roger Williams himself, (p. 57,) the father of American Anabaptism, "in March, 1639, was baptized by one of his brethren and then he baptized about ten more." Jacob Albright, of course, had quite as much right to originate a new ministry, (p. 275,) in the same way; which, however, is very much like a man pretending to lift himself up from the ground by his own breeches or boot-straps. So throughout. The idea of a historical continuity in the life of the Church, carries with it no weight whatever for the sect consciousness. It is felt to be as easy to start a new Church, as it is to get up a new moral or political association under any other name.

This turns, of course, at bottom, on a want of all true and steady faith in the Church itself as such. The Church is declared in the Creed to be an object of faith, a necessary part of Christianity. As such it is a divine supernatural fact, a concrete reality, an actual objective power in the world, which men have no ability whatever to make or unmake at their own pleasure. In this form it defines itself to be one, holy, catholic and apostolical. To be apprehended at all as it is, it must be apprehended under these attributes, as the inseparable adjuncts of the fact which faith is here brought to embrace. To conceive of the Church as an institution *not* holy, not formed for holiness and not requiring it, would be at once to give up its existence altogether as affirmed in the Creed. And just so it must lose its true power for faith, if it be conceived of as *not* one and universal and historical, not formed for all this, and not demanding it throughout as an indispensable part of its idea. Only where such a sense of the Church prevails, can the danger and guilt of schism be felt at all, or any hindrance be raised at all to the easy multiplication of sects. In its very constitution, accordingly, the sect spirit is an unchurchly spirit. It turns the Church into a phantom; values it at best only as an abstraction; transforms the whole high and awful mystery into the creature of its own brain. The book before us is full of evidence and illustration, in regard to this point. Sect Christianity is not the Christianity of the Creed, or at best it is this Christianity under a most mutilated form. Of this proof enough is found in the fact that wherever the sect spirit prevails the Creed falls into disuse. It may be still spoken of respectfully perhaps when spoken of at all; but what sect repeats it, or recognises in it the mirror of its own consciousness? The Creed has become almost universally a dead letter, in the religion of sects. There are, no doubt, thousands of so called evangelical ministers in our country at this time, to say nothing of their congregations, who could not even repeat it correctly, were they called on suddenly to do so, as a test of their Christian knowledge.

As thus unchurchly, the sect system tends to destroy all faith in the holy sacraments. No one can well fail to be struck with this, in studying its own account of itself in this History of Religious Denominations. Our view of the sacraments is always conditioned by our sense of the mystery comprehended in the idea of the Church, and forms thus, of course, at the same time, a simple, but sure, touchstone of our faith in the Church itself. The idea of divine sacraments, mystically exhibiting the super-

natural realities they represent as things actually at hand, and the
idea of a divine Church as proclaimed in the Creed, go hand in
hand together. The sect mind, therefore, in proportion as it has
come to be unchurchly and simply private and individual, is
always necessarily to the same extent unsacramental. The forms
of the sacraments may be retained, but the true inward meaning
of them is more or less lost. One broad and most instructive
evidence of this, is found in the fact that the sect spirit left to
itself, invariably runs towards the baptistic theory; which proceeds throughout on the assumption, that the sacraments carry
in their constitution no objective mystical force whatever. It is
not by accident, merely, that almost every new sect that rises, is
led, sooner or later, to reject infant baptism; the sect principle
flows legitimately to this result, and it can never, indeed, stop
short of it without inconsistency and contradiction. The Baptists
take Christian baptism to be a sign only (p. 46) of Christian profession, which has no significance except as it is preceded by the
grace it represents, as something previously at hand in the person
who receives it; in which view, naturally enough, they contend
that it can never be applied, with propriety, to unconscious infants.
The Lord's supper, of course, (p. 52,) is only another sign of the
same sort. This is plausible; falls in with common sense; and
we are not surprised to hear, accordingly, that where mixed communion prevails in some parts of England, (p. 67,) "the sentiments and practice of the Baptists are so far introduced among
the members of pædobaptist churches, that comparatively few of
their pastors can say very much against the Baptists." The thing
doth eat like a cancer; sending its roots oftentimes far in advance
of its open presence, where the true substance of sacramental
faith is gone, and only the form of it left in its room. Mr. Winebrenner makes the "Church of God" believe in "three positive
ordinances of perpetual standing"—sacraments have a wonderful
tendency to rationalize themselves into mere *ordinances* in the
sect vocabulary—"viz: *Baptism, Feet washing,* and the *Lord's
supper*" (p. 178). All for believers only, and not for children.
We find a much better triplicity of Protestant sacraments, if we
must have three, in the creed of the African Methodists, (p. 403,)
where they are made to be, "the Lord's supper, Baptism, and

Holy Matrimony"—the last left without any farther definition.
Campbellism started in pædobaptist connections, on the broad
basis of the Bible and justification solely by Christ's merits, not
meaning to add a new sect to those already existing, (p. 225)
but hoping rather to put an end to sects. In due time, however,
the baptistic question came in its way. Thomas Campbell, father
of Alexander, undertook to preach it right, according to his old
Scotch Seceder faith ; but the Bible and private judgment proved
too strong, to be ruled down in such style. His discussion " convinced a number of his hearers, (p. 226,) that the practice of infant baptism could not be sustained by adequate scripture evidence ;" and worst of all " his son and coadjutor, Alexander,
especially," was after a full examination of the subject, led to the
conclusion, not only that the baptism of infants was without
Scriptural authority, but that immersion in water, upon a true
profession of faith in Christ, alone constituted Christian baptism."
On conferring with his oldest sister, she was found to be already
on the same ground ; and by the time a Baptist minister was at
hand to immerse them, strange to say, the old gentleman himself, and a considerable part of his congregation, had become so
" forcibly impressed with the same convictions," that they were
all prepared to go together into the water. This is curious and
instructive. With the premises of Campbellism, which are the
premises of all unhistorical, unchurchly Christianity, it could not
honestly come to any other conclusion. The wonder is not,
that such Christianity should run so often into this baptistical
rationalism, the next thing to the Quaker spiritualization of the
sacraments into sheer nothing ; but rather, that it should be able
in any case, to stop short of it as the natural end of its thinking.
Look, for instance, at the pains taken, p. 488, 489, in the name
of the New School Presbyterian Church, to set aside the whole
idea of anything like a true supernatural force mystically lodged
in the Church itself ; ordination only the " recognition of one
whom God has *already* by his providence and grace put into the
ministry ;" no intrinsic force in *any* rite ; no grace in union with
the outward symbols of either sacrament, (all in plump opposition to the Westminster standards); no other influence from them,
other than " that which results from a wise adaptation for enforc-

ing truth, by striking symbols, and creating hallowed associations!" Surely it needs no very great depth of thought to see,
that all such constitutionally unsacramental religion can owe it
only to the most dead outward tradition, if it is kept in any case
from passing over in due form to the Baptist ranks. Its pædo-
baptism is little better than a solemn sham.

Another striking feature of sect Christianity, which finds ample illustration in Mr. Rupp's book, is the tendency it has to drive
all religion into a system of outward notions and abstractions.
It is apt indeed, as we all know, to lay great stress on its practical
and spiritual character. But its spirituality and practicality lack
the force, that belongs properly to a truly divine life. They hold
not so much in the actual apprehension of divine realities by
faith, as in the mere notion of them by the imagination. They
come not so much to an inward living union with the very life
of the soul, as they are accepted by it rather in an external, mechanical way, as something different altogether from itself and
out of itself. Religious truth so apprehended is always abstract,
and not concrete. Sect Christianity, which makes so much of
the individual mind and so little of all that is objective, can never
avoid these abstractions. The individual mind, in its view, must
take truth out of the Bible; there it is offered in an outward way,
for this purpose; we have only to satisfy ourselves first, rationally,
that the Bible is inspired; all turns afterwards on extracting from
it our faith and practice. The idea of a living revelation in the
Bible, which must authenticate it and unfold its true sense, is but
dimly, if at all, perceived. The Bible is turned thus into an
outward Jewish rule, and religion is made to have its merit mainly
in the acknowledgment of its authority under such view. The
text, and nothing but the text, becomes its motto and hobby,
which it is ready to harp upon continually in praise of its own
dutiful obedience. It needs no great sagacity to see, from the
Bible itself, that this is *not* the way in which it proposes itself as
our rule of faith and practice. It is not made like a catechism;
it is no formal directory of things to be done and things to be left
undone. It goes on the assumption throughout that Christianity
is a living fact, a divine reality, which must be expected to act
out its own significance in a free way, and through the medium

of whose self-interpreting life only the Bible can come to its true application and force. But all this the spirit now before us most obstinately ignores. It affects to go by line and plummet; and all sorts of exegetical violence and trickery are resorted to, for the purpose of saving to appearance, in its own favor, the credit of its own false and servile maxim. The result is pitiful dishonesty, and endless crimination and altercation, on all sides. The most heartless and hollow of all theological controversies, are those which turn on this unhistorical and outwardly mechanical use of the Scriptures. Congregationalism affects in this way to be the *very* truth of the New Testament, as it lies open to plain common sense. The Baptists, however, charge it with being false to its own principle, in allowing infant baptism, for which there is no rule or precedent, but at most a presumption only, in the sacred rule book; and beyond all controversy the Baptists here are right. If Christianity be such an abstract letter, " the law of baptism" must be taken as a positive institution whose whole worth lies in our obediential respect to the authority prescribing it, and which we have no right, therefore, to stretch a particle beyond what is expressed in the precept. But we have other Baptists again, who charge the regular Baptists with being themselves unfaithful to the Protestant rule; and who find it necessary, accordingly, to become more Bible stiff still. The Seventh Day Baptists, for instance, can find no express authority in the New Testament for the change of the Sabbath to the first day of the week; which indeed can be found there by nobody else, as little as any such authority for the baptism of infants. It is all in order, therefore, when we hear them say in true Baptist and Jewish style: " This Sabbath he has imposed upon us by a power which belongs to himself alone; and it is perpetually obligatory on us to sanctify *that day*, until He himself abrogates us from the service" (p. 121,). Full as conclusive, certainly, as the everlasting changes rung on the same string, in opposition to the comprehension of infants in Christ's covenant. With equal consistency, these Bible Christians " celebrate the Lords's supper at night, in imitation of our Saviour; washing at the same time each other's feet, agreeably to his command and example." Among other Bible proofs for the perpetuity of the original Sabbath, they refer us to the texts: " The Sabbath was made for man," and " The Son of Man is Lord even of the Sabbath day," (p. 104, 107,) ; precious exemplifications of the abstract method now under consideration ; though, in truth, not a whit worse than a great many stereotyped tricks of the same sort in use with more respectable denominations, by which an incidental expression, oftentimes of the most ambiguous interpretation, is gravely made a peg on which to hang the whole weight of a doctrine or institution, which it is counted downright heresy to dispute.

Altogether, sect christianity has a wonderful propensity to substitute the abstract and mechanical for the living and concrete, on all sides; as might be extensively illustrated from the book before us, if the limits of our present article allowed. It must ever be so, where the sense of the historical, objective, sacramental and churchly, in the fact of Christianity, is wanting, and the ultimate measure of it sought in the exercises of the single mind separately considered. " Christianity," says Campbellism, p. 231, " is a system of religion and morality instituted by Jesus Christ, principally taught by his Apostles, and recorded in the New Testament. It has for its immediate object the amelioration of the character and condition of man, morally and religiously considered. It consists in the knowledge, belief and obedience, of the testimony and law of Jesus Christ, as taught by his apostles and recorded in the New Testament—Are not law and obedience, testimony and faith, relative terms, so that neither of the latter can exist without the former ? . . . Is not testimony necessarily confined to facts, and law to authority ? . . . Wherefore, in every case, faith must necessarily consist in belief of facts ; and obedience in a practical compliance with the expressed will or dictates of authority. By facts, is here meant, some things said or done. *Conclusion*: Upon the whole, these things being so, it necessarily follows, that Christianity, being a divine institution, there can be nothing human in it; consequently, it has nothing to do with the doctrines and commandments of men ; but simply and solely with the belief and obedience of the *expressly recorded* testimony and will of God, contained in the holy Scriptures, and enjoined by the authority of the Saviour and his holy prophets upon the Christian community." This must be allowed to express well, what may be styled the reigning theory of Christianity among our modern sects. But now, with all due respect to Mr. Campbell, (who has this honorable apology, indeed, in our mind, that he has made more conscience of following out his principle to its proper consequences, than many others, who denounce his consequences, while they make common cause with him in his principle); with all due respect, we say, to President Campbell, this is not Christianity, but in its best view Judaism; and when made to stand for the conception of Christianity, it always involves, though it may be under the guise of an abstract supernaturalism, the very power of Rationalism itself; which only needs suitable scientific sea-room, to run out finally into all the results of its past significant and truly instructive history in Germany. Of this we have not a shadow of doubt. Christianity is no such outward statute-book of things to be believed and things to be done. It is " the law of life in Christ Jesus." It is a new constitution of grace and truth starting in Christ's *person*, and perpetuating itself in this form, as a most real historical fact, by the Church. The difference between this conception and the other, (Moses and Christ, John i. 17, John the Baptist and Christ, Matth. iii. 11, ix. 11,) is very great; and we only wish that Mr. Campbell, and many others, could be led to revolve it solemnly and earnestly in their minds. What if it might be found to be the true Ariadne thread in the end, that should conduct them forth from the horrible sect labyrinth into the clear sunlight of catholicity, which they have been so unsuccessfully struggling to reach in a different way.

There is much besides to be learned from this History of Denominations, for the right understanding and appreciation of the sect spirit. We are admonished, however, by the length of our article, to dwell no farther at present on details. What we have to say farther, will be presented hereafter in the form of certain general reflections, which come over us painfully from the contemplation of the subject as a whole.

                                                    J. W. N,

THE

MERCERSBURG REVIEW.

NOVEMBER, 1849.

NO. VI.

ART. XXXIX.—The Sect System.

History of all the Religious Denominations, &c., *Second improved and portrait edition of Rupp's work, published by John Winebrenner, V. D. M.* Harrisburg, Pa.

Second Article.

1. Our sect system is exceedingly *irrational.* We can conceive of divisions in the church that might be in a certain sense rational and necessary, and so capable of some scientific representation. The original distinction of Protestantism from Catholicism, and the resolution of the first again into the two great confessions Lutheran and Reformed, have this character. They have their ground in the idea of Christianity itself; they form necessary *momenta*, or moving forces, in the process by which this idea is carried forward to its final completion; they can be studied accordingly, and understood, in the way, for instance, of comparative symbolism. But nothing of this sort can be affirmed of our reigning modern sects. No idea underlies them, by which they can be said to have a right to exist. Their appearance is in defiance and scorn of all such objective reason. It is their boast, to be sprung for the most part of mere private judgment and private

will. They start generally, by their own confession, in the
most outward and accidental occasions. A Jacob Albright is
awakened, and finding no congenial religious connections immediately at hand, makes his subjectivity the basis of a new sect,
which in due time swells into an evangelical church. A John
Winebrenner takes it into his head, that every body is wrong but
himself, and being put out of the old church, complacently offers
himself to the world as the nucleus of a new one, that may be
expected to work better. Elder Randall is pushed aside by the Regular Baptists, and forthwith originates the Freewill Baptists. Mr.
Cowherd (p. 124,) is led to inculcate the doctrine of abstinence
from the flesh of animals. as well as total abstinence from all intoxicating liquors, " on the testimony of the Bible," and has many
other private fancies besides on the same testimony; and so we get
the *Bible Christian Church;* still happily in the wilderness and
out of sight. Dr. Abner Jones, of Vermont, has "a peculiar travel of mind in relation to sectarian names and human creeds,"
and to rectify the evil sets in motion a sect of his own, which
falls in afterwards with two other equally providential accidents,
and helps in this way to form the body calling themselves " Christians." And so it goes, to the end of the chapter. Can anything
well be more accidental and capricious, than the rise of sects in
this way ? Who does not see, that we might as reasonably have
five hundred in such form, as fifty or sixty ? Have there not
been hundreds of men, who had just as much vocation in their
circumstances as Albright or Winebrenner, to found new churches,
that might have had just as much character and meaning too, as
theirs, or possibly a good deal more? It is the easiest thing in
the world to moot new questions in religion, scores of them, that
might just as fully justify division as half of those that have
already led to it, provided only the proper zeal were got up in
some quarter to push them out to such extreme, " for conscience'
sake," and to put honor on the Bible. Will any pretend to reduce
such a system to any sort of intelligible method or scheme? It
has none. It is supremely irrational, so far as all inward reason
goes, by its very constitution. We might as well pretend to sys-
tematize and genealogize the clouds, driven hither and thither by
all conflicting winds. It is a chaos, that excludes all science.

Who will dream here of a Sect Symbolism, generically unfold-
ing the inward sense of each upstart body, as related to all the
rest and to the whole system, its historical necessity, its comple-
mental contribution to the full idea of Protestantism?   Who
will find it needful for the right understanding of theology, to
pursue the history of its doctrines through the mazes of our present
sectarianism, as held, for instance by the United Brethren, the
Cumberland Presbyterians, and all manner of Baptists; in the
same way that all true theology does require undoubtedly such
a prosecution of doctrines, through the life of the ancient Greek
Church, the life of the Roman Church, and that of the original Protestant Church under both its grand confessional distinctions.   Take one wing only of the system, the Scotch Secession,
which has been accustomed from the first to make the greatest account of its own *theological* significance, in this way; and
what after all, we ask soberly, is the value of all its witnessings
put together, in this country, for the cause of universal Christianity, whether in theory or practice?   Is there any inward reason
in its divisions and subdivisions, its abortive unions and consequent new sections, till the whole has become a tangled web in the
end which it is a perfect weariness of the flesh to pretend to unra-
vel?   Altogether we have some ten or twelve bodies in this country,
(possibly more,) conscience split for the glory of God, who stand
unitedly, while severally excluding one another, not only on the
Bible, the sure foundation of all sects, but on the Presbyterian
sense of the Bible also as embodied in the Westminster Confession.   *Can* there be any meaning or reason in such a phenomenon?   Has historical theology any real interest whatever in the
questions that lie between Old Covenanters, New Covenanters,
Associate Seceders, Associate Reformed Seceders, and Reformed
Associate Reformed Seceders, clear out to the tip end of orthodoxy
in the last *wee* Associate Presbytery of Pennsylvania?   To ask
the question, is to provoke a smile.   Who understands this field
of church history?   Who cares to thrust himself into its briery
waste?   Do these sects understand themselves?   Is there, in truth,
anything in them *to be* understood; or that is likely to weigh a
feather hereafter, under any separate view, in the mind of God's
Universal Church?   Alas, for the *unreason* of our reigning sect
system!

2. The evil just noticed is greatly aggravated by the considoration, that very few sects remain *constant* at all to their own origin, or make it their business to understand and maintain them. If this change were the result of a true inward process, serving to develope the sense of some mission they had at first, it might be all very well; but every body may easily enough see, that this is not the case. The movement is altogether negative and outward, and amounts to nothing. Once formed, the body floats hither and thither according to circumstances, till finally its original moorings are lost sight of almost entirely ; only it still carries its old name and has gradually accumulated a certain historical substance of its own, a body of recollections and traditions, shibboleths and hobbies, prejudices and pedantries; whereby all manner of selfish interests and ends are enlisted for its support, and room made for a few men in the saddle, by humoring its fancies, to rule and guide it almost at their pleasure. Thus the original irrationality of sects is made for the most part more irrational still, looses any little grain of reason it may have had at first, by the meaningless fluctuations of their subsequent history. The starters of a sect, fifty years afterwards, in many cases, would hardly recognize their own progeny. Happy is the sect, that is able to define at all its own distinctive position, or that can give any show of reason whatever for its existence, under such form as it actually carries. In the great majority of cases, this cannot be done even by the ministers themselves. And then as to the people, poor sheep in the hands of their leaders and pastors, what can *they* be expected to know of their own denominational " whereabouts," or of its rational necessity, in the general pellmell of conflicting " persuasions" with which they are surrounded? As a general thing they know nothing about it.

3. The system is constitutionally *tyrannical.* Every sect pretends indeed to make men free. But only consider what sects are ; self-constituted ecclesiastical organizations, called forth ordinarily by private judgment and caprice, and devoted to some onesided christian interest, under perhaps the most superficial and narrow view ; educated polemically to a certain fanatical zeal for their own separatistic honor and credit ; and bent on impressing their own " image and superscription," on all that fall be-

neath their ghostly power.   Are these the circumstances that
favor liberality and independence?   The man who puts his conscience in the keeping of a sect, is no longer free.   It might as
well be in the keeping of a Roman priest.   In many cases indeed this were far better.   Have the Baptists no traditions?   Is
there no slavery of intellect and heart among the United Brethren?   Pshaw!   The very last place in which to look for true
spiritual emancipation, the freedom of a divinely, self-poised catholic mind, is the communion of sects.

4. The narrowness and tyranny of the sect spirit, unfriendly
to all generous christian life, is of fatal force in particular against
the cultivation of *theology*, without which in the end it is not possible for the church to have any true prosperity.   Theology can
be no science, except as it has to do with the whole of Christianity,
and is thus at once both churchly and historical in the full sense
of these terms.   The sect life, by its very conception, kills it, by
turning it into a petrifaction or causing it to evaporate in the way
of thin abstraction.   Facts here are very plain.   Sects, as they
actually exist, have no theology, save as now mentioned ; the miserable residuum only, so far as it may have any value at all, of
the church life they had to start upon in the beginning, carried
along with them as a mere outward tradition.   Sects have no
pleasure in theology, as a science.   It has nothing to expect from
this quarter.   It is no libel on our American sects in particular,
to say that they have not thus far contributed anything at all to
the advance of this most noble and excellent of all sciences ; and
it needs no prophet's gift to say, that they never will do so in time
to come.   If any service has been rendered to it in any quarter,
it has been by such as have been able to surmount the system in
some measure, forcing their way upwards into a more catholic
region.   No sectarian theology can ever be of any permanent
value.

5. The sect plague has no tendency to work out its own *cure* ;
unless it be in the way of a deadly malady, that ends itself by
ending the life on which it has come to fasten.   It is vain to look
for a reduction of the number of sects, by their voluntary amal-
gamation.   No two have yet been able to make themselves
one.   The difficulty is not in their theological differences.   These

are for the most part of very little practical force ; with the great mass of the people, we may say, indeed, of absolutely no force at all.   In nine cases out of ten it is a matter of sheer accident, that this man is an Albright and his neighbor a Cumberland Presbyterian, that one phase of the Baptist faith prevails here and another phase of it ten miles off.   All this, however makes no matter ; and it would make very little matter, if it were brought to be never so clear that the causes of separation in any case had completely fallen away.   There would still be no union. It is the curse of the system, that it can never of itself break the chains it has thus forged for its own slaves.   On the contrary, it tends perpetually from bad to to worse.   It is easier by far to divide one sect into two, than it is to splice two sects into one.   There is not the least reason to expect accordingly, that the system will ever reform itself into any better shape.   Is is plain moreover that it has no necessary end; on the contrary, its capabilities and possibilities are indefinitely boundless.   No multiplication of sects can exhaust the principle from which they spring.

6.   It is well to note how generally the sect system adheres to the article of *justification by faith,* and how prone it is to run this side of Christianity out to a false extreme, either in the way of dead antinomianism or wild fanatacism.   With many persons, at this time, the test of all soundness in religion is made to stand in the idea of salvation by grace as opposed to works, Christ's righteousness set over to our account in an outward way, and a corresponding experience more or less magical in the case of those who receive it, which goes under the name of evangelical conversion.   But now it falls in precisely with the abstract mechanism of the sect mind, to throw itself mainly on this view of religion, to the exclusion or at least vast undervaluation of all that is comprised in the mystery of christianity as the power of a new creation historically at hand in the church.   It is common for sects, accordingly, to make a parade of their zeal, in such style, for the doctrines of grace and the interests of vital godliness ; and this is often taken at once for a sufficient passport in their favor, as though any body of religionists professing faith in free justification and violent conversion, must needs be part and parcel of Christ's Church, however unchurchly in all other

respects. But surely for a sober mind, it should be enough to expose the fallacy of such thinking, to look over the array of sects
which is here presented to our view, and see how easy it is for almost the whole of them, if need be, to legitimate their pretensions in this way. All fragments of the Scotch Secession of
course are one here, however divided in their " testimonies" at
other points. They make election the principle of christianity,
turn justification by faith into a complete abstraction, and so nullify the law in one form, only to come too generally under the
yoke of it again in another. The Baptists, through all their divisions, meet here also as on common ground ; with antinomian
tendency in one direction ; with a tendency to fanatacism in
another direction ; but with common intolerance, all round, to
every view of religion that is not found to harmonize with their
own abstract scheme. The Winebrennerians hold justification by
faith without works, (p. 177,) and are great in their way for revivals and wholesale conversions. So of course the Albright Brethren (p. 277.) So the United Brethren in Christ (p.564.) These
and other sects indeed ambitiously strive to outdo one another, in
the business of saving souls in the most approved style, " getting
them through" as it is called, according to the abstract scheme
now noticed. The one grand requisite for fellowship in the
Campbellite communion is, (p. 225,) " an entire reliance upon
the merits of Christ alone for justification ;" it is founded we are
told, (p. 223,) " upon the two great distinguishing principles of
the Lutheran Reformation, *viz:* the Bible alone as the rule of
faith, to the entire exclusion of tradition, and the relying only upon
that justification that is obtained through faith in Jesus Christ."
Even the " Chrstians," with no faith in Christ's divinity, and the
Universalists too, when it suits, can go in for some sort of abstract
magical justification, and on the strength of it bring into play the
common revival machinery with quite good success. All this
surely deserves to be well laid to heart. There are, it is but too
plain, " depths of Satan" here, as well as in other quarters,
against which we need to stand solemnly on our guard. Let no
one feel that it is safe to go with a sect, simply because it may
seem to be *evangelical,* (O most abused word,) in this quacksalvery
style. What can it be worth, if it be dissociated wholly from
the old church consciousness embodied in the creed ?

7. For one who has come at all to understand the constitution of this abstract supernaturalism, it can produce no surprise to find the sect system marked universally by a *rationalistic* tendency. A Rationalism that denies the supernatural altogether, and a Supernaturalism that will not allow it to enter into any concrete union with the natural, are at bottom much of the same nature; and the last needs only the force of true consecutive thinking always, to pass over peacefully into the arms of the first. Sects start usually in abstract supernaturalism, with an affectation of hyper-spiritual perfection. But the rationalistic element comes at once into view, both in their thinking and practice. This is clearly exemplified in the Baptistic scheme, as already noticed; a divine statute book, outwardly certified to be from heaven; christian *laws* drawn forth from it in a like outward way; the mechanism of salvation brought nigh to men all outwardly again, in the form of thought or credited report; its application magically affected by an outward impulsion from God's Spirit, carrying the soul through a certain process of states and feelings. No sacramental grace. No true union with the life of Christ. So with sects generally. Their idea of private judgment; their notion of religious freedom; their low opinion of the sacraments; their indifference to all earnest theology; their propensity to drive religion by might and by power, rather than by the still small voice of God's Spirit; all betray a rationalistic habit of mind, and lean inwardly to still more decidedly rationalistic consequences and results. When Mr. Campbell makes Christianity to be " simply and solely," (p. 233,) the belief of certain testimony, and obedience to certain laws, outwardly offered to men in the Bible, what less is it, we ask, than the very genius of Rationalism itself; although most of the other sects probably would accept the same definition, as altogether satisfactory and sufficient. The sect life tends to destroy faith, as it is notoriously unfriendly also to every thing like reverence. It is not strange at all to see it running out into " Christianism;" or to hear, in certain quarters, of converts being taken into the church, (so called,) without baptism! There is too much reason to fear, that the virus of a low vulgar insensibility to the divine fact of Christianity has come to pervade the popular mind, in some sections of our country,

under the forms and shams of this unchurchly religionism far beyond what most persons have ever been led to imagine or suspect.

8. It is encouraging however, as well as curious, to see how the sect system is made to lend *testimony* throughout, against itself, to the idea of the Holy Catholic Church; not unlike the devils in the New Testament, who were forced to acknowledge Christ, while fighting against him or fleeing from his presence. Every sect, in spite of itself, is forced to acknowledge, at least indirectly, the necessary attributes of the Church, as one, holy, catholic, and apostolical. It cannot be a *mere* particular corporation, society or persuasion, however much in some views it may seem disposed to be nothing more. To stand at all, it must put on the character of a church, and then carry out as it best can what this character is felt by a sort of inward necessity, to imply and require. Some sects openly claim the prerogatives and powers of the Universal Church, as belonging to themselves alone, in such a way as to exclude all that is not of their own communion; and this certainly is the most consistent course. Generally however no such claim is made; but the sect professes to look upon itself only as a tribe of the true Israel, a section or wing in the sacramental host of God's elect. And yet it goes on, in these circumstances, to arrogate to itself within its own bounds full church powers; such powers as have no meaning, except as conditioned by the idea of a catholic or whole church; powers which cannot be fairly asserted, without virtual limitation upon the equal independence of sister sects. The inward ecclesiastical economy of every sect, as to its ordinations, admission of members, church censure, supervision of both faith and practice, &c., is so ordered as to involve throughout the assumption of an absolute and final and exclusive supremacy in matters of religion. The idea of the Church, however dimly and obscurely present, will not allow it to be otherwise. It *must* be one and universal, the *whole*, that of necessity excludes all beyond its own sphere. In this way every sect, so far as it can be called a church at all, becomes necessarily a caricature of the catholicity with which it pretends to make war, and so, like every other caricature, bears witness to the truth, which is thus distorted by it and brought into con-

tempt. In some cases, we have surprising confessions in favor
of the true idea of the Church, where they might seem to be
wholly out of place. Mr. Winebrenner (p. 175,) insists on visi-
bility, unity, sanctity, universality and perpetuity, as the necessary attributes of the church. " An invisible church that some
divines speak of,' he tells us, " is altogether an anomaly in christian theology " So again: " The union of sects, into one general
evangelical alliance, or into one human organization diverse in
character, faith and practice, from the one true church of God, as
characterized in the Bible, we have no belief in nor sympathy
for." So we meet in Mr. Alexander Campbell many traces
of a sound and right feeling here, which we may well regret
to find overwhelmed again, and made of no effect, by the
power of the unhistorical sect mind which is allowed after all to
prevail in his system.

9. The posture of sects, being such as now described, involves
them unavoidably in endless *inconsistency* and *contradiction.*
There is a lie always at the bottom of it, from which it can never fully make its escape. It is the part pretending to be the whole,
while it proclaims itself still to be nothing more than a part. The
sect acknowledges the christian consciousness to be something
deeper, more comprehensive, more absolutely necessary and real,
than its own modification of it as a sect ; and yet, this modification, the relative and partial sect consciousness, is in fact exalted above the other and clothed with powers which appertain of
right only to the idea of christianity in full. The sect wills itself above the church, calls itself modestly *a* church, as one of
many ; but then goes on, almost in the same breath, to play itself
off as *the* church, virtually sinking all other catholicity into a
fiction as opposed to such high usurpation. Here is a tremendous contradiction, which runs through the entire system. The
very features it is most ready to quarrel with in Romanism, it
thrusts upon us again in new shape as its own. It hates church
tradition ; will hear of no binding force in church history ; but
straightway manufactures a log chain of authority in the very
same form, out of the little yesterday of its own life, which it
binds mercilessly on the neck of all its subjects. It will have no
saints nor fathers ; but forthwith offers us instead its own foun-

ders and leaders, and makes it well nigh blasphemy to speak a word in their dispraise. It is great for private judgment; which it takes mighty good care however to regulate, by bit and bridle, to one single track, and that generally of the most narrow sort. It is loud for the Bible, an open Bible, the Bible *alone ;* but only as read through the medium of its own theological habit, and wo to the wight who may presume to read it in any other way. So throughout. The very things it protests and fights against in the church of Rome, it is ready the next moment to assert in its own favor, under some altered form ; only with this difference that the old *catholic* truth which in every case underlies the Roman abuse, is with sects generally treated as part of that abuse itself, so that the new exercise of power brings no such sacred sanction along with it for the pious heart. It is counted dreadful that the church should be placed under the *human* headship of the pope, or of a pope and council ; but has not every sect its human headship—whether one man, five men or twenty is of no account —whose supremacy is complete in all its religious affairs, only by its own confession *without* right divine ? This headship, moreover, with all its pretended humility, is in no case slow to assume the exercise of divine powers. Popery, we are told with horror, presumes to fix doctrines, make laws, use keys &c., all in virtue of its own right and power, instead of simply following the letter of the Bible. And what sect, we ask, is not continually doing the same thing, in substantially the same way ? Has not each sect its system of doctrines, or at least of notions, derived through its own prophetical headship, its particular founder and standing leaders, from the divine record, and legislated into authority by its own circle of reading and teaching, as absolutely as any faith that prevails in Rome ? Has it not besides its *index expurgatorius* too, in fact if not in form, its particular world of religious thought hedged in carefully by its approved books and tracts, or possibly by a powerful " book establishment" even, that contrives to monopolize in great measure the business of thinking for the body at large? Rome, it is said, dares to create ecclesiastical rules, ceremonies, rites, &c. And what sect is it, that has not done the same thing ? The Holy Church Catholic, by its very idea, includes in itself the whole power of the Saviour's

Mediatorial life, under its three functions, prophetical, priestly and kingly. To say that these functions are exercised by Christ only under an outward and separate form, and that the Church, his mystical Body, does not also include them in her constitution as " the fullness of him that filleth all in all," is a profound absurdity; an absurdity so profound indeed, that no religious body can assert it, and still claim to be a church, without at once falling into the most gross practical contradiction; that, namely, of repudiating the true powers of christianity in the only view in which they *are* true, and then trying to force them into its service again under another form that involves of necessity what is wrong and false. In claiming church rights and church powers accordingly, and in pretending to exercise church functions and satisfy church wants, every sect does in truth lay claim to a true prophetical, true priestly, and true kingly character, at the same time; as without all this, the other pretension is reduced to empty smoke. That is, every sect puts itself forward as an infallibly safe expositor of the true sense of Christianity and the Bible, a perfectly trustworthy and sufficient depository of God's grace and the sure medium of reconciliation with him for sinners, the legatee in full of the commission of the keys as originally given to Peter and his fellow apostles. And yet on the other hand, no such divine powers are acknowledged, as necessary at all to constitute the Church; and other sects are allowed to have just as much right to play prophet, priest and king, in the same ecclesiastical style, as the body in question; which at once turns all such exercise of church functions into a merely human assumption, resting on no general necessary ground whatever, that is, into the very essence of popery itself. In such perpetual self-contradiction is the sect system doomed everywhere to move, by trying to uphold the conception of the Church, while it shows itself at war with all the attributes that enter into its constitution.

Every sect, in claiming to be a church, claims rights and powers which it has no ability whatever, to make good, and invites a faith and trust for which it can offer no sort of commensurate ground in its actual constitution. Take, for exemplification, the large and respectable body of the Narraganset Brethren. Of its origin, tenets and ways, the case does not require that we should speak. Enough that it rose in the way of protest against errors and defects which were supposed to prevail in the rest of the Christian world, threw itself on the sole guidance of the Bible, and has all along shown itself very zealous for evangelical religion and its own revivals. It allows now that there are other churches besides itself in the world; that the sects generally, are such churches; and is ready indeed, on fit occasion, to make a great parade of liberality and toleration, in the way of shaking hands with other denominations, to express what it conceives to be the " communion of saints." Still it puts itself forward, for all who can be induced to listen to its claims, as the comprehension in full of what the idea of the Church requires; that is, it arrogates to itself prerogatives and resources, which are absolutely universal in their nature, and as such exclusive of every like claim in any other quarter. The sect calls on all men, as they value their salvation, to take refuge in her communion. She does not simply offer them the Bible, but along with it her own tradition also, her sacraments, her ministrations of grace. She is not content to make them christians, but seeks to make them also Narragansets. Her mission is to spread and build up Narragansetism. This for her is identical with absolute and complete Christianity; she expects the whole world to become Narragansets, if not before, at least in the blessed millenium. This same feeling she tries to infuse into every soul, that falls within the range of her ecclesiastical domain; and she exacts from them accordingly, at the same time, full faith in her separate sufficiency for all church purposes and ends. She assumes in regard to them the full stewardship of Christ's house. She makes herself responsible for their souls, engaging if they do but trust her guidance and care to see them safe into heaven. She carries the keys of the kingdom of heaven, to bind and to loose, to open and shut, at her own pleasure. All this implies *universal* validity in her acts, validity for all men and not simply for some men; and in no other view can it ever be the object of Christian faith and trust. But see now the contradiction of the whole case. Narragansetism does not pretend to assert these universal powers in a truly universal way, but only within a given circle, the compass namely of her own membership. It is the church, with all its divine resources, for one man who has got into its communion, but not at all for another, his neighbor, who belongs to another communion. It is charged with the salvation of one it may be in a family, where all the rest are cared for in a wholly different way. It exacts a faith and obedience of one, which it never thinks of requiring in the case of another. It calls for sacrifices and services in the first case, all for the glory of God in the promotion of Narraganseism, which it never dreams of demanding or exacting in the second. Its privileges and opportunities are for Narragansets only, not for Christians generally, save as they are willing to put on the Narraganset livery, and so make this to be identical with the profession of Christ. The censures of the sect too are taken by herself to be of universal force for those on whom they fall ; although acknowledged to be of no force whatever, should it be pretended to hurl them over the sect fence, into any part of the Christian world that lies beyond. Thus one man is excommunicated, put out of the whole church, by a power which would be only laughed at if it undertook to disturb in the least the ecclesiastical relations of another, close beside him, only within another communion, involved in precisely the same offence. Nay, the man who is thus amenable to Narraganset jurisdiction to day, may to-morrow clear himself of it completely by taking letters of dismission from his sect, with all its universal powers, and passing over to the jurisdiction of some other evangelical body, which exercises the same universal powers, with equal independence, in like circumscribed and particularistic style.

How *can* church powers carry with them any truly necessary and universal force, such as all church faith is felt to demand, exercised in this arbitrary and conventional way? Plainly, in this whole order of things, the church has no necessary existence whatever, but is the creature and product simply of the men who belong to it, with such powers as they may be pleased to lodge in it for present use. There is a sore contradiction here in our whole sect system, the thorn of which those only can fail to feel sharply, who have never yet been brought earnestly to reflect on the true nature of the Church itself. No wonder that sects find it hard often to distinguish themselves from mere voluntary societies, in the service of morality and religion. No wonder, that their sacraments sink so

readily into rationalistic signs, and that the assertion of supernatural objective powers, as something immanent in the constitution
of the Church itself, is apt to fill them with offence.   It is hard
indeed to conceive of all this in the communion of a sect, which I
am at full liberty to forsake to morrow, if I so please, for the communion of another.   How can I yield to such a body ever, as
such, the faith and homage that are due to the Church as a divine reality, and which crave the presence of this Church in full
as a necessary object, to make room for their exercise ?   If I may
thus leave one sect, why not twenty ; and if twenty, why not
all ?   On what principle of common sense am I bound to confine my ecclesiastical vagrancy to the range of actually existing sects, (accidents as they are too generally at best,) instead
of bidding adieu at once to the whole of them, and originating
a new communion, more to my taste, in the bosom say of my
own house ?   To all such questions the sect system can make no
satisfactory reply.   It tends, with inward necessity from the beginning, to subvert completely the whole idea of the Church.

10. It is owing in part at least, no doubt, to the vast inward lie
which the sect system thus carries in its very constitution, that its
influence is found to be so *unfavorable actually to honesty and
godly sincerity*, in the case of those who surrender themselves to
its power.   This is a wide subject, which we will not pretend
here to take up in its details.   All experience however shows,
that the sect mind, as such, has a strange tendency to run into
low cunning, disingenuous trickery and jesuitic policy.   Religion degenerates with it into a trade, in which men come to terms
with God on the subject of their own salvation, and lay away
their spiritual acquisitions as a sort of outward property for convenient use.   The object is required to bend and bow to the subject ; becomes a thing indeed for private appropriation, and under such partial apprehension is made to stand falsely for what is
the whole.   Sect piety is constitutionally unequal, inconsistent,
fantastic and pedantic.   It never has been, and never can be,
sound, calm, full, catholic and free.   By the very falsehood of
substituting the sect for the Church, it is involved necessarily
in hypocrisy, which reaches always with fearful power at last into
its entire life.   It has a tendency universally to run into sham.

It abounds notoriously in cant.   It is full of hollow pretensions, phrases and forms that have parted with all life.   It delights in all sorts of quackery.   Nor is this dishonesty confined to the sphere of religion ; it is very apt to infect the whole life.   Hypocrisy towards God begets naturally unfaithfulness towards men. It is not meant of course to charge all sectarian christianity with the moral defect now noticed.   We speak only of the *tendency* it has this way.   Good men, in the bosom of a sect, may rise superior to the danger ; but in doing so, they lay aside to the same extent the sect consciousness itself, and are brought into conflict thus with its ordinary pretensions and claims.   On all sides, however, we have examples enough of the bad power, which belongs to the system in the general view here presented.   This book of sects sheds no small amount of illustration on their habit of carnal policy and jesuitic calculation.   Still wider evidence of it is to be found every day, in our common sectarian religious press. What sectarian paper is trusted beyond the limits of its own denomination, on any question involving sectarian interests and relations?   It seems almost the necessary character of every such publication, to be disingenuous and unfair ; without thought, it may be, or premeditation ; which itself, however, serves only the more fully to show how completely natural such want of catholic integrity is, for the whole system out of which it so easily and readily springs.

11. It is truly amazing, that any person should pretend to justify the sect system, as either agreeable to the true idea of Christianity or conducive to its interests.   Some, however, still do so openly ; while a much larger number would seem to acquiesce in the thought, indirectly, at least, and by implication.   Every such imagination, however, is itself, but a sign and proof of the evil nature of the system, for which it thus seeks to raise an apology; for it carries in itself, we may say, the principle of annihilation in the end, for all that is comprehended in the faith of the holy catholic church.   Not only is our sect system in flat contradiction to the letter of the New Testament; it is at war besides with the divine constitution of Christianity itself.   It wrongs the idea of the Church, withdraws it as an object of faith from the Christian world, and in this way mars and spoils the symmetry, and full-

ness, and force, of the Christian life throughout. The bad fruits
of the system, in this view, stare us in the face from all sides.
Our theology is sickly, lame and lean. Our piety is angular and
hard, running much into narrow technicalities and traditionary
forms. Every denomination has its own small world of theory
and experience, which it affects to regard as universal Christianity,
without the least account of the other little worlds of like sort,
with which it is surrounded. It is gross falsehood, to say that
the influence of sects on one another is wholesome, and favorable to the general cause of Christianity. Their emulation is not
holy ; and any gain that may seem to come of it, is no better
than " the hire of a whore or the price of a dog" brought into the
house of the Lord, which he has declared to be an abomination
in his sight (Deut. xxiii. 18). It is not by any such rivalry and
strife, that the glorious gospel may be expected to prevail in the
world. All zeal for religion is rotten, and will be found at last
to stink, that springs not from a true interest in religion for its
own sake. Our sects do not love each other. Their relation to
each other, at best, is one of indifference. To a fearful extent,
it is one of quiet malignity and hatred. What sect takes any
active interest in the welfare of another, rejoices in its prosperity,
sympathizes with its griefs and trials, makes common cause with
it in its enterprises and works? Every body knows, rather, that
the charity of sects stops short for the most part with the lines of
circumvallation that surround for each one its own camp, and
that it is cold as winter towards all that lies beyond. The jeal-
ousies and collisions of sects, not loud, mainly, but in the form
rather, of quiet still fanaticism, are the source of endless religious
mischief throughout the land. Altogether the system is a plague
that calls for mourning and lamentation in every direction.

12. For one who has come to make earnest with the church
question, and who 'has courage to face things as they are in the
way of steady firm thought, the whole present state of sect christianity is full of *difficulty* and *discouragement*. In the first place,
it is not possible for 'him to identify any one sect with the idea of
the whole Church. Whether he be a Methodist, or a Presbyterian, or a Lutheran, or of any other denomination, he sees clearly
that it is a desperate business to think of making out a full agree-

ment with primitive christianity in favor of his own body. He owns too, at any rate that other bodies are included in the Church, as it now stands. Of course, his own is but a part of the Church, not numerically only, but also constitutionally. Hence it must be regarded, when taken by itself, as a one-sided and defective manifestation of the Christian life; and so the consciousness, or state of mind, which it serves to produce, and in which distinctively it stands, can never be rested in as evangelically complete. It is not possible thus for a true church consciousness, and the particular sect consciousness, Presbyterianism, Lutheranism, or any other, to fall together as commensurate spheres of life; the first is something far more wide and deep than the second, and cannot be asked to yield to this as ultimate in any way, without the sense of incongruity and contradiction. Then again, it becomes impossible, of course, to acquiesce in the denominational position as final and conclusive. No position can be so regarded, that is not felt to be identical with the absolute idea of Christianity, the true sense of it as a whole. What earnest minded man now seriously expects that his particular denomination, Methodist, Presbyterian, or any other, is destined to swallow up at last all other types of Christianity, and so rule the universal world? Nor is the case relieved at all, by imagining the different sects, as they now stand, to continue collectively in permanent force. It is not possible at all for a truly thoughtful spirit, to settle itself in this as the legitimate and normal state of the Church. The very sense of sect, as related to the sense of the Church, requires that the first should pass away. The whole sect system then is interimistic, and can be rightly endured only as it is regarded in this light. And yet the system itself is opposed to every such thought. It cannot will its own destruction. Every sect demands of its members a faith and trust, as we have already seen, which imply that it is to be taken as absolute and perpetual. It plays, in its place, the part of Christ's one universal Church. Here, then, is a difficulty. To cleave to the sect as an ultimate interest, in the way it requires, is to be divorced in spirit necessarily, to the same extent, from the true idea of Christ's kingdom, whose perfect coming cannot possibly be in such form. To become catholic, on the other hand, is necessarily to rise above the standpoint of the mere sect, and to lose the power thus of that devotion to its interests, separately considered, which it can never fail to exact notwithstanding, as the test and measure, in such relation, even, of universal Christianity itself. How much of embarrassment and confusion is involved in all this, the more especially as the sect system has no tendency whatever to surmount its own contradiction, but carries in itself the principle only of endless disintegration, many are made to feel at this time beyond what they are well able to express.

J. W. N.

EDITORIAL INTRODUCTION TO "EARLY CHRISTIANITY"

In the third and fourth volumes of the *Mercersburg Review*
(1851-1852) Nevin published two of his most important articles,
"Early Christianity" and "Cyprian." The former was published
in three parts, the latter in four parts. "Early Christianity"
is reproduced on the following pages as it originally appeared.

Nevin's consideration of the nature of the church led him
to a study of early Christianity. He was particularly concerned about the manner in which nineteenth century American Protestantism measured up to the thought and practice of the primitive church. His articles of 1851-1852 reveal the burden of
his conclusions. They display great respect for the earlier
fathers of the church whose ecclesiology and views on the
sacraments Nevin found much to his own liking. While both
Roman Catholicism and Protestantism fell short of the "full
idea of Christianity," the embryo of which is found in the
early church and its fathers, it appeared to Nevin that Roman
Catholicism was closer to it. As a matter of fact, on the
basis of his patristic research, Nevin found himself more and
more attracted to the doctrine and practice of Roman Catholicism. He did not hesitate to conceal these sympathies in his
writings and correspondence. This angered many of his colleagues in the German Reformed Church and produced lively
polemics.

In 1851, due to financial pressures on the seminary, heavy
responsibilities connected with its administration, and his own
theological uncertainty concerning the "Catholic" question,
Nevin submitted his resignation as Professor of Theology. It
was formally, though reluctantly, accepted by the Synod of 1852.
Nevin continued as President of Marshall College until its re-

moval to Lancaster in 1853. "Early Christianity" marks a major
transition in the development of Nevin's thought and his role
in the seminary.

EARLY CHRISTIANITY.

In an interesting letter of the Rev. Dr. Bacon, written recently from Lyons in France and published in the N. Y. "Independent" and the "American and Foreign Christian Union," we meet with the following passages referring to the present and past religious character of that ancient and venerable city.

"Before I left home I resolved that, if it were possible, I would visit Lyons in my travels, and see for myself what God has wrought there for the revival and advancement of true religion. That city, as you know, is the centre of a great and powerful organization for the propagation of the Roman Catholic faith—an organization second only to the Propaganda at Rome in the extent of its missions and the amount of its resources. In that city, too, the Roman Catholic religion is more flourishing, with the indications of living zeal, and more deeply seated in the affections of the people, than in any other city on the continent of Europe. The fact, then, so often reported to us, that there a Protestant Evangelical Church has been gathered, and that in the midst of such a population evangelical labors have been crowned with signal success, is a fact which the Christian traveler may well turn aside to see."

"Ever since my childhood the name of Lyons has been associated in my thoughts, with the faith and patience of the saints who suffered there as witnesses for Christ in the second century. The story of the sufferings and constancy of Pothinus, Blandina, Perpetua, and others, is upon record in the epistle from the Christians of Lyons and Vienne, to their brethren in Asia Minor, with whom they appear to have been closely connected—a document which is familiar to the readers of Milner's Church History, and which is among the earliest and most authentic remains of Christian antiquity. It was an interesting thought that I was now for the first time upon ground that had been consecrated by the struggle of primitive Christianity, and watered with the blood of martyrs, some of whom had looked upon the faces of Christ's immediate followers. And now, among the 200,000 inhabitants of Lyons, are there any living remains of the Gospel for which the primitive martyrs suffered, and which gave them the victory? The archbishop of Lyons and Vienne is honored by the Roman Catholic Church as the successor of Pothinus and St. Irenæus; but how slight the resemblance between the pompous and showy worship now performed under the roof of that old cathedral, and the simple prayers and songs of the few disciples who were wont to meet here in some obscure chamber "with their bishops and deacons," seventeen hundred years ago. Where are the successors of those primitive Christians?

"It was with such thoughts that I went forth on the morning of the Lord's day to find the Evangelical Chapel in the *Rue de l'Arbre Sec.* I looked in at the cathedral and at other churches, splendid with pictures and images, as I past by, and beheld their devotions; and it seemed to me that the city could hardly have been more given to idolatry in the palmy days of Pagan Rome, than it is at this day. In these magnificent structures the Christian traveler looks in vain for anything like what he has learned from the New Testament. The worship, instead of being offered exclusively and directly in Christ's name to the one living and true God, is offered to deified mortals, and chiefly to Mary, "the mother of God." Instead of being addressed only to an invisible God, who is a spirit, and who must be worshipped in spirit and in truth, it is offered to images and pictures, (and those, for the most part, of no superior description,) and to dead men's bones. Not in such places, nor where such worship is offered, are we to look for the true succession from the apostles and primitive martyrs, the true Catholic Church, which is the body of Christ."

Dr. Bacon's letter is addressed to an Association of Benevolent Ladies in New Haven, whose contributions have gone for a number of years past, through the Foreign Evangelical Society, (now the Am. and For. Chr. Union,) towards the support of an evangelical missionary in Lyons. In that city, containing with its immediate environs at least 300,000 inhabitants—next to Paris, the most populous and influential city of France—the great centre of Papal influence—the truth, according to Dr. Baird, has made greater progress within the last twenty years than in any other city of the same country. "The work began in 1825, or even earlier, in the efforts of a pious Swiss Protestant shoemaker. In the humble apartment of this poor man little meetings were held for reading the Scriptures and prayer. It was at these meetings, we believe, that Mr. Moureton, the brave grenadier of Napoleon, (who was in the battle of Leipsic, and several others in the later years of the reign of that wonderful man,) was converted." There was of course a considerable body of Protestantism there before; but this unfortunately had ceased to be evangelical; like the Protestantism of France generally had glided into dead rationalistic formality. The church here noticed is a wholly new and independent movement. The pious grenadier, Mr. Moureton, in the capacity of a deacon and colporteur, has done much to promote it for a series of years by his labors among the laboring population of Lyons and its suburbs. The Rev. Adolphe Monod, settled as one of the pastors of the regular Protestant church in 1829, was soon after " brought to the saving knowledge of Christ, and began to preach the true Gospel with great zeal and power ;" the resut of which was, that the worldly-minded consistory of the church took offence, and soon after deposed him from his office. In this way he became the head of the small evangelical interest just noticed, which now assumed the character of a separate church, and has since grown into its present importance. It is remarkable however, that this improved Protestantism has derived but little of its material from the ranks of the old Protestantism. " Mr. Monod soon found that the new church was to be increased not so much by bringing back the degenerate Protestants from their rationalism to the simplicity of the gospel, as by conversions from among the Roman Catholics. Thus his enterprise became from the outset a work of evangelism among the manufacturing population of the city and its crowded suburbs. Into that field of labor he entered with great zeal and great success. And when, on the removal of Mr. Monod to Paris a few years ago, he was succeeded by Mr. Fisch, the work went on with undiminished prosperity"—that is, the work of turning Catholics into a much better sort of Protestants than could be made generally from the Protestant body itself. Dr. Bacon describes the congregation as very plain, made up for the most part of common laboring people of the lower class, but still as much resembling in its intelligent appearance and simple worship what he had been accustomed to in Puritan America; so that he felt himself, stranger though he was, among brethren of the same household of faith. In the afternoon, he attended a meeting of the brotherhood for mutual conference and inquiry.

" It was held in a school-room, and very much resembled a Congregational church meeting in New England. There was however one obvious difference. Those brethren were not merely concerned with the working of a system defined and understood in all its details, and familiar to them from their childhood. With the New Testament in their hands, they were inquiring after principles and rules of church order; and the question which then chiefly occupied their attention, and seemed somewhat to divide their opinions, was whether the government of their church should be in part committed to a body of elders, or retained entire in the hands of the assembled brethren. As I listened to the discussion, I could not but admire the free and manly yet fraternal spirit in which it was conducted. And as I saw what a school for the development of various intellectual gifts as well as for the culture of Christian affection, that church had been under its simple democratic organization, I felt quite sure that those brethren, with all their confidence in their teachers, would not be easily persuaded to subvert a system to which they were already so greatly indebted, or to divest themselves of the right of freely debating and voting on all their interests and duties as a church."

The letter states, that there are now in the city and suburbs four chapels, in addition to the mother church, one with a distinct pastor the other three missionary preaching places—that four ministers, several evangelists and a number of colporteurs, are constantly employed—that the total number of communicants in 1850 was 440, while about 2500 persons were more or less directly connected with the evangelical community; whereupon the excellent and much respected writer concludes:

" I think that in these facts the ladies who formerly contributed to aid the good work at Lyons, will find evidence that their coöperation was not in vain. Rarely, have I enjoyed anything more than I enjoyed my visit to that missionary and apostolical church. Nor do I know where to look for a more satisfactory representation of the ideal of primitive Christianity than may be found in the city which was made illustrious so long ago by the labors of Irenæus, and by the martyrdom of Pothinus and Blandina."

In reading this, we were reminded of certain notices of the same place, in somewhat similar style, from the pen of the Rev. Daniel Wilson, (then of Islington, but better known since as Bishop of Calcutta,) in his work entitled " Travels on the Continent of Europe in the Summer of 1823;" as also of certain parallel passages in the same work, relating to the early and later Christianity of the celebrated city of Milan. Take in the case of Lyons the following extracts :

" This morning I have visited St. Irenée, the site of the ancient city, though now only a suburb. I here visited the Roman baths at the Ursuline Monastery (formerly so, for all the monasteries and convents were abolished at the Revolution.) These baths consist of a series of numerous dark vaults, communicating with each other. about twenty feet under ground ; but no longer interesting, except from their antiquity. I then went to what was the garden of the Minimes, and saw the remains of the Roman Amphitheatre, where the early Christians were exposed to the wild beasts. This scene affected me extremely. The form of the Amphitheatre remains, after a lapse of sixteen or seventeen centuries. Some traces may be discovered of the rising seats of turf, and several dilapidated brick vaults seem to indicate the places where the wild beasts, and perhaps the holy martyrs, were guarded. It is capable of holding an immense assemblage—perhaps 30 or 40,000 persons. A still more elevated range of seats, to which you ascend by decayed stone steps, seem to have been the place allotted for the magistrates and regulators of the barbarous shows. A peaceful vineyard now flourishes where these scenes of horror once reigned. The tender garden shrub springs in the seats and vaults. The undisturbed wild flowers perfume the air. A stranger now and then visits the spot, and calmly inquires if that was the Amphitheatre which once filled all Christendom with lamentation. What a monster is persecution, whether Pagan, Popish, or Protestant! And yet, till the beginning of the last century, it was hardly banished from the general habits of Europe. Would to God that even now it could be said to be utterly rooted out!

"I visited, after this, the church of St. Irenée, built in the time of the Romans, when the liberty of public worship was refused the Christians. It is subterraneous, and contains the bones of the many thousand Christians who were martyred in the year 202, under the emperor Severus. It is of this noble army of martyrs that Milner gives such an affecting account. An inscription on the church states, that St. Pothinus was sent by Polycarp, and founded it; and was martyred under the emperor Antoninus; that St. Irenæus succeeded him, and converted an infinite multitude of Pagans, and suffered martyrdom, together with nineteen thousand Christians, besides women and children, in the year 202; and that in the year 470, the church was beautified. I have not an exact recollection of what Milner says, and therefore may be wrong in giving credit to some of these particulars; but I have a strong impression that the main facts agree with the tradition on the spot; and I confess, I beheld the scene with veneration. I could almost forgive the processions which are twice in the year made to this sacred place, if it were not for the excessive ignorance and superstition attending them.

"Near to this church are some fine remains of a Roman aqueduct, for conveying water to the city, built at the time of Julius Cæsar. A convent of three hundred nuns has arisen since the peace, in the same place, of the order of St. Michel, where many younger daughters are sent from the best families, to be got out of the way, just the same as under the ancient regime. In saying this, I do not forget that the education in many of the convents is, in some respects, excellent, and that the larger number of young persons are placed there merely for a few years for that purpose. Still the whole system is decidedly bad, and unfriendly to the highest purposes of a generous education."

———

"Upon looking carefully into Milner's Ecclesiastical History, since I came home, I find there were two early persecutions of the

Christians at Vienne and Lyons (neighboring French towns,) one about the year of our Lord 169, under the emperor Marcus Antoninus; the second under Septimus Severus, about the year 202. The first of these is best known, and the accounts in Milner refer to it. The scene of its cruel executions was the Amphitheatre which I visited as I have above mentioned. The second is not so credibly attested, but at the same time may on the whole be believed to have taken place. The church of St. Irenée relates exclusively to it. Pothinus was bishop of Lyons during the first cruelties; he had been a disciple of the blessed Polycarp, the contemporary of the apostle John. He perished about the year 169, being upwards of ninety years of age; he had been sent, in all probability, by Polycarp from Smyrna to found these French churches; for the merchants of Smyrna and Lyons were the chief navigators of the Mediterranean sea. This could not be very long before the persecution burst out. He was accompanied in his apostolical labors by Irenæus, an Asiatic Greek also, who wrote the interesting and authentic account of the first acts of the martyrs, preserved by Eusebius, and given so well by Milner. Irenæus succeeded Pothinus as bishop, and suffered martyrdom in the persecution of 202."

The animus of the writer in all this, the inward posture with which he looks upon the past and its relation to the present, comes out more clearly in the notice he takes of Milan and its distinguished prelates St. Ambrose and St. Charles Borromeo.

"*Sunday morning, Sept.* 14.—This is one of my melancholy Sundays. An immense Catholic town of one hundred and fifty thousand souls—the ecclesiastical apparatus enormous; about two hundred churches, eighty convents, and one hundred religious houses—compare this with the Protestant establishment of Birmingham or Manchester, which fall as far short of what such a crowded population fairly demands, as the Milan establishment exceeds it. We might surely learn something in England of the duty of greater zeal and attention to our pure form of Christianity, from the excessive diligence of the Catholics in their corrupt superstitions.

"I feel a peculiar veneration for Milan on two accounts: St. Ambrose, whom Milner dwells on with such commendations, was the light of this city in the fourth century; Carlo Borromeo, whose benevolence exceeds all description, was archbishop here in the sixteenth. This last I know at present little of; but Ambrose was one of the most humble and spiritual of the fathers of the church, two or three centuries before Popery, properly speaking, began. In this city Ambrose preached: it was here Austin heard him, attracted by the fame of his eloquence. It was here also, that Angilbertus, bishop of Milan in the ninth century, refused to own the supremacy of the Pope; indeed, the church of Milan did not submit to the Roman see till two hundred years afterwards. May God raise up another Ambrose to purify and recall the city and churches, which he instructed thirteen or fourteen centuries ago! Nothing is impossible with God; but Popery seems to infatuate this people. On the church of Milan notices are affixed, that whoever causes a mass to be said there, may deliver any one he chooses from purgatory. In the mean time, this debasing superstition goes hand in hand with secret infidelity and unblushing vice."

"St. Ambrose died in the year 397, in the 57th year of his age, and the 23d of his episcopate. He has been charged with leaning too much towards the incipient superstitions of his day, and thus unconsciously of helping forward the growth of monastic bondage and prelatical pride. Something of this charge may be true; but he lived and died firm and unbending in all the fundamentals of divine truth. He loved the Saviour. He depended on his merits only for justification. He relied on the illumination and grace of the Holy Spirit. He delighted in communion with God. A rich unction of godliness rests on his writings; and he was one of the most fervent, humble, laborious, and charitable of all Christian bishops."

"I have witnessed to-day, with grief and indignation, all the superstitions of Popery in their full triumph. In other towns, the neighborhood of Protestantism has been some check on the display of idolatry; but here in Italy, where a Protesant is scarcely tolerated, except in the chapels of ambassadors, you see what things tend to; Popery has its unimpeded course; every thing follows the guidance and authority of the prevailing taste in religion.

"At half-past ten this morning we went to the cathedral, where seats were obtained for us in the gallery near the altar. We saw the whole of the proceedings at High Mass—priests almost without end—incense—singing—music—processions—perpetual changes of dress—four persons with mitres, whom the people called the little bishops—a crowd of people coming in and going out, and staring around them; but not one prayer, nor one verse of the Holy Scriptures intelligible to the people, not even if they knew Latin; nor one word of a sermon; in short, it was nothing more nor less than a PAGAN SHOW.

"We returned to our inn, and, after our English service, we went to see the catechising. This was founded by Borromeo, in the sixteenth century, and is one of the peculiarities of the diocese of Milan. The children meet in classes of ten or twenty, drawn up between the pillars of the vast cathedral, and separated from each other by curtains; the boys on one side, the girls on the other. In all the churches of the city there are classes also. Many grown people were mingled with the children. A priest, and sometimes a layman, sat in the midst of each class, and seemed to be explaining familiarly the Christian religion. The sight was quite interesting. Tables for learning to write were placed in different recesses. The children were exceedingly attentive. At the door of each school, the words, *pax vobis*, peace be unto you, were inscribed on a board; the names of the scholars were also on boards. Each school had a small pulpit, with a green cloth in front, bearing the Borromean motto, *Humilitas.*

" Now what can, in itself, be more excellent than all this? But mark the corruption of Popery: these poor children are all made members of a fraternity, and purchase indulgences for their sins by coming to school. A brief of the Pope, dated 1609, affords a perpetual indulgence to the children in a sort of running lease of six thousand years, eight thousand years, &c., and these indulgences are applicable to the recovering of souls out of purgatory; the prayers also before school are full of error and idolatry. All this I saw with my own eyes and heard with my own ears; for I was curious to understand the bearings of these celebrated schools. Thus is the infant mind fettered and imprisoned.

" Still I do not doubt that much good may be done on the whole —the Catholic catechisms contain the foundation of the Christian religion, a general view of Scripture history, explanations of the creation and redemption of mankind, some good instructions on the moral law, sound statements on the divinity of Christ, and the Holy Trinity; some acknowledgments of the fall of man, and the necessity of the grace of God's Holy Spirit; with inculcations of repentance, contrition, humility, self-denial, watchfulness, and preparation for death and judgment. These catechisms are not brief summaries, but rather full explanations of religion; making up small volumes of fifty or more pages. In the frontispiece of the catechism for the diocese of Geneva is the following affecting sentence, under the figure of our Lord, " Son amour et mon crime ont mis Jésus à mort"—a sentiment which cannot but produce good. Still all is wofully mixed up with superstition, and error, and human traditions; and the consequence of this mixture is, that vital truths are so associated in the mind, from early youth, with the follies of Popery, that even the most pious men of that communion do not enough distinguish between them. If you deny transubstantiation, they suppose you disbelieve the divinity of Christ; if you avow that you are not a Papist, they suppose that you are a heretic, and have renounced the faith, &c. It was thus that such eminent Christians as Pascal, Nicole, Quesnel, Fénélon, and the great men of the Jansenist school, lived and died in the church of Rome. " A voluntary humility," as well as the " worshipping of angels,"—Coloss. ii. 18—may well be noted by St. Paul as an error, which ought zealously to be excluded from the Christian church."

" I was vexed on returning to England, and consulting my books, that I had been so long ignorant of the history and character of Borromeo. He is considered by the Roman Catholic writers as the model of all virtues, and the great restorer of ecclesiastical discipline in the sixteenth century. I have not been able to satisfy myself in what degree he was a true Christian, in the Scriptural sense of the word. That he was devoted to the superstitions of Popery, and was a firm upholder of the Roman see, cannot be doubted ; but I have no access to his sermons or letters, so as to judge whether any living embers of the faith and love of Christ were smothered at the bottom of these superstitions. His habits of devotion, his self-denial, his zeal, his fortitude, his humility, and especially his unbounded and almost unparalleled benevolence, which are ascribed to him by universal consent, would lead one to hope that, notwithstanding " the wood, and hay, and stubble," accumulated on it, he was building on the true " foundation, Christ Jesus."—1 Cor. iii. 11, 12.

" He was born at Arona in 1538, in a small apartment which I saw behind the church ; and was of one of the noblest and most opulent families of Italy. At the age of eleven he had several livings given him by his uncle the Cardinal de Medicis, who was elected Pope in 1549. In his twenty-third year he was created cardinal by the same pontiff, and managed the proceedings of the council of Trent, as well as the chief temporal affairs of the Pope, for some years. This I consider as by far the most unfavorable part of Borromeo's life, as to the cultivation of personal piety. Such employments at Rome must have initiated him into all the system of that artful and secular court—and he who was intrusted to draw up the Trent catechism, must at that time have had little real Christian knowledge or feeling. However, in 1565 he left Rome, and went to reside at Milan, of which he had been made archbishop.

" Here begins the bright part of Borromeo's history. He had now to preside over the largest diocese of Italy, consisting of not less than eight hundred and fifty parishes, many of them in the wildest regions of the Alps. He began by resigning all his other preferments, by giving up to his family his chief estates, and by dividing the revenues of his archbishopric into three parts—one for the poor—another for the building and reparation of churches —the third for his domestic expenditure as bishop ; all the accounts of which he submitted annually to the examination of his clergy. He next totally renounced the splendor in which he had lived at Rome, reduced the number of his servants, forbade the use of silk garments in his palace, rendered his household a pattern of edification, slept himself on boards, prolonged his watchings and prayers to a late hour of the night, wore an under dress coarse and common, and devoted himself to perpetual fasts and abstinences.

" He then entered on the task of restoring decayed discipline and order throughout his vast diocese. To this end he was indefatigable in visiting himself every parish under his care, held frequent ecclesiastical synods, and established a permanent council, which met monthly to inspect and regulate the conduct of the priests. In this manner his cotemporaries agree in asserting, that he removed various scandals which prevailed amongst all classes of the faithful, abolished many superstitious usages, and checked the ignorance and abuses of the secular and regular clergy.

" His fortitude in carrying through his reforms, notwithstanding the violent opposition which he met with from all quarters, deserves remark. On one occasion an assassin was hired, who shot at him, whilst kneeling in prayer, in the archiepiscopal palace. Borromeo, unmoved, continued his devotions; and, when he rose from his knees, the bullet, which had been aimed at his back, but had been caught in the lawn sleeves of his dress, fell at his feet.

" His charities were unbounded. He built ten colleges, five hospitals, and schools and public fountains without number. Besides this, he bestowed annually the sum of thirty thousand crowns on the poor; and in various cases of public distress in the course of his life, as much as two hundred thousand crowns more.

" In the meantime, his personal virtues, his lowliness, his self-command, his forgiveness of injuries, his temperance, his prudence, his sanctity, the consistency of his whole character, (I speak after his biographers, whose veracity, I believe, is not questioned,) gave him such weight, that he not only rendered his immense diocese a model of good order and discipline, after an anarchy of eighty years, during which its archbishops had not resided, but extended his influence over the neighboring dioceses, and pushed his regulations throughout a great part of France and Germany.

" Perhaps his conduct during a pestilence which raged for six months at Milan is amongst the actions of his life which may lead one the most to hope that this benevolent and tender-hearted prelate was indeed animated with the fear and love of his Saviour. Nothing could restrain him from visiting his sick and dying flock, during the raging of this fatal malady : when his clergy entreated him to consult his own safety, he replied, that nothing more became a bishop than to face danger at the call of his duty. He was continually found in the most infected spots, administering consolation both to the bodies and souls of his perishing people; and he sold all the small remains of his ancient splendor, and even his bed, to give the produce to the distressed.

" The institution, or rather invention of Sunday schools, is again a further evidence of something more than a superstitious state of heart. Nothing could be so novel as such institutions in the sixteenth century, and nothing so beneficial. When we recollect the public admiration which has rested on such schools in our own Protestant and enlightened country, though planned scarcely fifty years back, we may estimate the piety of mind, the vigor and penetration of judgment, which could lead a Catholic archbishop and cardinal to institute them two hundred years ago, and to place them on a footing which has continued to the present day. May I not add, that possibly some of the superstitious usages now attached to these schools may have grown up since the time of Borromeo. Certainly the indulgences which I saw were of the date of 1609, five-and-twenty years after his death ; for the reader must be informed that, in the year 1584, this benevolent bishop fell a victim to fever caught in the mountainous parishes of his diocese, which he was visiting in his usual course.

" As a preacher he was most laborious. Though he had an impediment in his speech, and a difficulty in finding words to express readily his meaning, he overcame these hindrances, and preached most assiduously on Sundays and festivals at Milan. His biographers say, that the higher classes in the city were offended with him, and did not frequent his sermons; but that the common people flocked with eargerness to hear him. Perhaps something of what the Apostle calls "the offence of the cross," may be traced in this. It does not at all lessen my hope of Borromeo's piety, that the rich and great did not follow him.

" Such is a faint sketch of some of the chief events in the life of Charles Borromeo. My materials are scanty, especially as to the spiritual state of his heart and affections. It is for God only to judge on this subject: but charity rejoices to hope all things in such a case. I acknowledge that his simple and sublime motto, HUMILITAS, is very affecting to my mind. I trust it was the expression of his real character ; and that his submission to the usurpations of the Romish church may have arisen from that faulty prostration of the understanding to human authority, which is so apt to engraft itself, under circumstances like those of Borromeo, on scriptural lowliness of spirit. Oh, if he had more fully studied and obeyed his Bible, and had read with honest candor the treatises of his great contempararies, the reformers of Germany and Switzerland, he might, perhaps, have become the LUTHER or ZUINGLE, instead of, what ho actually was, only the FENELON of Italy."

The reference made in the foregoing extract to *indulgences* shows the writer, with all his education, to be one of those who stick in the vulgar notion still of this doctrine, and in spite of all evidence to the contrary insist on forcing upon the Roman church an abomination here which she continually disowns.

The idea of an indulgence to commit sin, a license in form to do wrong, is a pure fiction got up by the seething brain of fanaticism to make Popery odious; and is just as little entitled to regard at best, as the charge brought against Presbyterians for instance of holding and teaching, that there are infants in hell not a span long. An indulgence has not even the force of a pardon for past sin, however repented of truly by the sinner. It is a wholly different conception, which we have no right to drag hither and thither to suit our own prejudice, but are bound in common honesty, if we must oppose it, to understand and handle at all events in the sense of its own system, and not in another sense.

One can hardly help feeling somewhat amused with the evident embarrassment, in which the good vicar of Islington finds himself with his facts. He has in his mind a certain scheme of religion, what he conceives to be the clear sense of the Gospel in regard to this great interest, which is at war with the whole idea he has formed of Romanism; to such an extent, that he feels bound to think of this last only as a system of unmitigated abominations, a wholesale apostacy from the truth, and such a tissue of foolery and impiety in the name of religion as can scarcely be reconciled with the opinion, that there are any pious persons at all within its communion. He finds it a great deal easier to admit the true godliness of ten "witnesses" opposing the church in the middle ages, even though it should be among such a sect as the Albigenses, than to be entirely satisfied with that of one only, quietly submitting to the authority of this church, believing in transubstantiation, and praying to saints and images, in its bosom. And still he is a good man, anxious to find his own ideal of evangelical piety as broadly as possible diffused in the history of the world, and cordially disposed to acknowledge and honor it wherever it comes in his way. With the instance of Ambrose, in the case before us, he can get along without any *very* serious difficulty, taking Milner's Church History for his guide, and holding fast always to the common Anglican theory of a marked distinction, between the Christianity of the first four or five centuries and that of the thousand years following. There are things hard to understand in the piety of Ambrose and Augustine, even as we have it portrayed to us in Milner; for which however an apology is found in the supposition, that standing as they did on the borders of the great apostacy which was to follow, they came accidentally here and there within the folds of its impending shadow, without still belonging to it properly in the substance of their faith. But the idea

of any similar exhibition of apostolical religion from the same
see of Milan, under the full-blown Papacy and in open communion with its corruptions—and all this too in the middle of
the sixteenth century, and in the person of one who had been
employed to draw up the Roman Catechism for the Council of
Trent—was altogether another matter, and something not provided for plainly in any way by our tourist's previous theory.
The good account he hears of St. Borromeo perplexes him.
He finds it impossible to unite in his mind the image of a truly
holy archbishop, such as he is described to have been, with the
mummery and superstition of the modern Milan, (a city wholly
given to idolatry,) which yet hardly could have been much better in the age of the Reformation, when presided over by this
canonized man.   Did he not hear the trumpet of the Reformation, giving no uncertain sound just over the Alps?   And how
then could he refuse to make common cause with it against
Rome and the Pope?   The bishop that was to be of Calcutta
cannot understand it ; but being, as we have said a good man,
he makes it a point on his return home to look into the character of this same Borromeo, with such literary helps as he can
find for this purpose ; when, lo, to his own great surprise, not to
say amiable confusion, it appears that there is no reason whatever to question the extraordinary sanctity of the man, so far as
least as the outward show of consecration to works of piety is
concerned.   So the Rev. Daniel Wilson, in the exercise of that
charity which hopeth all things and believeth all things, feels
himself constrained to bear open testimony to its reality ; the
only question being still, whether the seeming sanctity after all
had any proper root in the doctrine of justification by faith, the
one great principle of religion in its true Protestant form.   On
this point a lingering doubt remains, which could be properly
dissipated only by studying the character in question in the mirror of his own written thoughts ; a privilege, which our author
had not still enjoyed, when he first published his travels.   Subsequently however it came in his way to look into the soul of
the Catholic saint in this way ; and now every doubt as to the
genuineness of his piety was forced to retire ; so that in the second edition of the same book, we have finally a free, full and
altogether joyful acknowledgment of the fact, that in the person
of Borromeo the Roman communion actually produced, so late
as the 16th century. out of its own bosom and as it were in the
very face of the Reformation itself, a veritable saint of like station and piety with the great St. Ambrose of the fourth century, and worthy even to be set in some sort of comparison with

the Protestant saints, Zuingli, Luther, and Calvin. Under huge incrustations of Popish superstition, may be clearly traced still, in this extraordinary case, the lineaments of a truly evangelical faith, an actual diamond of grace, formed no one can tell how in the very heart of what might seem to be most fully at war with its whole nature. The case is set down accordingly as a sort of grand exception to common history, the next thing to a *lusus naturæ* in the world of grace. Anselm, Bernard, Thomas a Kempis, Fenelon, and a few other like celebrities perhaps, names " rari nantes in gurgite vasto," are referred habitually to the same convenient category or rubric. They are spiritual curiosities, which no one should be expected fully to understand or explain.

In all this, however, we have two utterly false conceptions at work in the mind of the vicar of Islington himself. In the first place, his estimate of the extent to which real piety has existed in the Catholic church, both before the Reformation and since, is in no sort of agreement with the truth. In the second place, his imagination that this piety is in no sense the proper product of the Catholic religion as such, but something violently exceptional rather to its natural course, is not a whit less visionary and unsound.

Both these notions, we know, enter largely into our common Protestant thinking. But this does not make them right. They form in conjunction a mere blind prejudice, which like every other prejudice of this sort is sure to prove hurtful, in the end, to the cause it seems to favor and serve. Of all styles of upholding Protestantism, we may say, that is absolutely the worst, which can see no sense or truth whatever in Catholicism, but holds itself bound to make it at every point as bad as possible, and to fight off with tooth and nail every word that may be spoken in its praise. Such wholesale and extreme pugnacity, may be very convenient; as it calls for no discrimination, it requires of course neither learning nor thought, but can be played off under all circumstances, by almost any polemic, with about the same good effect. Its strength consists mainly in calling nick-names, in repeating outrageous charges without regard to any contradiction from the other side, in thrumming over threadbare common-places received by tradition from the easy credulity of times past, in huge exaggerations, and vast distortions, and bold insulting insinuations thrown out at random in any and every direction.[1] But however convenient all this may be, re-

---

[1] As a single exemplification, take the *Ladies'* petition got up a few months

quiring little reading, and less thought, and no politeness nor
charity whatever, it is high time to see that it is a system of tac-
tics, which needs in truth only a slight change of circumstances
at any time to work just the opposite way from that in which it
is meant to work. The vanity and impotency of it must become apparent, in proportion precisely as men are brought to
look at things with their own eyes; and then the result is, that
sensible and well-bred people, not those who go by the text book
of a sect, but such as move in a wider range of thought and
have some better knowledge of the world, political and literary
men, seeing how they have been imposed upon by the current
slang, are very apt to be taken with a sort of quiet disgust towards the whole interest which they find to be thus badly defend-

---

since for the Legislature of Pennsylvania, in the city of Philadelphia, under the auspices of the notorious Giustiniani, calling for the suppression of
nunneries, under the gross insinuation of their being only seats of licen-
tiousness and sin. Strange "ladies" they must have been, that could lend
their names to such an infamous libel on the purity of their own sex. The
like insult directed towards the Episcopalians, Methodists or Presbyterians,
would have at once drawn upon itself the angry frown of society, as a
breach of all decency as well as charity. But as directed against the *Catholics* only, the blackguardism of the thing was generally not felt. Certain
evangelical papers caught up even with great gusto, as a capital hit, the
flying report that the Legislature had referred the petition to the Committee
on Vice and Immorality. Now if *any* ground had ever been given for
scandal in the history of American nunneries, one might have some patience with such ribald ruffianism, hiding its malignity under the cloak of
religion. But what well informed person needs to be told, that every apology of this sort is wanting? All attempts yet made to blast the good name
of these institutions among us, have recoiled with signal discomfiture on
the heads of those who have acted as leaders in the vile crusade. It is
enough to refer to Charlestown, Pittsburg, and Montreal—to the *memory* of
Miss Reed, Dr. Brownlee and Maria Monk. On the other hand, the good
works of these religious houses have been too manifold and plain in every
direction, to be at all rationally called in question. Now in all seriousness
we ask, what right in these circumstances have people pretending to be
themselves respectable and pious, to vilify and calumniate the inmates of
such institutions in the way of which we now speak, as though they had
forfeited all claim to the most ordinary courtesies of well bred life? Just
as little right, we say confidently, as any gentleman has to outrage in the
same way any Ladies' Seminary whatever that is to be found in the land.—
This same Giustiniani is the apostle of German Catholicism, as it has been
called, or Rongianism, in this country; whose *wonderful* success in found-
ing churches in New York, Rochester, Buffalo and Philadelphia, has been
duly trumpeted and glorified in times past by a part of our religious press;
though the same papers have never considered it necessary to let us know,
how completely the infidel sham has in each case run out since into clear
smoke. He has now gone to Italy, we are told, to help set things right in
that unfortunate part of the world.

ed, and so to look favorably in the same measure on the other side, as being at so many points plainly an injured and persecuted cause. To make our opposition to Romanism of any weight, the first condition would seem to be clearly that we should have made ourselves acquainted with it on its own ground, that we should have taken some pains to learn from the system itself what it means and wills. But of all that army of zealots, who hold themselves perfectly prepared to demolish it at a blow through the stage or press, how few are there probably who have ever felt it necessary to get their facts from other than the most common Protestant sources? Take indeed our ministers generally. Has one in fifty of them ever examined seriously a Catholic work of divinity, whether didactic, practical or historical? An ordinary anti-popery assault implies no preparation of this sort whatever; but rather a dogged purpose only, not to hear or believe a single word the Catholics say for themselves, while everything contrary to this is forced upon them from other quarters, as the voice and sense of their system. The sooner all such fanatical indecencies can be brought to an end, the better. They help not Protestantism, but serve only to involve it in reproach.

To return to the two imaginations already named. It is a sheer prejudice to suppose, in the first place, that cases of sanctity and true godliness have been, or are now, of only rare and extraordinary occurrence in the Roman communion. Any one who is willing at all to look into the actual history of the church, to listen to its own voice, to study its institutions, to make himself acquainted with its works, will soon find reason enough to rejoice in a widely different and far more favorable view. The single institution of the " Sisters of Charity," with its manifold services of mercy and love, is of itself fact enough to upset, for any thoughtful mind, the vulgar idea that Romanism is without religion, and a source of evil only without any good. This is however but one among many illustrations looking the same way, which the charity, "that rejoiceth not in iniquity but in the truth," need never be at a loss to find in the same church. That must be a stout bigotry indeed, which is able to turn aside the force of all such examples, by resolving them into self-righteousness or mercenary motives of any still lower kind. It has its fit parallel only in the calumnies, that were used in the first ages to blacken the virtues of Christianity into crimes among the heathen.

But in the second place it is just as blind a prejudice again, to suppose that the piety of the Roman church, such as it is, springs not from the proper life of the system itsely, but is there rather by accident, and as something out of place, and so to speak in spite of the unfriendly connections with which it is surrounded; so that if it could only be torn up from the soil in which it thus happens to stand, and transplanted into a truly evangelical liberty, it might be expected to thrive and flourish at a much better rate. The native and as it were normal tendency of Catholicism, in the view of this prejudice, is not to piety at all, but only to superstition and sin; for it is taken to be a systematic conspiracy against the doctrines of grace from the beginning; and hence when we meet with the phenomenon of a truly evangelical spirit here and there in its communion, as in the case of Pascal or Fenelon, we are bound to see in it a wonderful exception to established law, and to admire so much the more the power of the evangelical principle, which is sufficient even in such untoward circumstances to bring to pass so great a miracle. No one however can study the subject to any extent for himself, without being led to see that the very reverse of all this is the truth. Catholicism is inwardly fitted for the production of its own forms of piety, and owes them to no foreign source or influence whatever. Its saints are not exotics, that pine after other climes and skies, but products of home growth, answerable in all respects to the conditions that surround them. To place them in other relations would be, not to advance, but to cripple their life. Borromeo was constitutionally a Catholic in his piety, and not a Protestant. The same may be said of Fenelon, of Philip de Neri, of Anselm and Bernard, of Ambrose, and of the old church fathers generally. The piety of all of them has a complexion, which is materially different from any that we meet with in the modern Protestant world. We mean not by this to call in question the reality of this last, or its high worth; all we wish to say is, that it is of another character and order, and that what we find of saintliness in the Roman church is strictly and legitimately from itself and not from abroad. To Protestantize it even in imagination, is to turn it into caricature and to eviscerate it at last of its very life. What could the early fathers do with themselves in New England? Such an institution as that of the Sisters of Charity can never be transferred to purely Protestant ground; as no such ground either could ever have given it birth. Attempts are made in our own time to furnish a Protestant version of the same idea, under what claims to be a higher and more evangelical form; for the purpose of supplying an evident want. But nothing of this sort will ever equal the original design, or be more indeed than a

weak and stunted copy of this on the most narrow and ephe-
meral scale. It is only in the bosom of ideas, principles and
associations, which are Catholic distinctively and *not* Protestant,
that charity of this sort finds itself perfectly at home. And
just so it is with the piety of this church in general. It is fairly
and truly native to the soil from which it springs. That church,
with all its supposed errors and sins, has ever had power in its
own way to produce a large amount of very lovely religion.
If it has been the mother of abominations, it has been unquestionably the mother also of martyrs and saints. It is a sorry
business to pretend to deny this, or to try to falsify the fact into
the smallest possible dimensions, for the sake of some miserable
pre-conception with which it will not agree. We do but belittle
ourselves, when we resort to strategy so poor as that. To deal
with Romanism to any purpose, we must get rid of the notion
that it carries in it no truth, no grace, no principle of religious
activity and life ; that it is as bad as infidelity, if not a good
deal worse ;[1] that it lacks all the attributes of a church, and is

---

[1] We clip the following from an editorial of the *New York Observer*, called
forth not long ago by a sermon which Archbishop Hughes preached on his
return from Europe, as the paper sneeringly adds, " without the Cardinal's
hat " It is curiously characteristic.
" The Tribune finds fault with Bishop Hughes, for resisting the progress
of Socialism in Europe. Between Romanism and Socialism there is little
to choose, so far as the moral improvement of the people is concerned.
They are essentially Anti-Christian, and many wise and good men regard
infidelity as the least evil of the two, when the choice must be between it
and Popery. We have therefore regarded it as one of the phenomena of
the times, worth observing and recording, that the leaders of the Romanizing and the Fourierite parties in this country, are now discussing the comparative worth of their two schemes, for the improvement of mankind.
We regard them both with equal detestation, and in the controversy now in
progress, are quite indifferent as to the issue."
The same editorial reproaches the sermon, in the beginning, with betraying a want of sympathy with the liberty spirit that is now at work in Europe. So in general our American anti-popery is ever ready to fall in with
the revolutionary tendency abroad, as though it must necessarily be both
patriotic and pious—needing only plenty of *Bibles* to tame the whirlwind
and keep it right. And yet notoriously this movement is prevailingly irreligious, radical, socialistic and infidel, threatening the foundations of all
government and society. So it is regarded by the Catholic church ; which
is powerfully resisting it, and forms at this time, we verily believe, a most
necessary bulwark in the old world against its terrible progress But this
the N. Y. Observer denounces, as hostility to the cause of liberty and the
rights of man ; while it goes on the next moment to make Catholicism just
as bad as Socialism itself. We have heard before of the same sentiment
being uttered in high places. But it is for all this none the less a truly
abominable sentiment, that must sooner or later quail before the frown of

purely a synagogue of Satan or a mere human confederacy, for worldly and unhallowed ends. One wing of the Presbyterian church has it is true openly committed itself to this bold position, in pronouncing what they stigmatize as *Romish* baptism to be without force—unchurching virtually thus the whole church as it stood at the birth of the Reformation and for at least twelve hundred years before, and making such men as Augustine and Chrysostom, as well as Luther and Calvin of a later day, to be no better than unbaptized heathens, so far as any idea of covenant or sacramental grace is concerned; for it is notorious, that the baptism in question goes back, with all its objectionable features, not only to the fourth century, but beyond that to the days of Cyprian even and Tertullian. But no such *brutum fulmen* as this can stand. All history laughs it to scorn. The vitality of Romanism at this very time, and the evidently growing confusion of Protestantism, all the world over, show it to be idle as the passing wind. It is no time, in the crisis to which things are now coming, to think of settling the question between Protestantism and Rome, in this extravagant and fanatical way. There must be honesty enough to see and own good on the side of this *hated* church, as well as a keen scent for its sores. Take it simply as it appears in our own country, struggling finally into full organization, after years of crushing difficulty and persecution; and need we say, that it has merit and respectability enough in a religious view to give it some right to the same sort of genteel respect at least, that is felt to be proper towards almost every sect besides? Is its hierarchy at this time

intelligent and good men. A few years since Dr. Hengstenberg of Berlin, whose zeal for Protestantism none can question who have any knowledge of the man, was heavily pressed on this very point by a party which made a merit of treating Romanism in the same way—Protestants of the rationalistic no-religion school, who were disposed to place religion in mere opposition and contradiction to the Catholic church. But he had courage to say to such spirit, " Get thee behind me, Satan;" and to proclaim to the world that there is no comparison to be thought of between Infidelity and Catholicism, and that when it comes to a war with the first, all our affections and sympathies are bound to go joyfully with the last, as one grand division simply of the great army of faith to which all true Protestants as well as all true Catholics belong. The heartless fanaticism of the N. Y. Observer not only *infidelizes* such men as Bishops Chevereux, England, Eccleston, Hughes, Kenrick, &c., (any of them good enough to compare with the Rev. Sydney E. Morse & Co., any day,) and Sisters of Mercy, Sisters of Charity, &c., in large number, in our own time; but goes away back to other times also, and swamps all the fathers and martyrs, after the first two centuries at least, in the same Acherontian lake.

a whit behind that of the Episcopal church, in point of learning, piety, or official diligence and zeal? Has any church
among us produced better specimens of apostolical sanctity, than
the first bishop of Boston for instance or the first bishop of
Charleston, and others also that might easily be named ; men,
whose virtues adorn the history of the country, and whose par-
allels are not so readily offered in other communions, that we
can afford for this reason to pass their memory into ungrateful
oblivion. It is not easy to read the writings of Bishop England,
glowing with the eloquence of noble gentlemanly feeling as they
do on almost every page, and not be filled with indignation, as
well as moved even to tears at times, with the gross and cruel
wrong which has been heaped upon the Catholics among us
from the beginning, in the holy name of religion. What *right*,
we ask again, have the zealots of other churches to lay aside
here the laws of common courtesy, and to be just as rude and
scurrilous as they please? What right have rabid pens, or still
more rabid tongues, to make religion in this form the synonyme
of impiety and unbelief, and when confronted with clear proofs
and living examples of the contrary, to resolve all into hypocrisy, or happy inconsistency, as though it were not possible for
piety to grow forth in any way from such a system? Some go
so far as to tell us even, that no intelligent priest or layman in
the Catholic church can seriously believe what he professes to
believe. This however is such unmannerly rudeness as deserves
no answer, come from what quarter it may.

But what we have in view now more particularly, is to expose
the fallacy that lies in the extracts we have given from Dr. Bacon and Bishop Wilson, with regard to the nature of early
Christianity, as compared with that particular modern scheme
of religion, which they dignify with the title Evangelical, and
which is for each of them the only true and perfect sense of
the Gospel. Both writers assume, that there existed in the beginning, back of the corruptions and abuses of Romanism, and
subsequently to the time of the Apostles, a certain golden age,
longer or shorter, of comparatively pure religious faith, which
truly represented still the simplicity and spirituality of the proper divine model of the church, as we have it plainly exhibited
to us in the New Testament ; and that this was in all material
respects of one character precisely with what they now approve
as the best style of Protestantism. But never was there a more
perfect mistake.

It may be easy enough to show, that there are many points of
difference between early Christianity and Romanism, as we find

this established in later times. But this fact is by no means sufficient to show, that the first was to the same extent in agreement with modern Protestantism, whether in the Episcopalian
or in the Congregational form. It is clear on the contrary, that
no such agreement has ever had place, but that modern Protestantism is still farther away from this older faith than the system by which it is supposed to have been supplanted in the
middle ages. No defence of Protestantism can well be more
insufficient and unsound, than that by which it is set forth as a
pure *repristination* simply of what Christianity was at the beginning, either in the fourth century, or the third, or the second.
It will always be found on examination to have no such character in fact; and every attempt to force upon the world any imagination of the sort, in favor of either Episcopacy, or Presbyterianism, or Independency, in favor of all or of any one of the
three score and ten sects which at this time follow the Bible as
their sole rule of faith, must only serve in the end by its palpable falsehood to bring suspicion and doubt on the whole cause
which is thus badly upheld. Whatever differences there may
be between the first ages and those that followed, it is still plain
enough that the course of things was from the very start *towards*
that order at least, which afterwards prevailed; that this later
order therefore stands bound by true historical connection with
what went before; and that Protestantism accordingly, as a still
more advanced period in the general movement of history, holds
a living relation to the first period only through the medium of
the second, and is just as little a copy of the one in form as it is
of the other. This we sincerely believe is the only ground, on
which may be set up any rational defence of the great revolution of the 16th century, (unsupported as it stands by miracles
or inspiration,) in conjunction with a true faith in the Divine
character of the church. It is the theory of historical development, which assumes the possibility and necessity of a transition
on the part of the church through various stages of form, (as in
all growth,) for the very purpose of bringing out more and more
fully always the true inward sense of its life, which has been
one and the same from the beginning. When Romanists refuse
every such view, and insist that their whole system has been
handed down from the time of the Apostles, it *seems* not easy
certainly to admit the pretence. But when Protestants also refuse the view, and pretend to give us things, in their several by
no means harmonious systems, just as they were in the first
ages of the church, the pretension is still more glaringly rash
and false. However it may be with Romanism, it is certain that

Protestantism can never make good its claims on any such ground. And yet it will not do, to give up all historical connection with the church as it first started, and as it stood afterwards for fifteen hundred years—at least not without an overwhelming *Thus saith the Lord* in the form of miracles. The only escape then is in the formula of the same and yet not the same, legitimate growth, historical development. If this cannot stand, if it be found at war with the true idea of a Divine revelation, we for our part must give up all faith in Protestantism, and bow as we best can to the authority of the Roman church ; for an interest which resolves itself virtually into infidelity, as Protestantism under every other view in which it can be put seems to us to do clearly, has no right, as in the end also it can have no power, to stand

It needs but little knowledge of history certainly, to see that Christianity as it stood in the fourth century, and in the first part of the fifth, in the time of Jerome and Ambrose and Augustine, in the time of Chrysostom and Basil and the Gregories, was something very different from modern Protestantism, and that it bore in truth a very near resemblance in all material points to the later religion of the Roman church. This is most clear of course as regards full Puritanism, in the form it carries in New England ; but it is equally true in fact of the Anglican system also, and this whether we take it in the low church or high church view. Episcopalians are indeed fond of making a great distinction, between the first four or five centuries and the ages that follow ; telling us with much self-complacency, that the early church thus far was comparatively pure, that the Roman apostacy came in afterwards marring and blotting the fair face which things had before, and that the English church distinguished itself at the Reformation by its moderation and sound critical judgment, in discriminating here properly between the purity of the primitive faith and its subsequent adulterations. According to the most churchly view, the Reformation was for Anglicanism no revolution properly speaking at all, but the simple clearing away of some previous abuses, and a self-righting of the English church as a whole once more into its old habit and course. But this is altogether a most lame and desperate hypothesis. All history gives it the lie. The boasted discrimination of the English Protestantism vanishes into thin air, the moment we come to inquire into its actual origin and rise. Never was there a great movement, in which accident, caprice, and mere human passion, more clearly prevailed as factors, over the forces of calm judgment and sound reason. If under the political auspices that ruled it, the system was indeed so fortunate as to hit the true mean in the way pretended, while all the Protestant world besides missed it, the advantage must be ascribed to its good luck far more than to its good judgment. The case however becomes still worse, when we look into the real nature of the advantage which is to be referred to this good luck. The main feature of it is episcopacy, with a king at the head of it instead of a pope. In virtue of this constitution, and some few peculiarities besides, Anglicanism piques itself on being a *jure divino* succession of the old English branch of the Church Catholic, while for want of such accidents other Protestant bodies, it is held, have no right to put in any similar claim. The charm lies in the notion of the episcopate, handed down by outward succession, as a sort of primary Divinely appointed mark and seal of the true church.

But what would such men as Cyprian, Ambrose, or Augustine, have thought of the glorification of the episcopate, with all that may go along with it in the English system besides, in any such outward style as this? They did indeed put a high value on episcopacy and some other things that Anglicanism contends for; but only as these interests were themselves comprehended in what they held to be a still wider and deeper system of truth. Episcopacy torn from the idea of that glorious unity, with which alone was felt to go the actual presence of Divine powers in the church, would have been for either of these fathers as perfectly powerless an institution for church ends, as any other scheme of government whatever. The plea then of falling back here to the ground of the first four or five centuries, is for the vindication even of this *accident* itself a false plea; for the episcopacy of that time, and its other points of agreement with modern Anglicanism, were mere circumstances in a wider scheme of thought, which this same Anglicanism disowns now as antichristian and false. If it had a right to reform thus far, and might do so without losing its identity as a part of the church, no good reason can be shown why it had not as much right, if it saw proper, to reform still farther. The rupture with Catholicism is the grand point; over against which, the accident of retaining episcopacy, and some other fragments of the old system, dwindles into insignificance.

For in truth there is no return here to anything more than fragments of the early system, even in the dead view now mentioned. It is as pure a fiction as ever entered a good man's head, to dream as Bishop Wilson does that his favorite scheme of evangelical Episcopalianism prevailed in the fourth century;

and the case is not materially improved, by simply changing the dream into an Oxford or Tractarian shape. The whole idea of a marked chasm anywhere about the fifth century, dividing an older purer style of Christianity from the system that meets us in the middle ages, much as English episcopacy stands related to the papacy, is no better than a chimera ; history is all against it ; we might just as rationally pretend to fix any such dividing line in the eighth century or in the tenth.

According to Bishop Wilson, Ambrose was somewhat infected with the *incipient* superstitions of his day ; but still " lived and died firm and unbending in all the fundamentals of divine truth;" by which is meant, that he looked to the merits of Christ for salvation, and built his religion on the doctrine of justification by faith, taking the Bible for his text book and guide, after the most approved evangelical fashion of the present time. " Ambrose was one of the most humble and spiritual of the fathers of the church," we are told, " two or three centuries before Popery properly speaking began." Even as late as the ninth century, the church of Milan is represented as still holding out against the claims of the Papacy ; and not till two hundred years after that indeed, does the writer allow it to have submitted to the Roman see, and in this way to have been drawn fully and finally into the vortex of its corruptions. But if anything in the world can be said to be historically clear, it is the fact that with the close of the fourth century and the coming in of the fifth, the Primacy of the Roman See was admitted and acknowledged in all parts of the Christian world. This is granted by Barrow himself, in his great work on the Supremacy ; though he tries to set aside the force of the fact, by resolving it into motives and reasons to suit his own cause. The promise of our Saviour to Peter, is always taken by the fathers in the sense that he was to be the centre of unity for the church, and in the language of Chrysostom to have the presidency of it throughout the whole earth. Ambrose and Augustine both recognise this distinction of Peter, over and over again, in the clearest and strongest terms. To be joined in communion with the see of Rome was in the view of this period to be in the bosom of the true church ; to be out of that communion was to be in schism. It was not enough to be in union with any other bishop or body of bishops ; the sacrament of unity was held to be of force only, as having regard to the church in its universal character ; and this involved necessarily the idea of one universal centre, which by general consent was to be found in Rome only, and no where else.[1]

_____

[1] St. Ambrose relates in praise to his brother Satirus, that on reaching

Examples of the actual exercise of supreme power on the part
of the Popes, in the fourth and fifth centuries, are so frequent
and numerous, that nothing short of the most wilful obstinacy
can pretend to treat them as of no account. In every great
question of the time, whether rising in the East or in the West,
all eyes show themselves every ready to turn towards the *cathe-
dra Petri*, as the last resort for counsel and adjudication; all
controversies, either in the way of appeal or complaint, or for
the ratification of decisions given in other quarters, are made to
come directly or indirectly in the end before this tribunal, and
reach their final and conclusive settlement only through its intervention. The Popes, in these cases, take it for granted themselves, that the power which they exercise belongs to them of
right, in virtue of the prerogative of their see; there is no appearance whatever of effort or of usurpation, in the part they
allow themselves to act; it seems to fall to them as naturally, as
the functions of a magistrate or judge in any case are felt to go
along with the office to which they belong. And the whole
world apparently regards the primacy, in the same way, as a
thing of course, a matter fully settled and established in the constitution of the Christian church. We hear of no objection to
it, no protest against it, as a new and daring presumption, or as
a departure from the earlier order of Christianity.[1] The whole

----

shore after shipwreck, he was careful to inquire, whether the bishop of the
place "agreed in faith with the Catholic bishops, that is with the Roman
Church"—assuming communion with Rome thus to be a test of orthodoxy
and catholicity.

[1] It is common to refer to the strong terms, in which St. Gregory the Great
opposed the use of the title, "Universal Bishop," on the part of John the
Faster, Bishop of Constantinople, as a proof that no similar character was
then thought of in favor of the Roman see. But this is altogether too late,
to be of the least historical force in any such view. The evidences of the
acknowledgment of the primacy of Rome long before this on all sides, are
too overwhelming a great deal to be for a moment disturbed, by the mere
sound of what is here paraded as a contrary testimony. Gregory disliked
the pretension of the title; it had for him a haughty sound, which fell not
in with his sense of the respect that was due to other bishops. Even Peter, "the first member of the holy universal church, to whom the care of
the whole church was committed," was to be regarded still as one among
his brethren, and not as a single and exclusive head. In rejecting this title,
Gregory certainly did not disclaim any superior authority in himself, as
successor of Peter; for he himself affirmed the contrary in the most positive terms, and exercised in the most marked manner the powers of an actual ruler of the whole church. "Assuredly," says Mr. Allies in his attempt to uphold the Church of England, "if there was any Pontiff who,
like St. Leo, held the most strong and deeply rooted convictions as to the

nature of the case implies, as strongly as any historical conditions and relations well could, that this precisely and no other order had been handed down from a time, beyond which no memory of man to the contrary then reached. So perfectly idle is the dream, that Popery, taken in the sense of an acknowledgment of the primacy of the Roman see, and of its right to be regarded as the centre of church unity, came in only some two or three centuries after the age of Ambrose, and was not fully admitted into Milan even before the eleventh century.

The idea of the primacy itself however, in the view now presented, was from the first but one necessary part of that general doctrine of the church, which the modern evangelical school is ever ready to denounce, as the introduction of Romanism and a complete falling away from the primitive scheme of faith. It implies of course episcopacy; but it implies also a great deal more. At the ground of it lies the conception of a truly Divine character belonging to the Church as a whole, and not to be separated from the attributes of unity and universality; the idea of the church thus as one, holy, and catholic; the idea of an actual continuation of Christ's presence and power in the church, according to the terms of the original apostolic commission; the idea of sacramental grace, the power of absolution, the working of miracles to the end of time, and a real communion of saints extending to the departed dead as well as to those still living on the earth. It is perfectly certain accordingly, that in the fourth and fifth centuries, all these and other naturally related conceptions, running very directly into the Roman corruptions as they are called of a later period, were in full operation and force; and this in no sporadic exceptional or accidental way merely, but with universal authority and as belonging to the inmost life and substance of the great mystery of Christianity. The fathers of this glorious period did indeed hold " all the fundamentals of divine truth," as Bishop Wilson is charitable enough to suppose; but they held them in no such order and view, as they are made to carry in the theory which Bishop Wilson would fain make to be the reigning sense of their faith, in spite of the " incipient superstitions" with which it was outwardly disfigured. We owe it to ourselves here to see and own the full truth. The

---

prerogatives of the Roman see, it was St. Gregory." His letters abound with admonitions, injunctions, threats, and decrees, directed to bishops in every part of the church, all of whom he treated as brethren whilst they were blameless; if they erred, admonishing them as a father; and punishing them as a judge when they proved delinquent.

religion of these fathers was not of the shape and type now usually known as evangelical, and paraded commonly as the best style of Protestantism. They knew nothing of the view which makes the Bible and Private Judgment the principle of Christianity or the only rule of faith. They took Christianity to be a supernatural system, propounded by the Saviour to his Apostles, and handed down from them as a living tradition (including the Bible) by the Church. The order of doctrine for them was the Apostles' Creed. They looked upon the sacraments as mysteries; taking baptism to be for the remission of sins, and seeing in the " tremendous sacrament of the altar" the real presence of the Redeemer's glorified body, and a new exhibition continually of the one sacrifice that takes away sin. All was reality, not merely shadow and type. They acknowledged the divine character of the Christian priesthood, the necessity of confession, the grace of ministerial absolution. They believed in purgatory, and considered it "a holy and wholesome thought to pray for the dead that they may be loosed from their sins." They held that the intercession of saints is salutary for the living in the other world, as well as in the present; and they made it a part of their piety accordingly to seek the aid of departed saints, as well as of angels, by addressing to them direct invocations for this purpose. They counted it a part of their religion also to venerate and cherish the monuments and relics of departed saints and martyrs, and were firmly persuaded that miracles were often performed through the instrumentality of such relics, as well as on fit occasions also in other ways; for of the continuance of miracles in the church, they never dreamed of making any question. They set a high value on the merit of celibacy and voluntary poverty, chosen in the service of the kingdom of God; and both by doctrine and example did what they could to recommend the monastic life, as at once honorable to religion and eminently suited to promote the spiritual welfare of men. All these things too went together, in their view, as so many parts and constituents of a single religious system; and the only voices that ventured here and there to make them the subject of doubt or contradiction, as in the case of Aerius, Jovinian and Vigilantius, were quickly cried down from every side as absolutely heretical and profane.

In the bosom of this system stood, not outwardly and by accident only, but as true representatives of its very soul and life, such men as Athanasius, Chrysostom, Basil the Great, Cyril of Jerusalem, Gregory of Nazianzen and Gregory of Nyssa, Ephraim the Syrian, Hilary of Poictiers, Jerome, Ambrose, and

Augustine. They held the fundamentals certainly of the Gospel ; but they held them in connexion with a vast deal that modern evangelical Protestantism is in the habit of denouncing as the worst Roman corruption, and what is most stumbling of all they made it a fundamental point to hold the supposed better parts of their faith just in this bad connection and no other. The piety even of Ambrose and Augustine is steeped in what this modern school sets down as rank heathenish superstition. The slightest inspection of historical documents is sufficient to convince any unprejudiced mind of this fact. No one can read attentively even the Confessions of Augustine, the work in which Milner and others affect to find a full parallel to the *experience* of true religion in the modern unchurchly style, without being made to feel that there is no room in truth for any such imagination. The two orders of thought are materially different. The very *crisis* of conversion in the case of the African father, turns on the principle of absolute and unconditional submission to the supernatural authority of the *Church*, in a form that would be considered anything but evangelical with the Pietistic or Methodistic tendency of the present time.

The ground taken here then by Bishop Wilson, and by the whole low church or no church so called evangelical interest, still bent on claiming some sort of genealogical affinity with the orthodoxy and piety of the fourth and fifth centuries, is clearly and palpably false. But how is it with Puseyism or Anglicanism in the high view, pretending to find in this early period its own pattern of Episcopacy, as distinguished from what it conceives to be those later innovations of the Papacy which it pompously condemns and rejects? Alas, the whole theory is brittle as glass, and falls to pieces with the first tap of the critic's hammer. Nothing can well be more arbitrary, than the way in which this system proceeds with church antiquity, choosing this feature and refusing that, just as it may happen to square or not square with the previously settled accident of its own constitution. It is stiff for the episcopate, without being able to see that the idea of its divine right rests from the start in a view of the church, which involves with equal force and often asserts the same necessity for the primacy. It builds a doctrine here and a practice there on the universal tradition of this classic time, this golden era of sound church feeling and faith ; but without any reason, other than its own pleasure and whim, thrusts out of the way other doctrines and practices embraced in the same universal tradition with even greater clearness and force. The whole hypothesis is untrue. There is no such chasm between this classic period

and the time following as it pretends, and least of all in the form
of any such discrimination of doctrines and practices as it needs
to prop up its own cause. The fathers of the fourth and fifth
centuries were not Protestants of either the Anglican or the
Puritan school. They would have felt themselves lost, and
away from home altogether, in the arms of English Episcopalianism, as well as in the more bony and stern embrace of Scotch
Presbyterianism.[1]

New England Puritanism of course, as represented by Dr.
Bacon, is quite willing to admit the general truth of what has
now been said in relation to the age of Ambrose and Augustine;
though at times ready enough still to talk of these fathers and
their fellows, as though it took them to be in the main of its
own communion and faith. Much even that Episcopalian Protestantism finds to be good here, this more unchurchly system
has no hesitation in treating as part and parcel of the "great
apostacy," which so soon turned the whole truth of Christianity
into a strange lie. The fourth century was miserably corrupt.
Even the third carries in many respects a very questionable face.
But still we are not to give up entirely the idea of a truly golden
age, representing for a time at least, however short, the true
original simplicity of the Gospel, as the same has been happily
resuscitated once again in these last days, particularly among the
churches of New England. In the second century somewhere,
or even reaching over this a little here and there into the third,
back of popery and prelacy, the theory ventures to assume what

---

[1] "Did St. Athanasius or St. Ambrose come suddenly to life, it cannot be
doubted what communion they would mistake for their own. All surely
will agree that these fathers, with whatever difference of opinion, whatever
protests if we will, would find themselves more at home with such men as
St. Bernard or St. Ignatius Loyola, or with the lonely priest in his lodgings,
or the holy sisterhood of mercy, or the unlettered crowd before the altar,
than with the rulers or the members of any other religious community.
And may we not add, that were the two saints, who once sojourned, in ex-
ile or on embassage, at Treves, to come more northward still, and to travel
until they reached another fair city, seated among groves, green meadows,
and calm streams, the holy brothers would turn from many a high aisle
and solemn cloister which they found there, and ask the way to some small
chapel where mass was said in the populous alley or forlorn suburb? And,
on the other hand, can any one who has but heard his name, and cursorily
read his history, doubt for one instant how the people of England in turn,
'we, our princes, our priests, and our prophets,' Lords and Commons, Uni-
versities, Ecclesiastical Courts, marts of commerce, great towns, country
parishes, would deal with Athanasius—Athanasius who spent his long years
in fighting against kings for a theological term?"—*Newman, Essay on Development.*

all historical documents fail to make clear, the existence namely of a strictly evangelical church, founded on Protestant principles, (the Bible the only rule of doctrine, justification by faith, the clergy of one order, the people the fountain of all church power,) breathing a Protestant spirit, and carrying men to heaven without sacramental mummery or mysticism in the common sense Puritan way of the present time. So we have seen Dr. Bacon pleasing himself with the imagination, that the Christianity of Lyons in the second century, in the days of Pothinus and Irenæus, and of course also the faith and piety of the church generally in a still earlier part of the same century, in the days of Ignatius and Polycarp, corresponded in all material respects with the modern ecclesiastical life of Connecticut and Massachusetts. Is there any more ground for this fancy, than can be urged in favor of the one we have just now dismissed? We believe not. It rests throughout on a mere hypothesis, which involves in the end a purely arbitrary construction of history, just as wild and bold, to our view, as any that has been offered to us, from a different standpoint, by Strauss or Baur. Into this part of the subject however, the limits necessarily imposed on us at present will not permit us to enter. We hope to be able to return to it, in a second article, some time hereafter.

J. W. N.

THE

MERCERSBURG REVIEW.

NOVEMBER, 1851.

VOL. III.---NO. VI.

EARLY CHRISTIANITY.

Second Article.

THE general Puritan theory of Early Christianity may be reduced to the following propositions:

1st. That it started in the beginning under the same form substantially, both in doctrine and practice, which is now known
and honored as Evangelical Protestantism without prelacy. The
doctrine was orthodox, as distinguished from all heresies that are
at war with the doctrines of the Trinity, human depravity, and
the atonement. The principle of the Bible and private judgment lay at the bottom of the whole system. The worship was
much in the modern style of Scotland or New England. So
was it also with the government or polity of the churches. All
was vastly rational and spiritual. Even Presbyterianism, according to the Congregationalists, was not yet born. The Baptists carry the nudity farther still. But all agree, that the church
notions of later times were unknown. There was no papacy,
no episcopacy, no priesthood, no liturgy, no thought of a supernatural virtue in baptism, no dream of anything like the mystery of the real presence in the awful sacrament of the altar. The
primitive piety was quite of another order from all this. It was

neither hierarchical nor mystical, but ran in the channel rather of popular freedom, democratic right, and common sense.

2nd. That this happy state of things, established under the authority of the Apostles and in their time universally prevalent in the churches, was unfortunately of only very short duration. How long it lasted is by no means clear. After the destruction of Jerusalem, we have for a time almost no historical notices whatever that serve to reveal to us the actual condition of the church; and such testimony as we have, with the going out of the first century and the coming in of the second, have so questionable a look at certain points, that it is hard to know how far they are to be trusted anywhere. It became the policy of later times to corrupt and suppress documents. The theory thus is of necessity thrown here on presumption and hypothesis. Two broad facts for it however are settled and given; first, that the church started right in the beginning, and secondly, that on coming fully into view again in the third century it is found to be strangely wrong, fairly on the tide in truth of the prelatical system with its whole sea of corruptions and abominations. Between these dates then must be assumed an apostacy or fall, somewhat like that which turned our first parents out of paradise into the common world. When or how the doleful change took place, in the absence of all reliable historical evidence, can only be made out by conjecture; and here naturally the theory is subject in different hands to some variations. The Presbyterian, Congregational, and Baptist schemes or constructions, are not just the same. All however make the paradisiacal period of the church very short. It is hard to find even one whole century for it after the destruction of Jerusalem; though in a vague loose way it is common to speak of it, as reaching through the second century and some little distance perhaps into the third.

3d. That the change thus early commenced was in truth in full opposition to the original sense and design of Christianity, and involved in principle from the start the grand apostacy that afterwards became complete in the church of Rome, and which is graphically foretold in those passages of the New Testament that speak of antichrist, the mystical Babylon, and the man of sin. The Baptists include in this corruption more than the Congregationalists; and these again include in it more than the Presbyterians, taking Presbytery itself in fact, and that idea of the church which *once* went along with it, for the first stage of the downward progress; but as to what lies beyond this, the vast world of notions and practices namely that go to make up the prelatical system as we find it in full force in the days of Cyprian, the whole Puritan body of course is but of one mind. It is throughout an usurpation only and an abuse, against the Bible, against apostolical and primitive example, against the entire genius and spirit of evangelical religion. It belongs to an order of thought and habit of life, which however countenanced by many good men in the beginning, must be regarded as constitutionally at variance with the first principles of the Gospel, as antichristian and worldly ; the natural and only proper end of which, in the course of two or three centuries, was the complete failure of the church in its original form. It became the synagogue of Satan. Christianity went out in dismal eclipse for a thousand years, with only a few tapers, dimly burning here and there in vallies and corners, to keep up some faint remembrance of that glorious day-spring from on high with which it had visited the nations in the beginning.

4th. That the long night of this fearful captivity came to an end finally, through the great mercy of God, by the event of the Reformation ; which was brought to pass by the diligent study of the Bible, the original codex of Christianity, under the awakening and guiding influence of the Holy Ghost, and consisted simply in a resuscitation of the life and doctrine of the primitive church, which had been so long buried beneath the corruptions of the great Roman apostacy. The Reformation, in this view, was not properly the historical product and continuation of the life of the church itself, or what was called the church, as it stood before It was a revolutionary rebellion rather against this as something totally false and wrong, by which it was violently set aside to make room for a new order of things altogether. If it be asked, by what authority Luther and the other reformers undertook to bring in so vast a change, the answer is that they had the authority of the Bible. This and this only, is the religion of Protestants. Popery was antichrist ; the Bible teaches plainly a different religion, which must have prevailed in the beginning, and which Popery had contrived to suppress ; and what better right than this fact then could the reformers have or need, to fight against it, to overturn it as far as they were able, and to set up the religion of the Bible, the primitive evangelical religion, in its room and place ? Such was their warrant, and such as far as it went their good and excellent work. It is not strange however, coming out of such thick darkness as they had in their rear, that they were not themselves able at once to see clearly all that needed to be done in this great restoration ; to say nothing of such outward political limitations as they had to contend with for instance in England. Luther stuck miserably in the mud of Romanism to the last. Even Calvin had his sacramental crotchets, and talks strangely at times of the church. Anglicanism remained out and out semi-popery. Hence the need of new reformation. This we have in Puritanism; which itself also has required some time to come to that perfection of Bible simplicity and truth, which it now happily presents in this country, especially in New England— and most of all, if we take their own word for it, in the wide communion of the Baptists. Here finally, after so long a sleep, the fair image of original Christianity, as it once gladdened the assemblies of the faithful in the days of Ignatius, Polycarp, Irenæus, and the blessed martyrs of Lyons and Vienne, has come forth as it were from the catacombs, to put to shame that frightful mask which has for so many centuries cheated the world in its name and stead. And what is better still, there is some ground now also to hope, since we have got into the mid-dle of the nineteenth century and Anglo-Saxon mind is in a fair way to rule the world, that this second edition and experiment of a pure faith and true church will be more successful than the first; and that Christ will find it proper *now*, in these last days, to be with his church always, and to make good thus his own promise that the gates of hell shall not prevail against it, as they might seem to have done before, till Shiloh come or to the end of the world.

Such in a general view, we say, is the Puritan theory of the past history of the church, and such is the relation in which it imagines Protestantism to stand to Primitive Christianity. The theory and the fancy we believe to be both together absolutely visionary and false. More than that, they are eminently suited to overthrow at last the credit of Protestantism itself, and along with this to upset all faith in Christianity as being really and truly such a revelation as it claims to be for the salvation of the world. Grant the premises of this wild hypothesis, and infideli-ty may proceed at once to draw its own conclusions with unan-swerable force.

It is truly amazing, before looking at the facts of history at all, that the holders of the hypothesis are not troubled some by the very *prodigiousness* of the conceptions that enter into its composition. They appear to be quite easy and at home, for the most part, in the fabric of their peculiar historical system, as though it were the most natural and reasonable structure in the world; and yet never was fabric of this sort probably so put together, as to furnish by its very texture more just cause for anxiety and distrust. The theory, instead of being natural and reasonable, is as much against nature and reason as can well be conceived. Let any thinking man put out of his mind the mere habit of looking at the past through the medium of the theory itself, so as to bring home to himself clearly in an abstract way the elements and combinations of which it is constructed, and he must feel surely that no scheme could well be, in an *a priori* view, less probable or worthy of trust. Every presumption is against it. If believed at all by the earnestly thoughtful, it can be only through stress of overwhelming evidence, making it a sin to doubt. The unthoughtful of course feel no such difficulty. Their faith is easy, just because it is hollow and blind.

Only look at the scheme in its own light. All previous history looked to the coming of Christ, and prepared the way for it, as the grand central fact of religion and so of the world's life. The Old Testament revelation, through thousands of years, made room for the magnificent and awful mystery. At length it came, the Fact of all facts, full of grace and truth, heralded by angels, surrounded with miracles, binding earth to heaven, and laying the foundations of a new creation of whose splendors and glories there should be no end. Christ died for our sins, and rose again for our justification. His apostles were solemnly commissioned to preach the gospel throughout the world. On the day of Pentecost, they were armed with supernatural power from on high for this purpose ; and the history of the Christian Church was opened under a form, that carried in it the largest promise of universal victory and success in following time. With this promise corresponded in full the progress of the new cause, in the age of the apostles and for a short time afterwards. The Gospel was rapidly published throughout the Roman world. The ascended Redeemer at the right hand of God, made head over all things to the church, gave proof of his exaltation and power by causing his kingdom to spread and prevail, in the face of all opposition whether Jewish or Pagan. The whole course of things seemed to show clearly, that the powers of a higher world were at work in the glorious movement, and that it embodied in itself the will and counsel of heaven itself for the full accomplishment of the end towards which it reached. It is usual indeed to make this early success of Christianity one of the external proofs of its divine origin, a real supernatural seal of its truth, like that of miracles. One would naturally suppose, that such a beginning must have led to some sound and true result, in harmony with its own heavenly conditions. But, according to the hypothesis now before us, the very opposite of this took place. Hardly had the last of the apostles gone to heaven, before signs of apostacy began to show themselves in the bosom of the infant church, threatening to overthrow and defeat entirely its original design. In the midst of its early triumphs, whilst it had still strength to perform miracles and exhibit martyrdoms on all sides in favor of the truth, the leaven of this malignant corruption went forward, strangely enough, in the most active and virulent way; infecting and poisoning, more and more, the very vitals of the church; till in the course of a single century from the death of St. John, perhaps indeed much sooner, the entire course of its life was changed from what it had been at first, and turned into a false direction. Traces of the original faith and piety are still to be found indeed in the third and fourth and fifth centuries, the echoes and reminiscences as it were, more and more faint, of the better age which had gone before; but these were exceptional now to the central tendency, rather than its true and genuine fruit; the power that prevailed, and that was fast carrying all things its own way, almost without question or protest, was the " mystery of iniquity," that same great anti-christian apostacy in principle and drift, which in due time afterwards culminated in the Pope, and brought upon the world the darkness of the middle ages. The eclipse came not at once in its full strength; but still, from the very start, it was the beginning of the total obscurity that followed, and looked to this steadily as its end. So in truth Satan in the end fairly prevailed over Christ. The church fell, not partially and transiently only, but universally, in its collective and corporate character, with an apostacy that was to reach through twelve hundred years. Had it not been for some copies of the Bible here and there, in the hands of a few obscure and persecuted witnesses for the truth, the light of Christianity would have become absolutely extinct; for the so called catholic church, in league plainly with the powers of hell, and with the sovereignty of the world in its hands, showed itself bent for ages on the accomplishment precisely of this terrible result. Never was there so glorious a morning, so suddenly lost and forgotten in think impenetrable clouds! The grandeur of the enterprise is equalled only by the greatness of its failure. And what is that fearful whisper that seems to steal upon us, in view of it, from the very depths of the bottomless pit: " This man began to build, and was not *able* to finish?" But here again the hypothesis is ready with its own answer. The failure was not final. So long as the Bible lived, there was still room for hope; and at last accordingly, " in the fulness of time," after centuries upon centuries of ecclesiastical chaos, God was pleased

to say once more, " Let there be light," and there *was* light.
The reformers of the 16th century drew forth from the sacred
volume, by the help of God's Spirit, the true scheme and pattern
of the christian faith, as it was in the beginning. The spell of
ages was broken. Christ gave tokens that he was again at the
head of his church. The unfinished work of the first and second centuries was once more actively and vigorously resumed.
In the form of Protestantism, it may *now* be expected, after so
long a time, to go forward conquering and to conquer, until all
enemies are subdued under the Saviour's feet. True, Popery is
not still dead, and Protestantism itself is getting into huge difficulties; but we must now have faith in Christ's headship over
his church, and in his promise that the gates of hell shall never
prevail against it; so as to be firmly persuaded, in spite of all
fears and discouragements, that the right course which things
have at last taken must certainly prove successful in the end,
and that he who sits king in Zion will not rest till he shall have
brought forth judgment unto victory.

Will any sober minded man pretend to say, that this, in itself
considered, is not a strange and unnatural hypothesis, which it
is exceedingly hard to reconcile, either with the divine origin of
the church, or with its divine mission, or with the divine presence in it of Him, who is represented as having the government
of the world on his shoulders for its defence and salvation ?

But the case becomes yet more difficult, when we look into
the sacred oracles which lie back of the actual history of the
church, and find that instead of lending any countenance to this
scheme prospectively, they set before us in the most plain and
unquestionable terms an altogether different prospect. Some
few passages, we know, have been impressed by a strained and
violent exegesis into the service of the theory, by being made in
sound at least to foretell a general apostacy of the church, the
features of which it has been pretended to identify in the Papal
communion; and it is not uncommon to hear the enemies of
Popery appealing to these perversions of scripture as the very
voice of inspiration itself, and charging those who question the
infallibility of their gloss with setting themselves against the authority of God's word. But the day for such arbitrary and unhistorical interpretation, it may be trusted, is now fast coming to
an end. On the field of science at least, it is fairly and fully
exploded. No real biblical scholar, in any part of the world, is
found willing to endorse the vulgar anti-popery sense of these
pet texts. On the other hand, however, there are many single
passages and texts, which clearly foretell the unfailing stability

of the church, through all ages, on to the end of time. And what perhaps is of still more account, the whole drift and scope of the Bible look always in the same direction, and in this direction only.

Even under the Old Testament, it was a standing article of faith that the theocracy could not fail. But this perpetuity was itself the type only of that higher and better state, in which the Jewish theocracy was to become complete finally as the New Testament church. [1] If it lay in the conception of the old that it should not prove a failure, much more must this be taken to lie in the conception of the new. It is to the times of the Messiah in this view emphatically, that the predictions and promises of the Old Testament in relation to the coming fortunes of the church especially refer. All join in the assurance, that the kingdom then to be set up should be an everlasting kingdom, and that of its dominion and glory there should be no end. Nothing could well be more foreign from the old Messianic scheme, than the imagination that the enlargement of Jacob, by the coming of Shiloh, was to give place almost immediately again to a long night of captivity and bondage, ten times worse than that of Babylon, from which there was to be no escape for more than a thousand years. And just as little can any such view be reconciled with the plan of Christianity, as it meets us in the New Testament. This proceeds everywhere on the assumption, that the kingdom of God, or the church, as now established among men, was destined, not to fall but to stand, not to pass away like the streams of the desert, but to be as the waters of the sanctuary rather, in Ezekiel's vision, an ever deepening and perpetual river. There are, it is true, predictions enough of trials, heresies, apostacies and corruptions; but the idea is never for a moment allowed, that these should prevail in any such universal way as the theory before us pretends. On the contrary, the strongest assurances are given, that this should not be the case.

These stand forth most conspicuously and solemnly, in those wonderful passages from the mouth of the blessed Saviour himself, which form as it were the charter of the church and its heavenly commission to the end of time. " Thou art Peter; and upon this rock I will build my church; and the *gates of hell shall not prevail against it*" Matth. xvi. 18. The use which the Romanists make of this text, must not blind us to its true magnificence and grandeur. It is still scripture; and we are bound, as good Protestants, to pause with some reverence before it, and to inquire with seriousness what it actually does mean. Take it as we may, it looks certainly like a most explicit pledge, in terms of unusual solemnity and deliberation, that the church should endure on its first foundation, that is with true historical succession from its own beginning, through all ages. Of the same tenor again precisely is the apostolic commission, after our Saviour's resurrection and just before his ascension: " All power is given unto me in heaven and in earth: Go ye *therefore*, and teach all nations, baptizing them in the name of the Father, and of the Son, and of the Holy Ghost; teaching them to observe all things whatsoever I have commanded you: And, lo, *I am with you alway, even* unto the end of the world" Matth. xxviii: 18–20. Here again we have scripture, under a most majestic and commanding form. Has it any meaning answerable to its magnificent terms, or is it a mere flourish of Oriental figures which mean the next thing to nothing? Words could hardly be put together in a way more significantly suited to express the idea, that the object of this commission was one which could not possibly suffer failure or defeat. The enterprise in view is conditioned by the fact, that all power is in the Saviour's hands, that he is head over all things, as Paul expresses it, to the church; and all conceivable difficulties attending it, as in the case of Moses when sent to bring Israel out of Egypt, are reduced to nothing by the one overwhelming consideration, " Lo, I am with you always," engaging the entire plenitude of this power for its never ending success. It is useless to dwell on other testimonies that look immediately in the same direction. If these capital and classical passages have no power to fix attention or constrain belief, it is not to be imagined that any amount of scriptural evidence besides will be felt to carry with it any real weight.

It is very certain, that only the most wilful and stubborn prejudice can fail to see, how utterly at war the Bible is with the notion of a quickly apostatizing and totally failing church, in any view answerable to the strange Puritan hypothesis which we have now under consideration. No such notion accordingly ever entered the mind of the primitive church itself. It was for a time supposed indeed that the end of the world was near at hand, and that the resurrection state or millenium would soon appear; and it was only gradually, that this view gave place to the idea of a long course of history preparing the way for Christ's second coming. But neither in the one form nor in the other, was the thought ever admitted that the church itself might collapse or go into universal dismal eclipse. That would have been counted downright infidelity. The promise to Peter and the apostolic commission were never taken but in one sense; and that appeared to be so plain, that no one but an unbeliever, it was supposed, could ever think of seriously calling it in question. It became accordingly, as we all know, an element of the primitive faith, an article of the early creed, to believe in the being of the holy·catholic church as an indestructible fact, a divine mystery that could never fail or pass away.

The biblical doctrine on this subject is so clear indeed, that even the most unhistorical advocates of the Puritan theory are themselves constrained to allow it; though they take care to put it into a shape to suit their own preconceived scheme. Nothing is more common than to hear them talk of the unfailing and enduring character of the church, of its being founded on a rock, and of Christ's presence with it always for its protection and defence; they ·are willing to say with the ancient creed, when necessary, "We believe in the church as one, holy, catholic and apostolical." But by all this they mean in the end, not the church in any outward and visible view, not the historical organization known under this name and claiming these titles from the third century down to the sixteenth, but a supposed succession of hidden and scattered witnesses, in the so called catholic church partly, but more generally after a time on the outside of it, handing down what the theory is pleased to call a pure faith, in conflict with the reigning system, and in the way of more or less direct protest against it as an anti-christian usurpation. It is of the invisible church only, they tell us, the secret "election in Israel," that the glorious things spoken of Zion are to be understood. The church was in the wilderness for a thousand years before the Reformation, among the Waldenses, Albigenses, Henricians, Paulicians, and such like; God was never altogether without a handful of people somewhere, that refused to bow the knee to Baal. No such evasion however is of any force in truth, for getting clear of the difficulty which we have here in view. It turns in the first place on a mere arbitrary assumption, borrowed from the clouds, and got up palpably to serve a purpose, without the least regard to historical facts and dates; an assumption that is doomed therefore, by necessary consequence, to dissolve before the light of history more and more into mere fog and mist. These sects of the middle ages are bad stuff at best, for making out the romance of a pure Christianity, from the fifth century to the fifteenth, on the outside of the Roman church. But allowing them to have been as good as the theory before us affects to believe, and granting it besides a fair proportion of sporadic exceptional cases of piety, in the reigning church itself, to fill up the thin and airy succession, what sound mind can be satisfied still to take *this* for any fitting verification of the glowing predictions of the Old Testament, any true fulfilment of the high sounding promises and pledges that are contained in the New? No *such* construction of these predictions and promises certainly ever entered into the mind of the primitive church itself; the construction is perfectly foreign from the sense of the ancient creed; and we may safely say, that nothing short of the most powerful prejudice in favor of a previously established theory can account in any case, for its being accepted as in the least degree satisfactory or probable. The whole is a subterfuge plainly, got up to escape the clear and proper sense of the Bible, and not an honest commentary by any means designed to meet this sense in a fair and open way.

The difficulty then stands before us still in its full strength. The helplessness of the plea thus put in to turn aside its force, only serves to give it greater weight. The more we bring the case home in an actual way to our thoughts, the more are we likely to be confounded with its palpable monstrosity. Puritanism puts an enormous tax upon our faith from the very outset, when it requires us to believe things so contradictory and mutually destructive as are here brought together in one and the same theory or scheme. That the church should have such a history behind it as that of the Old Testament, such a glorious array of miracles, types, prophecies, heralding and foreshadowing its advent, for thousands of years, as the desire of all nations, the last sense and grand fulfilment of all previous revelations; that its actual inauguration in the world should be so every way worthy of this stupendous world embracing proem, in the mystery of the incarnation itself, ("God manifest in the flesh, justified in the Spirit, &c." 1 Tim. v: 16.), in "promises exceedingly great and precious," and high guaranties from the throne of heaven, in signs and wonders and miracles, and in wide pentecostal triumphs throughout the Roman empire; that Christianity should start thus, under such divine auspices, the glorified Saviour head over all things for its single cause and sake, and ever present by his Spirit in the midst of it according to his own word, and by infallible tokens also making his presence known and felt on all sides; that the church in these circumstances should look upon itself as an institution founded upon a rock, and make it an article of faith that its charter could not fail: and yet, that in fact all began to fail, to go into confusion, to run towards apostacy, before the end of the second century; that this fearful tendency, in spite of Christ's headship in heaven and his, *Lo, I am with you always,* on earth, through fires of martyrdom and unheard of sacrifices for the faith once delivered to the saints, so far prevailed actually as in the course of two or three centuries more to turn this whole faith into a lie ; that the church in short, under its original corporate character, ran out historically into a complete and universal failure, so as to be for a whole millenium of the most horrible spiritual darkness and desolation, a mere synagogue of Satan, the enemy of all truth and righteousness, seeking only to pull down and destroy what Christ (King in Zion Ps. ii : 1–6) was still trying to build here and there, by such people as the Paulicians and Albigenses : All this taken together, we say, requires such a cormorant credulity for its full reception, that the most careless minds, when brought to think only a little for themselves, are very likely to start back aghast from the scheme, and may well be excused for gently asking, By what authority and right does it pretend so to lord it over our faith ?

It would seem reasonable to expect in so improbable a case, that the main positions of the theory at least would be so supported by clear historical proof, as to carry with them some sort of coercive force for such as are willing and anxious to know the truth. An apostacy so profound and total should be properly attested in some way, by historical testimonies and monuments. Allowing it to have come in gradually, this only gives us the more right to expect and demand the evidence of which we now speak. So vast a revolution, in such view, implies of necessity a moral struggle, a conflict of principles and aims, a tumult of inharmonious and opposing forces. To say that the primitive church yielded passively to the great apostacy from the beginning, without contradiction or protest, is to make it from the very first, not "the pillar and ground of the truth," but the mother of error itself ; to conceive of it as built, not on a rock beating back the strong floods of hell, but on the mere sand at the mercy of all winds and waves. The least we can ask then, is to have set before us in history some traces of this grand ecclesiastical catastrophe, by which all our *a priori* conceptions of Christianity are so confounded, and our faith in its divine origin and heavenly commission is so terribly tried. And as we should have clear proof in this way of the failure of the church in the beginning, it would seem but reasonable also that we should not be left to take the Reformation on trust subsequently as a merely human work. Allow the continuous stability of the church, as a divine institution carrying in itself down to that time the promises and gifts with which it was freighted in the beginning, and we may at least try to justify Protestantism as a true product of this historical life itself; in which view it might need no higher warrant perhaps for its vindication.   But give up the historical succession, by taking the ground that the church had failed for a thousand years, except among sects from which it is notorious Protestantism did *not* spring, and that the Reformation was in truth a new setting up of Christianity parallel with its first setting up by the Apostles; and then really we see not, why the proper credentials of a truly apostolical commission should be wanting in the second case more than in the first. Luther himself did not hesitate to pose the radicalism of the Anabaptists with this test: " If they have a commission from God, let them prove it by *miracles*." But if the Reformation itself is to be taken for what this Puritan theory makes it, we must say it was quite as much a new church as the enterprise of Storck and Munzer, and needed quite as much the argument of miracles for its support.

But now when we look into the actual course of history, we find it in no agreement whatever with these reasonable presumptions and anticipations, as directed either towards the end of this supposed failure of the church or towards its beginning.   The Reformation, we all know, lacked entirely the seal of miracles, the only truly apostolical warrant for a really apostolical work. In this respect it bore no resemblance to the mission of Elijah, the restorer of Moses in the apostate kingdom of Israel.   That such an apostacy, reaching through a thousand years, should finally be set right in this way, is not a little strange.   On the other hand however, the coming in of the apostacy is more strangely conditioned still.   Never was a revolution so vast and important, so broad and deep in its course, so sweepingly disastrous in its effects.   We may apply to it without exaggeration the strong figure: " In those days the sun shall be darkened, and the moon shall not give her light, and the stars of heaven shall fall, and the powers that are in heaven shall be shaken." The church, having in charge the most vital interests of a fallen world, proved recreant to her solemn trust, fell from her high estate, and became literally the seat of Antichrist and a synagogue of Satan.   Thus fearfully radical, the revolution was at the same time no less dreadfully universal.   And yet, strange to say, no one can tell when or how it came to pass.   We have indeed certain schemes that pretend to be such an explanation. But these, when examined, are found to be purely fanciful attempts to solve the demands of a theory already adopted, rather than the exhibition of actual historical grounds for the theory itself. It is assumed in the first place that a certain form of religion, Puritanism for instance, is taught in the New Testament, and therefore that it must have prevailed in the apostolical and primitive church; it is very evident in the next place, that a wholly different form of religion prevailed in the church of the third and fourth centuries, a system intrinsically at war with Puritanism and leading directly towards full Catholicism; here then the fact of an apostacy is supposed to be historically established, and any combination now is taken to be rational and legitimate that serves at all to bind the two sides of it plausibly together. So we have various pretty plans or methods, that of the Quakers, that of the Baptists, that of the Independents, that of the Presbyterians, and coming down somewhat farther that also of the Episcopalians, setting forth with more or less particularity how the corruption of pure Christianity in the first ages took place, first one step and then another, till at last the face of it was totally altered and changed; but if we call for the direct proof of these fine spun contructions, we find it to be either wanting altogether, or at best to consist in a few stray words, picked up here and there without regard to the general formation from which they are taken, and of such slippery and extremely brittle sense, that one may well feel astounded to see what weight they are made to bear. It seems to be counted sufficient for the most part, if no direct proof can be quoted the other way, or if the force of any such quotation can be ingeniously set aside. If Irenæus speak not of infant baptism in terms that cut off all captious debate, the Baptists hold it a good argument that the baptism of infants in his time was unknown. If Justin Martyr teach not diocesan episcopacy in the same terms with Cyprian, the Presbyterians lay hold of him as a good witness that the ambition of prelacy was not yet born. If the primacy of the Roman see be not positively declared by the earliest fathers in round set phrase, the Episcopalians take it as so much testimony that this usurpation, as they call it, came in at a later day. If it appear that the Apostles' Creed is not quoted in its full present form before the fourth century, Puritanism chuckles over the nice discovery, and on the strength of it proceeds at once to deny its apostolical and primitive authority, treating its article of the church as a figment, and seeing in it the germs at least of all sorts of Popish error and delusion. And so it goes throughout the chapter. It never seems to enter the head of these self-complacent theorizers, that the burden of proof lies of right first and foremost upon themselves; that the difficulty of making out clear and plain testimony in every case for the negative of their arbitrary positions, is not in and of itself any testimony whatever in favor of these positions ; that the *indifference* of the argument in this form, the mere want of positive and direct testimony either way, is itself in truth a most powerful presumption, not in favor of their theories, but against them, and in favor only of the cause to which they are variously opposed. The grand difficulty is just to see, how so great an apostacy as is here supposed to have had place, turning the fair bride of the Lamb in so short a time into the similitude of a harlot, should have gone forward through its several stages or steps, as laid down in either of these schemes, and yet have left no trace of its dire revolutionary march on the historic page!

That false tendencies might begin to work in a pure state of the church, is not hard to believe. But the case before us involves immeasurably more than this. These tendencies are taken to be from the start in full opposition to the genius and spirit of the Gospel ; they work rapidly in fact towards its overthrow ; they bring in by degrees new ideas and practices altogether, the fruit of cunning secular pride and borrowed from Judaism or Paganism, that go directly to undermine and break up the simple evangelical system of earlier times ; and yet they provoke no opposition, excite no alarm, but make an easy prey of the whole church, as it would seem, without a protesting cry or a contradictory stroke. The ministers took the lead in the bad movement, and the people fell in passively with their wrong guidance. All sorts of pious lies and forgeries were resorted to for its support ; and the daughter of Zion was either too silly to perceive the fraud, or too sleepy to lay it seriously to heart. The old faith died thus, and gave no sign. The apostacy came in without an effort or a struggle. True, as we are told, it had stages and degrees. But each new stage found a generation ready to accept it, as the undoubted sense of the faith they had received from their fathers. The work went silently but surely forward always in the same false direction. It carried along with it the universal church. When this comes fully into view in the fourth century, we find, not a part of it merely, but the entire body fully committed to the sacramental, liturgical, churchly and priestly system, with the full persuasion that the whole of it had come down from the earliest times. All history may be defied, to furnish any parallel to such a revolution, any change political or religious at once so vast and yet so entirely without noise. It passes before us like a scene of magic. As some one has observed, it is as though the world on some one night had gone to bed Protestant or Puritan, and on waking the next morning found itself thoroughly and universally Catholic.

Only think of a single province, such as modern New England for instance, in the course of one or two hundred years throwing off the whole type of its religion in this way, and with general consent accepting another of diametrically opposite character and cast, without a single monument to inform posterity how the thing was done. Think of her associations and consociations, with their system of parity and rank democracy, passing over in so short a time to a well ordered hierarchy, revolving round a single centre. Think of her free prayers losing themselves in liturgical forms, her naked spiritualism stooping to clothe itself with the mummery of outward ceremonies and rites, crossings, bowings, sprinklings, with all the paraphernalia of a truly pontifical worship. Think of her sacraments turning from barren signs into supernatural mysteries, of the simple memorial of the Lord's supper in particular assuming the character of a real sacrifice for the sins of the living and the dead, and running into the bold and utterly confounding tenet of transubstantiation. Think of her mission of worldly prudence, utility, materialism and common sense, running out into the glorification of monasticism, voluntary poverty, the angelical life of celibates and virgins. Imagine these and other kindred transformations, we say, accomplished between the days of Dr. Increase Mather and those of President Dwight, and all so smoothly and quietly as to leave no trace, not a solitary record or sign of resistance, protestation, division or dissent, to inform posterity in any case when or how the change took place. Would it not be a moral miracle, transcending entirely the common order of history? But in the hypothesis before us, the miracle goes far beyond this. It embraces not one province only, but many, widely separated in space, and differing in every social and national respect. It is universal Christendom, from Britain to Africa, from Spain to India, that is found to have yielded simultaneously to the spirit of defection and revolt, as though it had been animated through all its borders with one and the same principle of evil, bewildering its senses and hurrying it among the tombs. Nothing could better show the universality of the supposed apostacy, and the deep root it had taken previously in the mind and life of the church, than the grand divisions that took place in the fourth and fifth centuries; giving rise to rival communions on a vast scale, some of which have upheld themselves down to the present time. These could not of course consent in any such innovation after they fell asunder ; on the contrary, the laws of party and sect would have been sure to bring out a loud complaint of the change, if anything of the sort lay within the reach of knowledge before. But the Arians and Donatists brought no charge here against the Catholics. The Nestorians and Monophysites went out and founded new churches, which remain to this day ; but they carried along with them the characteristic peculiarities of the Roman system, which they have never ceased since to regard as of truly apostolical force and date. These have indeed become for the most part mere petrifactions or dead fossil remains ; but in this character they still bear powerful and unanswerable testimony to the fact of which we now speak, the universal and unquestioned authority of this system throughout Christendom in the fourth century. No language written on rocks for this purpose, could be more sure or plain.

The contrast in which this noiseless revolution stands with the known vigilance of the church in other things, serves to make it still more striking and strange. Christianity in the beginning was anything but a passive and inert system, which offered itself like wax to every impression from abroad. It had a most intense life of its own, power to assimilate and reject in the sea of elements with which it was surrounded, the force of self-conservation over against all dissolving agencies, as never any system of thought or life before. It is just this organific and all subduing character that forms the grand argument from history, for its divine origin and heavenly truth. Neander has it continually in view. What subtle speculations were not tried, in the first centuries on the part of the Gnostics, Manicheans, Sabellians, Arians, and others, to corrupt the truth ; and yet how promptly and vigorously all these innovations were met and repelled. It was not reflection either that led the way in these contests with heresy, but a fine tact rather and living instinct for the orthodoxy to which they were always opposed. Danger was felt with keen inward sensibility even afar off, and no time was lost in sounding an alarm. There is no lack accordingly of historical witnesses and monuments, to show here what actually took place. They abound in the form of contro·versies, councils, heretical parties, and wide-spread long enduring schisms. And yet in the midst of all this vigilant activity, if we are to believe our Puritan hypothesis, the great apostacy of Popery came in upon the universal church so quietly that no one now can lay his hand on the origin of a single one of all its manifold forms of corruption and abuse. It gave rise to no controversy, created no party, led to no schism. The Argus-eyed jealousy of the heretical sects themselves was blinded and deceived. They saw not the wholesale treason which was going forward in such bold and impudent style; and it was allowed by all of them accordingly to pass, without one syllable of remonstrance or rebuke.

But this is not all. The prodigiousness of the theory goes still farther. It is by the Bible it pretends to be sure that the church started on the Puritan model, and that this later state of it therefore must be counted a grand falling away from its first and only true form. But now the Bible itself comes down to us through the hands of this same apostate church, which made no conscience, we are sometimes told, of forging and falsifying documents, to almost any extent, for the purpose of carrying out its own wrong; and we have absolutely to take it on trust from the credit solely of this suspicious source. This is particularly clear, in the case of the New Testament, the main authority of course for the question here in debate. What authority was it that fixed the sacred canon, determining in the beginning what books were to be taken as inspired, and what other books not a few were to be rejected as apocryphal or false? The authority precisely of that very organization, which these same canonical writings are now brought forward to convict of palpable wholesale unfaithfulness to its own trust; and which was in the full career of such sad apostacy indeed, while diligently and as it would seem most faithfully fulfilling this great commission, for the use of the world in later ages. The work of settling the canon began in the second century, but was not fully completed before the fourth; and then it was by the tradition and authority of the church simply that the work, regarded through all this time as one and the same, was brought thus to its final consummation. We have already seen however, where the church stood in the fourth century, and in what direction all its forces were tending in the third. Is it not strange, that we should be under obligation to such a growing mystery of iniquity for so excellent and holy a gift, and that coming to us in this way we can still be so sure that every line of it is inspired, so as to make it the only rule of our faith? Is it not strange that the very Church, which had still divine tact enough for the delicate function of settling the canon, had at the same time no power to see or feel her own glaring departures from the light of this infallible rule, but actually gloried in it as the oracle and voucher of her claims;—not dreaming how, after the lapse of twelve hundred years, it should blaze forth into quite another signification, and be a swift witness against herself, as the whore of Babylon, the mother of abominations and lies.

Nor does the wonder stop here. The faithful execution of
this most responsible task of settling the canon, and handing
down an uncorrupted Bible, for the use of all following time,
is not the only merit of the ancient church. These ages of
apostacy, as they are here considered, were at the same time, by
general acknowledgment, ages of extraordinary faith and power. Miracles abounded. Charity had no limits. Zeal stopped
at no sacrifices, however hard or great. The blood of martyrs
flowed in torrents. The heroism of confessors braved every
danger. Bishops ruled at the peril of their lives. In the catalogue of Roman popes, no less than thirty before the time of
Constantine, that is, the whole list that far with only two or
three exceptions, wear the crown of martyrdom. Nor was this
zeal outward only, the fanaticism of a name or a sect. Along
with it burned, as we have seen before, a glowing interest in the
truth, an inextinguishable ardor in maintaining the faith once
delivered to the saints. Heresies quailed from its presence.
Schisms withered under its blasting rebuke. Thus, in the midst
of all opposition, it went forward from strength to strength, till
in the beginning of the fourth century finally we behold it fairly
seated on the throne of the Cesars. And this outward victory,
as Neander will tell us, was but a faint symbol of the far more
important revolution it had already accomplished in the empire
of human thought, the interior world of the spirit. Here was
brought to pass, in the same time, a true creation from the bosom
of chaos, such as the world had never seen before, over which
the morning stars sang together and the sons of God shouted for
joy. In foundation and principle at least, old things, whether
of philosophy, or of art, or of morality and social life, were passed away, and, lo, all things had become new. This is the grand
argument for Christianity from its *miraculous success ;* of which
Puritanism, when it suits, is ready to make as loud use as any
part of the church besides, as though it really believed this ancient glory to be in some way after all truly and properly its own.
And yet by the same Puritanism we are told again, when another object is in view, that the cause which thus conquered the
world by manifest supernatural power, was itself so deserted and
abandoned by its glorified King, as to be all the while rushing
at the same time towards universal apostacy and ruin, by the
mystery of sin which it carried in its own womb !
And then again, when this mystery came fully out, and the
apostacy stood completely revealed in the form of full grown
and undisguised Popery, followed as we all know by the long
deep night of the middle ages, there was still no end to the mor-

al wonders of which we now speak. The Papacy itself is a wonder of wonders. There is nothing like it in all history besides. So all will feel, who stop to *think* about it in more than a fool's way. History too, even in Protestant hands, is coming more and more to do justice to the vast and mighty merits of the system in past times, bringing in light upon it, and scaring away the owls and bats that have so long been accustomed to hoot and flit here at their own will. These ages of darkness as they are called, were still, to an extent now hard to understand, ages also of faith. The church still had, as in earlier days, her miracles, her martyrdoms, her missionary zeal, her holy bishops and saints, her works of charity and love, her care for sound doctrine, her sense of a heavenly commission, and her more than human power to convert and subdue nations. True, the world was dark, very dark and very wild; and its corruptions were powerfully felt at times in her own bosom ; but no one but a simpleton or a knave will pretend to make this barbarism *her* work, or to lay it as a crime to *her* charge. She was the rock that beat back its proud waves. She was the power of order and law, the fountain of a new civilization, in the midst of its tumultuating chaos. Take the conversion of Saxon England in the time of Gregory the Great. and the long work of moral organization with which it was followed in succeeding centuries. Look at the missionaries that proceeded from this island, apostolical bishops and holy monks, in the seventh and eighth centuries, planting churches successfully in the countries of the Rhine. Consider the entire evangelization of the new barbarous Europe. Is it not a work fairly parallel, to say the least, with the conquest of the old Roman empire in the first ages? Is not the argument of " miraculous success" quite as strong here as there? Think again of the theology of this old Catholic church, of its body of ethics, of its canon law. The cathedral of Cologne is no such work as this last ; the dome of St. Peter is less sublimely grand than the first. How wonderful, that the theological determinations of the fifth and sixth centuries, in the midst of endless agitation and strife, should fall so steadily the right way ; and also that these true conclusions should seem to hang so constantly, in the last instance, on the mind and voice of Rome. And then in the ages that followed, how wonderful again, that when there was but small power to build, nothing should be done at least to unsettle and pull down the edifice of sound doctrine as it stood before. However much of rubbish the Reformation found occasion to remove, it was still compelled to do homage to the main body of the Roman theolo-

gy as orthodox and right; and to this day Protestantism has no
valid mission in the world, any farther than it is willing to build
on this old foundation. Its distinctive doctrines are of no force,
except in organic union with the grand scheme of truth, which
is exhibited in the ancient creeds and in the decisions of the first
general councils. Cut off from this root, taken out from the
stream of this only sure and safe tradition, even the authority of
the Bible becomes uncertain, and the article of justification by
faith itself is turned into a perilous lie. In every view, we may
say, the work and mission of the church after the fourth century continue to be, as they were before, the most wonderful and
solemn fact in the world. And yet, according to the theory now
in hand, it was no longer an apostatizing church merely, but a
body fully apostate, fallen from the truth, opposed to righteousness, in league with Satan, and systematically bent on destroy-
ing all that Christ came into the world to build. Antichrist, the
man of sin, reigned terribly supreme, " sitting in the temple of
God, and opposing and exalting himself above all that is called
God or that is worshipped." How truly confounding the incon-
gruous combination ! How perfectly self-satirical the incoherent
face of the contradiction !

The theory is false. It rests on no historical bottom. The
scriptures are against it. All sound religious feeling is at war
with it. Facts of every sort conspire to prove it untrue. It is
a sheer hypothesis, a sort of Protestant myth we may call it, got
up to serve a purpose, and hardened by time and tradition now
into the form of a sacred prejudice; or rather it is an arbitrary
construction, that seeks to turn into mere myth and fable the
true history of the church. In this view we have said, that it
may fairly challenge comparison with the famous critical systems of such men as Strauss and Baur. Indeed these are in
some respects more plausible. They take the ground, that
Christianity as we have it now in the New Testament is a product properly of the second century, rather than the true birth historically of the first; that the original facts and doctrines were far
more simple ; that the religious imagination of the infant church,
or the spirit of controversy among its Jewish and Gentile parties,
idealized all into new shape and form ; and that most of our
canonical books were then forged according to this new and
higher scheme, and piously fathered upon the apostles to give
them more credit and weight. Monstrous as this representation
is, it is truly wonderful what a show of learning, critical and
historical, can be urged in its favor, enough almost to deceive at
times the very elect themselves. And yet it is a wild theory,

which needs no other force to upset it in the end than the simple persuasion, that the church itself is of divine origin, and not the most abominable imposture that ever has appeared in the world. The article : " I believe in the holy catholic church," which must ever precede in the order of faith, as Augustine tells us, that other article : " I believe in the holy inspired bible," wherever it really prevails in the heart, scatters to the wind all imaginable sophistries and subtleties in this form. The logic of Hegel before it, becomes no better than a spider's web. The true answer to Strauss, as well as to the whole Tübingen school, is an act of faith in the mystery of Christianity itself, as we have this concretely set forth in the ancient creed. But now what better after all, as tried by the touchstone of such faith, is the Puritan theory at which we are now looking? Is it not equally borrowed from the clouds, and at the same time equally fatal to all firm and full confidence in the supernatural origin and mission of the church, whose history it pretends to follow in so strange a way? To allow the suppositions of Strauss or of Baur, is from the very outset to drag down Christianity from the skies, and to make its whole signification not only human merely and earthly, but grossly carnal also and devilish. It is morally impossible to conceive of its rise and growth in any such style, and yet look upon it as a direct revelation in any way from heaven. The two conceptions are incompatible, and go at once to destroy each other. And just so also, we say, to allow the historical suppositions of Puritanism, is to convert the divine origin of the church into a fiction or a dream. Even such a scheme of history as we have in Mosheim for instance, or in the text book of Gieseler with all its show of authorities, is intrinsically at war with any real faith in this mystery, and can never fail to undermine it where no antidote is in the way. The sense of authorities, the force even of facts, turns always on the standpoint from which they are viewed. An infidel hypothesis necessarily sees all persons and things in the light of its own evil and false eye. Both Mosheim and Gieseler in this way are very little better than Gibbon. To accept their disposition and combination of facts, is of necessity to give up secretly the whole idea, that the glorious things spoken of Zion in the beginning ever had any truth. But the common Puritan scheme goes farther still in this infidel direction. It outrages all moral verisimilitude, and joins together such contraries as by no possibility *can* cohere in the same real and firm belief. What sane mind can bring its theory of the wholesale errors and corruptions of the early church, into any sort of harmony with the assured feeling, that the heavenly and supernatural conditions of its presence in the world were ever in any real sense what they are described as being, either in the New Testament or in the ancient creeds? There is not the least doubt, but that the theory in fact tends directly to destroy all such assurance, by the monstrous and violent incompatibility of its own terms. This does not imply indeed a formal giving up of the point in question, as an article of so called faith. That is the true logical end of the contradiction. But all men have not logic; and it is quite possible to carry out the rationalism in another form. The article may be shorn of all historical connections, and thrust out from the real world altogether, so that the supernatural in the case shall have ·no actual being whatever in the bosom of the natural, but be only as a cloud or dream floating over it and beyond it in Gnostic or Nestorian style. In such shape it may be possible still, to believe in a holy catholic church, which was from the very start the mere foot-ball of Satan. But in the same way it is possible also to believe, that the moon is made of green cheese.

And so we come finally to the conclusion, towards which this discussion has been looking and reaching all along, that there never was in truth any such identity as Puritanism dreams between the early church and its own modern self. Its hypothesis of the vast and terrible revolution by which all is taken to have fallen so soon into another type, is unnatural, unhistorical, irreligious, and fairly incredible; and we have a right to infer accordingly that its primary premise is false. No such primeval state ever existed, as makes it necessary to consider the whole subsequent history of the church an apostacy only and a grand universal lie. Dr. Bacon and others are entirely mistaken, when they imagine any counterpart to New England Congregationalism in the days of Ignatius and Polycarp, or please themselves with the thought that the martyrs of Lyons and Vienne, in the second century, suffered for just such views of truth as are now preached in the pulpits of Connecticut and Massachusetts. An overwhelming presumption of the contrary lies before us in the later history of the church; and it needs only some proper freedom from prejudice, we will now add, to find this presumption abundantly confirmed by the historical data of this older period itself. True, these are comparatively sparse, and often a good deal indefinite and vague; and it is not impossible for an adroit criticism, on this account, to twist them to its own mind—especially if it have *carte blanche* to treat as interpolation or corruption every passage that may prove refractory in the process. But the violence of all such criticism appears plainly enough on its own front, and when it has made the most of its cause in this way, the proofs that stand in clear force against it are still amply sufficient for the purpose now affirmed. The force of the argument is sometimes enfeebled and obscured, by fixing attention too exclusively on single points and particular phrases and texts. But what the case requires, is a steady regard to the broad issue in question as a whole, and a fair estimate of the testimony or evidence concerned under the like universal view. It is not necessary to stickle for this or that point separately considered; nor is it worth while to waste either ink or breath, in settling the credit or fixing the sense of one clause here and another there, in the remains of Clemens Romanus, Ignatius, or Irenæus. The main question in controversy is of far wider scope and range than any such particular eddies raised in its bosom, and is capable of being brought to some general conclusion in a much more comprehensive and summary way. It regards not so much mere prelacy, or the use of a liturgy in this or that particular form, or the positive practice of infant baptism at a given time, or the mode in which the water was applied in this sacrament whether in the case of infants or adults, or the acknowledgment of transubstantiation and the sacrifice of the mass—it regards not so much any one or all of these and such like points separately taken, we say, as it does rather the whole idea and scheme of the church, in which all such points are comprehended, and from which they derive necessarily in the end their proper significance and import. The determination of these single points, we know, is of no small consequence, where it can be fairly reached, for the settlement also of this general and main question. But what we wish to say is, that in the case before us the main question is not thrown absolutely or conclusively on any particular issues of this sort, which it may be possible for a small criticism to envelope here and there in dust or smoke. The general spirit and form of early Christianity are capable of being understood from its few historical remains, especially when taken in connection with the tradition of following times, in such manner as fairly to overwhelm the nibbling of such mouse-like criticism at particular points, instead of being dependent upon it at all in any way for their own authority. The sense of the whole here is so clear and plain, that we have the best right to use it as a key or guide for the interpretation of the parts. Take for instance the Baptistic points of immersion and the exclusion of infants from the church; all turns finally on the light in which the sacrament of baptism itself was regarded, and so on the view taken of the supernatural constitution of Christianity; and it requires nothing more than the most general acquaintance with the first age of the church, and the writings that have come down to us from that time, to see and feel surely that the whole standpoint of Christianity then was completely different from that of the Baptists in the present day; so that no proof they may ever seem to have for their favorite hobbies can have any force at all to identify the one position with the other. Allowing the points of correspond-ence they claim to be real, to what can it amount still so long as it is plain, that the whole inward posture of the early church was in contradiction to the unmystical, unsacramental and un-churchly system, in which the Baptists now glory as pre emi-nently their own? The best and most sufficient defence against this system after all, is simply to be somewhat imbued with the general soul of the primitive church, as it looks forth upon us from the writings of Ignatius, Justin Martyr, Irenæus and Ter-tullian. With any such preparation, no one can be in danger of mistaking the modern fiction for the ancient truth. They belong to different worlds; and only to be at home in the one, is necessarily to feel the other in the same measure foreign and strange.

It is in this general way that we propose now, to try briefly the whole question here offered for our consideration. May the Puritan system as a whole, whether carried out in the Baptistic or in the Congregational or in the Presbyterian form, or allowed even to get as far as low-church Episcopalianism, be regarded as constitutionally one and the same with what Christianity was in the second century, and so by implication in the latter part also of the first? To settle this question, we need not go minutely into the Ignatian controversy, or any other of like accidental and mechanical character. Strike out as an interpolation every passage in Ignatius that goes directly for episcopacy, and for the argument now in hand but little is lost from the weight that truly and properly belongs to him as a witness. For a really thoughtful mind, this weight lies in no such texts nakedly tak-en, but in the reigning drift and complexion of the epistles as a whole. A very short writing in this way, such for instance as Pliny's celebrated letter to Trajan, where there is any power whatever to reproduce in the mind its historical surroundings, may convey by its total representation far more than any criti-cism can reach by mere verbal dissection. In this way it is very easy, we think, to bring the question here propounded to a full and conclusive settlement. Whatever Christianity may have been in the second century, and in the age immediately following that of the Apostles, it was not the system that is now known and honored as Puritanism, and least of all was it this system under its most approved and complete form as it reigns at the present time in New England.

I. In the first place, it rested throughout on a wholly different conception of the *Church*. With Puritanism, the church is acknowledged to be divine, as having been founded originally by Christ, and as standing still in some way under the superintendence of his Spirit. But this supernatural character, in the end, resolves itself very much into an unhistorical abstraction. The church is not conceived of as a real outward as well as inward constitution, having in such view of its own organism as a single whole, and keeping up a true identity with itself in space and time. It is of the nature rather of a school; the divinity of it falls back entirely upon its doctrine; or rather on the Bible which is taken to contain this doctrine, while men are left to draw it from this source, as they best can, in a perfectly human way. The only realization of the church after all in the world, thus, is in the form of an invisible communion, representing all those who are happy enough, under the guidance of the Holy Ghost, to find the truth. In the way of such inward spiritual experience, on the part of individuals, there is room to speak still of supernatural operations reaching over into the sphere of our present life; but to dream of any other supernaturalism in the church than this, is counted dangerous superstition. The idea of the church in this way is stripped of all mystery; it falls to the level of any other social or political institution; to believe in it is just as easy, as to believe in the Copernican system or the Parliament of Great Britain. It is neither catholic nor apostolical, except as Aristotle's philosophy may be called Aristotelian for all who are satisfied that he was the author of it. No divine obligation, no supernatural necessity, accordingly, is felt to go along with any actual organization bearing this name; a thousand organizations, wholly independent of one another, may have equal right to such distinction; and though all should fail even for centuries, it would be perfectly possible to restore the machinery again in full force, at any time, and with all its original powers, by the help simply of the Bible, the true *magna charta* of man's rights and privileges in this form. The divine character of the church is in no sense parallel, for Puritanism, with the divine character of the bible. It holds it for a sort of profanity to make any such account of its heavenly authority. Theoretically and practically, Puritanism treats the actual church as a simply human institution, the work of man's hands, and of divine force at the last only as civil government is of such force, or in the sense rather of the republican maxim, "The voice of the people is the voice of God." The powers of the organization, and so of course the offices by which they are to be executed, are held to come, not from above, but from below. It is made the glory of Christianity to be purely and intensely democratic. No *jure divino* constitution is to be allowed to the ministry, no superhuman force to its functions. The people are the fountain of right, and the basis of all order and law. Congregationalism completes itself in full Independency. All comes thus to the platform of common sense; all goes by popular judgment and popular vote.

Now it is not the truth or worth of this theory, in itself considered, that we are here required to discuss; we merely affirm, that it is in no sort of harmony with the idea of the church which prevailed in the second century. This might be confidently inferred indeed from the simple fact, acknowledged on all sides, that the ruling features of the later church system come fully into view in the next century, as the only scheme known or thought of throughout the Christian world. To imagine the Puritan ideal, as we have it now exemplified in New England, turning itself over, by complete somerset, in the course of one century, into the pattern of things presented for instance in Cyprian or the Apostolical Constitutions, without so much as a historical whisper to show when or how the prodigious revolution was brought to pass, is much like pretending to take Gulliver's travels or the stories of Sinbad the Sailor for sober truth. But besides this, the authorities of the second century itself are full against the whole fancy which is here in question. The drift and spirit of every writing that has come down to us from this time, look quite a different way. To read Ignatius, or Polycarp, or Justin Martyr, or Irenæus, or Tertullian, is to feel ourselves surrounded in the very act with a churchly element, a sense of the mystical and supernatural, which falls in easily enough with the later faith of the primitive church, but not at all with the keen clear air of modern Puritanism, as this sweeps either the heaths of Scotland or the bleak hills of New England. We need not stop here to settle the precise polity of the church at every point, in the age after the Apostles. It is enough to know, that all proceeded on a view of its supernatural rights and powers, which was exactly the reverse of what we have found to be the Puritan scheme. The church was considered a mystery, an object of faith, a supernatural fact in the world, not based at all on the will of men, but on the commission of Christ, the force of which it was held extended from the Apostles forward through all time. It was taken to rest on the ministry, which was regarded accordingly as having its origin and authority, not from the people, but from God. The idea of a democratic or simply popular constitution in the case finds no countenance in the New Testament; this proceeds throughout on the assumption rather that the powers both of doct██████ ████ern-ment, for the church, start from above and not ███ ███ ██; the apostolate is the root of all following ministerial offices and functions. And fully conformable with this, is the theory and the actual order of the church in the period of which we now speak. We may appeal here even to Clement of Rome in the latter part of the first century, who in a memorable passage, (*Ep. I. ad Corinth.* c. 42–44.) urges the duty of submission to church rulers, on the ground of a divine order in their office, parallel with that of the Levitical priesthood under the Old Testament, of which God had shown himself so jealous through the ministry of his servant Moses.[1] To quote Ignatius on the same general point, may be taken as perfectly superfluous. It is not merely where he bears direct witness for episcopacy, that his testimony is of weight; the force of it lies rather in the universal tone of his several epistles. It is sometimes said, that the episcopal passages have the air of being interpolations, thrust into the text from a later age. But any one may readily see the contrary, who will take the trouble of reading the text with his own eyes, for the purpose of getting out of it its own sense instead of putting into it a sense to suit himself. Their is nothing whatever in these passages at variance with the reigning tone of the epistles, but on the contrary they are in full keeping with this throughout.[2] There is hardly a sentence or a line indeed

---

[1] "The apostles had their office from Christ," he tells us, "Christ from God; they were sent by him as he was sent by God. Both in right order according to God's will." Clothed with full power after his resurrection, they went forth and founded churches on all sides, appointing tried men to preside over them as bishops and deacons, which was only fulfilling the sense of ancient prophecy, Is. lx: 17 This they did, in virtue of their own commission, to prevent contentions such as they knew were likely to arise; and not only did they appoint these first officers, but "they made arrangement also for the future, that when these should die other approved men should succeed to their place."

[2] This is well shown by that most profound and acute critic, Dr. *Richard Rothe*, in his work entitled "Die Anfänge der christlichen Kirche," where the authority of these epistles, and the whole subject of the constitution of the early church, are handled in a truly masterly style.

in Ignatius, that is not in spirit fully opposite to Puritanism, on the great question of the church. He has in his mind always the mystical order of the creed, according to which the fact of the incarnation underlies in a real way the fact of the church, as the carrying out of the same wonder for faith. In correspondence with the real union of divinity and humanity in Christ, his mystical body must have a real historical and visible being in the world as well as an invisible spiritual character, and this must of necessity carry along with it in such view the attributes of unity and catholicity, as the signature of its superhuman authority. Hence the stress laid on the hierarchy, as the bond, not from below but from above, of that glorious *sacramentum unitatis* on which was felt to hang the virtue and value of all grace in the church besides. Hence the holy martyr's horror of all schism. Obedience to the church is, in his view, obedience to Christ; to be out of communion with the bishop, in rupture with the one altar he guards and represents, is to have no part at the same time in the kingdom of God.[1] The unity must be somatic, as well as spiritual.[2] To fall away from this bond, is taken to be a falling away to the same extent from the lively sense of the mystery of the incarnation, a species of Gnosticism which turned the flesh of the Son of God into a mere phantom, and so robbed the Gospel of its heavenly power. For those who resolve Christ in this way into a phantom or abstraction, according to Ignatius, make themselves in the end to be without either substance or strength; all true christian strength comes from an apprehension of the whole mystery here in view as something historically and enduringly real. With this agrees again, as all know, the teaching of Irenæus in the latter part of the second century, as it has come down to us particularly in his celebrated work against heretics; and the same views substantially are presented to us also by Tertullian and Clement of Alexandria.

II. The contrary schemes of the church just noticed, involve with a sort of inward logical necessity different and contrary views also of the *ministry*, and of its relations to the body of the people. Puritanism makes the ministers of religion to be much like county or town officers, or sees in them at best only good religious counsellors and teachers, whom the people create

---

[1] Μη πλανασθε αδελφοι μου ει τις σχιζοντι ακουλουθει βασιλειαν Θεου ου κληρονομει, Ad Philad. c. 3.

[2] ινα ενωσις η σωματικη τε και πνευματικη, Ad Magnes. c. 1, 13.

for their own use and follow as far as to themselves may seem good. It spurns the whole idea of a divinely established hierarchy, drawing its rights and powers from heaven, and forming in its corporate character the bond of unity for the church, the ground of its perpetual stability, and the channel of all communications of grace to it from Him who is its glorified head. Every view of this sort runs counter to the democracy of the system, and does violence to its rationalism and common sense. It has no power constitutionally to believe in any really supernatural order reaching here below the time of the Apostles; and it must have accordingly the same guaranties for freedom precisely, which it is accustomed to ask and lean upon in the case of purely human and civil relations. Hence the vast account it makes of the popular element in all ecclesiastical interests and concerns, its zeal for the parity of the clergy, its deep seated hostility to the idea of the priesthood, as well as to all pontifical allusions or associations, in any connection with the work of the christian ministry.

But now how different from all such thinking, is the light in which the ministry is found to stand in the second century. We need not go into any minute examination of the ecclesiastical polity which then prevailed. The question is not primarily whether there were three orders of clergy, or two, or only one; whether the bishops of Ignatius were diocesan in the modern sense, or simply parochial; but this rather, What relation did the overseership of the church bear to the mass of its members? And this, we say confidently, was neither Congregational *nor* Presbyterian, in the established sense of these distinctions at the present time. Let any one look into the writers already named, especially Ignatius and Irenæus, so as to catch at all their general tone and spirit, and he will feel it to be no better than burlesque, when Dr. Bacon allows himself to transfer to the scene of Smyrna or Lyons, in the second century, the picture he himself gives us of what he takes to be the repristination of the primitive church in this latter city in our own day.[1] The imag-

---

[1] "The meeting which I attended was a meeting of the brotherhood for mutual conference and inquiry. It was held in a school-room, and very much resembled a Congregational church meeting in New England. There was, however, one obvious difference. Those brethren were not merely concerned with the working of a system defined and understood in all its details, and familiar to them from their childhood. With the New Testament in their hands, they were inquiring after principles and rules of church order; and the question which then chiefly occupied their attention, and seemed somewhat to divide their opinions, was whether the govern-

ination of any such ecclesiastical republicanism, is completely
foreign we may say from the whole spirit of this ancient period.
Only look at the way in which Irenæus speaks of the episcopate
and the apostolical succession, as the grand bulwark of truth
against all heresy and schism ; not once or twice merely, but
whenever the subject comes in his way ; showing the view to be
inseparably joined with the entire scheme of Christianity in his
mind. It is not to be disguised moreover, that the episcopate is
viewed by him as a general corporation, having its centre of
unity in the church of Rome. Against the novelty of heretics,
he appeals to the clear succession of the catholic sees generally
from the time of the Apostles ; but then sums all up, by singling
out the Roman church, founded by the most glorious apostles
Peter and Paul, and having a certain principality for the church
at large, as furnishing in its line of bishops a sure tradition of
the faith held by the universal body from the beginning.[2] Take
this system of church government as we may, it is the very reverse of all such independency and popularity as are made to be
the basis of ecclesiastical order in New England. Congregationalism lays no such stress on the episcopate or overseership of
the church, regarded as an organic corporation, bound together
always by a common centre, and having authority by unbroken
tradition from the Apostles. And just as little have we here the

---

ment of their church should be in part committed to a body of elders, or remain entire in the hands of the assembled brethren. As I listened to the dis-
cussions, I could not but admire the free and manly, yet fraternal spirit in
which it was conducted. And as I saw what a school for the development
of various intellectual gifts, as well as for the culture of Christian affection, that church had been under its simple democratic organization. I felt
quite sure that those brethren, with all their confidence in their teachers,
would not be easily persuaded to subvert a system to which they were already so greatly indebted, or to divest themselves of the right of freely
debating and voting on all their interests and duties as a church."——
" Rarely, have I enjoyed anything more than I enjoyed my visit to that missionary and apostolical church. Nor do I know where to look for a more
satisfactory representation of the ideal and primitive Christianity, than in
the city which was made illustrious so long ago by the labors of Irenæus,
and by the martyrdom of Pothinus and Blandina."—*Letter from Lyons.*

[2] " Sed quoniam valde longum est, in hoc tali volumine omnium ecclesia-
rum enumerare successiones : maximae et antiquissimae et omnibus cog-
nitae, a gloriosissimis duobus Apostolis Petro et Paulo Romae fundatae et
constitutae ecclesiae, eam quam habet ab Apostolis traditionem et annun-
tiatam hominibus fidem per successiones episcoporum pervenientem usque
ad nos indicantes, confundimus omnes eos, &c.—Ad hanc enim ecclesiam
propter potiorem principalitatem necesse est omnem convenire ecclesiam, &c."——
Adv. haeres. III. 3, §, 2.

type of modern Presbyterianism.   The bishops of Ignatius, Polycarp, and Irenæus, however small may have been their charges, were not simply Presbyterian pastors.   They have altogether a different look, and hold an entirely different relation to the people over whom they preside.   Their rule is not indeed lordly, but neither is it simply representative and democratic; it is patriarchal rather, but at the same time an actual episcopate or oversight, derived from the chief Shepherd, at once supreme and self-sacrificing, in the full spirit of 1 Pet. v: 1–4.   The order altogether is that of a hierarchy.   The pastors are at the same time priests; and pontifical ideas fall in with their ministry easily and naturally from every side.   The altar at which they serve is not merely a cold metaphor; and the sacrifice they offer upon it is mystical indeed, but nevertheless awfully and sublimely real.   In one word, the system contains in element and germ at least the whole theory of the church that is more fully presented to us afterwards, in the writings of Cyprian and Augustine.   There is no contradiction between the two schemes. The first flows over without any sort of violence or effort into the last; and becomes hard to understand, only when inquisitorial theorists put it to the rack, for the purpose of forcing from it a sense and voice which are not its own.[1]

III.   This leads us naturally to the consideration of a third general and broadly palpable difference between Puritanism and the early church, that namely which appears in the view they take of the *holy sacraments.*   The modern system owns no real mystery either in baptism or the Lord's supper.   It takes them indeed for divine institutions; but the sense of them is altogether natural only and human.   They carry in them no objective force, have no power whatever to present what they represent; they are taken to be signs only or pictures of a grace, which exists not in the sacraments themselves, but out of them and beyond them under a wholly different form.   Any virtue they have is from the activity of the worshipper's mind, moved it may be by the Spirit of God to make good use of the outward and natural help to devotional thoughts and affections, which is thus placed within its reach.   All beyond this is held to be superstition; and the sacramental system in particular of the Catholic church, as well as the whole doctrine of the real pres-

---

[1] This is shown, with what appears to us to be the most triumphant evidence, by Richard Rothe, in the great work to which we have before referred, *Die Anfänge d. chr. Kirche,* particularly in the third book.

ence in its Protestant form also, is denounced and discarded as a purely diabolical figment, brought in under the Papacy in complete contradiction to the original sense of the Gospel, and without the least ground or reason in the practice of the church as it stood in the beginning.

It might seem plain to any child, that if any such low view had prevailed in the second century, it must have required a miracle to place the entire church, in its doctrine of the sacraments, where we find it to be in the fourth century, or to lead it over even in half a dozen centuries to so astounding a tenet as that of transubstantiation, with like universal and at the same time profoundly noiseless and peaceful revolution. But the second century can easily enough speak here for itself. And so clear and full in truth is its voice on the whole subject, that we venture to say no one can listen to it attentively, having any sort of confidence at the same time in the true apostolicity of its faith, and not be inspired with a feeling of downright horror, in view of the deep yawning gulph by which this is found to be sundered from what we have just now seen to be the modern system. Right or wrong, Puritanism is in its sacramental doctrine a grand apostacy, not only from what Protestantism was designed to be in the beginning, but also from the faith of the early church as it stood in the days of Pothinus and Irenæus. The martyrs of Lyons must have drawn back aghast from the view of baptism and the holy eucharist now commonly prevalent in New England ; while their venerable bishops, no doubt, would have placed it in one category with the numerous heresies of the time, that went directly to overthrow the real appearance of Christ in the flesh.

Passing over baptism, let us fix our attention on the sacrament of the blessed eucharist. Nothing can be clearer at first glance, than that the fathers of this period make vastly more of the institution than is at all answerable to the natural and simple light in which it is regarded by Puritanism. They lay great stress on its doctrinal significance, as being in some vital way related to the mystery of the incarnation, and conditioning the whole faith and life of the church ; and they seldom refer to it, without bringing into view the idea of its mystical supernatural import. Ignatius takes the real presence of the eucharist to be organically related to the truth and realness of the Saviour's humanity, and upbraids the docetic Gnostics, (who acknowledged thus also the force of the connection,) with abstaining from the institution, because they would not believe that Christ had ever assumed anything more than the show of a human body.

" They refrain from the service," he writes, " on account of their not confessing *that the eucharist is the flesh of our Saviour Jesus Christ,* which suffered for our sins and which the Father in his goodness raised from the dead. Contradicting the gift of God they die in their contention; but it would be their interest to love, so that they too might rise again." [1] In another place, (ad Ephes. c. 20.) Ignatius calls the eucharist the " medicine of immortality" (φαρμακον ἀθανασιας) and the " antidote of death" (ἀντιδοτον τοῦ μη ἀποθανειν); phrases that are sufficiently explained by the last clause of the foregoing quotation, where the risen flesh of the Saviour is made to be the power that is to reanimate also our mortal bodies. But if there were any doubt as to the doctrine of Ignatius here, or as to its agreement with the reigning faith of the church at the time, it must vanish certainly before the ample and plain testimony of Irenæus.

With this father again, the doctrine of the eucharist is made to be of extraordinary practical and theoretical account. It is not a circumstance merely in the general system of faith, but appears as a truly living and divinely efficacious link, between the mystery of the incarnation on one side and the coming resurrection of our bodies on another; showing plainly that these connections as sugested by Ignatius, were not fanciful or casual, but rooted in the reigning belief of the church. The Gnostics generally held the material world to be intrinsically evil, and so not capable of coming into any real union with the new creation by Christ. They would not allow accordingly that the Saviour took a real human body; and they could not admit of course then the resurrection of the body, in the case of his people. It was a principle with them, that the body as such constitutionally excluded the idea of immortality. Against these errors Irenæus affirms the goodness of the natural creation, the truth of Christ's incarnation, and the commensurateness of his redemption with the whole nature of man, as being able to save the body in the way of future resurrection no less than the soul. One grand source of argument is found in the mystery of the holy supper, which it is taken for granted that these heretics, in common with the church, acknowledged to be a bond of communication with Christ's substantial flesh and blood. However disposed they might be by their spiritualistic system to take these

---

[1] Εὐχαριστιας και προσε χης ἀπεχονται δια το μη ὁμολογειν, την εὐχαριστιαν σαρκα εἰναι τοῦ σωτηρος ἡμων Ἰησοῦ Χριστοῦ, την ὑπερ ἁμαρτιων ἡμων παθοῦσαν, ἡν τη χρηστοτητι ὁ πατηρ ἡγειρεν. Οἱ ἀντιλεγοντες τη δωρεα τοῦ Θεοῦ συζητοῦν:ες ἀποθνησκουσι· συνεφερε δε αὐτοις ἀγαπαν, ἱνα και ἀναστωσιν.—Ad Smyrn. c. 7.

terms in an improper and merely figurative sense, it seems that
they were still compelled to yield here to the pressure of the
catholic faith, and to admit thus an actual presence of the Saviour's
glorified body, whatever that might be, in this sublime mystery ;
and no evidence could well be stronger than this, for the universal and vital authority of this faith in the church itself at the
time.   To deny the possibility of the resurrection, according to
Irenaeus, involves this consequence : " That neither the cup of
the eucharist is the communication of his blood, nor the bread
which we break the communication of his body ; for it is not
blood, unless it be from his veins and his flesh, and the rest of
that human substance, by which he became truly the Word of
God."   Again : " Since we are members of him, and live from
the natural creation, which he furnishes to us for this end, causing his sun to rise and sending rain according to his own pleasure ; he has proclaimed the cup which is of the natural creation to be his own blood, from which he moistens our blood, and
has established the bread which is of this creation to be his own
body from which he nourishes our bodies."   And still farther :
" When therefore the natural cup and bread, by receiving the
word of God at consecration, are made the eucharist of the blood
and body of Christ, by which the substance of our flesh is advanced and upheld, how can they deny that the flesh is capable
of the gift of God, which is eternal life, since it is nourished by
the blood and body of Christ and is his member ?   Even as the
blessed Apostle says in his Epistle to the Ephesians, *We are
members of his body, of his flesh and of his bones ;* not speaking of the spiritual and invisible man, (for spirit has neither
bones nor flesh,) but of that constitution which is truly human,
consisting of flesh and nerves and bones, which is nourished
from the cup that is his blood and from the bread that is his
body.   And as the slip of the vine laid in the ground brings
forth fruit in its time, and the grain of wheat falling into the
earth and undergoing decomposition rises manifoldly by God's
Spirit, through which all things are upheld ; which then by the
wisdom of God come to be for the use of man, and receiving
the word of consecration become the eucharist, which is the
body and blood of Christ : so also our bodies nourished by this,
and laid away in the earth and dissolved into it shall rise again
in their time, the Word of God bestowing the resurrection upon
them to the glory of God the Father." [1]   In another place, Iren-

---

[1] Adv. haeres. v. 2, §. 2, 3.

aeus calls upon the heretics either to give up the errors now noticed, or else to abstain from the eucharist, as some of the earlier
Docetae actually did in the time of Ignatius, according to what
we have seen before. "How can they say," he exclaims, "that
the flesh perishes and attains not to life, which is nourished by
the body and blood of the Lord? Let them change their view,
or refrain from offering these things. Our view, on the contrary, agrees with the eucharist, and the eucharist again confirms
our view. For we offer to him things that are his own, setting
forth congruously the communion and unity, and confessing the
resurrection of the flesh and spirit. For as the bread from the
earth, when it has received the invocation of God, is now no
longer bread, but the eucharist consisting of two things, an earthly and a celestial; so also our bodies receiving the eucharist are
no longer corruptible, having the hope of the resurrection to
everlasting life." [1]

So much for the real presence of the Saviour's glorified humanity in the holy supper. Can there be any doubt in the face
of these passages, whether such a mystery was held by the early church, or whether it was considered to be of necessary force
as a part of the faith originally delivered to the saints? We see
too, how the service was regarded as carrying in it the force of a
sacrifice or oblation, analogous with the offerings of the altar
under the Old Testament; an idea which Irenæus elsewhere
utters in full and distinct terms, applying to the case, in the spirit
of later centuries, the memorable passage, Mal. i: 10, 11, where
it is said: "From the rising of the sun even unto the going
down of the same, my name shall be great among the Gentiles;
and in every place incense shall be offered unto my name, and
a pure offering; for my name shall be great among the heathen,
saith the Lord of Hosts." But what student of antiquity needs
to be told, that the eucharist in this early period carried in it a
significance and solemnity, of which no rational account can be
given, except on the ground that such powers as those now
mentioned were supposed to go along with its celebration? [2]

We inquire not now into the truth of this old sacramental
doctrine; neither is it necessary to define in what mode precisely it understood the mystery of the real presence to take place.
It is enough to know, that the mystery itself was universally

[1] Adv. haeres. iv. 18. §. 5.

[2] See an interesting and clear representation of the testimony of Irenæus
on the whole subject in *Möhler's Patrologie*, pp. 377–391.

received, as of fundamental consequence in the christian system; and that the doctrine therefore stood in no sort of harmony with the common Puritan view of the present time.   The
martyrs of Lyons and Vienne died in full hope of the resurrection; but this hope was based on a species of realistic sacramen-
talism here, which we feel very sure would bring upon them
now through all New England the charge of gross superstition,
and leave no room for them whatever within the magic ring of
its "evangelical sects."

IV. A like wide contrast between the early system and the
modern comes into view, in the next place, when we look at
their different theories in regard to the *rule of faith*.

It is a primary maxim with Puritanism, that the Bible alone
is the rule and ground of all religion, of all that men are required to believe or do in the service of God.   In this sacred volume,
we are told, God has been pleased to place his word in full, by
special inspiration, as a supernatural directory for the use of the
world to the end of time; for the very purpose of providing a
sufficient authority for faith, that might be independent of all
human judgment and will.   If it be asked, how the Bible is to
be interpreted and made available as a rule of faith, the answer
is that every man must interpret it as he best can for his own use,
under the guidance of God's Spirit, and with such helps as he
may happen to have at his command.   In other words, the ultimate tribunal for the exposition of God's word is private judgment.   No other tribunal can be regarded as of any legitimate
authority or right.   All tradition especially, pretending in any
way to over-rule private judgment, is to be firmly rejected as
something inimical to the rights of reason and conscience.   What
men can see to be taught in the scriptures is to be of force for
them as revelation, and what they cannot see to be so taught
there is to be of no such force.   The great matter accordingly
is to place the bible in every man's hands, and to have him able
to read it, that he may then follow it in his own way.   The
idea seems to be, that the bible was published in the first place
as a sort of divine formulary or text book for the world to follow
in matters of religion, and that the church rested on no other
ground in the beginning for its practices or doctrines, appealing
to it and building upon it in a perfectly free and original way
after the fashion of our modern sects; in which view it is to be
counted still the foundation and pillar of the truth, so that the
dissemination of its printed text throughout the world, without
note or comment, is the one thing specially needful and specially to be relied upon for the full victory of Christianity, from sea
to sea and from the river to the ends of the earth.

This theory has many difficulties. To place a divine text at the mercy of private judgment, looks very much like making it a mere nose of wax. Men deal not thus with the authority of other laws and constitutions. All the world over the sense of written statutes is ruled more or less by the power of an unwritten living tradition, (such as the " common law" of England and this country,) which at the same time is applied to the case by some public tribunal, and *not* by every man at his own pleasure. So deeply seated indeed is this order in our very nature, that it is never surmounted even by those who in the case before us pretend to set it aside. Puritanism never in truth allows the bible *alone* to be the religion of Protestants. Every sect has its tradition, its system of opinions and habits, handed forward by education, just as much as the Catholic church itself, through which as a medium the written word is studied and understood at every point. In no other way could it exist as a historical body at all. The private judgment of a good Presbyterian is always carried, from infancy on to old age, in the bosom of a general Presbyterian stream of thought, that has been flowing in its own separate channel from the origin of this communion in the days of John Knox ; and the same thing precisely is true of the Methodists, as well as of all the other scores of sects that in as many variant ways follow the same infallible rule of faith and practice. It cannot well escape observation again, that the bible itself lends no sort of countenance to the hypothesis, which turns it thus in such abstract style into the sum total of all God's mind and will, mechanically laid down for man's use, like the directions for the building of the tabernacle in the book of Exodus. It never speaks of itself as being either a system of divinity or a confession of faith. It has no such form, but shows as clearly as possible an altogether different construction and design. Nay more, it is perfectly certain from the New Testament itself, that Christianity was *not* made to rest on any such foundation in the beginning, but on a living authority, which started in Christ and passed over from him to the ministry of the church. This is as plain as words could well make it, from Matth. xvi: 18, 19 ; Matth. xxviii: 18, 20 ; Eph. ii: 19, 22, and 1 Tim. iii: 15, 16. On the basis of the apostolical commission, backed by heavenly miraculous authority, and entering into no negotiation whatever with the world's private judgment, the early church was in fact planted and built throughout the Roman empire. The books of the New Testament came afterwards as part and parcel of the glorious revelation committed to her hands; and it was not till the fourth century, as we have before seen, that the arduous and responsible task of settling the canon was brought to a complete close, although the main parts of it were acknowledged and in general use probably before the middle of the second.

These are difficulties, we say, which from the Puritan stand-point it is by no means easy to meet. But we do not press them at present. What we wish to hold up to view is the clearly evident fact, that the church of the second century was not Puritan but Catholic, in its conception of the rule of faith, concurring here in its whole habit of thought with the order that actually prevailed, as just now stated, in the first planting of Christianity in the world. The sacred books are indeed referred to with high veneration in this age, as they are in all subsequent times of the Catholic church, but never under any such abstract and independent view, as they are made to carry in the private-judgment sect system of the present day. Of a bible, out of which every man was to fetch the doctrines and practices of religion as he best could with the bucket of his own common sense, these early Christians had not so much as the most remote imagination. They own the inspiration of the scriptures and appeal to them as the norm and measure of their faith; but it is only and always as they are taken to be comprehended in that general tradition of infallible truth, which had come down from the Apostles in a living way by the church. The bible was for them the word of God, not on the outside of the church, and as a book dropped from the skies for all sorts of men to use in their own way, but in the bosom of the church alone, and in organic union with that great system of revelation of which this was acknowledged to be the pillar and ground. Sundered from that organism, cut off from the living stream of catholic tradition, the holy oracles in the hands of heretics were considered as shorn of all their force. Such men as Irenæus and Tertullian had no idea of sitting down, and debating points of doctrine with the Gnostics out of the bible, in any way owning at all their right to appeal to it as an independent rule; just as little as it ever entered into their heads probably to put the people, " with the New Testament in their hands," on inquiring " into the principles and rules of church government," after the democratic fashion of the nineteenth century. They will not allow the heretics to put their cause on any ground of this sort; they cut them off by prescription, that is, by the clear title of the regular church to the succession or tradition of Christianity, as it had been handed down, under the broad seal of its original charter, from the time of the Apostles. Some notice has been taken before of the way, in which which Irenæus appeals to the known apostolical succession of the bishops in his time, and their collective voice in favor of the truth, bringing all to centre and culminate in Rome as the principal see. This constitution, and no other, is with him the organ of unity both in doctrine and government; all else is heresy and schism. " It is necessary to hearken to the presbyters in the church," he tells us (Adv. haer. iv. c. 20), who have the succession from the Apostles, and along with the succession of the episcopate have received the certain gift of truth according to the good pleasure of the Father." Again (iv. c. 33, §. 8.): " The true knowledge (γνῶσις) is the doctrine of the Apostles, and the ancient constitution (σύστημα) of the church in the whole world, and the character of the body of Christ according to the successions of the bishops, to whom they (the Apostles) have committed the church in every place." The paths of heresy are many and variable, but the doctrine of the church is one and unchanging all over the world ; " she preserves the traditionary faith, though spread throughout the earth, with the greatest care, as if she occupied but one house ; and believes it, as if she had but one soul and one heart ; and proclaims, teaches, hands it forward, with marvellous agreement, as if she had but one mouth. The languages used are indeed different, but the matter of the tradition is still one and the same" (i. 10. 2. comp. v. 20. §. 1.). Again (iii. 4. §. 1.): " If the Apostles had left us no writings, ought we not still to follow the rule of that tradition, which they handed over to those to whom they committed the churches? To this rule many nations of barbarians do hold in fact, which believe in Christ, and have his salvation inscribed by the Holy Ghost without ink or paper on their hearts, carefully following the tradition &c." Specially striking is the passage, L. iii. c. 24. §. 1., where this tradition is made to carry in it a divine element, rendering it infallible ; gathering itself up into the mystery of that faith " which we have received and hold from our church, and which the Spirit of God continually renovates, like a precious jewel in a good casket, imparting to it the quality of his own perennial youth." Such is the testimony of Irenæus. Tertullian is, if possible, still stronger in the same churchly strain. He will know nothing of any private argumentation, from the scriptures or any other source ; all must yield to the smashing weight of ecclesiastical tradition. Christianity is built, not on a book, but on a living system handed down from the day of Pentecost. Truth is fellowship with the churches derived by regular succession from the Apostles ; they have collectively but one doctrine ; and whatever disowns this order, is without farther examination to be rejected as false. His whole tract on the *Prescription of Heretics* rests on this view, and might be quoted here with effect. The heretics have no right to appeal to the scriptures. These belong only to the church. She may say to them: 'Who are you? Whence do you come? What business have you strangers with my property? By what right are you, Marcion, felling my trees? By what authority are you, Valentine, turning the course of my streams? Under what pretence are you, Apelles, removing my land-marks? The estate is mine; why do you other persons presume to work it and use it at your pleasure? The estate is mine; I have the ancient, prior possession of it; have the title deeds from the original owners. I am the heir of the Apostles; they made their will, with all proper solemnities, in my favor, while they disinherited and cast you off as strangers and enemies." Tertullian had no idea of making exegesis the mother of faith.[1]

Is it necessary to say, that the faith of the second century, as here portrayed, is something very different from the reigning evangelical scheme of the present day? No honest student of history, we think, can fail to see and confess, that the doctrine of Irenæus and Tertullian on the relation of the bible to the church is essentially one and the same with that which is clearly presented afterwards by Chrysostom and Augustine, and that in sound at least it is very much like the Catholic doctrine as opposed to Protestantism in modern times.

V. Take next the *order of doctrine*. Single truths have their proper value and force, not merely in themselves separately taken, but in the place they occupy as parts of the whole system to which they belong. Much depends then on the order in which they are held. The doctrinal scheme of the early church has come down to us in the Apostles' Creed. Into the question of the origin of this symbol, it is not necessary now to enter. Its universal prevalence in the fourth century is itself argument enough for a thinking mind, that it must have come down from time immemorial before in substantially the same form; but independently of this, it is abundantly plain from the writers of the second century, that the whole theology of that period was shaped in the mind of the church on this model at least, and on no other. But this at once conditions and determines its uni-

---

[1] See Rothe's work before quoted; also Möhler's Patrologie, pp. 344–357, 737–748.

versal character, setting it in close affinity with the later theology of the Catholic church, and placing it in broad contrariety to the Puritan scheme of doctrine as we now meet with it in New England. Puritanism, by its abstract spiritualistic character, has lost the power to a great extent of understanding both the old creed, and the catholic theology of which it was the foundation ; and with a certain feeling of superior maturity is disposed generally to put the whole away as somewhat childish and out of date. The objection is not so much to single points in themselves considered ; for most of these may be translated into some good modern sense ; but it holds rather against the order in which they are put together, the architecture of the creed, its reigning animus, its too much of one thing and its too little or nothing at all of another. The sound of it is uncomfortably mystical, sacramental and churchly. Puritanism knows very well in its inmost soul, that no *such* creed is the symbol exactly of that form of belief which it now parades as its own, and as being at the same time the only true and perfect sense of the bible. It would never have produced any creed of this sort. It sees all truth in a different order, and holds it in quite other proportions and relations. When it undertakes to give us a creed in fact, (as it is ready to do commonly at a moment's warning and to any order,) the product is something very different from the ancient symbol of the Apostles.[1]

---

[1] See an article entitled " Puritanism and the Creed," in the Mercersburg Review for November 1849, published at the same time also as a separate tract. It will be remembered, that the *Puritan Recorder*, of Boston, plainly acknowledged " that the Creed and Puritanism have not a kindred spirit," and that only by courtesy it found a place originally in Puritan formularies and catechisms. " Its life and spirit," it was said, " never entered into the life of the Puritan churches ; and consequently it now exists among us as some fossil relic of by-gone ages. And we look with a sort of pity upon those who are laboring to infuse life into it, and to set it up as a living ruler in the church. We are free to confess, that this Creed has forsaken the Puritans, and gone over to become the idol and strength of all branches of anti-puritanism. And there are good reasons ; for Puritanism builds on the Scriptures, and this Creed teaches, in several respects, anti-scriptural doctrines." It should have been said rather, that Puritanism has forsaken the Creed ; breaking away at the same time from the faith of the universal church as it stood in the second century, and while it accepts the bible from the hands of this same church, cooly turning round and saying to it: You never understood your own scriptures ; *we* know what they mean, and you and your creed may go to the tomb of the Capulets. We have never heard of any repudiation of this monstrous sentiment, on the part of the interest thus represented by the Puritan Recorder, and take it for granted therefore that it is nothing more than a true picture after all of what must be considered here a general falling away from the *regula fidei* of the primitive church.

There is a real difference, as regards the *tout ensemble* of Christian doctrine between the Patristic system and Protestantism in its original proper form. More than one has felt something of the experience given in the following striking passage from Thiersch. " It is a strange impression," he remarks in his work on the *Canon*, p. 280, " that the church fathers make on one who first enters on the study of them, under the full force of a merely Protestant consciousness. So fared it with the writer himself. Nurtured on the best that the old Protestant books of devotion contain, and trained theologically in the doctrines and interpretations of the orthodox period of Protestantism, he turned finally to the fathers. Well does he remember how strange it appeared to him in the beginning, to find here nothing of those truths, which formed the spring of his whole religious life, nothing of the way the sinner must tread to arrive at peace and an assurance of the Divine favor, nothing of Christ's merit as the only ground of forgiveness, nothing of continual repentance and ever new recourse to the fountain of free grace, nothing of the high confidence of the justified believer. Instead of this, he found that all weight was laid on the incarnation of the Divine Logos, on the right knowledge of the great object of worship, on the objective mystery of the Trinity and of Christ's Person, on the connection between creation, redemption, and the future restoration of the creature along with the glorification also of man's body, on the freedom of man and on the reality of the operations of Divine grace in the sacraments. But he was enabled gradually to live himself into this old mode of thought, and without giving up what is true and inalienable in the Lutheran Protestant consciousness, to correct its onesidedness by a living appropriation of the theology of the fathers. He soon saw, that over against the errors of the present time, its pantheism and fatalism, its spiritualism and misapprehension of the significance of the corporeal, the church needs a decided taking up again of what is true in the Patristic scheme of thought, and an assimilation of her whole life to the ancient model—in spirit and idea first, as outward relations are not at once under human control. This old primitive church stood out to his view more and more in its full splendor, in its sublime beauty, of which only fragmentary lineaments are to be recognised in the churches, confessions and sects, of the present day."

Thiersch here finds Protestantism itself materially different from early Christianity; while he holds it however, in its legitimate character, capable of a living conjunction with the ancient faith, though carrying in itself a fearful tendency to fall away from it altogether; a tendency, which is now getting the mastery of it in truth in many places, and that needs to be counteracted by a return to former ideas. What he has his eye upon immediately is the rationalism surrounding him in Germany. But the tendency is not limited to that form of open unbelief. It lies in all unchurchly religion. It animates the whole sect system. It forms the proper soul of Puritanism. This is not original Protestantism, carrying in it the *possibility* merely of a full dissociation from the mind of the ancient church; but it is this possibility actually realized. It is a growth completely to the one side, which refuses now all organic agreement with the trunk of Christian doctrine as this stood in the beginning. The two schemes of thought are quite apart, and can never be made to fit together with any sort of symmetry or ease. Puritanism, by its very constitution, ignores and abjures the *old* sense of the Apostles' Creed.

VI. Look finally at the subject of *faith in miracles*. It is well known, that the early church not only believed firmly in the miracles of Christ and his Apostles, as well as in those of the Old Testament, but had a most firm persuasion also that the same power was still actively displayed in her own bosom, and that it lay in her commission in truth to look for its revelation, as occasion might require, " always to the end of the world." It is generally admitted even among Protestants not openly rationalistic, (though some feel it necessary with the celebrated Dr. Conyers Middleton to take different ground through fear of Popery,) that many supernatural signs and wonders were wrought in the service of Christianity during the first three ages. But what we have to do with just now is not so much the actual truth of these miracles, as the state of mind on the part of the church itself, by which they were considered possible, and which led to their being readily received on all sides as nothing more than the natural and proper fruit of the new religion. The apologists appeal to them boldly as notorious facts. Both Irenæus and Tertullian challenge the heretics to prove their authority by miracles, as the church did hers in every direction; and the proofs mentioned are such as giving sight to the blind and hearing to the deaf, casting out devils, healing sicknesses, and even raising the dead to life. To question the fact of miracles in the church, would have been in this period equivalent to downright infidelity. It lay in the whole sense the church then had of the realness and nearness of the supernatural world, in her felt apprehension of the living communion in which she stood with it through Christ, that such demonstrations of its presence should be regarded as most perfectly possible, and in some sort as a matter of course. Her idea of *faith* was such, as of itself involved this from the very start.

But who needs to be told, how different from all this the tone of thought is that now pervades the universal empire of Puritanism? The difference is not in the mere want of miracles; though that is something too for a thoughtful mind; it appears rather, under a more alarming and affecting view, in the want of power to exercise faith in anything of the sort. Puritanism pretends indeed to great faith in the invisible and supernatural; just as the Gnostics did also in ancient times. But its faith, like theirs, is in the language of Ignatius wonderfully asomatic and unreal. The action of the supernatural is remanded by it to the world of mere thought. God works miracles now in the souls of his people; and away back in the shadow land of the past, he wrought them by special dispensation also under a more outward form. But the age of such proper wonders is long since past. It is unsafe to speak of them after the third century, and not very wise to lay much stress on them even in the second. All pretensions to anything of the sort may be set down at once, and without any examination, as purely " lying wonders." Such we all know to be the reigning habit of thought here, with this popular system. Dr. Middleton's theory suits it to a tittle, and is drawn as it were from its very soul. Puritanism has no faith in miracles answerable at all to what prevailed in the early church, no power we may say to believe them in the same way. Its inward relation to the world from which miracles come, is by no means the same. The difference is not in the judgment exercised in regard to this particular miracle or that, but in the total frame of the mind with regard to the universal subject. This is not faith, but absolute scepticism, just as complete as anything we meet with in Gibbon, Voltaire, or Hume.[1]

The martyrs of Lyons knew nothing of such scepticism. It required another sense of the " powers of the world to come,"

---

[1] Both the N. Y. Observer and the N. Y. Churchman, representing but too faithfully we fear the spirit of their respective communions, noticed not long since with pure derision a sermon by Dr. Forbes, the late convert to Romanism, in defence of the idea that Christ has continued to fulfil his promise of miracles in the later ages of the church. The misery of all this is, not that this or that wonder of popular belief in the Catholic church may be shown to be false and ridiculous, but that the basis on which alone any such popular beliefs are made possible, the sense namely of the supernatural order of Christianity as a real and ever present fountain of the miraculous in the church, is rationalistically undermined and destroyed.

to carry so many simple and plain persons, with such triumphant courage, through the scenes that are described in the account of their martyrdom. They had no difficulty in admitting the reality of signs and wonders in the church. Nay, these had place in connexion with their own sufferings, and are reported by Irenæus, (the supposed writer of the account,) as carrying in them nothing incredible whatever. Blandina, a weak slave, was regarded as being upheld, quite beyond the common course of nature, in the terrible torments through which she was made to pass, from the break of day till night. The deacon Sanctus was tortured with hot plates of brass and in other ways, till his body became so covered with wounds and bruises that the very figure of it was lost; a few days after which he was brought out again, when it was supposed that the inflammation of his sores would cause him, under the repetition of the same cruelties, either to yield at once or expire. But " to the amazement of all, his body under the latter torments recovered its former strength and shape, and the exact use of all his limbs was restored; so that by this miracle of the grace of Jesus Christ, what was designed as an additional pain, proved an absolute and effectual cure." The martyrs appeared to move in a perfect nimbus of supernatural grace; even "their bodies sent forth such an agreeable and pleasant savor, as gave occasion to think that they used perfumes."[1] The wild beasts of the amphitheatre, to which she was exposed, could not be provoked to touch Blandina. One of the martyrs " had a revelation" in regard to another, which this last made it his business dutifully to follow. What remained of the bodies, after the terrible tragedy, was burned to ashes, and thrown into the waters of the Rhone; but it was believed, that a part of these ashes was afterwards miraculously recovered, and the relics were deposited under the altar of the church which anciently bore the name of the Apostles of Lyons.

We say nothing of the credibility of these statements, nothing of the opinion we should have of what they pretend to describe. We hold them up simply as a picture of the mind that was in the church in the days of Pothinus and Irenæus; and in view

---

[1] It is related in the acts of the martyrdom of St. Polycarp, written by the church of Smyrna, that when fire was set to the pile prepared to burn him the " flames forming themselves into an arch, like the sails of a ship swelled with the wind, gently encircled the body of the martyr, which stood in the middle, resembling not roasted flesh, but purified gold or silver, appearing bright through the flames; and his body *sending forth such a fragrancy,* that we seemed to smell *precious spices.*"

of it we have no hesitation in saying, that Dr. Bacon is altogether mistaken, when he finds its *facsimile,* either in Mr. Fisch's evangelical congregation of the present Lyons, or under the keen sharp features of Puritanism in any part of New England.

It would be easy to extend this contrast to other points. Veneration for the *relics* of deceased saints comes into view, as far back as our eye can reach. The bones of Ignatius, who was martyred at Rome under Trajan in the beginning of the second century, were carefully gathered up after his death, we are told, and carried back to Antioch his episcopal see. According to Chrysostom, they were borne in triumph on the shoulders of all the cities through Asia Minor. In Antioch they were placed finally in a church distinguished by his name, which St. Chrysostom encourages people in his day to visit, as having been to many the means of undoubted help both spiritually and corporally. In the case of Polycarp, the church of Smyrna writes that the malice of the devil was exerted to prevent his relics being carried off by the Christians; "for many desired to do it, to show their respect to his body." At the suggestion of the Jews, the proconsul was advised not to give the body into their hands, lest they should pass from the worship of the crucified one to the worship of Polycarp; "not knowing," say the acts, "that we can never forsake Christ, nor adore any other, though we love the martyrs, as his disciples and imitators, for the great love they bore their king and master." The corpse accordingly was reduced to ashes. "We afterwards took up the bones," the church adds, "more precious than the richest jewels or gold, and deposited them decently in a place, at which may God grant us to assemble with joy, to celebrate the birthday of the martyr." How different all this is from the spirit of modern Puritanism, even a child may see and feel. But the veneration for relics is itself only the proof and sign of a great deal more, embraced in the article of the "communion of saints" as it was held in the early church, every vestige of which has disappeared from the thinking of this later system. It is equally evident again, that the church of the second century attributed a peculiar merit to the state of celibacy and virginity, embraced for the glory of God and in the service of religion, which falls in fully with the tone of thought we find afterwards established in the Roman Catholic communion, but is as much at war as can well be imagined with the entire genius of Puritanism in every form and shape. It is not necessary, however, to push the comparison any farther, in the consideration of these or of other kindred points. Our general purpose is abundantly answered, our cause more than made out, by the topics of proof and illustration already presented.

The Puritan hypothesis, we now repeat, is false. There never was any such period of unchurchly evangelicalism as it assumes, in the history of early Christianity. Its whole dream of a golden age, answerable to its own taste and fashion, after the time of the New Testament and back of what it takes to be the grand apostacy that comes into view in the third century, is as perfectly baseless as any vision could well be. It rests upon mere air. It has not a syllable of true historical evidence in its favor; while the universal drift of proof is directly against it. Those then who will have it that New England Puritanism is the true image of what Christianity was at the start, and that the church tendency as it appears in universal force afterwards was from the start a corruption only, must take still higher ground than even this dizzy imagination; they must make up their mind, with the heroic Baptists, to look upon the history of the church as a grand falling away from its original design and type, as soon as it passed out of the hands of the Apostles, and long before the last of these in fact had gone to his rest. To this the theory comes in the end; and with the great body of those who hold it, this probably is the sense that always lurks in it at the bottom. But we need have no hesitation surely in saying, that every view of *this* sort is fatal to the credibility of the Gospel. It is only Gnosticism in disguise.

Our faith in the realness of Christianity will not allow us to bear the thought, that it fell from the very outset into the gulph-stream of a total apostacy, which carried the universal church, without resistance or knowledge, right onward always to the shipwreck of a thousand years—while Christ was showing himself by infallible signs both present and awake in the vessel, and miracles of faith and zeal prevailed on every side. It will not do; the whole supposition is monstrous. Puritanism is mistaken. It is a thousand times safer to interpret the meaning of Christianity from its own actual history in the beginning, than it is to sit at the feet now of any such modern authority, spinning the sense of it from the clouds. As to the likelihood of apostacy and wholesale error, in the main difference between the two forms of teaching, we believe the chances to be immeasurably in favor of antiquity and against the modern authority. It is far easier to believe Puritanism an apostacy, in its rejection of the *mystery* of the church and its sacraments, than it is to brand the universal faith of the second and third centuries with any such character, for the acknowledgment of this mystery as

something quite above the range of reason and common sense.
We choose to go here with the early church. We do not believe that it fell into apostacy, as a whole, from the very outset
of its course; that it mistook fundamentally the sense and meaning of the faith delivered to it by the Apostles; that it was almost immediately overpowered by a new and foreign idea, a
" mystery of iniquity" that turned it finally into the synagogue
of Satan. We detest and abhor any imagination of this sort;
and pray God that our children may be kept from every such
miserable tradition, as a true snare of the Devil that looks directly to rationalism and infidelity. There were faults and corruptions no doubt in the history of the church; but there was no
such falling away from its own proper and primitive idea, as
Puritanism finds it necessary constantly to assert. The reigning course of Christianity was right, and in full conformity with
the will of Him who so visibly presided over it " on the right
hand of the Majesty on high." The habit of doctrine and worship in which such men as Augustine, Ambrose, Chrysostom,
Cyprian stood, which animated the martyrs of Lyons and Vienne,
and glowed in the seraphic ardor of Polycarp and Ignatius,
must have been in the main, not diabolical, not superstitious,
but true to the genius of the Gospel as it was " first spoken by
the Lord and confirmed by them that heard him—God also
bearing them witness both with signs and wonders, and with di-
vers miracles, and gifts of the Holy Ghost, according to his own
will." This implies of course that even the Papacy itself, *towards* which at least the whole system was carried with intrinsic
necessity from the beginning, came in with reason and right,
and had a mission to fulfil in the service of Christianity that
could not have been fulfilled as well in any other way. No one
indeed can study the history of the church soberly, it seems to
us, without seeing this in the actual course of events. The
grand bulwark of the true religion, through the whole period of
the middle ages, was beyond all question the ecclesiastical organization that centered in the popes or bishops of Rome.
Without this, the church would have fallen to pieces, hundreds
of years before the Reformation. Only suppose the Papacy to
have been overwhelmed by Mohammedanism, or by the German emperors, or by the wild fury of the Albigenses and other
such Manichean sects, and what would there have been left of
the glorious mystery of Christianity as it first stood, either to reform or mend in the sixteenth century?

If the cause of Protestantism then is to be successfully maintained, it must be on some other ground than the common Puri-

tan assumption, that it is just what Christianity was in the beginning, and that all variations from it in antiquity are to be set to the account of a devilish apostacy, of which Popery was at last the consummation and end. Come what may of the Reformation, there are certain general maxims of faith here which we can never safely renounce. We must hold fast to the divine origin of the church, and to its divine continuity from the beginning down to the present time. We must see and admit, that Protestantism is no return simply to Primitive Christianity. Its connection with this is *through* the Roman Catholic church only, as the real continuation of the older system. In no other view can it be acknowledged, as the historical and legitimate succession of this ancient faith. This implies, however, that the life of Protestantism must be one with the life of the church as it stood previously. It is to be taken as different from this indeed in the rejection of many accidental corruptions, but not in distinctive substance and spirit. Its doctrines and habits must be felt to grow forth, with true inward vitality, from the faith that has been accredited as divine from the beginning, by the promise and miraculous providence of Christ. Puritanism then, by abjuring this historical and organic relationship to the ancient church, does what it can in truth to ruin the cause of genuine Protestantism. It brings in another Gospel. It throws us on the terrible dilemma: " Either Ancient Christianity was intrinsically false, or Protestantism is a bold imposture "; for it makes this last to be the pure negation and contradiction of the first. But when it comes to this, what sound mind can pause in its choice ? To create such a dilemma, we say then, is to fight against the Reformation. Puritanism, carrying upon its hard front these formidable horns, is no better than treason and death to Protestantism.

J. W. N.

THE

MERCERSBURG REVIEW.

JANUARY, 1852.

VOL. IV.----NO. I.

EARLY CHRISTIANITY.

Third Article.[1]

To make our discussion properly complete, it is still necessary to bring into view, more particularly than has yet been done, the practical bearings and issues of the whole subject.

---

[1] 1. *Ancient Christianity, and the Doctrines of the Oxford Tracts for the Times.* By the Author of "Spiritual Despotism." Fourth Edition. London, 1844. 2 vols. 8vo.

2. *Die Anfänge der Christlichen Kirche und ihrer Verfassung.* Ein geschichtlicher Versuch von RICHARD ROTHE, Professor der Theol. &c. Erster Band. Wittemberg, 1837.

3. *The Principle of Protestantism as related to the Present State of the Church.* By PHILIP SCHAFF, Ph. D. Chambersburg, 1845.

4. *What is Church History? A Vindication of the idea of Historical Development.* By PHILIP SCHAFF. Philadelphia, 1846.

5. *An Essay on the Development of Christian Doctrine.* By JOHN HENRY NEWMAN. American Edition, 1846.

6. *Vorlesungen über Katholicismus und Protestantismus.* Von HEINRICH W. J. THIERSCH, Doctor der Philosophie und Theologie, ordentl. Prof. d. Theol. an der Universität Marburg. Erlangen, 1848.

It is rather a sorry commentary on the reigning knowledge of ecclesiastical history among us, that the statements made in our first article with regard to the Christianity of the fourth and fifth centuries, should have given rise in certain quarters to so much scandal and offence. We have been represented as betraying the cause of Protestantism, and making huge strides towards Romanism, by the mere fact of venturing such statements themselves; as though they were of either novel or questionable character, or must necessarily and at once imply a full approval of the points which as a matter of simple history they are found to grant and allow. Our positions here are not theological, but purely historical. They relate to a question of outward fact, to be settled in such form by proper testimony. How the fact may suit this or that theory of divinity, is another question altogether; and nothing can well be more childish and absurd, than to think of making this second inquiry the rule and measure of the other. Is our theology then to regulate and decide the meaning of history? Must this last have no voice whatever, save as it can be forced to speak in agreement with the first? Shall facts be concealed or denied, because they fall not in with a given scheme of belief? Ridiculous pretension. It breathes the very spirit, that is ordinarily attributed to the inquisition. We have heard of the case of Galileo; forced to do penance, as the story goes, for teaching that the earth moves round the sun, while the honor of the reigning theology was supposed to require rather, that the sun should be taken to move round the earth. The case before us is precisely of the same tyrannical complexion. Nay it is in some respects worse; for the facts of the Copernican system are by no means so near to us, and so capable of full verification in their own order, as the facts of history with which we are here concerned. The first may always be questioned with some show at least of reason; whereas to question these last is like pretending to call white black or black white.

We refer to what we have said of the religious system of the days of Ambrose and Augustine. "You tell us," exclaims some evangelical inquisitor, doing his best to look calm and mild as well as more than commonly pious, "that Christianity as it stood in the fourth century, and in the first part of the fifth, was something very different from modern Protestantism, and that it bore in truth a very near resemblance in all material points to the later religion of the Roman church."—That, Sir, is what we have said; and such precisely is our opinion.—"You go so far as to add, that were the fathers who then lived to return to

the world in our time, they would find themselves more at home
in the Papal than in the Protestant communion."—We have
not the least doubt of it, Sir, supposing them to return as they
were when they died ; their first movement would be towards
Romanism, and the most we could hope would be that, after
some time taken to understand the present state of things, they
might be prepared perhaps to pass forward to Protestantism, as
after all better and higher ground.—" You hold that these fathers, whom the whole Protestant world is accustomed to venerate
and laud as the glory of the ancient church, knew nothing of
the view which makes the bible and private judgment the principle of Christianity and the only source and rule of faith, acknowledged the central dignity of the bishop of Rome, believed
in baptismal regeneration, the mystery of the real presence, purgatory and prayers for the dead, venerated relics, had full faith
in the continuation of miracles, and glorified celibacy, voluntary
poverty, and the monastic life, as at once honorable to religion
and eminently suited to promote the spiritual welfare of men."
—Certainly, Sir, we do hold all this, and are prepared to furnish
any amount of proof for it that may be reasonably required.—
" Then you endorse the worst abominations of the Roman system."—Softly, Sir Inquisitor, not quite so fast ; that is not the
question in any way under consideration.   The matter here to
be settled is not what we or you may think of these points.
The simple inquiry is, Are the positions true ?   Whatever may
be thought of them theologically, are they *historically* true ?
They are merely historical positions.   They affirm certain facts
of history as facts, and in no other way.   If the positions in this
view are wrong, if it can be shown that the facts were not as
they affirm, let us have proof of it, proper historical proof, and
we shall consider it a privilege to acknowledge and retract our
mistake.   But are *you* prepared, Inquisitorial Sir, for this reasonable task ?   Alas, no.   You have never read a page of one
of these early fathers; and you have never given any serious
attention to the history of the church in this period as it may be
studied from other sources; for if you had done so, it would not
be possible for you to assume the ridiculous attitude in which
you now stand.   You have never studied the subject; know
nothing about it; and yet here you are, in spite of all such
ignorance, pretending to dispose of it in the most dogmatical and
wholesale style, without the least regard whatever to actual facts.
The Romanizing spirit of the fourth and fifth centuries is too
clear, to admit of any sort of question or doubt.   You simply
expose your own want of everything like true scholarship, on

the field of church history, by imagining that there is any room for controversy in the case of so plain a fact.

Any respectable church historian may be appealed to as a witness in regard to this point. Gieseler, Neander, Mosheim, though not with the same spirit exactly, agree here in the same general representation, so far as the main fact is concerned. Quotations are unnecessary. It is agreed all round, that the prelatical and pontifical system was in full force in this period, that the sacraments were regarded as supernatural mysteries, that purgatory, prayers for the dead, and the worship of saints, were part and parcel of the reigning faith, that celibacy and monasticism were held in the highest honor, that an unbounded veneration for relics everywhere prevailed, and that miracles were received on all sides as events by no means uncommon or incredible in the church. Who indeed can be ignorant of this, who has only read Gibbon's History of the Decline and Fall of the Roman Empire? We may put what construction we please on the facts. We may explain them as we please. But it is perfectly idle to dispute them, or to pretend to set them aside. We might just as well quarrel with the constitution of nature. The fathers of the fourth and fifth centuries were not Puritan nor Protestant. They stood in the bosom of the Catholic system, the very same order of thought that completed itself afterwards in the Roman or Papal church. And their position there was not by accident merely or in a simply external way. It belonged to the very substance of their faith. Their christianity was constructed throughout from this standpoint alone. The strong supposition then of Dr. Newman is not a whit too strong for the actual character of the case. If Ambrose or Athanasius should now revisit the earth, with their old habit of mind, neither of them would be able to feel himself at home in any of our Protestant churches. They would fall in much more readily, for a time at least, with the doctrine and worship of the Catholics. And so on the other hand, neither of them would find the least toleration in any Protestant sect. Anglicans, Low Episcopalians, Presbyterians, Methodists, Congregationalists, Baptists, United Brethren, Quakers, and so on to the end of the chapter, would exclude them alike from their communion, or take them in at best as novices and babes requiring to be taught again the first principles of the doctrine of Christ. Let any one appear in New England, at the present time, in the spirit precisely and power of Athanasius, or Chrysostom, or Ambrose, or Augustine, and it is perfectly certain that he would find no countenance or favor in any quarter. Orthodoxy and Unitarianism would join hands in trying to put him down, as a pestilent fellow bent only on corrupting the faith of the churches. No evangelical sect would think of extending to him the right hand of fellowship. His name would be cast out as evil, he would be regarded as a Papist and an enemy of all true religion, in every direction. Such men as Jovinian and Vigilantius would find far more favor. These were the true Protestants, as Neander styles them, of the fourth century. But for this very reason they appeared wholly out of place in its bosom. The whole tone and temper of the time was against them. They were fairly overwhelmed as rationalistic heretics.[1]

We may charge all this, if we choose, to the ignorance and superstition of the age. We may be sorry or angry, as best suits our humor, that the facts of history should come before us in such disagreeable form. It is easy enough also to renounce the authority of the whole Christianity of this period, and to throw ourselves at once back upon the authority of the Bible. The fathers of the fourth and fifth centuries were not infallible; why should we then trouble ourselves with their fancies and ways, when we have the sure word of revelation itself to make us acquainted with all necessary truth? Such ground certainly we have a right to take, if we see proper. Only, in doing so, let us see and know clearly what we are about. Let us not pretend in this way to set aside the fact itself, from the force of which we thus try to make our escape. This is all we are concerned with at present; and this is something entirely independent of any construction that may be put upon it, or of any theological use to which it may be turned, in one direction or in another.

---

[1] "The most eminent of these worthy opposers of the reigning superstitions was *Jovinian*, an Italian monk, who, towards the conclusion of this century, taught first at Rome, and afterwards at Milan, that all those who kept the vows they made to Christ at their baptism, and lived according to those rules of piety and virtue laid down in the gospel, had an equal title to the rewards of futurity; and that, consequently, those who passed their days in unsociable celibacy, and severe mortifications and fastings, were in no respect more acceptable in the eye of God, than those who lived virtuously in the bonds of marriage, and nourished their bodies with moderation and temperance. These judicious opinions, which many began to adopt, were first condemned by the church of Rome, and afterwards by Ambrose, in a council held at Milan in the year 390. The emperor Honorius seconded the authoritative proceedings of the bishops by the violence of the secular arm, answered the judicious reasonings of Jovinian by the terror of coercive and penal laws, and banished this pretended heretic to the island *Boa*. Jovinian published his opinions in a book, against which Jerome, in the following century, wrote a most bitter and abusive treatise, which is still extant."—*Mosheim, Eccles. Hist. Cent. IV, Part II. Chapt. III.*

Make what we may of it, we owe it to truth here to acknowledge and confess the full existence of the fact itself. The
Christianity of the fourth and fifth centuries was more Roman
Catholic a great deal than Protestant. The best piety of this
period, as it meets us in such saints as Athanasius, Chrysostom
and Ambrose, is fairly steeped in what would be counted by the
common Puritanism of the present time rank heathenish superstition. Let us at all events have honesty enough to own here
what is the simple truth. Let us look the fact fairly and steadily
in the face, and then *as a fact* we may deal with it as seems
best.

We had no idea indeed, that what we have said with regard
to this point was likely to be disputed at all, or even to be found
particularly startling, in any section at least of Puritan Christianity. We thought it was a matter conceded and granted on
all hands, that not only the prelatical system, but all sorts of
Romanizing tendencies besides, were in full play as early as the
fourth century; and that no account was to be made of this period accordingly, as a source of testimony or evidence for any
other form of faith that might be supposed to have prevailed at
an earlier day. Puritanism, we thought, had settled it as a fixed
maxim, that the seeds of Popery were not only sown, but actively sprouting also and bearing most ugly fruit on all sides, in the
fourth and fifth centuries, the time of Ambrose and Augustine ;
and that *therefore* exactly no stress was to be laid on the voice
of any such fathers, wherever it seems to be pitched on the
Catholic key and to carry in it a plainly Catholic sound. Nothing is more familiar to us certainly than this line of argument.
What Independent is disturbed by the hierarchical ideas, that
are everywhere current in the age of Athanasius? What Baptist cares a fig for the usages of " time immemorial," that are
brought into view in the controversy between Pelagius and Augustine? What Presbyterian is put out of countenance in the
least, by any amount of proof urged against his favorite system,
from creeds or liturgies that date from the days of Arius or Nes-
torius? The ever ready answer to all such authority is, that it
is quite too late to be of any significance or force. The period
is given up as an age of wholesale departure from the truth.[1]

------

[1] " We can then admit, with Dr. N., that the Christianity of the fourth
century was something ' very different from modern Protestantism'—and
very different too from the truth and piety taught in the New Testament.
We can readily admit that those fathers, were they now to rise from the
dead with the same views they had when they fell asleep, would hardly
' find their home' in any of our Protestant churches. They would still have

The fathers of the fourth and fifth centuries, we are told, were all wofully infected with superstition and under the dominion of error. Patristic testimony in any case is not of much account, except as it falls in with what we may take to be the sense of the Bible ; but borrowed from the time now mentioned it is worth, on all points here in consideration, the next thing to nothing.

Take in exemplification a single passage from Dr. Miller's Letters on Episcopacy. " In examining the writings of the Fathers," he tells us, " I shall admit only the testimony of those

---

a hankering after the imaginary virtues of celibacy, and asceticism, and mystical interpretations, and baptism for the remission of original sin, and an insatiate passion for relics, and for the pretended miracles of monkery. We grant that the elements of Romanism were fermenting and growing rank in the ancient Church—the church of the fourth century ;—and we also admit in these elements, the development of the great Apostacy predicted by the Apostle.—If men cannot see evidences of the Apostacy, ' the falling away,' in the teaching and monkery and fanaticism of that age, it must be for the want of eyes to see, or power to discriminate between the graceful form of truth and its hideous caricatures ; or they must be the victims of a blinding credulity, which regards with reverential awe, every relic of antiquity."—*Christian Observer*, (*Philadelphia*,) *Nov.* 1851.

This is curious enough in its connexions. The occasion is Mr. Helffenstein's circular, calling on sister sects to take part with Dr. Berg and himself in their protest against the G. R. Synod, for not choosing to make our first article on *Early Christianity* cause for a process of Lynch law at our capital expense. Our amiable friend, Dr. Converse, so well known for his zeal against the assumptions of the Old School section of Presbyterianism, though too delicate to " intermeddle" with the ecclesiastical difficulties of another body, holds this a fair opportunity and call notwithstanding for stepping forward, in the character at once of both judge and jury, to regulate the affairs of the G. R. church. The body is not competent, it would seem, to act for itself. It has no right to its own historical character. It must be tried by a foreign standard, by Puritanism, by New School Presbyterianism, by "*American* Lutheranism," by all that is unsacramental and unchurchly in the land. And if it abide not *this* test, then all must be wrong. But what is it now that Mr. Helffenstein's circular finds to be so dreadful in the article on Early Christianity ? Simply this, that it makes the leading elements of Romanism to have been at work in the Nicene church, and denies the existence of any golden period answerable to modern Puritanism after the age of the N. Testament. And yet, what so horrifies Mr. H. here is fully granted, in the foregoing extract by the Philadelphia observer itself. With what then does the editor quarrel ? Had he read our article with his own eyes ? We presume not. And yet he undertakes to deal with it, and with the whole G. R. church besides, in this magisterial way, on the strength of the first wrong impression caught up from the *ex parte* statement of a foiled and passionate appellant, flying to his Editorial Bench for redress ! If this be either honorable or honest, there is need in truth that we should go to school again to learn " which be the first principles" of Christian Ethics.

who wrote within the *first two centuries.* Immediately after this period so many corruptions began to creep into the church ; so many of the most respectable Christian writers are known to have been heterodox in their opinions ; so much evidence appears, that even before the commencement of the third century, the Papacy began to exhibit its pretensions ; and such multiplied proofs of wide spreading degeneracy crowd into view, that the testimony of every subsequent writer is to be received with suspicion." This is the only proper Presbyterian view. Presbyterianism *must* take this ground, in order to have any solid bottom whatever. And still more must Congregationalism do so, under every form and shape. The universal voice of the fourth and fifth centuries looks wholly another way. The least that can be said of it is, that it goes in full for the prelatical and high church system at all points ; and Presbyterians and Independents are generally willing to allow that it goes for a great deal more than this system under its common Episcopalian form ; that it goes in fact for many of the leading features of Romanism, and that for Episcopalians therefore as an argument which proves too much it may be said properly to prove nothing.

In this light we find the subject handled indeed, even in the Episcopal church itself, by one of its parties in controversy with the other. The Puseyites, as they are called, and the High church party in general, have been disposed to build the authority of their system very much on the Nicene period of ecclesiastical antiquity ; taking it for granted, that while it exhibits, with unmistakeable clearness, all the traces of their theory as distinguished from every less churchly scheme, it may be regarded as standing equally clear from the abuses of Romanism, as these come into view along with the growth of the Papacy in later centuries. On the other side however it has been well and ably shown, that there is no room whatever for this last distinction in any such pretended form. In particular, the work entitled " Ancient Christianity," by Isaac Taylor, Esq., the author of " Spiritual Despotism" and other well known volumes, is wholly devoted to the object of proving that it is a most perfect mistake, to imagine anything like the counterpart of Anglican Protestantism as having existed in the fourth century, and that in truth what are usually considered the worst abuses of Romanism were already fully at work in this period ; nay, that in many respects the form under which they then appeared was decidedly worse altogether, than that which they carried subsequently in the middle ages. So far as the mere question of history goes, no one will pretend to question the competency of Mr. Taylor, as a truly learned and faithful witness. His testimony is given as the result of a very full and laborious personal examination of the writings of the early fathers themselves, and is supported throughout with a weight of authorities and examples that a man must be rash indeed to think of setting aside. The evidence is absolutely overwhelming, that the Nicene church was in all essential points of one mind and character with the Papal church of later times, and that where any difference is to be found, it was for the most part not in favor of the first, but against it rather, and in favor of this last. Let a few extracts serve here to show the ground taken and triumphantly maintained by this author, on the relation of these older and later schemes of Christianity, viewed thus as a question of simple historical fact and nothing more.

"Our ears have been so much and so long used to the sound (repeated by Protestant writers, one after another, and without any distinct reference to facts, and probably without any direct knowledge of them,) of the *progressive corruption* of Christianity, and the slow and steady advances of superstition and spiritual tyranny, that we are little prepared to admit a contrary statement, better sustained by evidence, as well as more significant in itself—namely, that, although councils, or the papal authority, from age to age, followed up, embodied and legalized certain opinions, usages, and practices, which had already been long prevalent in an undefined form, it very rarely pushed on far in advance of the feeling and custom of the times; but that, on the contrary, it rather followed in the wake of ancient superstitions, expressing in bulls, decretals, and canons (which were not seldom of a corrective kind) the inherited principles of the ecclesiastical body. Or to state the same general fact, as it is seen from another point of view, it will be found true that, if the sentiment and opinion of the church at different eras be regarded apart from the authorized expressions of the same, there will appear to have been far less of *progression* than we have been taught to suppose; and that, on the contrary, the notions and usages of a later, differ extremely little from those of an earlier age; or that, so far as they do differ, the advantage, in respect of morality and piety, is quite as often on the side of the later as of the earlier ages. If particular points be had in view, it may be affirmed that Popery is a practicable form, and a corrected expression, of the Christianity of the Nicene age."—*Ancient Christianity, Vol. I. p.* 63.

"A well-defined and authoritative system (involving elements of evil) is, I think, much to be preferred to an undefined system, involving the very same elements; and I firmly believe that it were, on the whole, better for a community to submit itself, without conditions, to the well-known Tridentine Popery, than to take up the Christianity of Ambrose, Basil, Gregory Nyssen, Chrysostom, Jerome, and Augustine. Personally, I would rather be a Christian after the fashion of Pascal and Arnold, than after that of Cyprian or Cyril; but how much rather after that of our own protestant worthies, who, although entangled by fond notions about the ancient church, were, in heart, and in the main bent of their lives, followers, not of the fathers, but of the apostles!"—*Vol. I. p.* 124, 125.

" In this sense then, and how much soever it may jar with notions that have been generally entertained, and whatever high offence the assertion may give to certain persons, I here distinctly repeat my affirmation that Romanism was a reform, (or if there be any other word of nearly the same meaning, but more agreeable to our ears,) a reform, or a correction of the Nicene church system. In thus reiterating this unacceptable assertion, I am prepared, if required to do so, to defend my ground by copious citations of historical and ecclesiastical evidence ; and particularly by an appeal to the writings of the early popes and to the acts of councils. As an inference from this advisedly-made assertion, I am prepared to say, that considered as a question affecting the morals of the people, it were better for us to return without reserve to the church of Rome, (horrid supposition as it is,) than to surrender ourselves to the system which Basil, Ambrose, Chrysostom, the Gregories, and Augustine bequeathed to the nations. Nicene church principles, as now attempted to be put in the room of the principles of the Reformation, if in some points *theologically* better, or less encumbered, than the Popery of the council of Trent, would as I verily believe more quickly and certainly deluge England with fanatical debauchery, than would *such* Romanism as the church of Rome would at this moment, gladly establish among us."—*Vol. II. p.* 69, 70.

" Popery then was a reform of the antecedent church system ; inasmuch as it created and employed a force, counteractive of the evils which that system, and which itself too, could not but generate. The great men of the fourth century believed, that the system contained within itself a counteractive power. A few years furnished lamentable evidence of the fallacy of such a belief. The popes snatched at the only alternative—the creating a power *exterior* to the system, and assuming to be independent of it, by virtue of the special authority vested in the successors of Peter. *This* scheme was practicable ; and Time has pronounced its eulogium. Terrible as is Popery, it is infinitely less terrible than its own naked substance, apart from its form. If at the present moment there are Popish nations in a moral condition almost as degraded as that into which Christendom at large had sunk in the fifth century, it is because the corrective energies of the papal hierarchy have long been dormant."—*Vol. II. p.* 71, 72.

" I have undertaken to show, by numerous and varied citations, not merely that the doctrine and practice of religious celibacy occupied a prominent place in the theological and ecclesiastical system of the Nicene church, a fact hardly needing to be proved, but that the institute was intimately and inseparably connected with, and that it powerfully affected, every other element of ancient Christianity, whether dogmatic, ethical, ritual, or hierarchical. If, then, such a connexion can be proved to have existed, we must either adopt its notions and usages in this essential particular, or must surrender very much of our veneration for ancient Christianity.

" The fact of the intimate connexion here affirmed is really not less obvious or easily established than that of the mere existence of the institute itself. Modern church writers may, indeed, have thrown the unpleasing subject into the back-ground, and so it may have attracted much less attention than its importance deserves; but we no sooner open the patristic folios than we find it confronting us, on almost every page; and if either the general averment were questioned, or the bearing of the celibate upon every part of ancient Christianity were denied, volumes might be filled with the proofs that attest the one as well as the other. Both these facts must be admitted by all unprejudiced inquirers who shall take the pains to look into the extant remains of Christian antiquity."—*Vol. I. p.* 131.

" Do not the fathers then worship God? do they not adore the Son of God? Assuredly: but when they muster all the forces of their eloquence, when they catch fire, and swell, as if inspired, whenever (I must be permitted to make the allusion, for it is really appropriate,) whenever they take their seat upon the tripod and begin to foam, the subject of the rhapsody is sure to be—' a blessed martyr,' it may be an apostle; or a recently departed ' doctor,' or, ' a virgin confessor;' or it is the relics of such a one, and the miraculous virtues of his sacred dust. If, in turning over these folios, the eye is any where caught by the frequency of interjections, such a page is quite as likely to be found to sparkle and flash with the commendations of the mother of God, or of her companion saints, as with the praises of the Son; and more often does the flood-tide of eloquence swell with the mysterious virtues of the sacraments than with the power and grace of the Saviour. The Saviour does indeed sit enthroned within the veil of the Christian temple; but what the Christian populace hear most about, is—the temple itself, and its embroideries, and its gildings, and its ministers, and its rites, and the saints that fill its niches. In a word, what was visible, and what was human, stood in front of what is invisible and divine; and when we find a system of blasphemous idolatry fully expanded in the middle ages, this system cannot, in any equity, be spoken of as any thing else than a following out of the adulatory rhapsodies of the great writers and preachers of the Nicene church."—*Vol. I. p.* 188.

" Let not the Protestant reader, who may lately have heard Ambrose named as one of the great three, to whom we are to look for our idea of finished Christianity, let him not be startled at this praying to a saint. Ambrose in the west, as well as Nazianzen, Nyssen, Chrysostom, in the east, and others, too many to name, had convinced himself that no prayers were so well expedited on high, as those which were presented by a saint and martyr already in the skies! In fact, a good choice as to the 'patrocinium,' was the main point in the business of prayer. These matters were, however, regulated by a certain propriety and conventional usage,—may we say, etiquette: it was not on every sort of occasion that the Virgin was to be troubled with the wants and wishes of mortals : each saint had, indeed, come to have his department ; and each was applied to in his particular line. In connexion with subjects such as this how can one be serious? unless indeed considerations are admitted that agitate the mind with emotions of indignation and disgust."—*Vol. I. p.* 212.

"It was, however, a consolation to Ambrose, in the loss of his brother, that he had lived to return to Milan, where the sacred dust would be at all times accessib'e, affording to him means of devotion of no ordinary value—'habeo sepulcrum,' says he, ' super quod jaceam, et *commendabiliorem* Deo futurum esse me credam, quod supra sancti corporis ossa requiescam.' Ambrose was truly a gainer by the death of his brother: for in place of his mere bodily presence, as a living coadjutor, he had the justifying merits of his bones, and the benefit of his intercession in heaven! Ungracious task indeed is it to adduce these instances of blasphemous superstition, as attaching to a name like that of Ambrose ; but what choice is left us when, as now, the Christian community, little suspecting what is implied in the advice, are enjoined to take their faith and practice from the divines of the Nicene age, and from Ambrose, Athanasius, and Basil, especially ?"—*Ib.*

" The florid orators, bishops and great divines of the fourth century, we find, one and all, throughout the east, throughout the west, throughout the African church, lauding and lifting to the skies whatever is formal in religion, whatever is external, accessory, ritual, ecclesiastical: it was upon *these* things that they spent their strength ; it was these that strung their energies, these that fired their souls. Virginity they put first and foremost ; then came maceration of the body, tears, psalm-singing, prostrations on the bare earth, humiliations, alms-giving, expiatory labours and sufferings, the kind offices of the saints in heaven, the wonder-working efficacy of the sacraments, the unutterable powers of the clergy : these were the rife and favoured themes of animated sermons, and of prolix treatises ; and such was the style, temper, spirit, and practice of the church, from the banks of the Tigris, to the shores of the Atlantic, and from the Scandinavian morasses, to the burning sands of the great desert; such, so far as our extant materials give us any information. And all this was what it should have been! and this is what now we should be tending toward!"—*Vol. I. p.* 265.

These are strong statements. But so far as historical facts are concerned, they are placed by our author beyond all contradiction. The Nicene Christianity bore no resemblance whatever to Protestantism. It carried in it all the principles of Romanism; so that this is to be considered in many respects an improvement on the older system, a regulation and correction of its abuses, and not by any means the bringing in of something always progressively worse. The model saint of the period is presented to us in the person of St. Antony, the "Patriarch of Monks." Asceticism is made to be the highest style of piety. The merit of celibacy, the glorification of virginity, veneration for relics, all sorts of miracles, the idea of purgatory, the worship of saints, prayers for the dead, submission to the authority of the church, and faith in the sacraments as truly supernatural mysteries, come everywhere into view as the universal staple of religious thought. All this is so clearly established by the historical monuments which have come down to us from this age, that he who runs may read—unless indeed he choose rather to shut his own eyes. And what are we to think then of those, who are ready to take offence with the declaration of so plain a truth, as though it involved a deadly stab at the whole cause of Protestantism, and were the next thing in fact to a full acknowledgment of the claims of Rome! Alas for our Protestantism, if it is to stand by the feeble arm of *such* defenders. The noise they make is found to be at last, the proclamation simply of their own shame.

It is simply ridiculous then to make any question about the reigning state of the church in the fourth and fifth centuries, as related to Romanism and Popery. Our representation has not been a whit too strong for the actual truth of the case, but may be considered as falling short of this altogether. It is the merest romance, when such a man as Bishop Wilson, or any other Evangelical Protestant of the present day, allows himself to dream that such men as Ambrose and Augustine were orthodox and pious after his own fashion, that the main elements of their religion were of a truly Protestant cast, and that they were in a great measure free from the ideas which afterwards took full possession of the church under what is called the Roman apostacy. Every imagination of this sort is a perfect illusion. These fathers, and along with them the entire church of their time, were in all material respects fully committed to the later Roman system; and at some points indeed stood farther off from Evangelical Protestantism than the full grown Popery of the eleventh and twelfth centuries. Let this truth then be known and kept in mind. Here at least is a fixed fact in church history, which only the most disgraceful ignorance can pretend to dispute. Let it be made familiar to our thoughts. Nicene Christianity, the system which the fourth century inherited from the third and handed forward to the fifth, was not Protestantism; much less Puritanism; bore no resemblance to this whatever; but in all essential principles and characteristics was nothing more nor less than Romanism itself. The great Athanasius, now in London or New York, would be found worshipping only at Catholic altars. Augustine would not be acknowledged by any evangelical sect. Chrysostom would feel the Puritanism of New England more inhospitable and dry than the Egyptian desert.

For his own immediate and main object then, the argument of Mr. Isaac Taylor, it seems to us, is unanswerably conclusive and overwhelming. Anglicanism builds its pretensions throughout on the position, that antiquity as far down as to the fifth century is in its favor, and at the same time against those features of Romanism which go beyond its measure; that these Roman features came in gradually at a later period, along with the rise of the Papacy, as innovations and corruptions; and that it is possible now to cast them all off as purely outward excrescences or incrustations, and so to find in the Nicene system a true picture of what the church was in the beginning, and the fair pattern at the same time of modern Episcopacy after the Oxford scheme. This whole position, it is perfectly certain, cannot stand. It is historically false. To trust it is only to lean upon a broken reed. There is no such distinction here as it asserts, between the older and later church systems. The Nicene Christianity was in its whole constitution of one order with Romanism. The worst corruptions, as they are usually called, of this later system, were all at work in the older system. They are not by any means the inventions and devices of the Papacy, as distinguished from the supposed Patriarchal or Episcopal order of more ancient times. The idea of a steadily growing apostacy and defection from such primitive state of the church, under the usurped dominion of Rome, is a purely arbitrary fiction, which the least true study of antiquity must soon scatter to the winds. In many things, the later order was a decided improvement on the order that went before. The Papacy was a wholesome reformatory and regulative power for the most part, in its relation to what are called Popish abuses and corruptions, rather than the proper fountain itself of these evils. They belonged to the inheritance it received from the Nicene age, the period in which modern Anglicanism now affects to glory as the model and pattern of an uncorrupted Christianity just like its own. All this, we say, Mr. Taylor makes perfectly clear. Puseyism, in his hands, is convicted of miserable pedantry. Its rule is too wide a great deal for its own pretensions. The line it pretends to draw between Nicene Episcopacy and *Popery* for the purpose of marking off a *jure divino* system of church principles to suit itself, is one that exists only in hypothesis and dream, and not at all in true history. Both historically and logically the premises of the fourth century complete themselves in the full Papal system, and under any form short of this are something, not better than such proper conclusion, but in all respects worse.

As far too as an argument may seem to hold in the relation of the church at different times to the reigning moral and social life in the midst of which it appears, the Nicene Christianity has nothing to plead in its own recommendation. It is a most gloomy picture in this view that Mr. Taylor gives us particularly of the fifth century, from Salvian and other writers. All sorts of immorality prevailed throughout the nominally Christian church. Society showed itself rotten to the core. The Goths and Vandals surpassed, in many cases, the morality of those who professed the true religion and participated in its sacraments. It is evident enough too from Chrysostom and others, that the state of things in the fourth century was much the same, the visible church being literally flooded with immorality and vice. Mr. Taylor brings this forward, as an exemplification of the natural and necessary operation of the Nicene theology. This is plainly a false use of the case. It had other causes sufficiently intelligible in the social state of the world at the time. But the fact is one, which on many accounts it is important to understand and hold in mind. Romanism in later times was not embosomed generally in moral associations so bad as those of this older period; and its worst social phases at the present time, as we are accustomed to think of them in connection with such countries as Spain or Italy or Austria, are far less revolting than the life of nominal Christendom in Europe generally, and throughout North Africa, in the days of Augustine. If modern Catholicism may be convicted of being a false religion on this ground, it is certain that the whole Christianity of the Nicene age is open to like condemnation, and with still greater effect, in precisely the same view.

So much for the Nicene age, according to the judgment of th's learned author. But he does not confine his view to this period. His knowledge of the laws of history could not permit him to doubt its organic union with the life of the period that went before; and his actual study of that earlier age has been of a kind to place this reasonable conclusion beyond all question. He confirms in full; accordingly, the general statement we have already made in relation to the Christianity also of the second and third centuries, as tried by the standard of modern Protestantism. The fourth century was a true continuation of the ecclesiastical forms and views of the third; and this again grew, by natural and legitimate birth, out of the bosom of the second. As far back as our historical notices reach, we find no trace this side of the New Testament of any church system at all answering to any Puritan scheme of the present time; no room or space however small in which to locate the hypothesis even of any such scheme; but very sufficient proof rather that the prevailing habit of thought looked all quite another way, and that in principle and tendency at least the infant church was carried from the very start towards the order of the third and fourth centuries, and through this, we may say, towards the medieval Catholicism in which that older system finally became complete. Listen for a moment again to the strong testimony of our English writer.

"At a time not more remote from the Apostolic age than we, of this generation, are from the times of Barrow, Tillotson, Taylor, Baxter, we find every element of the abuses of the twelfth century, and not the elements only, but some of those abuses in a ripened, nay, in a putrescent condition."—*Vol. I. p.* 70.

"I cannot however proceed to call in my next pair of witnesses, without adverting to a fact which forces itself upon every well informed and reflecting reader of the early Christian writers, I mean the much higher moral condition, and the more effective discipline of the Romish church in later times, than can with any truth be claimed for the ancient church, even during its era of suffering and depression. Our ears are stunned with the outcry against the 'corruptions of Popery.' I boldly say that Popery, foul as it is, and has ever been, in the mass, might yet fairly represent itself as a *reform upon early Christianity.* Do not accuse me of the wish to startle you with paradoxes. I will not swell my pages (which will have enough to bear) with quotations from modern books that are in the hands of most religious readers. In truth, volumes of unimpeachable evidence might be produced, establishing the fact, that

the *later* Romish church has had to boast eminent virtues, in connexion with her monastic institutions; and I think virtues, better
compacted, and more consistent than belonged to the earlier church."
——"Nothing can be more inequitable than to charge these horrors
upon Romanism. The church of Rome has done, in these instances, *the best it could,* to bring the cumbrous abomination bequeathed
to it by the saints and doctors and martyrs of the pristine age, into
a manageable condition. And if we are to hear much more of the
'corruptions of popery,' as opposed to 'primitive purity,' there
will be no alternative but freely to lay open the sewers of the early
church, and to allow them to disgorge their contents upon the
wholesome air."——"Before we reprobate popes, councils, and
Romanist saints, let us fairly see what sort of system it was which
the doctors and martyrs of the highest antiquity had delivered into
their care and custody. We Protestants are prompt enough to condemn the pontiffs, or St. Bernard; but let inquiry be made concerning the Christianity imbodied in the writings of those to whom
popes and doctors looked up, as their undoubted masters."—*Vol.
I. p.* 77–79.

"I have undertaken to adduce proof of the assertion, not only
that the doctrine of the merit of celibacy, and the consequent practices, are found in a mature state at an early age; but also—That,
at the earliest period at which we find this doctrine, and these practices, distinctly mentioned, they are referred to in such a manner
as to make it certain that they were, at that time, no novelties or
recent innovations. Now I am aware that a statement such as this,
if it shall appear to be borne out by evidence, will excite alarm in
some minds; the dissipation of erroneous impressions, is always a
critical and somewhat perilous operation; nevertheless dangers
much more to be feared, are incurred by a refusal to admit the full
and simple truth. Yet the alarm that may be felt in this instance,
at the first, may soon be removed; for although it were to appear
that certain capital errors of feeling, and practice, had seized the
church universal, at the very moment when the personal influence
of the apostles was withdrawn, yet such an admission will shake no
principle really important to our faith or comfort. In fact, too many
have been attaching their faith and comfort to a supposition, concerning pristine Christianity, which is totally illusory, and such as
can bear no examination—a supposition which must long ago have
been dispelled from all well informed minds, by the influence of
rational modes of dealing with historical materials, if it had not
been for the *conservative accident,* that the materials, which belong
to this particular department of history, have lain imbedded in re-
pulsive folios of Latin and Greek, to which very few, and those not
the most independent, or energetic in their habits of mind, have
had access. Certain utterly unfounded generalities, very delight-

ful had they possessed the recommendation of truth, have been a thousand times repeated, and seldom scrutinized.

" But the times of this ignorance are now passing away : and I think the zeal of the Oxford writers will have the effect, as an indirect means, of disabusing effectively, and for ever, the religious mind, in this country, and perhaps throughout Europe, of the inveterate illusions that have so long hung over the fields of Christian antiquity. It will be utterly impossible, much longer to make those things believed which we have been taught to consider as unquestionable; and the result must be, (how desirable a result) the compelling the Christian church, henceforward, to rest its faith and practice on the only solid foundation.

" The actual impression, moral and spiritual, made upon the Jewish and Pagan world by the preaching of the Apostles themselves, and of their personal colleagues, has, I fear, been overrated by the generality of Christians."——" And then, as to the period immediately following the death of the apostles, and of the men whom they personally appointed to govern the churches, we have too easily, and without any sufficient evidence, assumed the belief that a brightness and purity belonged to it, only a shade or two less than what we have attributed to the apostolic times. This belief, is, in fact, merely the correlative of the common Protestant notion concerning the progressive corruptions of Popery, it being a natural supposition that the higher we ascend toward the apostolic age, so much the more truth, simplicity, purity, must there have been in the church. Thus it is that we have allowed ourselves to theorize, when what we should have done, was simply to examine our documents.

" The opinion that has forced itself upon my own mind, is to this effect, that the period dating its commencement from the death of the last of the apostles, or apostolic men, was, altogether, as little deserving to be selected and proposed *as a pattern,* as any one of the first five of church history;—it had indeed its single points of excellence, and of a high order, but by no means shone in those consistent and exemplary qualities which should entitle it to the honour of being considered as a model to after ages. We need therefore neither feel surprise nor alarm, when we find, in particular instances, that the grossest errors of theory and practice, are to be traced to their origin in the first century. In such instances, for my own part, I can wonder at nothing but the infatuation of those who, fully informed as they must be of the actual facts, and benefited moreover by modern modes of thinking, can nevertheless so prostrate their understandings before the phantom—venerable antiquity, as to be inflamed with the desire of inducing the Christian world to imitate what really asks for apology and extenuation."—*Vol. I. p,* 102-104.

"In fact, I think, there are very few points of difference, distinguishing the Nicene church from either the earlier or the later church, within the compass of two hundred years on either side, which modern controvertists of any class would much care to insist upon, as of material consequence to their particular opinions."— *Vol. I. p.* 144.

These are serious admissions; and coming from such a source, they are entitled certainly to serious consideration. Let it be borne in mind, that we quote them simply in confirmation of a historical fact, without any regard now to the light in which this fact may be viewed, either by Mr. Taylor himself or by others, in its theological connections. It is of the highest importance, that we should make here a clear distinction, between what actually had place and what construction should be put upon it in a theory of church history. All we are concerned with at present, is the simple fact, (explain it or judge of it as we may,) that the Christianity of the second century was in no sense of one and the same order with modern Puritanism. How far precisely it may have anticipated the several features of the later Nicene system, is not entirely clear; but that it carried in it the elements and germs of this system, and looked towards it from the first with inward natural tendency, would seem to be beyond all doubt. The third century could not be what we find it to be in Cyprian and the Apostolical Constitutions, without some corresponding preparation at least in the age immediately preceding; and both the fact of such preparation, and its general nature, can be easily enough traced, as we have already shown, not merely to the time of Tertullian and Irenæus, but away back even to the days also of Polycarp and Ignatius. Let the *fact* then be fairly and honestly acknowledged; or else let it be disputed and set aside, if possible, on proper historical grounds. We present it as a simple point of history. We might wish it to be otherwise; but we feel that we have no power to make it otherwise, any more than we have to stop the earth from rolling round the sun, or to hush the alphabet of geology into dead silence. Facts themselves must not be treated as heresies, however we may feel disposed to treat the conclusions which are drawn from them.

But—we hear some one say—our appeal as to what constituted Early Christianity, in its oldest form, is to the New Testament itself. Let the writings of the Apostles themselves speak. The fathers sadly corrupted the truth, and mingled with it the dreams of pagan philosophy. Let those who choose rest in such false or doubtful authority; *we* go at once to the original founders of the church, and are content to learn what it was in the beginning from their lips.

All very good, we say in reply; all very good. But the point before us just now, is not the Christianity that may be taught in the New Testament, or that may have prevailed in the Apostolical age.[1] Our inquiry, as historical, has been directed throughout to the determination of what Christianity was *after* the age of the Apostles, first in the Nicene age, and then back of that again in the middle and first part of the second century. The facts regarded in these two cases, are by no means just the same; and our idea of the first must not be allowed to blind or distort our vision, as directed towards this last. *You* may not care indeed for any later state of the church; but that is no reason why such later state should not be allowed, as a fact of history at least, to appear in its own place and under its own form. If we do not need it for our faith, let us at all events not quarrel with it as a matter of simple knowledge.

The fact itself however, in whatever light we regard it theologically, is one of the greatest practical account, as necessarily conditioning our whole theory of church history, and more particularly the view we may take of the relation that holds between Catholicism and Protestantism.

We have from it first of all this general result, that Protestantism is not at all identical with early Christianity, in the form at least which it carries after the time of the Apostles. We do not of course urge this as an objection to Protestantism. There are, as we shall see presently, different ways of reconciling the fact with the supposition that it is after all the purest and best style of Christianity. If we except Newman, all the distinguished writers whose works are quoted at the beginning of the present article, have in view the vindication of the Protestant Reformation, over against the pretensions of the Roman church; and yet all of them agree with Newman himself, in believing the

---

[1] Those who take us to task for not ascending at once to the original records of Christianity, for the determination of what it was in its earliest and purest form, ought to remember that this whole discussion has had for its object from the beginning an altogether different inquiry—prompted in the first place by a particular position taken in the Rev. Dr. Bacon's Letter from Lyons; this namely, that the system of religion now prevalent in New England, is to be regarded as in all material points the same with that which existed at Lyons, and throughout the church generally, in the days of Pothinus and Irenæus.

modern form of religion to be in many respects very different
from that which prevailed either in the fourth century or in the
second.   Newman's own theory indeed makes the mere fact of
the disagreement to be of no conclusive force; since he himself
allows the idea of a real historical movement in the life of the
church, and must consider Protestantism therefore to be sufficiently justified on his own principles, if only it can be shown
to be a legitimate development out of the bosom of Christianity
as this stood before.

The general truth is clear.   Protestantism and Early Christianity are not the same.   Let it be observed, we speak not now
of early Christianity as it may be supposed to have been in the
age of the Apostles, but of its manifestation in the period following that age, as far back as our historical notices reach this
side of the New Testament.   We speak not of what it may
have been before the destruction of Jerusalem, or for a short
time afterwards, in the first century; but of what it is found to
have been, as a fact of history, in the second century as well as
in the third and fourth.   Let it be observed again also, that we
speak now not of inward essence but of outward form.   There
may be wide differences in the latter view, where a real sameness has place after all under the former view.   All we say is,
that Protestantism outwardly considered does not agree, in its
general constitution and form, with what we find Christianity to
have been after the time of the New Testament, as far back as
the middle of the second century as well as in the fourth and
third.   No one of our modern sects can show itself to be identical with this ancient church.   They may fall upon the still older
period of the New Testament, and claim to be in full agreement
with this; to all that we have nothing just now to say; but
they are not any of them what the church was in the days either
of Athanasius or of Cyprian or of Irenæus.   The church from
the fourth century back to the first part of the second was not
Congregationalism, nor Presbyterianism, nor Methodism, nor
Anglican Episcopalianism, nor any other phase of Protestantism
as it now stands.   It had its own changes great and serious during this period; but through them all it bears a certain sameness
of character peculiar to itself, with which none of these modern
systems is found to agree.   It carries in it from the beginning
elements and tendencies, from whatever source derived, that look
steadily towards Romanism, the later system in which all at last
actually reached their natural end.   Protestantism is not the repristination simply of any such ecclesiastical antiquity, (this side
of the New Testament,) whether under its later or its earlier

form. Its right to exist can never be put safely on any test of this sort.

So much we ought to see and openly confess. Nothing is gained, but much lost rather, by pretending to consider our modern position the same that was occupied by the primitive post-apostolical church. We cannot force facts; and it is always rash and impolitic to take ground directly or indirectly, that makes any such violence necessary for the support of our cause.

Granting then, as all who know anything of church history must, that Protestantism is not the restoration strictly of early (post-apostolical) Christianity, but that this ran naturally rather first into the Nicene system, and then through that again into the later Roman Catholic system, how is the cause of the Reformation to be vindicated as just and right? What view shall we take of this disagreement, (solemn historical fact as it is and not to be disguised nor ignored,) which shall not compromise the credit of Protestantism, but allow us to regard it still as worthy of our confidence and trust? Such is the great question, with the solution of which not a few of the best minds of our age are now seriously wrestling, as a problem of the deepest interest for the world. Only the superficial can fail to look upon it in this light.

Shall we cut the whole matter short, by casting off entirely the authority of the post-apostolical church from the second century down to the sixteenth and by throwing ourselves exclusively on the New Testament, as a sufficient warrant for the modern system, not only without antiquity, but against it also, to any extent that the case may require? This is the ground taken by Puritanism.[1] Its theory is, that Protestantism stands in no or-

---

[1] It is hardly necessary to say, that Puritanism, as we always take it, is by no means the same thing with Protestantism. It is of later appearance, a sort of *second growth* upon the original work of the Reformation; and its distinctive features in this view are by no means hard to understand. It is one side simply of the original whole of Protestantism, the Reformed tendency; not in polar union as this was at first with the Lutheran tendency, and so in organic connection with the proper historical life of the old Catholic church; but cut off from both these relations, and under such miserable unhistorical and unchurchly abstraction, now claiming pedantically to be the truth, the whole truth, and nothing but the truth, of all that Christianity has ever been in the world. It resolves all religion into private reason, by making this to be the only oracle of what is to be considered the divine sense of the Bible. It is always in this way rationalistic, even when it may seem to be most orthodox. It has no sense of a supernatural church, no faith in the holy sacraments, no sympathy with the reigning drift and tone of the ancient creed. It makes no account of Catholic Christianity.

ganic historical connection with the life of the Catholic church
as we find it before the Reformation; that the relation between
the two was one of simple contradiction; that the old church was
an entire apostacy from the Christianity of the New Testament;
and that this was reproduced in the sixteenth century, as an absolutely new creation, directly from its own original fountain and
source. The assumption is, that the church at an early period
fell away from its primitive purity, and came under the power
of a strange and dreadful apostacy, which completed itself finally in the Papacy and all the abominations usually charged upon
the church of Rome. The theory involves the idea of a steadily growing corruption, a continual progress from bad to worse.
The fourth century thus is taken to have been far more pure
than the twelfth. Still its general corruption also is not to be
denied. The third century too must have been strongly set in
the same false direction. But is there no part of the second,
that may be claimed as the pattern of evangelical piety in its
modern Protestant style? This is frequently taken for granted
in a quiet way, for the purpose of effect. But we have found
the assumption to be groundless. History knows nothing of any
such period, after the age of the Apostles, but on the contrary
shows the church, from the time it first comes into notice, to
have been plainly committed to the course of things that led onward directly to the Nicene system. So this Puritan theory, to
be fully true to itself, is willing in the end to give up *all* post-
apostolical antiquity. It is enough for it, to be certain that the
pattern of Protestantism is found in the New Testament. Grant
that a different order of religion is found to be at work immediately afterwards, in the ancient church, to what does the fact
amount in the face of this original rule, which the world can
now interpret for itself? So far as any such difference goes, we
have only to set it down from the first for an apostacy, the coming in of that grand catastrophe which afterwards turned the
church into a synagogue of hell. Protestantism sets the whole
process aside, overleaps the entire interval between the sixteenth

---

Anglicanism, in its eyes, is sheer foolery and falsehood. The sense of Lutheranism—*true* Lutheranism, and not the bastard spawn of Puritanism
itself usurping this venerable name—it has no power even to comprehend;
the whole system is a *terra incognita* to its brain. Even the old Calvinistic
or Reformed faith has passed quite beyond its horizon. And yet it now
claims to be the whole fact of Protestantism, and as such the whole truth
of Christianity! Preposterous assumption. Puritanism is indeed a great
fact too in its way; but it is not proper Protestantism. This is something
older, wider, greater, and as we believe also a great deal better.

century and the first, abjures antiquity clear back to the beginning, and claims to be a new and fresh copy simply of what Christianity was in the days of the Apostles.

This theory we have examined and found wanting. Its disposition of facts, in the first place, is loose and blind in the extreme. There is no such difference as it pretends, in the order of corruption, between the Popery of the middle ages and the period going before. We agree fully with Mr. Taylor, that this was in many respects an improvement on the older system. Then again, the main hypothesis in the case is in the highest degree unnatural and violent. It assumes a full *principial* failure of the church from the very start, an actual triumph of Satan over Christ in the very heart and bosom of his own kingdom, in the face of all God's promises to the contrary, in the face of the original charter and commission of this same church from Christ's own lips, and in spite of his continual headship over it at the right hand of the Father, with all power given unto him in heaven and in earth, to make good his word that the gates of hell should not prevail against it through all time. For the idea is, that the ancient church *did* fail, so as to lose finally the life with which it started; and that Protestantism therefore is no continuation of this life in any really historical way, but an actual return to the beginning, for the purpose of a new experiment of Christianity under a better and safer form. In this way Protestantism is made to be the contradiction and negation of all previous Christianity, back to the age of the Apostles. Its justification requires us to denounce and condemn all church antiquity. To be on good terms with it, we must renounce everything like hearty fellowship—if not with the names—at least with the real persons of the fathers, martyrs, and saints, of the first centuries, everything like true sympathy with their actual spirit and life. Then farther, the use which the theory makes of the Bible is by no means satisfactory; and is of such a wilful and arbitrary character indeed, as may well inspire a terrible doubt of its being more free from mistake after all than the use made of it by the ancient church. If all antiquity could so blunder here, for fifteen centuries, as to miss the entire sense of God's word, who will go bail for us that Puritanism may be trusted and followed now as a truly infallible guide? Finally, the scheme refuses to come into any sort of intelligible harmony with the course of church history. It supposes such a state of things as leaves no room for the idea of a divine life in the church, and makes it in fact to have been the enemy of all truth and righteousness. And yet the church has never been without the signs and proofs of Christ's supernatural presence in her midst, (according to his promise,) from the beginning.

Altogether thus, this Puritan theory runs directly towards infidelity. It puts together terms which are in their own nature incompatible; and in asking us to believe them, necessarily remands our faith into the world of mere abstractions and notions. On this account it is, that we have denounced it as secretly the foe of Protestantism. We say most deliberately, that a christianity which is not historical, not the continuation organically of the proper life of the church as it has existed from the beginning—but which abjures all connection with this life as something false, and sets itself in contradiction to it as a totally new and different existence—can have no right whatever to challenge our faith, as being the same supernatural fact that is set before us by the article of the church in the ancient creed. It seeks to turn that fact into a wholesale lie, by making such supposition the only alternative to its own truth. No defence of Protestantism in this form can stand. To make the Reformation a mere rebellion, a radical revolution, a violent breaking away from the whole authority of the past, is to give it a purely human or rather an actually diabolical character. It comes then just to this, that either the rebellion was diabolical or else the ancient church back to the second century was the work of the Devil and not Christ's work. We are shut up to the necessity of rejecting one, in order that we may choose the other; for they are opposite interests, and the case will not allow us to acknowledge both at once. But who that has any faith in the supernatural mystery of the church, as it came from Christ in the beginning, can submit to the claims of Protestantism put into any such shape as this? Who of any sound christian feeling will bear to give up all antiquity in such radical style, for the sake of a wholly new system starting only in the sixteenth century? This is Puritanism; but we are not willing to allow that it is Protestantism, that it expresses the meaning of the Reformation in its true original sense. Puritanism is absolutely unhistorical by principle and profession; but Protestantism, if it have any right to exist at all, is the true historical continuation of the ancient church. To force the other character upon it. is to kill it root and branch.

We are sorry to find that Mr. Isaac Taylor, with all his learning and good sense, is not able to clear himself of this false and untenable ground, in his controversy with the Oxford theology. He sets out indeed with what might seem to a very strong acknowledgment, of the dependence of the modern church upon that of antiquity. The following passages are of great point and force certainly, against the whole spirit of our reigning sect system at the present time, (wiser in its own conceit than seven men that can render a reason,) which only laughs at every sort of authority in such form, and counts *itself* to be nothing less than the direct embodiment of the bible over against all that the church has ever been before.

"Looking at the Christian world at large, it is my full conviction, that there is just now a far more urgent need of persuasives to the study of Christian history and literature, than of cautions against the abuse of such studies. Too many feel and speak as if they thought there were no continuity in their religion; or as if there were no universal church; or as if the individual Christian, with his pocket bible in his hand, need fix his eyes upon nothing but the little eddy of his personal emotions; or as if Christianity were not what it is its glory and its characteristic to be—*a religion of history.*

"Christianity, the pledge to man of eternity, is the occupant of all time; and not merely was it, itself, the ripening of the dispensations that had gone before it, but it was to be the home companion of the successive generations of man, until the consummation of all things. Not to know Christianity as the religion of all ages—as that which grasps and interprets the cycles of time, is to be in a condition like that of the man whose gloomy chamber admits only a single pencil of the universal radiance of noon."—*Vol. I. p.* 21, 22.

"If it be true that the general complexion of church history, through the course of long centuries, is such as to offend our preconceived notions, and to shock our spiritual tastes, and if, while we bend over the records of those dim eras, the promise of the Lord to be with his servants, still rings in our ears, as a doleful knell of hopes broken; if it be so, or as far as such may be the fact, the motive becomes more impressive and serious which impels us to acquire an authentic knowledge of this course of events, in all its details,—and if there are any who must acknowledge that they feel a peculiar repugnance in regard to church history, they are the very persons, more than any other, whom it behooves to school themselves in this kind of learning; for it seems more than barely probable, that this distaste springs from some ill affection of their own minds, demanding to be exposed and remedied. Such persons may well admit the supposition that they have hastily assumed certain notions of their Lord's principles of government, which are in fact unlike what, at length, they will find themselves to be subject to; and if so, the sooner they dispel any such false impressions, the better. On the face of the instance supposed, one should say, that any perplexities we may feel in regard to that course of events which constitutes the history of Christianity, probably spring from some deep-seated error of feeling, or of opinion, which, for our own sakes, we should carefully analyze."—*P.* 25.

" These indispensable studies, have, in fact, been revived of late, to a great extent. in our own, as well as other countries ; while the use and necessity of them are forced anew upon the minds of all by the rapid and unexpected advances of Romanism, whose ministers are taking advantage of that ignorance of antiquity which has too long been the reproach of Protestantism."—*P.* 28.

" These ' fathers,' thus grouped as a little band, by the objectors, were some of them men of as brilliant genius as any age has produced : some, commanding a flowing and vigorous eloquence, some, an extensive erudition, some, conversant with the great world, some, whose meditations had been ripened by years of seclusion, some of them the only historians of the times in which they lived, some, the chiefs of the philosophy of their age ; and, if we are to speak of the whole, as a series or body of writers, they are the men who, during a long era of deepening barbarism, still held the lamp of knowledge and learning, and, in fact, afford us almost all that we can now know, intimately. of the condition of the nations surrounding the Mediterranean, from the extinction of the classic fire, to the time of its rekindling in the fourteenth century. The church was the ark of all things that had life, during a deluge of a thousand years."—*P.* 34, 35.

" Nearly of the same quality, and usually advanced by the same parties, is the portentous insinuation, or the bold and appalling averment, that there was little or no genuine Christianity in the world from the times of Justin Martyr to those of Wicliffe, or of Luther ! and the inference from this assumption is, that we are far more likely to be led astray than edified by looking into the literature of this vast territory of religious darkness.

" I must leave it to those who entertain any such sombre belief as this, to repel, in the best manner they are able those fiery darts of infidelity which will not fail to be hurled at Christianity itself, as often as the opinion is professed. Such persons, too, must expound as they can, our Lord's parting promise to his servants."—*P.* 35.

" Christianity is absolute truth, bearing with various effect, from age to age, upon our distorted and discoloured human nature, but never so powerfully pervading the foreign substance it enters as to undergo no deflections itself, or to take no stains ; and as its influence varies, from age to age, in intensity, as well as in the particular direction it may take, so does it exhibit, from age to age, great variations of form and hue. But the men of any one age indulge too much the overweening temper that attaches always to human nature, when they say to themselves—*our* Christianity is absolute Christianity ; but that of such or such an age, was a mere shadow of it."—*P.* 36.

"The modern spirit of self-sufficiency seems to reach its climax in the contempt thrown by some upon those who, endowed with as much learning and acumen as ourselves, read the scriptures while the ink of the apostolic autographs had hardly faded."—*P.* 40.

"It is in fact a circumstance worthy to be noticed, that even the most ultra-protestant of ultra-protestants, if it happens to him to meet with a real real or apparent confirmation of his peculiar views, within the circle of ecclesiastical antiquity, shows no reluctance whatever in snatching at it, and in turning it to the best account he can, piously quoting Irenæus, or Tertullian, or Ignatius, like any good Romanist! It is—' the bible, and the bible alone, just when the evidence afforded, on some disputed point, by the writings of Ignatius, or Irenæus, or Tertullian, happens to tell in the wrong direction; otherwise, these 'papistical authorities' are good enough. —*P.* 52.

"It has been nothing so much as this inconsiderate 'bible alone' outcry, that has given modern Popery so long a reprieve in the heart of Protestant countries; and it is now the very same zeal, without discretion, that opens a fair field for the spread of the doctrines of the Oxford Tracts."—*P.* 54.

These, we say, are sound and true sentiments. But they are not well sustained by Mr. Taylor's own work. The only use he sees proper to make of ecclesiastical history after all, is such as is made of the testimony of a common witness in a court of law. The voice of the church is to him obly as the voice of the profane world, the authority of the fathers of one and the same order with the authority of Tacitus or Pliny. Antiquity may help us to the knowledge of some facts, but nothing more; to sit in judgment on the facts, to make out their true value, to accept them as grains of gold or reject them as heaps of trash, is the high prerogative of modern reason, acting in its triple office of lawyer, juryman, and judge. The rule or standard of judgment is indeed professedly the bible, God's infallible word; but the *tribunal* for interpreting and applying it, the highest and last resort therefore in all cases of controversy and appeal, is always the mind of the present age as distinguished from every age that has gone before. Mr. Taylor's standpoint is completely subjective. It is not the right position, for doing justice to any history; but least of all, for doing justice to the history of God's church. For if the church be what it professed to be at the start, and what it is acknowledged by the whole christian world to be in the creed, it is a supernatural constitution, and in such view must have a supernatural history. A divine church with a purely human history, is for faith a contradiction in terms. In

any such view however, it is something fairly monstrous to think
of turning the whole process into the play of simply human factors, and then requiring it to bend everywhere to the measure of
our modern judgment. But this precisely is what Mr. Isaac
Taylor allows himself to do. With the bible in hand, he finds
it a most easy and reasonable thing to rule out of court the universal voice of the church, from the second century if need be
to the sixteenth, wherever it refuses to chime in with his own
mind. In this way he falls in fact into the theory and method
of Puritanism, under the most perfectly arbitrary form. Protestantism in his hands ceases to be historical altogether, and
stands forward in direct antagonism to the life of the early church.
The relation between the two systems is made to be one of violent contradiction and opposition. It admits of no organic reconciliation. To make good the modern cause, antiquity is presented to us under attributes that destroy its whole title to our
confidence and respect. It becomes indeed an unintelligible
riddle. It is the church of Christ in the habiliments of hell;
or shall we call it rather a hideous vision of Satan himself, transformed for the time into an angel of light?

" Our brethren of the early church," Mr. Taylor himself tells
us (*Vol. I. p.* 37), " challenge our respect, as well as affection;
for theirs was the fervour of a steady faith in things unseen and
eternal; theirs often a meek patience and humility, under the
most grievous wrongs; theirs the courage to maintain a good
profession before the frowning face of philosophy, of secular
tyranny, and of splendid superstition; theirs was abstractedness
from the world, and a painful self-denial; theirs the most arduous and costly labours of love; theirs a munificence in charity,
altogether without example; theirs was a reverent and scrupu-
lous care of the sacred writings, and this merit, if they had had
no other, is of a superlative degree, and should entitle them to
the veneration and grateful regards of the modern church. How
little do many readers of the Bible, now-a-days, think of what
it cost the Christians of the second and third centuries, merely
to rescue and hide the sacred treasure from the rage of the
heathen !"

This is a beautiful and bright picture. But, alas, the historical analysis that follows turns it all into shame. Nothing can
well be more gloomy and oppressive to a truly christian mind,
than the light in which the fathers of these first centuries, together with the theology and piety of the ancient church generally,
are made to show themselves beneath the pencil of this brilliant
and fluent writer. False principles came in from the start, not

affecting simply the surface of the new religion, but carrying the poison of death into its very heart. Gnosticism, though resisted and conquered on the outside of the church, had a full triumph within. Out of it grew the ascetic system, false views of marriage, the glorification of virginity, monasticism, and all kindred views. The celibate corrupted the whole scheme of theology. Christianity itself is opposed to the Oriental theosophy, proceeding throughout on a different view of the world; and it vanquished this enemy in fact. But only, we are told, to take it again into its own bosom. " The catholic church opposed its substantial truths to these baseless and malignant speculations; and triumphed : but alas, it fell in triumphing." Gnosticism thus infused its own antichristian soul into the entire body of the Nicene theology.[1]   Parallel with this doctrinal corruption, ran a corresponding corruption of the whole life of religion practically considered. The true scheme of salvation was to a great extent lost. Repentance and justification by faith sunk out of sight, overwhelmed completely by a factitious religion of outward forms and rites. The sacraments were exaggerated into saving mysteries. Polytheism, expelled and subdued under its heathen character, rose into power again as Christian demonolatry, the worship of saints, relics and images; all in pure contradiction to the original genius of the gospel. Along with this system went the universal noise of prodigies and miracles. These were " lying wonders," piously contrived to keep up the credit of the reigning superstitions. They are not insulated instances merely of alleged supernatural agency, but form a *miraculous dispensation*, running on from year to year, and carrying along with it the ostensible faith and homage of the whole church. At the same time it is plain enough to modern common sense, that the dispensation was throughout an enormous cheat, kept up by the priesthood for their own ends. Even the best men of the church, such as the Nicene fathers generally, must have been more or less privy to these awfully wicked frauds.[2] St. Ambrose, for instance, must have first buried the

---

[1] " The massive walls of the church, like a hastily constructed coffer-dam, had repelled, from age to age, the angry billows of the Gnostic heresy, which could never open a free passage for themselves within the sacred enclosure. Nevertheless these waters, bitter and turbid, no sooner rose high around the shattered structure, than, through a thousand fissures, they penetrated, and in fact stood at one and the same mean level, within, where they were silently stagnant, as without, where they were in angry commotion."—*Vol. I. p.* 175.

[2] " It will be my painful task, to lay open the shameless frauds and im-

skeletons, during the night, which he pretended to discover the next day, by divine revelation, as the remains of the martyrs Gervasius and Protasius ; must have hired men to act the part of demoniacs, who should bear testimony to the truth of the discovery, drilling them well into their diabolical parts ; must have engaged Severus, the butcher, to feign himself restored to sight by touching the covering of the relics, as they were borne in solemn procession to their new resting place beneath the altar of the Ambrosian church. And yet Ambrose was one of the best and greatest men, belonging to the history of the ancient church.

With such a view of the theology and life of the fourth century, Mr. Taylor finds it natural and easy to charge the system directly with the universal decay of morals, that marked the last stage of the old Roman civilization. All came, by necessary derivation, from the " church principles" of the third and fourth centuries. The cause which Christ had founded for the salvation of the world, proved in the end like the breath of the Sirocco, sweeping it with an unmeasurable curse.[1]

This may suffice for our present purpose ; which is not to discuss directly the merit of our author's positions ; but simply to set them in contrast with the other side of his own picture of this same ancient Christianity, in argument and proof of the perfectly unhistorical character of his general scheme. A man may talk as he pleases about the glories of the early church, Christ's presence in it, and its victories over error and sin ; if he couple with it the idea of such wholesale falsehood and corruption as is here laid to its charge, all this praise is made absolutely void.[2]

---

pious miracle-mongering, by means of which the trade of the priests at these magnificent shrines was kept agoing ; frauds incomparably more discreditable than were any that had been practised in the heathen oracular temples. This is indeed a heavy theme ; and how sorrowful--how sickening, when a man like Chrysostom is found acting as the Hierophant of these mysteries of iniquity !"—*Vol. II. p.* 207.

[1] " Christianity, as restored by the Reformers, has gradually regenerated the countries which have freely entertained it ; while, on the contrary, Christianity, as debased by the Nicene divines, after quickly spending its healthful forces, only served to hurry the nations downward into—to use Salvian's language--'a sink of debauchery.' "—*Vol. II. p.* 37.

[2] " The ancient church having compromised the greatest truths, and thereby forfeited the guidance of the Spirit of Truth, rushed forward, without a check, on every path of artificial excitement ; and being at the same time urged by the circumstances of its precarious conflict with the expiring paganism, as well as with innumerable new-born heresies, to strengthen itself by the nefarious arts of popular influence—by factitious terrors, hopes, wonders, it regarded no scruples of honor, and threw the reins on the neck of fanatical extravagance."—*Vol. II.* 157. If this be true, what nonsense to speak of *such* a heaven-forsaken church, as being in any sense the ark of religion or the pillar and ground of the truth !

The two thoughts refuse to stand together. One necessarily excludes the other. Common history will not endure any such gross contradiction. But still less can it be reconciled with any faith in the history of the church, as a supernatural order. If Ambrose could so lend himself to the Devil, he was no saint. If the church generally was so terribly corrupt both in doctrine and practice, embodying in itself the worst principles of heathenism, God surely was not in the midst of it as a Saviour and King. It was, clear back to the third and even to the second century, the synagogue in truth of Satan, the unclean temple and home of Antichrist.

For the errors and corruptions here set to its account, are not represented as partial only or relative, the exaggerations or distortions merely of acknowledged truth and sound christian feeling. In that view, they might still be reconciled with the idea of a truly historical church, bearing in its bosom the supernatural presence of its glorified Head. Faith in the continuity of the church as a divine fact, (the proper mystery of the creed,) by no means requires us to overlook or deny the frailties and follies that necessarily belong to the human side of its history. But in the case before us, the human, which left to itself is always the diabolical also, is made absolutely to overwhelm the divine. All resolves itself pragmatically into the play of worldly factors, often of the most ignoble kind, in no real union whatever with heavenly factors in any way answerable to the promise, " Lo, I am with you always to the end of the world." At best the heavenly is sublimated into the notion only of God's providence, as it floats over *all* human history—a Gnostic conception, that falls immeasurably short of the mystery set before us in the creed. The errors and corruptions charged upon the church here, are such as strike at the very root of its inmost sanctuary, we may say, of its universal constitution and life. They are false, not by excess or distortion merely, but by principle; being nothing less, in truth, than the introduction of another gospel altogether, whose swift triumphs soon supplanted the original and proper sense of Christianity, from one end of its broad domain to the other.

If Protestantism then is to be defended successfully it can be neither on the ground that it is a repristination simply of early post-apostolical christianity, nor on the ground that it is an absolute nullification of this ancient faith, leaping over it with a single bound to the age of the Apostles.

We are shut up thus to the idea of *historical development*, as the only possible way of escape from the difficulty with which we are met in bringing the present here into comparison with the past. If the modern church must be the same in substance with the ancient church, a true continuation of its life as this has been in the world by divine promise from the beginning, while it is perfectly plain at the same time that a wide difference holds between the two systems as to form, the relation binding them together can only be one of living progress or growth. No other will satisfy these opposite conditions. Growth implies unity in the midst of change. That precisely is what we are to understand by historical development. We do not say now, that it is actually the true key to the problem of Protestantism. We say merely, that if this interest be at all capable of rational apology, in the face of its notorious disagreement with ancient christianity, it can be in this way only and in no other. If we are not at liberty to apply the law of organic progress to the case, there is no help for the cause of the Reformation, the facts being what we find them to be in actual history. Let those look to it, who pretend to be the most staunch friends of Protestantism by scouting the entire idea of any such law ; who will have it either that their own small version of Christianity in this form, as given in some one of our sects, is a true picture of what the church was in the beginning of the second century, or that it is against this altogether, and above it, as being the re-assertion at last of the original and proper sense of the New Testament, from which the whole course of history immediately afterwards fell away. Neither of these alternatives can stand. The present here is plainly not one with the past ; but just as little may it pretend to be the nullification of the past, or its plump contradiction.

Some pretend to identify this doctrine of development with the system of Romanism itself ; as though the only occasion for it were found in the variations through which it is supposed to have passed in reaching its present form. Nor have Romanists themselves been unwilling always, to allow it a certain amount of truth. It is not easy to deny certainly, that very considerable changes had place in the history of Christianity before the time of the Reformation ; and this might seem to be a natural and ready view, for surmounting the objection drawn from them against the stability and unity of the Catholic church. Mr. Newman, it is well known, has tried to turn the idea to account in this way, in his memorable Essay on the Development of Christian Doctrine. Few theological tracts, in the English language are more worthy of being read, or more likely to reward a diligent perusal with lasting benefit and fruit. The author

holds christianity to be an objective fact in the world, that must
be throughout identical with itself.[1]   Still that it has undergone
serious modifications in its outward form and aspect, he considers to be no less certain and clear.   To reconcile this semblance
of discrepancy then, he has recourse to what he calls the *theory
of developments*.   It is of the nature of a living idea to expand
itself, to take new form, as it comes by the course of history into
new relations requiring its application in new ways.   At the
same time however it carries in itself, from the start, the type and
norm of all that it is subsequently to become.   We must distinguish accordingly between a true development in such view and
a corruption which transforms the very substance of the idea
itself into something else.   Mr. Newman lays down no less than
seven tests, by which we may be guided and assisted in making
this important distinction ; and then goes on to apply the subject,
by illustrations drawn with great force and effect from the actual history of the church in past ages.   The whole theory, however, has been condemned by other Romanists, as being at war
with the true genius of the Catholic religion.   Mr. Brownson of
our own country in particular, it will be remembered, set himself
in vigorous opposition to it from the start.   Catholicism, as he
will have it, has known no change.   It is only Protestantism
that has moved away from what the church was in the begin-

[1] " Christianity is no dream of the study or the cloister.   It has long
since passed beyond the letter of documents and the reasonings of individual minds, and has become public property.—It has from the first had
an objective existence.—Its home is in the world.——The hypothesis,
indeed, has met with wide reception in these latter ages, that
Christianity does not fall within the province of history, that it is to
each man what each man thinks it to be, and nothing else.—Or again, it
has been maintained, or implied, that all existing denominations of christianity are wrong, none representing it as taught by Christ and his Apostles ;
that it died out of the world at its birth, and was forthwith succeeded by a
counterfeit or counterfeits which assumed its name, though they inherited
but a portion of its teaching ; that it has existed indeed among men ever
since, and exists at this day, but as a secret and hidden doctrine, which does
but revive here and there under a supernatural influence in the hearts of
individuals, and is manifested to the world only by glimpses or in gleams,
according to the number or the station of the illuminated, and their connexion with the history of their times."   All this however, the writer tells us
truly, is at best in itself a *hypothesis* only.   The only natural assumption is
the contrary, namely, " to take it for granted that the christianity of the
second, fourth, seventh, twelfth, sixteenth, and intermediate centuries, is in
its *substance* the very religion which Christ and his Apostles taught in the
first, whatever may be the modifications for good or for evil, which lapse
of years, or the vicissitudes of human affairs have impressed upon it.——
The *onus probandi* is with those who assert what it is unnatural to ezpect;
to be just able to doubt is no warrant for disbelieving."—*Introdu tion.*

ning, and that is still always in motion and never at rest. It is only Protestantism, that needs any such law of development to account for its changes; and to Protestantism alone, accordingly, the whole theory legitimately and of right belongs.[2]

Be this as it may, Protestantism at all events is still less able to get along without the help of some such theory than Roman-ism In no other way possibly, can it make good its claim to be the historical continuance at all of the supernatural fact which the church is allowed to have been in the beginning.[3] This is now felt by all, who deserve to be considered of any authority in the sphere of church history. The whole progress of this science at the present time, under the new impulse which has been given to it by Neander and others, is making it more and more ridiculous to think of upholding the cause of the Reformation under any other view. It *must* be one with the ancient church, to have any valid claim to its prerogatives and powers; but this it *can* be only in the way of historical growth. Give that up, and all is gone. Without the idea of development, the whole fact of Protestantism resolves itself into a fearful lie.

Those who wish to see this subject ably and happily handled, are referred to Professor Schaff's *Principle of Protestantism*, the special object of which is to exhibit and defend the idea of

------

[2] Mr. Brownson's judgment in this case is not to be taken, of course, as at once final and conclusive for the Catholic church. Mr. Newman's book was written before he became a Romanist in form; but it has been defended by some in that communion; and we do not find, that Mr. Newman himself, since his conversion, has renounced the general doctrine of it as wrong. On the contrary, if we understand him rightly, it is distinctly affirmed still in some of his recent lectures. Möhler has the same thought.

[3] Mr. Newman will tell us, that even in *this* way it is perfectly indefensible, as being not a true development at all of what Christianity was in the beginning, but its radical corruption. "Whatever be historical Christianity, it is not Protestantism; if ever there were a safe truth it is this.—Protestants can as little bear its Ante-nicene as its Post-tridentine period.—— So much must the Protestant grant, that if such a system of doctrine as he would now introduce ever existed in early times, it has been clean swept away as if by a deluge, suddenly, silently, and without memorial; by a deluge coming in a night, and utterly soaking, rotting, heaving up, and hurrying off every vestige of what it found in the church, before cock-crowing; so that 'when they rose in the morning,' her true seed 'were all dead corpses'—nay dead and buried—and without a grave-stone." This we may consider to be exaggeration and mistake; since it amounts to a full condemnation of Protestantism in every view, as being without all real root in the past life of the church, But it only shows the more strongly, what necessity there is of making out the line of a true historical succession in its favor, by a deeper and better apprehension if possible of this idea of development.

historical development in its application to the Protestant movement. This work we have noticed at some length on a former occasion. It was decried, on its first appearance, by a certain class of Protestants, as being inimical to the very cause it professed to defend. But it was only because the author had a far deeper insight into the necessities of his subject, than those who thus judged him were able to understand. They belonged to the unchurchly, unhistorical school, for which Christianity is a mere matter of opinion or notion, and which has no difficulty accordingly in setting all the laws of real history, as well as all the conditions of a truly supernatural church, at the most perfect defiance, in order to carry out its own dogmatical abstractions. Dr. Schaff had entered too far into the modern sense of history and the proper idea of the church, to be satisfied with any such poor and superficial habit of thought. He saw the absolute necessity of showing Protestantism to be historical, in the full modern force of this most significant term, for the purpose of vindicating its right to exist; and his work accordingly is a most honest and vigorous attempt to defend it on this ground. We have said before, what we now deliberately repeat, that it is the best apology for the cause of the Reformation which has yet appeared in this country. If this cause is to be successfully upheld at all, it can only be, we believe, on the general ground taken in this book. However it may be as regards details, the argument in its main course and scheme may be considered identical now with the very life of Protestantism. It is approved and endorsed in such view, we may say, by the whole weight of German theological science, as it appears in its best representatives at the present time. The Reformation, according to this scheme, was not a revolution, radically upsetting the church as it stood before. In that view it must have been a new religion, and would have needed miracles to support its claims. It was merely a disengagement of the old life of the church from the abuses, with which it became burdened in the course of time, and its advancement to a form more congenial, than that which it carried before, with the wants of the modern world. It was no nullification thus of previous history, no return simply to what christianity was supposed to have been in the beginning; its connection with that was still through the intervening history of the old Catholic church; and from the bosom of this church it sprang by true living derivation and birth. Protestantism is no repudiation then of ancient christianity, nor of the proper religious life of the middle ages. It owes its being to this old life, which was engaged for centuries before with its painful parturition. Here is the idea of historical development. But the theory goes farther still. Protestantism, the favorite child of Catholicism, is not itself a full realization of the true idea of Christianity. It has terrible defects upon it, malignant diseases, belonging as would seem to its very blood, which are growing always worse and worse, and threaten to bring upon it in the end full dissolution. It will not do then to rest in it as the absolute consummation of the church. To take it for that, is again to turn it palpably into a lie. As it was not the first form of Christianity, so neither may it be considered the last. It is itself a process of transition only towards a higher and better state of the church, which is still future though probably now near at hand, and the coming in of which may be expected to form an epoch in history quite as great at least as that of the Reformation itself. The result of this new development will be the recovery of Protestantism itself from the evils under which it now suffers, and in this way its full and final vindication by the judgment of history. It will be however, at the same time, a vindication of Catholicism also, as having been of true historical necessity in its day for the full working out of the problem which shall thus be conducted at last to its glorious solution. Such, we say, is the theory of *historical development*, as we have it applied in this interesting and able tract to the great question here brought into view; the question, namely, how Protestantism is to be set in harmony with the past history of the church, and with its true ideal as the kingdom of God, a supernatural polity of truth and righteousness among men.

This German idea of development, as we may call it, is not the same with that presented to us by Dr. Newman. The last is a continuous expansion and enlargement under the same form and in the same general direction; the process involves no disorder or contradiction in its own movement; it is the full sense always, as far as it goes, of what the church was in fact and intention from the beginning; it is the simple coming out of this sense, in a view answerable to the new relations of its history from age to age; each stage of development is by itself normal and full, and so of force for all time; all moves thus in the line of Catholicism only, without the possibility of growing into anything like Protestantism; on which account, accordingly, this must be regarded as a corruption of the original idea of Christianity, by which it is changed into another type and fashion altogether. It is not easy in truth to conceive of the old Catholic system blossoming into Protestantism, in the way of any such regular and direct growth; and there seems to be no room therefore, for the supposition, that Dr. Newman's conception of development goes against the pretensions of the Roman church.[4] The German theory however does do so, in the most emphatic manner. Its idea of growth is that of a process carried forward, by the action of different forces, working separately to some extent, and so it may be even onesidedly and contradictorily for a time, towards a concrete result representing in full unity at last the true meaning and power of the whole. Each part of the process then is regarded as necessary and right in its own order and time; but still only as *relatively* right, and as having need thus to complete itself, by passing ultimately into a higher form. Catholicism in this view is justified as a true and legitimate movement of the church; but it is taken to have been the explication of one side of Christianity mainly, rather than a full and proper representation of the fact as a whole; a process thus that naturally became excessive, and so wrong, in its own direction, preparing the way for a powerful reaction finally in the opposite direction. This reaction we have in Protestantism; which in such view springs from the old church, not just by uniform progress, but with a certain measure of violence, while yet it is found to be the product really and truly of its deeper life. Here again however, as before, the first result is only relatively good. The new tendency has become itself onesided, exorbitant, and full of wrong. Hence the need of still another crisis, (the signs of whose advent many seem already to see,)

---

[4] We meet with the same thought in Tertullian. "There is nothing," he tells us, "which does not advance by age. All things wait upon time; as the preacher saith, there is a time for every thing. Look at the natural world, and see the plant gradually ripening to its fruit, first a mere grain; from the grain arises the green stalk, and from the stalk shoots up the shrub; then the boughs and branches get strength, and the tree is complete; thence the swelling bud, and from the bud the blossom, and from the flower the fruit; which at the first crude and shapeless, by little and little proceeds, and attains its ripe softness and flavor. And so in religion, for it is the same God of nature and of religion; at first in its rudiments only, nature surmising something concerning God; then by the law and the prophets advanced to its infant state; then by the Gospel it reached the heats of youth; and now by the Comforter is moulded to its maturity." Tertullian speaks here as a Montanist, but the thought itself may be applied to the gradual expansion of the Catholic system. Isaac Taylor sets it down, in this view, as the foundation principle of Romanism (Vol. I. p. 93–96). He wrongs the church however, by charging it with the introduction of new revelations. The supposed innovations of the system came in always as the growth merely of what was at hand before. The expansion thus claimed to be organic, the actualization simply of the previously potential. It was a development in every case, professedly, and not a proper apocalypse.

which may arrest and correct this abuse, and open the way for a higher and better state of the church, in which both these great tendencies shall be brought at length happily to unite, revealing to the world the full sense of Christianity in a form now absolute and complete.

For a truly learned representation of this whole view, in its relations to other older schemes of ecclesiastical history, (for there has been a remarkable exemplification of the law of development in the progress of this science itself,) we beg leave to refer our readers to Professor Schaff's tract entitled, *What is Church History?* They will find it well worthy of their most careful and diligent perusal.

We have spoken before of Thiersch's "Lectures on Catholicism and Protestantism." They abound in original and fresh thought, pervaded throughout with a tone of the most earnest piety, though not altogether free at times from the excesses of an erratic fancy. The history of the church is with him also a grand and complicated process, exposed to powerful corruptions, and yet moving onward always towards the full consummation of its own original idea; which is not to be reached however without the intervention of a new supernatural apostolate, in all respects parallel with that which was employed for the first establishment of Christianity in the beginning. The church, he thinks, has passed through four great metamorphoses already, in coming to its present condition. First we have it under its *Old Catholic* form, as it existed between the age of the Apostles and the time of Constantine. Then it appears as the *Imperial (Græco-Roman)* church, in close connection with the state, and undergoing many corruptions and changes. Next it becomes the *Roman Catholic* church of the middle ages. Last of all it stands before us as the *Protestant* church. This was called forth, with a sort of inward necessity, by the corruptions and abuses of the Roman system; and it has its full historical justification, in the actual religious benefits it has conferred upon the world; benefits that may be said to show themselves even in the improved character of Romanism itself. Still it is but too plain, that Protestantism is not the full-successful solution of the problem of Christianity. It has not fulfilled the promise of its own beginning; and it carries in it no pledge now of any true religious millenium in time to come. Evils of tremendous character are lodged within its bosom. A reign of rationalism and unbelief has sprung out of it, for which the present course of things, in the view of Thiersch, offers no prospect of recovery or help. It is no relief, in such case, to know

that the Catholic church, in countries where it has no Protestantism as a rival at its side, such for instance as South America or
Spain, is in a moral condition equally if not still more deplorable. It is only the more sad, that neither *here* nor *there* the
proper face of the true church is to be discerned. " Whether
the Reformers, could they have seen the present posture of the
church that goes by their name, would have regretted and cursed
their own work, as has been often said, we know not ; but it is
certain that a keen eye and a strong faith are needed, in view of
the general declension that prevails, not to overlook the good
which is still left, and to see in it the germ of a better future.
Of such future however one of the most necessary conditions is
just this, that we should learn to maintain a proper bearing towards the Catholic church and its peculiarities." The self-sufficiency of both systems must come to an end, before room can
be made for that higher state of the church, which God may be
expected then to bring in by miraculous dispensation, restoring
all things to their proper form.

Professor Rothe takes a different view, conditioned by his
speculative construction of Christianity in its relations to Nature
and Humanity, as we have this fully brought out, with unparalleled architectonic power, in his *Theological Ethics.* The idea
of the church he takes to be accidental, rather than essential, to
the religious life of the world. The ultimate and only fully
normal order of man's existence is the state, the organism of his
moral relations, which can never be complete save as they are
brought in the end to embrace all that is included also in the
sense of religion. Such will be at last the actual consummation
of the process, by which our world is now fulfilling its original
destiny and design. The process itself however is conditioned
now by the fact of redemption, made necessary through sin.
This implies a new power brought into the world for its sanctification ; a power in such view different from the natural life of
the world, but fited at the same time to take possesion of this
life always more and more, and finally to transform it fully into
its own image. So far as Christianity continues in such distinction from the world naturally considered, it must have its own
organization as something distinct from the state, and as something necessarily also in conflict to a certain extent with its very
conception. This organization gives us the proper fact of the
church. Its relation to the state is at first one of broad opposition ; but in the nature of the case it is in this respect a changing and flowing relation ; for as the state receives into it more
and more the power of the christian life, through the agency of

the church, the mission and work of this last over against it shrink always into narrower bounds, so that the assertion of its authority becomes at last a source of oppression and restraint. In the end thus it comes naturally to a rebellion against the idea of the church, as an exclusive institute for the purposes of religion. This was the true sense of the Reformation. It involved the breaking up of the old Catholic doctrine of the church, as something good in its time but no longer answerable to the advanced age of the world, for the necessary purpose of securing free room and scope for the forces of religion under a different form, that namely which is presented to us in the constitution of the state. There is still indeed a demand for the action of the church, and but little prospect as yet that this demand will soon come to an end ; but the first step has been taken towards what is to be at last the true order of religion ; the vanishing nature of the church has begun to be apparent ; its former attributes are passing away ; we find it in a chaos of dissolution, the result of which will be in due time its universal absorption into the political organism which has been its rival from the beginning.[1]

This is truly a startling way of bringing the problem of Protestantism to a solution ; and it is no wonder perhaps that the religious world, even in Germany itself, where the church might seem indeed to be fast tumbling into ruins, has not been able yet to look upon the view with much favor. Still it is the view of a most earnestly religious man, who is at the same time one

---

[1] "There is bitter complaint made in our day, especially in Evangelical Christendom, of the decline of the church. With right and without right, as we choose to take it. With right ; for the church, *as a church*, is in reality falling always more and more into ruins, and how it may or can be helped up again, even with the best will on the side of government, is in no wise to be seen. Without right ; for this collapse of the church is just the consequence of the maturity and independence of the christian life, which thus breaks the old form that has become too strait for it, and escaping from its restraints runs joyfully towards its true element, the state. We will acknowledge unreservedly the decline of the church, but in the complaint which is made on this account we will take no part. As it seems to us, the general position in which we have tried to set the reader is the only one, from which one can survey the whole course of church history, without danger of falling out with its movement.——From this standpoint alone also, do we first reach a real justification of the Reformation against Catholicism. So long as the *church* is considered to be the highest and only proper realization of the christian life, the act must in truth be set down for a crime, by which the unity of the church, and so the church itself, has been and only could be dashed to pieces."— *Die Anfänge d. chr. Kirche, p.* 88.

of the profoundest thinkers and most learned scholars of the age, grappling here in all his strength with what he feels to be the very life question of Protestantism itself; and it well deserves attention in such light, if for no other reason yet at least for this, that it goes to show how real and serious the general problem is, which is here offered for our consideration. Puritanism, with its ordinary want of historical sensibility and its most superficial conception of the mystery of the church, may affect to find no difficulty in the whole subject, and can easily afford to dismiss every theory of this sort as a vain and superfluous speculation. It needs no solution for a knot, which it has no power to see. But for all this, the knot itself is there, and it is one of no common intricacy and force. Puritanism is ready at once to reject Rothe's resolution of the church into the state; but only because it does not admit at all the idea of the church in his sense, and in the old christian sense, as distinguished from the idea of the state. That whole idea is for it from the start a falsehood, the very *proton-pseudos* we may say of Romanism. Its highest order is only the state throughout, or man in the form of natural political society. The church has no absolute necessity; it is not of the essence of religion in any way; this holds in humanity as such under the political order; and it is the glory of Protestantism, as well as its only true sense, to assert such independence to the fullest extent. Hence many churches instead of one; any number of them indeed, to suit the world's taste; till the whole conception runs out finally into the open sea of no church whatever. And what less is this, we ask, than Rothe's version of the Reformation—the breaking up, namely, of the old doctrine of the holy catholic church, as we find it in the creed, and the first grand step towards its full formal dissolution at last in the all devouring idea of the state?

The whole theory, with all our respect for Rothe, *we* of course at once repudiate as unsound and false. How could the idea of the church be an object of faith, that is a supernatural mystery of like order with the other articles of the creed, if it were after all any such merely provisional and transient fact, (a downright *"figment"* the Puritan Recorder would say rather,) designed to pass away finally in another conception altogether? We might just as well resolve the resurrection of the body, with Hymeneus and Philetus, into the idea of a new moral life begun in the present world. It will not do to defend Protestantism, by surrendering Christianity. We are not willing to give up for it either history or the creed.

Rothe's error, we think, lies in the assumption, that the economy of the world naturally considered must be regarded as carrying in itself, from the beginning, all the necessary elements and conditions of a perfect humanity; in which view a real redemption must complete its work under the form of our present telluric life, (though not of course without the resurrection,) keeping itself to the organism of earth where the law of sin and death now reigns, and achieving a true and proper victory here on the theatre of the actual curse, instead of translating its subjects for this purpose, in a violent way, over into some altogether new and different order of being. A scientific apprehension of what the world is as a historical process or *cosmos*, would seem indeed to require that it should not be defeated in its highest end, the glorification of humanity, by the disorder of sin—that with reference to this it should not turn out a hopeless failure, an irrecoverable wreck, from which man must be extricated by an act of sheer power for the accomplishment of his salvation somewhere else. But we have no right to assume in this way, that the proper sense of the world in its natural order lies wholly in itself as an independent and separate system. The overshadowing embrace of a higher economy—the absolutely supernatural—we must believe rather to have been needed from the first to complete its process in the life of man. In such view, redemption is more than the carrying out of the natural order of the world to any merely natural end; and the church, as the medium of its work, is more than a provisionary institute simply for perfecting the scheme of the state, the highest form of man's life on the basis of nature as it now stands. The true destination of this lies beyond the present economy of nature in the sphere of the supernatural, in an order of things that fairly outleaps and transcends the whole system out of which grows now the constitution of political kingdoms and states. In the kingdom of heaven, the last and most perfect order of humanity, as "they neither marry nor are given in marriage," so also there will be neither Greek nor Jew, but the whole idea of nationality is to be taken up, as it would appear, into a far higher and wider conception, rooted not in nature but in grace. The church will not lose itself in the state; but it will be the state rather that shall be found then to have vanished away in the church.

We have then this result. Since Protestantism is not the same thing with primitive post-apostolical Christianity, but this last looks rather directly towards Romanism; and since, at the same time, Protestantism cannot be historically divorced from the first life of the church, and set in full rebellion against it, (if the church was originally what it claimed to be, a divine supernatural fact and not a hellish imposture,) without forfeiting all title to our faith and trust; there is but one view only in which it is possible to uphold rationally the modern system, and that is the view of historical development; which however must be so taken, that it shall not on the one side remain hopelessly bound to the limits of the Roman system, as in the hands of Dr. Newman, nor yet on the other side run itself out into a fair dissolution of the very idea with which it started, whether this be by the Hegelian dialectics of a man like Baur or by such more respectable theories as we have from the hands of Rothe and Thiersch. A development into sheer vacuity, is only another word for annihilation. If *that* be the true sense of Protestantism as related to the old mystery of the church, all defence of it for faith is gone. It must be a real historical continuation of the church, in the verity of its old supernatural existence, carrying along with it a true participation in its prerogatives and powers, or it is nothing.

It is not necessary now that we should be prepared to determine positively the true construction and proper significance of Protestantism beyond the result now stated, in order to make this result itself of practical account. It is of high account at all events to see what are the necessary conditions of the question which is to be solved, what are the terms and limits within which the solution must move, whatever view we may choose to take of it afterwards as restrained to such bounds. It is much only to have it settled in our minds, that the defence of Protestantism, if it is to be made good at all, must be conducted in a certain general way, whether any particular plan of such defence may be counted satisfactory or not. We propose at present no positive doctrine on the subject one way or another. That has not been the object at all of these articles. We have wished merely to show that the nature of Christianity, and the facts of history, require the argument for Protestantism to run in a certain line, if it is to be of any force; and that no different form of apology, in which this general necessity is overlooked or trampled under foot, can deserve to be regarded with respect. No view of Protestantism can be either sound or safe, which by setting it in absolute universal opposition to Catholicism makes it to be unhistorical, and so cuts it off from all lot or part in the inheritance of the past life of the church.

Nothing more than the sense of this plain truth is needed, to expose the vanity of all that system of polemics against the church of Rome, which proceeds on the assumption that it is purely and entirely false and corrupt, and that it deserves no hearing in truth, and much less anything like calm respect, whatever it may pretend to urge in its own defence.

We are all familiar with the anti-popery spirit under this radical and fanatical form. Our common religious press may be said to teem with it every week. It meets us on the street and in all public places. Our very piety is infected with it to a large extent, both in the sanctuary and in the domestic circle. The fountains of our charity are turned by it too often into wormwood and gall. Many appear to look upon it as one main part of their religion, a necessary evidence of their evangelical temper and habit, to hate and curse the Catholics. However it may be in any other direction, here at least they feel that they do well, as it would seem, to be angry, to show contempt, and to indulge misrepresentation and abuse, to their heart's full content. Nicknames are so put to the tongue, that they flow from it like the poison of asps without effort or thought. All too in Christ's sweet and holy name. The most abominable charges and criminations are trumpeted without proof, as though the bold repetition of them simply were enough in the end to make them good. No pains are taken to understand any doctrine or practice of the church, in the light of its own historical or theological relations; it is counted quite sufficient to drag every article in the most rude and vulgar way before the tribunal of the world's common sense, (alas, how *common* in many cases,) and to take the measure of its merits accordingly; as though the deepest mysteries of religion might be settled by such superficial and profane judgment, as it were at a moment's glance. All runs out easily thus into the most wholesale censure and reproach. Romanism is found to be, from beginning to end, a tissue of impiety and folly, at war with the most sacred interests of humanity, and in full contradiction to the will of God. It is a diabolical conspiracy against truth and righteousness. There is no reason in any of its institutions; they are founded on falsehood throughout; they subvert the whole sense of the gospel, and in their source and operation are purely antichristian, of one order we may say with infidelity itself. Such in general is the tenor of this popular theory.

But no such style of thinking can be maintained, where anything like a sound historical feeling has been brought into exercise in regard to the church. Those who look at Romanism only in this rabid and fanatical way, show themselves by the very fact to have no sense of the divine organization of Christianity as a perpetual living constitution in the world, and no apprehension of the necessity there is that Protestantism should be strictly and truly the product of this life, if it can have any right to exist at all. They make no account of history. Their view of Protestantism is such as cuts it off entirely from the concrete mystery of the church in past ages, and turns it thus into a mere abstraction. In this way it is essentially rationalistic and infidel; and it is ever ready accordingly to make common cause with open unbelief, in treating the whole real past of the church as a sort of universal cheat and lie. Faith in historical christianity at once upsets every such habit of thought; and in doing so necessarily begets a more just and tolerant spirit towards the present Catholic church. It does so in a two-fold view, first as it regards the past, and secondly as it throws its eye forward into the future.

As regards the past, the faith now mentioned feels itself bound to derive the life of Protestantism, genealogically, from the historical church of previous ages; which at the same time is clearly seen to carry in it the leading features of Romanism away back to the Nicene age, and in element or germ at least beyond that also up to the very middle of the second century. Now it need not follow from this, that all such features are to be approved as right and good for all time; nor even that they were in all cases right and good at any time. The very idea of the Reformation implies the contrary; for the meaning of it is, that many things belonging to the old church were either abuses in their own nature, or had grown to be such by the progress of history, which it was necessary at last to thrust wholly out of the way. But no one who has any sense of the divine constitution of the church can bring himself to look upon its whole past order and spirit, for this reason, as false and wrong; nor can he think of denouncing even what he may not be able to approve, in any such style of vituperation as our modern anti-popery sees fit to indulge in towards what it calls the abominations of Romanism. Here then it becomes at once impossible for any person of this sort, to sympathize with the vulgar method of fighting the Roman Catholics which we have now under consideration. Take it, for instance, as it comes before us in " Kirwan," or in the pages of the " Protestant Quarterly Review." It not only fights Romanism, but fights at the same time with fully equal effect the whole ancient church. The points on which it expends mainly its indignation, or ridicule, or scorn, are to a great extent distinctive, not of modern Romanism as such, but of the church as it has existed back to the fourth century, if not indeed to the first part of the second. The argument goes too far, and proves a great deal too much. It becomes immediately profane, by striking at all that has been esteemed most holy for the faith of christians, not simply in the middle ages, but in the ages also that went before. It turns the fathers into knaves and fools. It covers all ecclesiastical antiquity with disgrace. This is more than any sound mind, imbued with the slightest tinge of right historical feeling, can be expected patiently to endure. It is infidelity pretending to preach to us in the name of evangelical religion. If anti-popery is to be at the same time anti-christianity, in this blind irreverent style, the less we have to do with it the better. No such zeal for Protestantism can be entitled to any sort of respect. It carries the evidence of its own impotency on its very front. To have any knowledge of the past, and to perceive at all the organic continuity that must necessarily hold in the life of the church from age to age, through all transformations and changes, involves at once the clear perception also that this vulgar feeling towards Romanism is from beneath and not from above. We need not be slavishly bound by the authority of the past; but as believers in the divine reality of the church, we must consider it one of our first duties to treat its ancient history with reverence and respect. We may not join hands here with Ham, the father of Canaan. Those who do so, and who thus make Christianity vile, while they pretend to be spitting only upon the errors and superstitions of Rome, prove by this very fact that they are blind witnesses and teachers even in regard to Romanism itself. Whatever may be wrong here, *they* are not the men whom it is safe to follow as guides and leaders into a better way. They do not understand what they condemn. There is neither light nor love in their zeal. If our war against Romanism is to be so managed that it must be at the same time a war against all church antiquity, we may as well give up the contest. But to have any intelligent regard for the ancient church on the other hand, any feeling of religious fellowship with it, is to see that Romanism itself is no fair object for persecution in this radical and ribald style. We may oppose it still; but we will have some sense also of its just claims and merits. We will not spit upon it, nor cover it with spiteful and malignant slang. We will not feel, that love to Christ and hatred of the Pope are precisely one and the same thing.

But the future also comes in, through the medium of a right historical feeling, along with the past, to promote this same equitable and moderate tone of thought towards the Catholic church. To have faith in Protestantism at all as a development out of Catholicism, (the only view that allows any real faith in it what-

ever,) is to feel at the same time that it is not in and of itself the
last full result of the process to which it owes its birth ; that it has
not carried away with it the *whole* life of the church as it stood
before ; that what it lacks accordingly in this respect, can only
be made up to it hereafter in some way from the other side of
Christianity, as the same is still extant in the church of Rome.
The actual course of history is proving this, for all thinking men,
more and more. Protestantism, as it now stands, is not the end
of the Reformation. Who will dare to say of it, that any one
of its sects separately, or that all of its sects collectively, may be
taken for the full and whole sense of the holy catholic church,
the original mystery of the creed? It is but too plain, that it
falls far short of the proper idea of this mystery. The sect system, say what we may of it, is constitutionally at war with the
true being of the church, and tends always towards its dissolution. It can never stand therefore as a fixed and ultimate fact,
in the history of Christianity. If it be required in the progress
of this history at all, it can only be for the sake of some ulterior
order in which it is destined finally to pass away ; and so, no
system in which it is comprehended can ever be enduring, under
any such form. In the case of Protestantism, this constitutional instability is now a simple matter of fact which has become
too plain to be denied. The system is not fixed, but in motion ;
and the motion is for the time in the direction of complete self-
dissolution. Fools and bigots may shut their eyes, to the truth ;
but it is none the less clear for all this to such as are earnestly
thoughtful and truly wise. The fashion of this system passeth
away. We can have no rational faith in it then as an abiding
order, but only as we take it for a transitory scheme, whose breaking up is to make room in due time for another and far more
perfect state of the church, in which its disorders and miseries
shall finally be brought to an end. But to feel this, with any
sense of the historical rights of the ancient church, and with
any apprehension of what the Roman communion still is as distinguished from the Protestant, is to see and feel at the same
time that the new order in which Protestantism is to become
thus complete cannot be reached without the co-operation and
help of Romanism. However faulty this may be in its separate character, it still embodies in itself nevertheless certain principles and forms of life, derived from the past history of the
church, which are wanting to Protestantism as it now stands,
and which need to be incorporated with it in some way as the
proper and necessary complement of its own nature. The interest of Romanism is not so left behind, as to be no longer of

any account; it must come in hereafter to counterbalance and correct again the disorder and excess of the other system. To this issue it comes necessarily, we say, with the historical scheme now under consideration.

The issue itself however may be conceived of as coming to pass in different ways, accordingly as greater or less stress is laid on one or the other of the factors concerned in its production.

First, Protestantism may be taken for the grand reigning stream of Christianity, (though not the whole of it by any means,) into which finally the life of Catholicism is to pour itself as a wholesome qualifying power, yielding to it the palm of superior right and strength.

Or secondly, the two forces may be viewed as contrary sides merely of a dialectic process, in the Hegelian sense, which must be both alike taken up and so brought to an end *(aufgehoben)* in a new form of existence, that shall be at once the truth of both and yet something far higher and better than either.

Or lastly, it may be supposed that the principal succession of the proper church life lies after all in the channel of the Roman Catholic communion; while Protestantism is to be regarded still as a true outflow of the same life, legitimate and necessary in its time, which however must in the end fall back into the old Catholic stream in order to fulfil its own mission, bringing into the universal church thus a new spiritual tone which only such a crisis could enable it to reach.

Of these three hypotheses, the first of course falls in best with the natural presumption of all Protestants in favor of their own system. But so far as the vindication of Protestantism itself is concerned, on the scheme of historical development, it would hold good under any of the views now mentioned; for even the last implies the necessity of its presence, and the reality of its vocation, as a vast and mighty factor in the work by which the church is to be made finally complete. It is no part of our business now, however, to discuss the merits either of all or of any of these hypothetical constructions; what we have in view is simply to show, how the general historical view here in question, by which Protestantism is seen to be in its very nature a movement towards something more complete than its present state, and something which is to be reached only in the direction of Catholicism, must necessarily beget towards the Roman church a much more tolerant and favorable feeling than that which usually actuates the enemies of this communion.

We know well, what sort of offence some are likely to take with any statement of this kind. They count it for no small part of their righteousness, to hate the Roman Catholic church with a perfect hatred ; and they are ready to make it a grievous heresy in others, if they fall not in at once with this want of charity, or presume to take any view of the case that is less intolerant than their own. We have only to say however, that *we* have not so learned Christ ; and we know of no reason why we should passively succumb to the authority of any such arbitrary and intemperate spirit. It is no article of faith with us, no term of orthodoxy, to believe that the Pope as such is Antichrist, that the Roman church is Babylon, that a certain scheme of exegesis or a certain construction of church history, brought in to prop up this view, is to be received as of one and the same force with the authority of God's word itself. We have yet to learn, by what right any pretend to set up their exegetical or historical hobbies in such shape, the shibboleths at best of a mere party, for the universal law of Protestantism and the only measure of its faith. We claim for ourselves, and for all Protestants, the exercise here of some independent thought, and full liberty to judge of this whole subject as the case itself may seem to require. It is high time indeed, that the school to which we now refer should itself begin to see, that its Procrustean rule here is one that cannot stand. Anti popery, in this absolutely radical and unhistorical style, is not the whole and only true sense of Protestantism. Its fanatical war-whoop belongs to the outskirts of this camp at best, and not to its proper centre. The best Protestant piety, and we may say the entire Protestant learning, of the present time, fall not in at all with any such senseless yell, but stand in doubt of it more and more as being too often of the very same sound with open infidelity itself. Philology and history are working now mightily against this narrow school, all over the world, and not at all in its favor. Its only strength lies in its determination to ignore and resist, as it best can, the progress of true theological science. But this must soon prove also a crumbling trust. Historical studies in particular are already fast undermining its foundations, by the new trains of thought they are forcing on the mind of the world. The actual course of events too in our own age, is full of ominous meaning in the same direction.

Certain it is, that the present especially is no time for yielding tamely to the madness of any spirit, that seeks to build up Protestantism as the work of God, by denouncing Catholicism as purely and wholly the work of the Devil. Never before perhaps was the principle of unbelief so actively at work in the nominally christian world, for the overthrow of religion under every supernatural view. To make the matter worse, this principle is affecting to be itself the deepest and last sense of Christianity, the true end of its high and glorious mission for the redemption of the human race. Here undoubtedly we meet the real Antichrist of the present age, in a form that may well fill the world with apprehension and dread. It is at once rationalism (with the sect spirit) in the church, and radicalism in the state. Against this formidable enemy, the cause of Protestantism and the cause of Romanism are one and the same ; and wo be to us as Protestants, if we refuse to see and acknowledge the fact. To make Romanism itself infidelity, to deride its supernatural pretensions, to treat its mysteries as diabolical and profane, and to own no fellowship with its faith whatever, (in the common anti-popery style,) is almost unavoidably to come to a sort of truce at least, if not indeed open friendship, with the real infidelity to which it stands opposed, and that is now notoriously making war upon it in precisely the same form and fashion. It is a sad spectacle in truth, when any part of the Protestant church is seen smiling on the enemies of all religion, and even cheering them forward it may be in their work of destruction, simply because it is directed immediately against the church of Rome, as though *any* opposition to this were at once a service rendered to the other side. According to this style of thinking, it would be a gain for the cause of religion if Romanism were at once swept, by some sudden revolution, from the face of the earth, even if open infidelity for the time should be left in its place.[1] Shall we join hands with those who thus think and

---

[1] The want of spiritual discernment here with many Protestants is truly amazing. They are ready to bid God speed to any agency, however low and vile, that is turned against the Catholic church. Every vagabond that sets up the trade of abusing the Pope, finds some favor. Ronge, a few years since, was at once hailed as a second Luther, though his whole cause now lies in the gutter of infidelity. And how was Giustiniani lauded for his work, in getting up German churches of the same stamp in our own country. There is a fearful tendency among us even to make common cause with the revolutionary spirit in Europe, under its worst forms, just because it seeks to destroy priests as well as to put down kings. True, we all condemn Rationalism and Socialism in the abstract ; but we are wonderfully prone notwithstanding to look upon the cause in which they are enlisted as in itself a very good cause, which it becomes us as Republicans and Protestants to cheer and help. The cry of liberty and social rights deceives us. It becomes part of our religion to pray for the success of every revolution got up in the name of freedom, whatever else may be its merits. We fall in with the cant and slang of humanitarian patriotism on this subject, as though it were the true sense of Christ's blessed evangel ; and are

talk? God forbid. They are traitors to the cause of Protestantism, if this be indeed the cause of true Christianity. We abhor every such unholy alliance as is here offered to our view. We go with Rome against Infidelity, a thousand times more readily than with Infidelity against Rome. We are very sure too, that any Protestant feeling which is differently constituted at this point, must be throughout miserably defective and false. It proceeds on a wrong apprehension altogether of the true relation between Protestantism and Romanism; it stands in no sympathy or fellowship whatever with the Catholic life of other ages; it shows itself to be wanting thus in a material element of Christianity itself. Plume itself as it may on its own worth, it is of counterfeit quality in its very nature. Its elective affinities prove it to be false.

We now bring these articles to a close. In the way of general recapitulation, our whole subject may be exhibited in the following propositions.

1. It is an error to suppose, that Nicene Christianity as it existed in the fourth and fifth centuries was in any sense identical with modern Protestantism. It was in all material respects the same system that is presented to us in the later Roman church.

2. It is an error to suppose, that the Christianity of the second century, as we find it in the time of Irenæus or even in the days of Ignatius and Polycarp, was of one and the same order with modern Protestantism. Especially was it unlike this in the Puritan form. However it may have differed from the Nicene system, it was made up of elements and tendencies plainly which looked towards this all along as their logical end. It was the later system at least in principle and germ.

3. The difference which exists in the whole case turns not merely on any single outward institution, such as episcopacy, but extends to the ecclesiastical life as a whole. It is a vain pretence therefore, by which Anglicanism affects to be on this score a true and full copy of what the church was in the first

---

prepared then to denounce every voice that refuses to take up the same song, as false to the genius of America. Such religious papers as the N. Y. Observer make common chime here with the Tribune and Herald of the same city; and the very pulpit rings in many cases, with no uncertain sound in the same direction. But what can be more shallow than all this? Europe may need reform; no doubt does need it greatly. But how idle is it to look for anything of this sort, from the revolutionary spirit that is now bent on overturning its governments and institutions? To expect the regeneration of society from any such spirit, is itself a species of infidelity not to be excused.

ages. The universal posture and genius of the ancient church, its scheme of thought and modes of action, were different. Its life was constitutionally Catholic and not Protestant.

4. No scheme of Protestantism then can be vindicated, on the ground of its being a repristination simply of what Christianity was immediately after the age of the Apostles.

5. On the other hand however, to pretend that this post-apostolical Christianity was in no view the legitimate continuation of the New Testament church, but a full apostacy from this in principle from the very start; so that Protestantism is to be considered a new fact altogether, rooting itself in the bible, without any regard to history; is such an assumption, as goes to upset completely the supernatural mystery of the holy catholic church, in the form under which it is made to challenge our faith in the Apostles' Creed. To take away from the church its divine historical existence, is to turn it into a wretched Gnostic abstraction. To conceive of it as the mere foot-ball of Satan from the beginning, is to suppose Christ either totally unmindful of his own word that the gates of hell should not prevail against it, or else unable to make his word good. No theory can stand, which thus overthrows the truth of the church from the beginning.

6. Protestantism then, if it is to be rationally vindicated at all on the platform of faith, must be set in union with the original fact of Christianity through the medium of the actual history of this fact, as we have it in the progress of the old Catholic church from the second century down to the sixteenth. It must be historical, the product of the previous life of the church, in order to be true and worthy of trust. Whatever line of sects it may be possible to trump up on the outside of the church proper, down to the time of the Waldenses, it is well known that Protestantism was not derived from any such poor source in fact; and one of the greatest wrongs that can well be done to it, is to seek its apology in any such jejune and hollow succession. If it be not the genuine fruit of the best life that belonged to the old church itself, as Luther and his compeers believed, it can admit of no valid defence.

7. This however involves of necessity the idea of historical development; by which both Romanism and Protestantism are to be regarded as falling short of the full idea of Christianity, and as needing something beyond themselves for their own completion.

8. No opposition to Romanism can deserve respect, or carry with it any true weight, which is not based on some proper sense of its historical relations to early Christianity and to modern

Protestantism, in the view now stated. Without this qualification, anti-popery becomes altogether negative and destructional towards the Roman church, and is simply blind unhistorical radicalism of the very worst kind. Its war with Romanism, is a rude profane assault in truth upon all ecclesiastical antiquity. No such controversy can stand. History and theology must in due time sweep it from the field.

J. W. N.

The Vindication of the Revised Liturgy (The Order of Worship of 1866) was written at the request of twenty-one Elders of the Reformed Church after the meeting of the General Synod in Dayton in 1866. That meeting had been torn with controversy and dissension concerning the use of liturgical forms for the worship of the congregations.

The Liturgical Committee had presented the Provisional Liturgy in 1857 eight years after its appointment. The Synod of 1863 instructed the committee to present a revision at the 1866 meeting which they did under the title, *The Order of Worship for the Reformed Church in the United States*. It consisted of twenty-three sections and included orders of service for all occasions, a lectionary of printed gospels, epistles and collects, and scripture readings and prayers for the family.

The *Order* was the creation of the Eastern Synod of the church. The Ohio Synod, representing the western section of the church, was greatly opposed to a liturgy for the congregation and desired a directory of worship which would be used only by the pastor. They were in the process of creating such a manual. J. H. A. Bomberger, who was an original member of the Liturgical Committee of Eastern Synod, led the group opposed to the Revised Liturgy. He was supported by many of the western churchmen.

Some weeks before the meeting of the General Synod at Dayton, Bomberger had published a pamphlet, *The Revised Liturgy*, in which he denounced in violent terms all aspects of the *Order of Worship*. In a certain sense it was a reply to Nevin's *The Liturgical Question* published in 1862 which presented the theology and rationale of the work of the Liturgical Committee.

After much debate the General Synod at Dayton voted by a small majority to allow the usage of the *Order of Worship* in the congregations and families of the Reformed Church without interfering in any way with the freedom of congregations and pastors not to use it. However the debate was not over. Early in 1867 Nevin published the *Vindication* to answer Dr. Bomberger. In May of the same year Bomberger blasted the liturgical party with his pamphlet *Reformed Not Ritualistic*. The controversy continued until the General Synod of 1878 appointed a Peace Commission whose members were equally divided between the liturgical and anti-liturgical parties in the church.

Nevin's *Vindication* reviews the history of the Liturgical Committee as he participated in it and presents the theological foundations of its work. He reiterates the cardinal theological positions that came to be known as the Mercersburg Theology: Jesus Christ is the principle of Christianity in his Person, the Creed is the "regula fidei" of the Christian world, the Church as the Body of Christ in the world is objective and historical. Therefore worship must be churchly, liturgical and sacramental.

VINDICATION

OF THE

REVISED LITURGY,

HISTORICAL AND THEOLOGICAL.

BY THE

REV. J. W. NEVIN, D. D.

PHILADELPHIA;

JAS. B. RODGERS, PRINTER, 52 & 54 NORTH SIXTH STREET.

1867.

ELDERS' REQUEST.

DAYTON, December 1, 1866.

REV. J. W. NEVIN, D.D.

REV. AND DEAR BRO.:—

We, the undersigned, *Elders of the General Synod*, being impressed with the conviction, that the exhibition of the history, doctrines, and ruling spirit of the Revised Liturgy, presented in a tract entitled, "A History and Criticism of the Ritualistic Movement in the German Reformed Church, by Rev. J. H. A. Bomberger, D.D.," must be one-sided and unfair, and, therefore, calculated to do much harm in the Church; and desiring to have an expression of the views held by the other members of the Committee who prepared the Liturgy, would unite in earnestly requesting you to furnish us with a history of its preparation and a critical review of its merits, for publication.

Very respectfully yours,

A. B. Wingerd, Mercersburg	Classis.
D. S. Dieffenbacher, St. Paul's	"
J. Troxel, Westmoreland	"
John Zollinger, Illinois	"
Wm. A. Wilt, Zion's	"
T. J. Craig, Westmoreland	"
Geo. P. Wiestling, Lancaster	"
W. G. King, Clarion	"
N. D. Hauer, Maryland	"
D. C. Hammond, Maryland	"
Daniel Cort, Iowa	"
Jacob Bausman, Lancaster	"
D. B. Martin, Mercersburg	"
John Bowman, Mercersburg	"
Geo. Hill, East Susquehannah	"
Michael Brown, West Susquehanna	"
R. E. Addams, Lebanon	"
Samuel Zacharias, Zion's	"
D. Lupfer, Zion's	"
John W. Bachman, East Pennsylvania	"
John Meily, Lebanon	"

INTRODUCTION.

THE *Request* prefixed to this pamphlet sufficiently explains its occasion and object; while it is of a character also not only to justify, but even to demand and require its appearance. It is most true, that Dr. Bomberger's tract is "one-sided and unfair, and therefore calculated to do much harm in the Church." It was brought out hastily, just before the meeting of the late General Synod at Dayton, to serve a party purpose, and as part of a plan to pre-occupy the members of that body (particularly in the West), with a prejudice against the Revised Liturgy, which, it was hoped, might be sufficient to overwhelm and crush it before it could have a chance of coming before the people. It was, in this respect, like a political campaign document, let off on the eve of an election for effect; and it is characterized throughout by the spirit of reckless misrepresentation we usually meet with, and expect to meet with, in publications of this sort. Its criticisms on the Liturgy itself do not amount to much. They are vague, indefinite, and loose; turning, for the most part, on the use of invidious terms of reproach, and appeals to popular prejudice. But this is only a small part of its offence. By far the greater part of the tract is devoted to another object altogether. Under the pretence of giving a history of the Liturgy, it seeks to make capital against it by trying to show that it is a grand fraud, which has been practised upon the Church by the Committee intrusted with the work of its preparation.

In this view, it is an atrocious libel throughout upon the character of the Committee, as well as an insult to the Church at large, in whose service they have been working for so many years. All this was brought out clearly enough in the Synod at Dayton; and the political bomb-shell went off there without much execution. But the matter deserves unquestionably a still more public exposure. The voice of so large a portion of our Eastern lay delegation in attendance at Dayton deserves to be heard. I proceed, therefore, to the task of vindicating the Liturgy from the wrong that is done to it in this tract, both historically and theologically. The personalities which this must involve, to a certain extent, I should have preferred having nothing to do with; but I do not see how they are to be avoided.

As just intimated, what I have to say will fall naturally into two general parts; a defence of the Liturgy, or say rather of the movement leading to it, historically considered; secondly, a defence of the Liturgy, considered in its actual theological character. For the second part, I will take the liberty of using an article I have written on this subject for the resuscitated *Mercersburg Review.*

PART I.

HISTORICAL VINDICATION OF THE NEW LITURGY.

WORSHIP, in the use of prescribed forms, is not a new thing in the Reformed Church. Liturgies, of some sort, have had place within it from the beginning. They belonged to its church life in Europe, and they came over with the same church life to this country. At the same time, they were held to be a fair subject all along for change and improvement. No Liturgy was considered to be of perpetual force, even for the particular country or province in which it was used; much less for other countries. The liberty of primitive times here was practically asserted, as the proper liberty of the Protestant Church. The old Swiss Liturgies in this way changed. The old Liturgy of the Palatinate became antiquated, even in the Palatinate itself. There was a movement all along, in other words, towards the realization of something in worship, which it was felt had not been fully reached in existing forms. The grossly unliturgical tendencies of later times (Rationalistic in Germany, Methodistic in this country), belonged themselves to this movement. But they had no power to bring it to rest. They only served to urge it onward in its course, by deepening the sense of a want which they had no power to satisfy, and by causing it to be felt, that the true satisfaction for this want must be sought in some other way. Hence, among the "pious desires" of the Reformed Church in America, we find at work all along, very sensibly felt, the wish for a satisfactory Liturgy. The old Palatinate service was *not* satisfactory; and none of the services brought over from Europe, during the last century, were satisfactory. At the same time, the deeper consciousness of the Church refused to settle into contentment with the modern innovation of totally free prayer. Such worship had, indeed, forced itself into use on all sides; but the true genius of the Church, at bottom, resented it as something foreign and strange; and its voice was still heard, though in more or less smothered accents, calling out for a Liturgy that might be worthy of the name.

It was in response to this call, that the *Mayer Liturgy*, as it is called, made its appearance in 1837; the respectable work of a truly respectable man. But, as all know, it failed to satisfy the Church. Full opportunity was given for the trial of it. Nobody thought of opposing any bar to its use. No popular prejudice lay in its way; no outside jealousy stood ready to shout *Ritualism* in its face. But still it found almost no favor. Ministers and people consented in allowing it to fall well-nigh dead from the press. Why? "Because," says Dr. Bomberger, "it was unhappily not constructed after the pattern of our older Liturgies," and was "too much of an accommodation to the spirit of the times." That is, it did not please the times, because it went too much *with* the times, and refused to go full against them, as was done soon after, Dr. B. tells us, by the reactionary movement which was led off by the publication of the *Anxious Bench* in 1842. What the Doctor says, moreover, of its unhappy variation from our older Liturgies, is mere moonshine. No following of that pattern would have helped the matter a particle. There the older Liturgies were; it was an easy thing to bring any of them into use, if the wants of the Church could have been satisfied in that way. But they were not satisfactory; the Church was all the time feeling and reaching after something better; and the Mayer Liturgy proved a flat failure, just because it was not something better, but the same thing in fact—the continuation of a mode or manner of worship, which it was felt the life of the Church had outgrown, so as to need now a different style of worship altogether.

I well remember how Dr. Rauch used to speak of this Liturgy.

He had no patience with its external, mechanical character; especially after the various tinkerings it had to undergo before its final adoption. A Liturgy, he used to say, in his earnest, genial way, should be of one cast, a single creation, ruled throughout by the presence of one central idea; in this respect, like a poem, or other true work of art. But what had we here? Dead forms only, bound together in a dead way; from which it was vain to expect, therefore, that the breath of life should be kindled in the devotions of the sanctuary. Such a Liturgy, he thought, could do the Church harm only, and not good.

Some years passed after this, before any serious movement was made toward getting out a better Liturgy. In the view of many, the matter was not held to be of any very great account. They were willing to abide by the system of free prayer, as it had place in the Presbyterian Church. That, I may say, was prevailingly my own position. I was not liturgical in those days, though not opposed to forms of prayer. But there was in the German Reformed Church somehow the power of a different spirit, that would not be kept down, but still cried, "Give us a Liturgy, whereby we may be able to worship God, like our fathers, with one mouth, as well as with one heart." Thus the Classis of East Pennsylvania urged the subject upon the attention of the Synod, which met at Lancaster in 1847; stating its dissatisfaction with the Mayer Liturgy, and asking that either the Old Palatinate Liturgy, or some other, should be adopted, and made of general use in its place. The whole subject was hereupon referred to the several Classes for their consideration. They reported favorably to the object the following year; and the Synod of Hagerstown accordingly (1848), after a long and earnest discussion, placed the matter in the hands of a special Committee (Dr. J. H. A. Bomberger, Chairman), with instructions to report at the next annual meeting of Synod. This report was presented to the Synod of Norristown in 1849, vindicating at large the use of liturgical forms, and recommending the appointment of a Committee to present at the next meeting of Synod a plan or schedule for a Liturgy, such as the wishes of the Church were supposed to require. The report was

adopted; and a *Liturgical Committee,* as it came to be called
afterwards, was constituted, for the purpose of carrying its recommendation into effect.

The Committee consisted of the following persons: *Ministers,*
J. W. Nevin, Philip Schaff, Elias Heiner, B. C. Wolff, J. H. A.
Bomberger, H. Harbaugh, J. F. Berg; *Elders,* William Heyser,
J. C. Bucher, Dr. C. Schaeffer, and G. C. Welker.

Here properly starts, at the Synod of Norristown in 1849,
the particular Liturgical Movement, which, running through a
series of seventeen years, has issued finally in the Revised Liturgy as it now stands, and the history of which Dr. Bomberger
has contrived so strangely to fabricate into a wholesale slander,
of the vilest sort, against the Committee by whom it has been
produced.

Let no one imagine, however, that I propose to follow him in
the details of his pretended historical argument, with the view
of showing them untenable and false. That would be, indeed,
both time and labor thrown away. He abounds in special pleading, and wastes page after page on points, that are, when all is
done, of no account for the main issue in hand. He lays himself out largely to show that the Synod from time to time clearly
and plainly had one object in view, while the Committee was
just as clearly and plainly bent on carrying out another object;
and it is wonderful what an amount of petty, quibbling interpretation he employs to make the case appear in this false light.
There is a great parade of trying to bring out in this small way
the sense of particular documents and facts, as though this must
necessarily show historical veracity and candor. But who does
not know, how easy it is to make this sort of exactness in particulars the medium of wholesale misrepresentation in regard to
what is general? This is just what Dr. Bomberger has done; and
what is required, therefore, is not a rectification of his historical positions and points in detail, but a broad exposition rather
of the universal falsehood that runs through his tract. This
can be done, happily, without much trouble.

A simple statement of the theory, on which the Doctor con-
structs what he calls his History of the Ritualistic Movement

in the German Reformed Church, is enough to overthrow, for any reflecting mind, the credit of the whole thing. It is too monstrously absurd for any sober belief. It bears the stamp of wholesale falsification on its very face.

The theory runs as follows:—The Synod of the German Reformed Church proposed to have a new Liturgy, and appointed a Committee of supposed reliable men (Dr. Bomberger and Dr. Berg among them), to bring out the work. The Synod had, at the same time, a very clear conception of what it wanted and wished in this movement, and took pains, from year to year, to make the Committee understand exactly the character of the service they were expected to perform. Strangely enough, however, this Committee seemed to be possessed, from the beginning, with a determination *not* to do the very thing they were charged to do in this solemn way. Nay, worse than this; it soon became only too evident, that the Committee had deliberately made up their mind (Drs. Berg and Bomberger still among them), to do the very opposite of the thing they were thus charged to do; that they had, in other words, conceived the plan of another order of worship, a liturgical service altogether different from what the Synod was thinking and resolving about, and now set themselves systematically to the task of bringing the Synod to accept their scheme, instead of its own. It was a bold purpose, assuredly; but the men also were bold, who had it in hand; their position in the Church gave them mighty advantage; and the event has shown that their policy was at once far reaching and profound. They knew it was in vain to think of carrying their point with the Synod openly and directly. So they went to work stealthily, and with circuitous management and stratagem, to accomplish their object; content to wait through years, if only they might be sure of reaching it in the end. With this view, it became necessary, first of all, to stave off action in regard to the Liturgy; in order that time might be gained in this way for working the mind of the Church round, by skilful manipulation, to a new way of looking at the subject, and so room be made for palming off upon it at last what the Committee wished to give it, in place of what the Church itself wanted to have.

Such was the situation of things from the very beginning of this Liturgical Movement; and here it is we have the key, which, properly applied, is sufficient to unlock the secret sense of all its historical intricacies, as regards both the Committee and the Synod. The history of the movement is simply the progress of a curious game between these two bodies—all simplicity on the one side, and all duplicity (diabolically astute) on the other—in which the Committee succeeds in out-witting and out-generalling the Synod through seventeen weary, mortal years; so as to bring things to the melancholy pass they have now reached in the Revised Liturgy. Whether the Committee acted, or refused to act, it all meant the same thing. Their one grand object throughout, was to baffle and defeat the wishes of the Synod; and this they did with a vengeance. Never, surely, was Government, political or religious, so impudently bamboozled before. The Synod had the power all in its own hands; might have had things at any time its own way; could have said whenever it pleased: "Gentlemen of the Liturgical Committee, you have been appointed to do the work we want, in the way we want, and not in any other way; and if you do not choose to do it in this way, go about your business; we will appoint another Committee to do the work in your place." This the Synod could have said and done at any time; but just this the Synod never did say, and never would do. On the contrary, it persisted all along in holding this same refractory Committee to its task. Year after year, the Committee reported, according to Dr. Bomberger, that it was *not* doing what the Synod wanted; year after year, the Synod accepted the report, and continued the Committee in service—all the while reiterating, according to Dr. Bomberger, in spirit, at least, if not in form, its original instructions. No other Committee could serve its turn but this. No other, it was supposed, could produce a Liturgy to its satisfaction. In spite of all its miserable contumacy, tergiversation, and treasonable malpractice, no other was to be thought of for a moment as worthy of the same confidence. It must be either this Liturgical Committee or none. O marvellous Committee! No wonder there should be to Dr. Bomberger's vision "a serpent" in the Liturgy itself, when the magicians that produced it could exercise such basilisk enchantment over the senses of the venerable body they thus played fast and loose with, through a period of seventeen years.

The mere statement of such a theory as this, I repeat, is enough to cover it with confusion. It is outrageously preposterous. No man in his senses can believe it. Yet this is just what all comes to, in Dr. Bomberger's professed history of what he calls the ritualistic movement in the German Reformed Church. There is no true history in it. With all its talk about fairness and candor, documents and facts, it is nothing more than a caricature of history from beginning to end.

The movement inaugurated at Norristown in 1849, he says, contemplated no such Liturgy as we have now offered for our use. This is very true, and needs no argument whatever. The Committee was instructed to "examine the various Liturgies of the Reformed Churches, and other works published on this subject in later times, and specify, as far as this may be done, the particular forms that are believed to be needed, and furnish specimens also, such as may be regarded as called for in the circumstances of the Church in this country." All this, evidently, looks only to the conception of a book of forms for the pulpit; and falls far short of what the idea of a liturgical service has come to mean among us since that time. It is worthy of being noted, however, that even at this early stage of the movement, it was held that there should be no mere following of European examples in what was done, but a proper regard, also, to the circumstances of the Church in this country.

At the Synod of Martinsburg, the following year, 1850, the Liturgical Committee was heard from, as follows: "The Committee appointed to commence the preparation of a new Liturgy, respectfully report, that after such attention as they have been able to give to the subject, and in view of the general posture of the Church at the present time, they have not considered it expedient, as yet, to go forward with the work. Should it be felt necessary on the part of the Synod to bring out at once a new formulary for public use, it is believed that the

most advisable course for the present would be to give a translation simply of the old Liturgy of the Palatinate; although
the Committee are, by no means, of the mind, that this would
be the best ultimate form in which to provide for the great interest here in question. Altogether, it is felt, however, that
other questions now before the Church need first to be settled,
in order that it may become important really to bestow any full
and final care on this question of a new Liturgy."

All this, certainly, looks innocent enough. The Committee
felt that nothing they could make, in the way of compilation,
out of the Palatinate Liturgy and others, would prove satisfactory; and they gave this as a reason for their not having gone
forward with the work assigned them; while they say, at the
same time, that if Synod thought otherwise, and *must* have a
formulary of the sort proposed without farther delay, then the
Committee recommend simply the Old Palatinate Liturgy itself
as the best present provision for the case.

But see, now, how Dr. Bomberger manages to look at so
plain and simple a matter through his green, historical spectacles. Here, at the very outset, he tells us, we are met with
that diplomatic duplicity, which is found to characterize the
relations of the Committee to the Synod all along afterwards.
He has the impudence to say, without a particle of proof, that
"the real import of the reasons" assigned by the Committee,
"for not at once proceeding with their work," was not what
these seemed to mean at the time on their face. There was no
honesty in their report. "The Synod had not asked the Committee to investigate anew the subject of ecclesiastical ritualism;
to take into consideration the expediency or the advisableness
of going forward with the preparation of suitable forms; to
inquire into the present posture of the Church; or to raise other
similar side issues." What they did now, in doing nothing,
was the beginning of their refractoriness, and ominous of trouble. ⸸ This was the first instance in the history of this liturgical movement, in which the Committee, through the influence
of its leading members, set up its own opinions and wishes, in

opposition to those of the Synod and the Church; unhappily, it was not the last."

Is not this the sublimity of nonsense? Did not the Committee recommend the Palatinate Liturgy, if one must be had at once, as the best thing they felt themselves prepared to bring forward at that time? What was there, then, to hinder the Synod from adopting it, and urging the use of it upon the churches? The Committee stated frankly their own opinion, that this would not prove ultimately satisfactory; but the Synod was not bound, in any way, to have the same judgment. Why did it not go on, then, to have the Palatinate Liturgy translated and published? Plainly, because it thought, with the Committee, that the circumstances of the Church called for something different. No censure was passed on the Committee. They were continued in office and trust, as before.

One year after this, at the Synod of Lancaster, 1851, the Liturgical Committee again present themselves, and report no progress. They had not found the way open to do anything they could be satisfied with, in the work placed in their hands; and they had come to despair very much of their being able to produce any Liturgy that would prove generally and permanently satisfactory to the Church. This was especially my own feeling. I had not led the way at all in the movement; my heart was not in it with any special zeal; I was concerned with it only in obedience to the appointment of Synod; other interests appeared to me at the time to be of more serious account; and I had no faith in our being able to bring the work to any ultimate success. In these circumstances, I was not willing to stand charged with the responsibility of continuing Chairman of the Committee; and I asked the Synod, accordingly, to relieve me from this position; with the understanding that I would be willing to act with it still in a subordinate character. The request was granted, and Dr. Schaff was made Chairman in my place. The name of Prof. T. C. Porter, at the same time, was added to the Committee.

All this again looks innocent enough; for common eyes, there would seem to be no mystery about it whatever. But only see once more, what becomes of it, when subjected to the disordered vision of Dr. Bomberger. I get no credit for giving up the leadership of the Committee; on the contrary, it seems to be regarded rather as a stroke of policy, which was designed to help on the general object of obstructing the work the Synod was vainly struggling to get done; although happily, in this case, it seems again, the Synod saw through the *ruse*, and waved it handsomely to the one side. "It was probably understood," we are told, "by most of the clergymen at least of the Synod, why Dr. Nevin had been unable to carry out the wishes of the Church in the work of the Liturgy, and why he desired to be relieved from all responsibility as Chairman of the Committee. But the Synod showed no disposition to modify its views, in order to accommodate them to his opinions in the case. Had there been any thought of departing from the purpose and principles at first laid down by the Synod of Norristown, this would have been a fitting time to bring out such a thought. Instead, however, of betraying any tendency in this direction, the Synod held fast to its original design, accepted Dr. Nevin's resignation, appointed Dr. Schaff in his place, and impliedly, said: Now, brethren, we hope you will have no farther difficulty in pressing forward rapidly with the work, according to instructions previously given, but be able to report its early completion." How the plot thickens! How the history becomes clear as mud!

The hypothesis is, that the Committee have joined hands to thwart the Synod in its design to have a certain kind of Liturgy. Dr. Schaff and myself are at the bottom of the conspiracy; we have conceived the idea of reaching, at last, another order of worship altogether, and are doing all we can, theologically, to bring about such a result; we have engaged the Committee to hold back the liturgical movement; and my giving up the helm is only part of the play, intended to bring matters to a deadlock, and thus force the Synod to come into our views. The Synod has some dim sense, however, of the way things are going; winks significantly at the last sly trick in particular; places the rudder in the trustworthy hands of Dr. Schaff; leaves the impracticable Committee constituted, in all other respects,

as before; and bids a hearty God-speed to their labors, with instruction to "report as soon as possible." Is not that rich?

Dr. Schaff now went to work in earnest, and set the rest of
us to work also, in preparing forms. He had faith in the
movement; as for myself, I had, I confess, almost none. Still,
I tried to do my share of service, and spent hours in what was
found to be generally a tedious and irksome task. The work
involved, necessarily, liturgical studies; and these brought
with them a growing liturgical culture, which required an enlargement of the range, within which it was proposed, originally, to confine the course of the movement.

In the report of the Committee, made to the Synod of Baltimore in 1852, through Dr. Schaff, all this is brought fairly and
fully into view. It gave a plan of such a Liturgy as was proposed; set forth the principles on which it should be constructed,
and offered some specimens of what it was expected to contain.
In this report, the ground is taken distinctly, that the new
Liturgy ought not to be shaped simply after modern models,
reaching back no farther than the Reformation; that among
these later schemes of worship, "special reference ought to be
had to the Old Palatinate and other Reformed Liturgies of the
sixteenth century"; but that the general basis of the work
should be "the liturgical worship of the Primitive Church, as
far as this can be ascertained from the Holy Scriptures, the
oldest ecclesiastical writers, and the Liturgies of the Greek and
Latin Churches of the third and fourth centuries." Should
the principles proposed be conscientiously and wisely carried
out, the report, in conclusion, adds, "it is hoped that, by the
blessing of God, a Liturgy might be produced at last, which
will be a bond of union, both with the ancient Catholic Church
and the Reformation, and yet be the product of the religious
life of our denomination in its present state."

Dr. Bomberger troubles himself sorely with this famous Baltimore report. The Synod, he thinks, hardly knew what it
was about, when it was induced to adopt it. "There was no
time taken," he tells us, "to weigh its import. There was no
dissection of its several parts, no discussion of its pregnant pro-

2

positions. With all the saving, modifying clauses, which we shall show it contains, it cannot be denied, that it proposes great departures from the original design and purpose of the Synod." This is a great confession, coming from Dr. Bomberger. But he tries bravely again to do away with its damaging effect; by catching at all the "saving, modifying clauses" he can find in the case, and making use of them in the way of very small chicanery and special pleading, to show that after all the action of Synod here, does not mean as much as it seems to mean. Matters might have been worse. There is room for praise in what was done, as well as blame. The wisdom of the Synod shines beautifully through its folly; its unseemly haste is characterized, after all, by great caution. "It is very significant," our ecclesiastical Philadelphia lawyer tells us, "that its action is expressed in such cautious terms." "Hastily as this important report was disposed of, there is no such endorsement of its peculiar sentiments, no such committal even to the general basis and plan of liturgy now proposed, or to the proposed departures from the first purpose and aim of Synod in this whole movement, as should be considered sufficient to bind the Synod and the Church to all the details of the report, or to debar all modifications and objections which subsequent reflection might suggest." Precious crumbs of comfort for the chickens of the covenant, truly, in so hard a case! "It proves the wisdom of the body," it is added, "that it spoke with so much official reserve upon the subject. The report was simply adopted, without any expression on its merits." Only this, and nothing more; saving merely a resolution, bidding the Committee to go ahead with their work, and "to carry out the suggestions made at the close of their report." Only *this;* "even suppose the pound of flesh is rigorously exacted, and the Synod held relentlessly to the letter of the bond." *Only* this, O Shylock; and nothing more.

A truce, however, to this pleasantry. I have no mind to stand strictly upon the pound of flesh; and do not care at all to run a race of special pleading with Dr. Bomberger for the exact letter of this Baltimore bond. It may not mean, in the circumstances, all that it has been logically made to mean since.

It is very likely, the Synod did not closely weigh terms, and that, for a large part of it at least, the full import of its action was not, at the time, distinctly considered. But what then? Are we to suppose, that it had not at least a general sense of what it was about? This general sense, in the case, is all we care for; and it is, in fact, also all that is needed, to take the wind out of Dr. Bomberger's historical hobby, and to place the liturgical movement before us in its true light.

Movement there was in the matter, beyond all controversy or question. The Committee had moved; they make no secret of the fact; they come before the Synod, asking an enlargement of the terms of their commission. And now it appears that there has been movement also in the Synod. The confession the Committee make of their troubles is taken in good part. It ought not to have been so, according to Dr. Bomberger. "Who had directed them," he asks, "to make the study of medieval or still earlier liturgies and litanies an essential part of their work? Who had requested them to make selections of services from works issued before the Reformation? Not the Synod. On the contrary, not trusting to what might be taken for granted, the Synod, as we have seen, from the first, used the precaution of naming, definitely, the sources from which it expected the matter of the new Liturgy to be substantially drawn. These were genuine Reformed Liturgies from that of the Palatinate (1663) onwards." What business had the Committee, then, to be bewildering and befogging themselves, like wayward, truant children, with studies outside of these wholesome limits. "Above all, what propriety was there in seeking to involve the Synod and the Church in perplexities, by which, through their disregard of very definite instructions, they had become embarrassed? Neglecting to use the chart and compass put into their hands by the Church, they had become entangled in the wilderness. Why seek to entice the Church into that same wilderness, not to help them out, but to lodge or wander there with them?" The case is well put. All can see that. But, unfortunately, this Baltimore Synod would not look at the matter in that way. It did not get angry with the

Committee; did not scold it; did not bid it back, like a set of naughty children, to the bounds from which it had wilfully strayed. On the contrary, the Synod professed to be well pleased with the Committee; approved its wandering studies; had compassion on its perplexities; and generously granted all it asked in the way of enlarged powers. The Church, in other words, followed the Committee into the wilderness. Was there no movement in all this? Did the Synod of Baltimore stand, in regard to the liturgical question, just where the Synod of Norristown stood three years before? Could it possibly dream that it did so, in the surroundings of its action? No amount of pettifoggery can set aside, what all the world may so easily see to be the plain meaning of so plain a case.

The matter, however, admits and requires a still broader view than this. Whatever the Baltimore Synod meant by its action, that action was not final. It could not bind the Church, says Dr. Bomberger, against the reaction of better subsequent thought rearward. Just as little, say we, could it bind the Church against the movement of better subsequent thought forward. Our concern, in the case of these Baltimore principles and instructions, is, after all, not so much with what they meant for the Baltimore Synod itself, as with the sense in which they have been actually carried out since by the Liturgical Committee, under the eye and open sanction of more than a dozen later Synods. With regard to this, at all events, there can be no mistake. The liturgical movement, the true inward history of the new Liturgy, did not begin in 1852; and it was very far from having come to its end there.

The names of the Rev. Dr. D. Zacharias, and Elders G. Schæffer and J. Rodenmayer, were now substituted, in the Committee, for those of the Rev. Dr. Berg (who had gone into the Reformed Dutch Church), and the Elders, J. C. Bucher and Dr. C. Schæffer (deceased). There was added to it, also, the name of the Rev. Dr. Samuel R. Fisher.

Three years now passed, before we hear of another report from the Liturgical Committee. It was working to some extent; but not with any comfortable feeling of success. During part of the time, Dr. Schaff was in Europe. Much that was done was felt to be afterwards unsatisfactory. There was an accumulation of material, which brought with it no light or order in the work of construction. The more the Committee read and studied, and talked together, on the subject, the more they found that it was no small thing to make a Liturgy; and could only smile at the easy credulity with which it had been imagined at the first, that such a work might be carried through in the course of a single year. One great difficulty was, that the work seemed continually to unsettle and destroy itself. What was done, would not stay done; but had all the time to be done over again. In knowing the wreck of matter, and the crush of forms, through which the hard way of the Committee thus led them, one is tempted to think Dr. Bomberger half right; and to ask what business they had then to be troubling themselves with out of the way studies, which nobody required at their hands. Why should they have left the green pastures of ignorance, and the quiet waters of tradition, where they were first put to the working out of their task? Why, indeed, O foolish, straying, and now much-bewildered Liturgical Committee.

At the Synod of Chambersburg, however, in 1855, we meet them again; and are pleased to learn, from their report, that they have made progress, and are in a fair way to get their work before the Church in the course of the coming year. But the tone in which they speak of it is anything but sanguine. "A growing sense," they say, "of the great difficulty and responsibility of the task intrusted to their care, and of their insufficiency satisfactorily to perform it, has brought them to the conclusion strongly to dis-advise any final action of Synod, for some time to come, on this subject; which is so intimately interwoven with the most vital and sacred interests of the Church, and which is just now beginning to be seriously agitated also in various other Protestant denominations of our country. Their intention is simply to furnish, according to the best of their ability, a *provisional* liturgy, including a sufficient variety of forms for examination and optional use, until the Church be fully prepared, by practical experience, to bring it into such a shape and form as will best suit the wants of our ministers and congregations, and make it, under the blessing of God, a rich fountain of sound piety and fervent devotion for many generations."

The Synod, as usual, made the action of the Committee its own. The report was adopted; the proposition in regard to a provisional liturgy was approved; and order was taken to provide for its publication. At the same time, the Rev. Dr. E. V. Gerhart was added to the Committee.

The Committee went on working; but found it impossible still to bring their work to a close so soon as they had expected. Meeting after meeting was called; and session after session was devoted to the task of reviewing preparations, discussing principles, weighing thoughts, and measuring the proper sense of words. A most important educational discipline, all felt it to be who took part in it, not only in a liturgical but also in a theological view. But the discipline was laborious and discouraging. As before, it was hard to get things finally fixed. Reconstruction and reorganization seemed to have no end. At last, however, though not until another meeting of Synod had passed, the end did come; and the Committee met, for the last time as they trusted, in October, 1857, to subject their work to a final joint revision, and to superintend its rapid progress through the press.

This was an interesting occasion. The entire work, previously examined and agreed upon in parts, was now, after a new general review, adopted unanimously as a whole, in the form in which it became known afterwards as the *Provisional Liturgy*. It is a little curious, that the only notice we have of this meeting, and of the merits of the new Liturgy, published at the time, is from the pen of the same Dr. J. H. A. Bomberger, who sees in the whole Liturgical Movement now nothing less than a foul conspiracy against the dearest interests of the German Reformed Church. It is to be found in a long article which he published in the *German Reformed Messenger* of November 18, 1857, devoted wholly to the purpose of recommending the work. It can do no harm, to borrow here a few touches from this fine old historiographical sketch. They belong properly to our subject.

The Committee, it should have been stated, met in Philadelphia. The occasion was metropolitan. "Its final sessions," we are informed, "were held in the old consistory room of the Race street German Reformed Church, and around the same old walnut table, at which Schlatter, Wynckhaus, Hendel, Helffenstein, and Weiberg, all of blessed memory, had so often been seated, when presiding over the council of the congregation, or instructing the youth of their charge in the holy doctrines of our religion, as set forth in the Heidelberg Catechism. The sessions of the Committee were closed with a fervent thanksgiving prayer, and the singing of the doxology."

Now for the character of the work. "The *Plan* and *Principles* reported to the Synod of Baltimore in 1852, and then approved of"—it is thus the Dr. Bomberger of 1857 can talk— "have been faithfully adhered to in the execution of the work. Accordingly, while everything has been made to yield to the true standard and spirit of genuine Evangelical Protestantism, and especially to the Reformed type thereof, scope has been given to that liberal, catholic spirit, which constitutes one of the most glorious characteristics of an elevated Christian freedom, and is the beautiful contrast of every sort of bigotry and exclusiveness. 'All things are yours,' is the assurance of the Apostle. The Evangelical Catholic Christian, therefore, may appreciate every thing that is good, and make it auxiliary to his faith, his piety, and his love. He need despise, or reject, no age, no nation, no Church, no body of Christians who hold the truth in righteousness, but regard all with charity, and learn from all, with meek wisdom, whatever they may offer for his improvement. In this spirit, according to the Plan and Principles referred to, the Committee, like the prudent scribe (Matt. xiii: 52), seems to have endeavored to bring forth, out of the rich treasures of the Church, things old and new, that by all combined, the edification of Christ's flock may be secured. But the Christian liberality of spirit thus exercised

has been, we believe, limited at all points by ultimate reference to our old standard Palatinate Liturgy. So that while such modifications (in the general plan, in the specific forms, and in the pervading style), as were felt to be expedient and necessary, have been freely allowed, the new work will be found to be in essential agreement with the old. It may be said to be what the original framers of the Palatinate Liturgy would have made it, had they lived and labored in such a period as ours."—
"The book, like every thing else new, will have to be tried, before any right judgment can be passed upon it. If only it be tried in candor!"—"If only the sacramental, festival, and special forms of the new work should come into general public use in our Church, a greatly beneficial influence must be exerted. We have seen and read these forms, and feel confident that they will commend themselves to the warmest approval of all who will seriously and candidly study them."—"Although the forms for the administration of the sacraments are intended to be used chiefly by pastors and people collectively on the appropriate occasions, they will be found no less instructive for private perusal. Parents, who have been blessed with children, whom they have given to the Lord in baptism, would find much admonition and profit in the baptismal service. The reading of it at intervals, in their homes, and to their children, would keep all concerned in beneficial remembrance of what had been promised and done. And nothing, in the way of outward help, would be so well calculated (in the writer's full conviction) to promote the worthy and comfortable observance of the Holy Supper, as the devout perusal of the communion service on the evening, or several times during the week, before the sacramental Sunday."

Who would imagine this to be the very same Dr. J. H. A. Bomberger, that now breathes out threatenings and slaughter against the Liturgy in its revised form; who sees in it all manner of "Gorgons, and hydras, and chimeras dire;" and who especially denounces its baptismal and communion services (in no material point changed from what they were in 1857), as being surcharged with theological poison of the very worst kind!

At the Synod of Allentown in 1857, the Committee reported what was now done. The Provisional Liturgy was complete, and in the printer's hands. The report was adopted; and the following vote of thanks was passed at the same time, showing the light in which the services of the Committee were regarded. It does not sound much like alienation of confidence, or soured humor. The whole runs: " RESOLVED, That our most devout thanks are due to the Great Head of the Church, for having sustained the brethren of the Committee in their weighty labors, and for having gifted them with that spirit of cordial harmony essential to the success of such an undertaking. RESOLVED, That the thanks of this Synod are due, and are hereby tendered, to the brethren of the Committee, for the strict attention, the untiring perseverance, the self-denying labors, and the unwavering fidelity, which they have devoted to the work assigned to them, and that this Synod heartily commend them to the blessing of Almighty God, and to the warmest regard and love of the German Reformed Church." And yet, according to Dr. Bomberger, this same Committee (himself among them) had been fooling the Synod for eight long years; *not* doing all the time what the Synod wanted done; and now at last stood there insulting the Synod to its very face, with the offer of a Liturgy, the like of which nobody had dreamed of in 1849 at Norristown!

The Provisional Liturgy, of course, carried with it no binding authority of any kind for the churches. They were merely allowed to make use of it, in whole or in part, if they saw proper. It was put forth professedly as an experiment. By an understanding with the publishers, this arrangement was to run on for at least ten years.

I had no expectation myself, that the work would be generally adopted. It was not fitted for easy and smooth practice; it seemed to be too great a change for our churches; the very fact of its being an experiment, stood in the way of any general serious effort to bring it into use. Still I did not feel that the labors of the Committee had been thrown away. The work had its literary value. It might do good service educationally. It

was a relief to feel, at all events, that with it we had reached a
decent end for our long, weary pilgrimage in search of a Liturgy; for there was no reason to think we could now reach our
object in any other way. The Church might not be prepared
at all for this new order of worship; but it was just as clear,
that she could not now be satisfied with any such book of forms
as was thought of in the beginning. We were beyond that. We
had got into the wilderness together; and the best we could do
was to make up our minds now to stay there for forty years at
least, leaving it for the next generation to get up their own
Liturgy, should they think proper, in a way to please themselves. That was about the feeling in which I had come to settle
down comfortably in regard to the whole matter; and it gave
me any thing but pleasure to be rudely jostled out of it, a few
years later, by the cry that was raised for a *Revision.*

The Liturgy, in fact, did not get into any general use. In
that respect it proved a failure. Yet it was wonderful to see,
how it worked notwithstanding as a silent influence among us,
in favor of sound ideas on the subject of Christian worship. It
wrought a change, far and wide, in the spirit and form of our
sanctuary services. It served to deepen among us the power of
the liturgical movement, which had given it birth. It became
more and more apparent, that this movement could not be turned
back; could not be arrested, and made to stand still. Its only
redemption and deliverance lay in going forward.

Three years later, at the Synod of Lebanon, in 1860, the
Liturgical Committee made their final report, and were discharged. The subject of revision had now come to engage considerable attention; and this same Synod, accordingly, passed
an act referring the work to the examination of the Classes,
for the purpose of obtaining their judgment of what was desirable with regard to it in this view.

Meanwhile, however, the old treasonable practising of the
Committee against the Church was kept up, according to Dr.
Bomberger, even worse than before. The Committee, as such,
indeed, was discharged, and had no longer any existence; but
its members were as badly alive and awake as ever; and their

plan was now to have the work of revision deferred (as they had held back the work of preparation before, with masterly inactivity, through so many years), in the hope that the Provisional Liturgy, every where unpopular, might still go on nevertheless to infect the popular mind with its deleterious poison; so that the way should be open finally for revising it at last into the full-blown ritualism, which it had been in the heart of this conspiracy all along to compass and reach. And now let the world take note of "a remarkable phenomenon, having relation to the general movement, which appeared during the year 1861"—a sort of prodigy in the heavens, that might well cause children at least to stand aghast. The Liturgy would not take with the grown membership of the Church; the people refused to be educated by it out of their old notions and customs. So the defunct Committee, it would seem, said somehow among themselves: "Go to now; we will send forth a lying spirit among the children, whereby they can be reached and trained into the new ways. Children and youth are pliant and unsuspicious; they can be taught and moulded to any thing." A new Sunday-school Hymn Book, for which, unfortunately, there was only too much need at the time, with proper ritualistic apparatus, suggested itself as a proper medium for the end proposed; and a suitable organ to produce it was not long wanting. The plot, accordingly, was carried into effect. "Such a Hymn Book," we are solemnly informed, "was prepared by the Rev. Dr. Harbaugh, a member of the Liturgical Committee, and was sent forth on its Jesuitical mission." Was it not, then, by the instigation of the Committee? If not, pray, by *whose* instigation?

At the Synod of Easton, in 1861, the action of the several Classes on the question of revision, was reported at large. It did not amount to much. The Classes were greatly divided in their judgment; and so far as any suggestions were made in regard to what should be modified or changed, they were of too loose and indeterminate a character altogether to be of any practical account. The whole subject, in truth, was exceedingly confused. Nobody doubted the necessity of having the Liturgy revised sooner or later, if it was ever to come into general use; the only question was, whether the revision should go on immediately, or be postponed, for years at least, if not indefinitely. For reasons already given, I was myself in favor of indefinite postponement.

The proposition to take the work in hand at once, however, prevailed. After considerable discussion, the Synod took action as follows: "RESOLVED, That the Provisional Liturgy be placed in the hands of the original Committee for final revision; and that the Committee be instructed to consider the suggestions of the Classes as given in the minutes of their late meetings, and use them in the revision of their work, as far as the general variety of the work will allow, and in a way that shall not be inconsistent either with established liturgical principles and usages, or with the devotional or doctrinal genius of the German Reformed Church. That the Committee be requested to report at the next annual meeting of the Synod, if possible, with a view of bringing this devotional work to a consummation desired by the Church, during the Tricentennial commemoration of the Heidelberg Catechism."

To any unsophisticated mind, the sense of this proceeding is abundantly plain. It did not mean, that the Committee must fall back on the old Norristown instructions of 1849; that the Synod had not changed at all its views of what a Liturgy should be since that time; and that the course of the Committee, in not carrying them out heretofore, had been refractory and contumacious. Nothing of this sort. It meant plainly a reiteration of the Baltimore instructions of 1852; in the sense in which these had been distinctly understood and acted upon by the Committee afterwards; in the sense in which every body could see that they had been actually wrought into the constitution of the Provisional Liturgy. That was, in fact, an attempt to bring the liturgical life of the first ages into harmonious union with the devotional and doctrinal genius of the Reformed Church in modern times. And now the order of Synod is, not that it should be pulled to pieces under pretence of amendment, but that its organic unity should be preserved; so that, through all changes, it should remain substantially what it now was, and not be metamorphosed into something else of wholly different nature. This, unquestionably, is what the action of that Easton Synod means, and was intended to mean. And in token of it still farther, we have the old Committee called into existence again, to carry out the work; the very last agency, if Dr. Bomberger's misrepresentations were correct, that should have been thought of for any such purpose. It would have been easy to appoint a new Committee. But no; that would not do. Only the old Committee, it was supposed, could do proper justice to their own work. Let them have full power, therefore, to manage this liturgical question, as before. The Synod will have no other Committee.

Many will remember how earnestly I tried, at this time, to have my own name, at least, dropped from this new commission. I told the Synod, that I had no faith in the undertaking; that I did not think the Church was prepared to receive the Liturgy in any form we could give it; that I knew the proposed work would involve far more than the slight changes some talked of; that I was sure the Committee would not be able to get forward now with full agreement; that there was no reason then to expect that the Church generally would be satisfied with what was done; that in these circumstances the service appeared to me a thankless waste of labor and time; that I had no heart for it, and could not take part in it with any animation or zeal; and that my want of spirit in this way would make me a dead weight only on the cause I was expected to serve. All this I urged; and fairly begged, over and over again, to be excused from the appointment. But the Synod would not hearken to my prayer. The old Committee must serve; and I *must* serve with it—in spite of all I had done, according to Dr. Bomberger, to upset the order and change the life of the German Reformed Church, by this very liturgical movement, in previous years.

In the face of these broad facts, what becomes of the special pleading of such a man, put forward here again, as in the case of the Synod of Baltimore, to torture words and phrases into the service of his own fancies? Is it any thing better than so much idle wind?

When the Committee came together again, it turned out as I expected. There was a difference of opinion among them, in regard to the principles by which they were to be governed in their revision. Dr. Bomberger took one view of the subject, while the rest of the Committee in attendance took another. Three days, at least, were consumed in friendly discussion, and abortive attempts to get forward. Finally, it was felt necessary to refer the difficulty to Synod for settlement; whereupon the following action was unanimously adopted:

"WHEREAS, In the endeavor to revise the Provisional Liturgy, the Committee discover, after a long discussion, protracted through several days, that there is a radical difference of opinion among its members concerning the import of the resolutions of Synod; therefore, *Resolved*, That the Rev. Dr. J. W. Nevin prepare a report to Synod, setting forth a clear, definite, and full idea of both schemes of worship advocated in Committee, in order that Synod may understand the real question at issue, and state in explicit terms what it requires at our hands."

This took place in Lancaster. A meeting of the Committee was held subsequently in Lebanon, when the report thus called for was received, adopted, and ordered to be published for the consideration of the Church. Dr. Bomberger voted against this action. The report was presented to the next Synod, which met at Chambersburg in 1862, in the form of a tract, bearing the title: "The LITURGICAL QUESTION, with reference to the Provisional Liturgy of the German Reformed Church."

Much ado has been made about this tract. The object of it, however, is sufficiently plain. The liturgical interest among us had become embarassed by its own movement. There were mixed up in it two different conceptions of what a liturgy ought to be. We had started in 1849 with one; all of us, Committee and Synod, having in our mind at that time, almost entirely, the notion simply of a book of forms for the pulpit. But we were carried gradually beyond this, and came to feel more and more the meaning of worship in its proper congregational view; which brought with it, of course, the idea of a liturgy directed and adapted more particularly to this end; the idea, in other words, of a liturgy belonging, not properly to the pulpit, but to the altar. Not that these two conceptions were consciously distinguished in this way. On the contrary, they ran more or less into one another; only with a growing preponderance of favor toward the idea of altar worship—even where the meaning of it was not yet fully understood. Under the plastic force of this sentiment it was, that the Provisional Liturgy had finally taken form and shape. It was prevailingly an order of worship for the altar. It became this mainly through its communion service, which was made to rule and control the movement of all its other services. There were come few forms in it, indeed, and parts of forms, which were not strictly coherent with this scheme, but might be said to be of the character rather of mere pulpit services; and so far it may be admitted that Dr. Bomberger is right in ascribing what he calls a duplex character to the work. But he is egregiously wide of the mark, when he speaks of by far the greatest portion of it as being of the type now referred to; to such extent, he says, as "greatly to overshadow, and almost exclude the other;" and nothing could well be more ridiculous, than his notion of converting the whole into a good and acceptable form book for the pulpit, by simply doing away with the responses, and striking out or changing a few passages here and there, supposed to be of objectionable sound. It is all the other way; the reigning character of the Provisional Liturgy is that of an altar service, and what there is in it that does not fall in with this conception, is there only by exception, and in the way of compromise, as it were, with the opposite scheme. So at least the Committee felt, which had produced it, all except Dr. Bomberger; and so they understood the Synod to feel, in the direction it had given them to be governed in their revision by a proper regard to "the general unity of the work." It was felt, at the same time, however, that there might be, and probably was, a measure of confusion still in the mind of the Church with regard to the subject; and when Dr. Bomberger now joined issue with the rest of us on this fundamental question at the very threshold of our new work, there seemed to be but one course for us honestly and honorably to pursue. We would refer the question to Synod; and we would try to do this in such a way, as to cut off, if possible, all room for mistake, and to bring out the mind of the Synod in such sort that there should be no room to dispute about it afterwards. This was the object of the tract now under consideration; and it was purposely written in the form which seemed best suited to reach that object.

To Dr. Bomberger's jaundiced vision, this tract, like everything else done or left undone by the Committee, was part of our plan, either to cajole or dragoon the Church into the scheme of ritualism we were forging for its neck. But in that view, never surely did a band of conspirators play a more stupid game. For what course could the Committee have taken, that was more likely than just the publication of this tract, to rouse against them and their work all the anti-liturgical, or merely semi-liturgical spirit there was in the Church? Was it not a perfect godsend, in this respect, to Dr. Bomberger himself? Has it not been the armory, from which he has stolen his best thunder against the Liturgy ever since? Have not its "concessions" been held up, on all sides, to the people, as enough to damage and damn the work before all examination? Were we not gravely told at Dayton, by more than one respectable declaimer, that the Liturgical Committee had in this tract charged themselves with a design to revolutionize, radically, the ecclesiastical life of the German Reformed Church, and madly asked the Synod of Chambersburg, at the same time, to cooperate with them in carrying out their nefarious purpose? What truly magnificent cunning! What marvellous profundity of art!

Any honest person can see that the tract, instead of being an attempt to seduce the Synod into the views of the Committee, was, in fact, a most honest effort to place the whole subject in a light, which might preclude all blind judgment in regard to it, and bring the Synod to act upon it in the most free and independent way. Speaking for myself again, I may say that I hardly expected or wished the Synod to fall in with the high view of altar worship presented in the tract. Had that body been prepared to say, "We want no such worship as that," I would have been content, and more than content, to be discharged from all further concern in the case. As it was, I was determined, at all events, that there should be no farther misunderstanding, if there had been any before, of what the Committee had been doing thus far, and of what they intended to do still, if they were required to go on with this work. With this view, the case was put in the most extreme light. The distinction between the two orders of worship (pulpit liturgy and altar liturgy) was drawn in clear lines; and in a way which has caused it to be understood since, and practically laid to heart, as it had not been before. The idea of an altar liturgy was declared to be alone worthy of respect. Then it was openly said, in substance: "This idea has governed the work of the Committee thus far, in conformity, as they have supposed, with the instructions of the Synod of Baltimore, in 1852; the Provisional Liturgy is an altar liturgy, in the sense of this tract; and it cannot be made to be any thing else, without destruction of its organic unity and wholeness. That, at least, is the judgment of the Liturgical Committee. It is for the Synod, then, to know and to say, what its real wishes are in this posture of the case. Shall the liturgical movement go on still in the line of this Provisional Liturgy, as thus determined by the sense of the Committee that framed it; or shall it be now stopped here, and turned into another and wholly different course?"

Dr. Bomberger, in the meantime, had been at work, in his own way, to out-plot the Committee. He had taken it into his head, that he could, himself, do up in short order what the Church wanted in this business of revision; and came, accordingly, prepared with a scheme of alterations and amendments, which he fondly hoped the Synod might be ready at once to adopt, and so end the whole matter. Of all this, he said not a word to the Committee, when he met with them previously in regular session, at Chambersburg; but sprung the whole sud-

3

denly upon Synod itself, in most unparliamentary style, by means of what he was pleased to call a minority report, in opposition to the report of the Committee. His proposed revision, however, found no favor! It only served to show how absurd it was to think of manufacturing the Provisional Liturgy into different shape in that mechanical way. There were not probably three members of the Synod who would have been willing to vote for the piebald affair. No vote, however, was taken upon it. There was an animated debate on the general subject of the Liturgy, continuing through three days; at the end of which it was decided, with overwhelming voice, that the way was not open for taking any further action in regard to the Provisional Liturgy at that time; that the optional use of it, as previously allowed, should be continued till the end of ten years from the time of its first publication; and that the whole question of its revision should be indefinitely postponed. The Liturgical Committee was thus dissolved a second time.

This took place in 1862. In the fall of 1863, the General Synod of the Reformed Church held its first meeting in Pittsburg. Here the subject was again called up, in connection with a request in regard to it from the Western Synod. Liberty was granted to this Synod to go on and prepare a new Liturgy, such as, in their view, might suit the wants of the Church; while it was recommended, at the same time, that the Eastern Synod also should go forward with the revision of its Liturgy according to its own judgment, so that it might come before the General Synod in complete form, with a view to final action upon the whole subject.

In conformity with this recommendation, the Eastern Synod, which met at Lancaster the following year, 1864, resolved that a Committee should be appointed to revise the Provisional Liturgy, so as to have it in readiness for being presented in the way required, to the next General Synod.

But only see now what a mess is made of all this by Dr. Bomberger, in his morbid desire to criminate the Liturgical Committee. Their relation to the Synod throughout, in his view, was one of disobedience and perverse unfaithfulness.

The work which Synod had expressly put upon them, three years before, they had failed to perform. Nay, they had even succeeded at Chambersburg, in 1862, in getting it indefinitely postponed; thus "gaining their point," we are told, which was *time,* in the interest of their "extreme ritualistic views." How the Synod could stand such treatment, was wonderful; yet stand it the Synod did, even to the extent of itself doing, unasked, in this last case, all the Committee secretly wished; wearied and worried out of all patience, it would seem, by the contradiction it was called to endure, and ready, at last, to do any thing, just for the privilege of being allowed to adjourn. Now, however, in 1864, one is pleased to find a much-abused Church freeing herself at long last from the badgering and browbeating to which she has been subjected, by her public servants, for so many years. In all conscience, the tragi-comic drama has been carried far enough; let it, then, come to an end. "It was evident," says Dr. Bomberger, speaking of the crisis to which things had come, "that no farther delay would be tolerated. Patient as the Church had always shown itself, even almost to weakness, toward the private views and desires of some of her leading men, and tolerant of what often wore the semblance of disobedience and dictation—tolerant as scarcely any other Church had ever been in similar circumstances—it was manifest that the action of the last two Synods (the General and the Eastern), plainly meant that the work must now be done." All praise, especially to the Lancaster Synod of 1864; it knows what it means in this business; and it means now to have it done.

Now then, first of all, for the agency to be employed in the resumption of the work. The old Committee is officially dead, and out of the way; *twice* plucked up by the roots; and after all its past offences, we might imagine, not to be thought of again in the present case. Let there be at least a wholesome reconstruction, leaving out a part of the old membership, and bringing into the room of it a new membership in sympathy with Dr. Bomberger. But can we believe our senses? This Lancaster Synod reiterates the madness of the Easton Synod. It is the old Liturgical Committee, which is once more summoned to go forward with their old work. Not a man of them is excused; and strangest of all, to fill the places of the Rev. Dr. Heiner and Elder Heyser (deceased), we find now added to the Committee the names of the Rev. Thomas G. Apple and Dr. L. H. Steiner; men known by every body to be in no sympathy whatever with Dr. Bomberger in his late minority stand-point, but, on the contrary, in full sympathy with the majority standpoint opposed by him—and *for that very reason also* dignified with this appointment!

In this new commission, says Dr. Bomberger, "no instructions are given for the guidance and government of the Committee; but it is presumed, that no one will call in question the continued force of previous directions." That is (according to his monstrous hypothesis), after all that had gone before; after the Baltimore instructions, and the sense put upon them by the Committee; after the preparation of the Provisional Liturgy openly on this scheme; after the Easton instructions in regard to a revision, and the way in which these also were openly taken by the Committee; and above all, after the strong, not to say extreme statement they had made of their views in the tract offered to the Synod of Chambersburg: after all this, we say, the Synod of Lancaster, now in 1864, having re-constituted the same Committee, and filled out its vacancies with men known to be of one mind with it in all it had been doing and trying to do thus far; and now saying to it, without farther direction, "Go on, and complete your work;" did not mean at all that they should follow out their past profession of principles and views, but intended just the opposite of this—namely, that they had been wrong all along, and were now expected to take up and perfect their unfinished work, in what Dr. Bomberger held to be the way the Church had wanted it from the beginning. Simply to state the case, is to make it ridiculous.

It is, in truth, sheer nonsense. The Synod knew perfectly well where the Committee stood in regard to the whole subject, and with this knowledge re-appointed them, and bid them resume their work, without one syllable of qualifying direction.

How was it possible, in these circumstances, that the Committee should not take this for a full and formal authorization to go on as they had been doing before, and to perfect their work in its own order and kind, not by pulling it to pieces, but by bringing it into round unity and harmony within itself as an altar liturgy? They did so understand the Synod, and addressed themselves now vigorously to the task assigned them, with full determination to carry it out in this way.

Dr. Bomberger, however, was still obstinate. When the Committee met, he took his old ground again; maintained that we were utterly mistaken in supposing our scheme of revision to be approved by the Church; contended that Synod had, in fact (God knows when or where), endorsed *his* scheme, as the only one to be thought of in the case; and wondered now, that all the rest of us should not give up at once to his single judgment, where we were so clearly wrong, and he himself so clearly right. We could not, of course, yield to this; and after some friendly talk on the subject, it was concluded that we, who were the majority, and the next thing to the whole of the Committee, should go on with the work of revision in our own way; while Dr. Bomberger would simply co-operate with us as far as he could, without being understood to recede at all from his protest against what seemed to him wrong. He himself urged us to go forward in this way; and for a time continued to work with us, as pleasantly as could be desired.

But this did not last. As the revision advanced, and gave promise of being successfully carried through in its own line, Dr. Bomberger found it more than he could stomach. His discontent appears to have reached its climax, when the Committee reported progress to the Synod of Lewisburg, in 1865, and submitted their new forms for common Sunday Service and for the Holy Communion, as specimens of the manner in which they were carrying on their work. "No opinion upon the merits of these forms," he says, "was expressed by Synod." This is very true. But this silence, in the circumstances, amounted to a great deal. Dr. Bomberger was there, and made a violent speech against the course the Committee were pursuing; so eloquently depicting the mischief which was to come of it, that one good brother, at least (innocent of much previous knowledge on the subject), was led to cry out, it is said, in a sort of panic fright, "Mr. President, can't we stop the Liturgy?" He tells us now, moreover, in his historical tract, that these very specimen forms are the worst part of what he considers worthy of condemnation in the Revised Liturgy. The Lord's day service is, in his view, "intensely ritualistic;" and the Communion service is denounced as "essentially inconsistent with the devotional genius of the Reformed Church, and utterly irreconcilable with the apostolic and primitive conception of the ordinance;" although it is, in fact, in no particular point different from the form in the Provisional Liturgy, which this same Dr. Bomberger consented to in 1857, and publicly commended to the Church as being not only good, but very good—"*nothing* in the way of outward help being so well calculated indeed (in his full conviction), to promote the worthy and comfortable observance of the Holy Supper, as the devout perusal" of just this service. These two pattern services, we say, the Synod had before it in 1865 at Lewisburg, with the benefit of Dr. Bomberger's damnatory criticism. And what now did the Synod do? "Expressed no opinion!" we are told. Oh, no, nothing of that sort; only paid no attention to Dr. Bomberger's damnatory criticism; and instead of *stopping* the Liturgy, ordered it on to completion. That was *all* the Synod did.

That was enough, however, for Dr. Bomberger. He sent us word by letter afterwards, that he could take no farther part with us in our work; we were not doing, he would still have it, what Synod wanted us to do; and so he would appeal to Synod against us when it next met. A sort of appellation, one might say, from Philip drunk, to the same Philip when it was hoped he might be sober.

The Committee went on, and finished their work; finished it greatly to their own satisfaction; not simply because they were through with it, but because they felt that they had been successful in bringing the book into a form suitable to the wants of the Church, and likely now to come at last into general use.

In this respect, my own feeling with regard to the Revised Liturgy was altogether different, from what it had ever been with regard to the Provisional Liturgy.

Thus completed, the work was presented, with a very brief report, to the Synod, which met last October at York, under the title: *An Order of Worship for the Reformed Church.* No sooner was this done, than Dr. Bomberger was on his feet again, to spring upon the house another of his unparliamentary interruptions, in the form of a long, elaborate, minority counter-report; which was offered as an apology for his not having acted with the Committee, but amounted, in fact, to a wholesale onslaught upon the work itself, and a most libellous defamation of the views and motives of all, who had been concerned in bringing it out. A libel, which has since been repeated deliberately and at large, in his history of what he calls the Ritualistic Movement in the German Reformed Church. It is wonderful with what effrontery, in this counter-report of his at York, he charges the entire Liturgical Committee (all except himself), as having been engaged, throughout, in a course of clear disobedience to the will and command of Synod, while *he*, singly and alone, had been laboring all along to set our refractory skulls right—but laboring, alas, in vain. He *could* not work with the Committee, it seems, because the Committee, ten against one, would not think as he did, but stubbornly insisted on thinking for themselves. Hence, these tears. "In this spirit, and for such reasons," he whines, "I come back to this Synod to-day from the mission upon which you sent me. I could not perform the duties of that mission in what I am most fully persuaded is the spirit and letter of your instructions, because my associates in the work"—thick-headed, stiff-necked jurymen as they all are—"would not aid me in such an execution of our trust. I would not perform them in any other way, not even to gratify any most favorite, subjective, personal views and tastes, because I believed that to do so involved disobedience to my ecclesiastical superior,"—the Synod, namely, which had been, all along, backing the Committee in their course—

"disloyalty to my Church, and infinite hazard to our spiritual peace and edification."

The action of the Synod of York, on the Revised Liturgy, is comprehended in a special report, adopted in regard to it, which may be allowed to speak for itself. After a brief general review of the liturgical movement, and the instructions of Synod with reference to it from time to time, the report goes on to say of the Committee and their work, as follows:

"These instructions, after much diligent labor, have been faithfully carried out, and, as the result of their labors, continued for the last three years, embracing forty-five sessions in all, we have now before us the Revised Liturgy, printed and prepared for the examination of Synod. The work bears on its face the indications of unwearied patience and perseverance, of self-denying toil, of an elevated and devotional taste, of much study and reflection, and an undeniable purpose to serve the Church and the cause of Christ. It is questionable, whether more labor and earnestness of purpose have ever been bestowed on any similar work, in Europe or in this country."—"The Liturgy, now presented to the Church, is fully as much the work of the Synod as of the Committee. It must be conceded, that the Committee have acted with prudence and respect for the instructions of Synod, at each step they have undertaken in the prosecution of their labors, and that all along they have been prompted and urged forward in their work by the special action of the Synod. It is, therefore, the legitimate child of this Synod. Whether it will ever come into general use among our congregations or not, it is evident that for all time to come, it will be a monument to the learning, ability, piety, and devotion of its authors to the liturgical idea, which they have so well comprehended."

Then follow these three resolutions:

"1. *Resolved*, That our thanks are due, and are hereby rendered, to the great Head of the Church, that this work, so far as Synod is concerned with it, has been brought to a termination."

"2. *Resolved*, That the thanks of the Synod are hereby tendered to the Committee, for the zeal, ability, and unrequited toil, which they have displayed in the prosecution of their work, from the beginning to the end.

"3. *Resolved*, That the Revised Liturgy be referred to the General Synod for action, and that, in the meantime, the optional use of the Revised Liturgy be authorized, in the place of the Provisional Liturgy, within the limits of the Eastern Synod, until the whole question be finally settled by the various Classes and the General Synod, according to the Constitution of our Church."

By this action, the new Liturgy came into the hands of the late General Synod at Dayton, in conformity with the order issued three years before, by the General Synod of Pittsburg; and now it was, that its friends were brought first fully to see, what manner of spirit it was that actuated and ruled the opposition, which had begun to work against it. This opposition sought nothing less than the destruction of the young child's life. Although it had been declared all along, that it was such an order of worship as the people did not want, and never could be brought to receive with any sort of favor, yet, now that it stood there asking barely permission to live, and nothing more, it was felt that this would be unsafe. Who could tell what power might be slumbering in that gentle, peaceful form, after all? "Herod, and all Jerusalem with him, was troubled;" and so the fiat went forth, not openly altogether, but, as it were, in secret: "Let the Liturgy die, before it is well born; let it pass away as a hidden, untimely birth, and become thus as though it had never been."

We have seen before, that permission had been granted to the Western Synod, to form a Liturgy of their own. They had not liked the Provisional Liturgy of the East; let them get up, then, a different order of worship to suit themselves, and have it ready to present, also, to the next General Synod. They did put their hand to this task. A Liturgical Committee was appointed to carry it forward; which also went bravely to work, and in due time got forth some interesting specimens of what they were able to do in this line. But there the movement

came to an inglorious end.   The specimen forms did not prove
satisfactory, either to the public at large or to the Committee
themselves.   The *Complete Manual,* as it was christened beforehand, got no farther toward completeness; and so, when we
came together in General Synod at Dayton, we found no such
work of the Western Synod there, but only an official act on
their minutes, asking for more time to get it ready.

What we did find there very soon, however, was a pretty
general determination on the part of these Western brethren to
put out of the way the Revised Liturgy of the Eastern Church,
now happily brought within their clutches, as it might seem,
for this very purpose.

Whence, we may well ask, such unbecoming animosity in
breasts otherwise generous and good?   Partly, of course, from
what we may call the natural opposition of the Western religious spirit to the whole idea of worship, under a liturgical
form.   But partly, also, beyond all doubt, from the factious in-
dustry and zeal of Dr. Bomberger and his clique in the East;
who all along, but more especially of late, had been working upon
this prejudice, and trying to persuade the Church in the West,
that all things were going wrong in the Eastern Synod, both
theologically and ecclesiastically; and that the salvation of the
German Reformed Church, in America, now depended on the
rising star of empire in the Synod of Ohio and the Adjacent
States.   This factious element had claimed, indeed, as we have
seen, to be the reigning power in the Eastern Synod itself; but
it had an uncomfortable sense still, of having been always, more
or less, worsted there in its anti-liturgical conflicts; and it was
a great satisfaction for it now, therefore, to think of joining
hands with this ultramontane jealousy at Dayton, so as to roll
off from the German Reformed Church, at once and forever,
the reproach now resting upon it from the liturgical movement.
No pains, accordingly, were spared, to win the political game.
Dr. Bomberger's tract, on the "Ritualistic Movement," was
got out hastily, and circulated far and wide.   The *Western
Missionary* was set to sounding a continuous alarm on the same
theme.   Ominous, bad-sounding words, were made to fall on all

sides upon the ears of the people. Appeals were addressed to their prejudices and their fears. All was done that could be done, to have the Liturgy prejudged and condemned, before it was either seen or read.

We all felt this when we got to Dayton. There was an element at work around us, that boded no good, but harm only, to the new Order of Worship. The opposition to it was strong; and it was called to give account of itself at what was, in one sense, a foreign bar. The Western delegation was full; the delegation from the East, especially in the case of the Elders, was only partially present. It was painfully evident, moreover, that the Western delegation itself had no power, as things stood in the West, to be entirely independent and free. Men could not vote in all cases as they might wish; but had to do it, in some cases at least, as they *must*.

Still would the brethren of the Western Synod seriously join hands with a miserable faction of the Eastern Synod, to subvert at one blow, in such a case as this, a work which had cost this last so many years of care and labor? That was hardly to be imagined beforehand; and I must confess it filled me with surprise, when I found that this, and nothing less than this, was what these Western brethren really proposed to do. We had it all brought out at last in the minority report, as it was called, on the subject of the Revised Liturgy, which every effort was made to have substituted for the majority report allowing its optional use. In this minority paper, drawn up by Professor Good of Tiffin, a long show of reasons was offered to prove that the Liturgy would not answer for the use of the Church; and on the ground of these reasons, preferred without any real examination of the book, the Synod was now asked to give judgment against it, without farther knowledge or inquiry; and to put it, along with the unfinished and abortive material of the Western Synod, into the hands of a new Committee; who should then go on to cut and patch all, at their pleasure, into some unknown shape, which, it was hoped, might satisfy at last the liturgical necessities of the German Reformed Church.

Could any thing well be more ironically absurd? It was more

than absurd, however; it was monstrous. Only look at the
case. Here was the Eastern Synod, which had been working
now through seventeen years to make a Liturgy. Its best
strength, talent, learning, piety, patience, and perseverance, had
been expended upon the object. Finally, after so long a time,
the movement was felt to be crowned with success. It had
issued the Revised Liturgy, which was now submitted to
the General Synod, according to previous order, with the
proud feeling of a duty well performed. For no one presumed
to call in question the general merits of the book. It was allowed on all hands to be of the first order in its kind. It was,
in this respect, an ornament and honor to the Church to which
it owed its being. And how, now, was it proposed to receive
the work in the General Synod? The proposition, in plain
English, was nothing more nor less than this; that the General
Synod should take the work out of the hands of the Eastern
Synod, and just then and there, without farther ceremony, crush
it ignominiously out of existence. What! without ever looking
at it in the way of examination? without giving it so much as a
chance to be known and judged on its own merits? Exactly
so; let it perish without any troublesome and useless formality
of this sort. But how is it expected that this can be done?
Will the brethren of the Eastern Synod consent to be robbed of
what has cost them so much, in such summary and ruthless
style? It matters not; the book is now in the hands of the
General Synod; only let the brethren of the West, by a sec-
tional vote, join hand in hand with Dr. Bomberger and his company, and they will be able, it is to be hoped, to do with it what
they please. Still, on what plea is all this violence to be done?
What crime is charged upon the Liturgy? What evil has it
wrought, to justify such wholesale rejection? How are those
who are asked to join in this vote (ministers and elders), to
know that it deserves such merciless treatment at their hands?
Their knowledge is not needed; their ignorance will answer just
as well; nay, the less they know of the matter, the better. They
will be the more sure to vote then, as they are wanted to vote.
Not one Western minister in ten, it is true, has examined the

book; not one Western elder in ten, probably, has so much as even looked into it. But what of all that? Have they not Dr. Bomberger's word for it, that it is full of all sorts of mischief? Has he not published a tract to put it down? Has not this been echoed by the "Western Missionary?" Are not Professors Good and Rust, and Williard, all here to make speeches against it? What need have we farther for witnesses? The power seems to be providentially in our hands. No time so favorable for the deed we meditate may ever occur again. Let the Revised Liturgy of the Eastern Synod die!

A beautiful spectacle truly, was it not, this attempt to turn the General Synod, at its second meeting, into an organ, through which the Synod of the West might be able to rule, as with a rod of iron, the mother Synod of the East!

One cannot help wondering and asking, what would have come of the radical proceeding, if it had been crowned with success. How would the brethren have disposed of the Liturgy, once fairly in their hands? It was to have gone into the hands of a new Committee, to be taken to pieces and reconstructed at their pleasure. But where was the Committee to be found for such work? The old Committee, of course, could not have been thought of in the case; neither was it to be imagined that any member of it would consent to take part in the service, unless it were Dr. Bomberger. Still farther, no friend of the Liturgy in the Eastern Synod could have had any thing to do with it. It must have been, then, mainly a Western Committee, composed of such men as the Brethren Williard, J. H. Good, Rust, and M. Stern, in conjunction with Dr. Bomberger, and one or two others that may be imagined, from the East. The respectability of such a Committee, in itself considered, need not be called in question. But the idea of placing the finished work of the Eastern Synod in its hands, as so much *material* simply, along with the botched stuff previously prepared in the West, to be extemporized now into new and better form! *Spectatum admissi risum teneatis, amici?*

Our good Western brethren have reason to be thankful, that the farce was not allowed to play itself out to this ridiculous

length. Some of them, no doubt, are already ashamed of what
they tried to do at Dayton, and pleased with their own defeat;
and it will not be strange at all, if before the meeting of the
next General Synod in Philadelphia, the cause of the Liturgy
shall be found to be quite as strong in the West, as it has now
shown itself to be in the East.

In the circumstances which have been described, it was a
great victory that was wrought in favor of this cause at Dayton;
far beyond all it might appear to be to superficial observation.
The friends of the Liturgy knew then, and know now, that the
vote in its favor meant a great deal more than the difference
simply of the yeas and nays recorded in it; and the enemies of
the Liturgy know the same thing. The true significance of the
vote lies in the fact, that it was a struggle of the East to save
its own cause here, against a faction which sought, by help of
the West, to destroy it—a struggle, at the same time, which had
to be maintained on Western ground. In this character, the
stand made in favor of the Liturgy was powerfully felt in the
West itself. There was a moral superiority gained by the argument in its behalf, which told upon the General Synod, and upon
the outside community, with far wider and deeper effect than
any counting of votes; which has been working for good since,
and which will continue to work for good still through a long
time to come. But more important than all this, was the way
the conflict served to bring out the thought and feeling of the
Eastern Synod in regard to the great interest which was here
at stake, and to show clearly where it stood, and intended to
stand, on the issue which had been raised concerning it. The
only vote that could be considered of material account in the case
was the vote of the East, including the Westmoreland Classis.
It was properly an Eastern question that was to be decided.
The voice of the West in regard to it meant nothing; because
it was uttered, to a large extent, in profound ignorance of the
subject, and under the power of blind, unreasoning prejudice.
The Liturgy belonged properly to the Eastern Synod; was the
child of the Eastern Synod; had its native home in the Eastern
Synod; and by the judgment of the Eastern Synod was destined

finally to stand or fall. In this view, as all may easily see, the vote of the Eastern delegation at Dayton was an overwhelming decision in its favor. What an extinguisher on Dr. Bomberger's slanderous tract; the burden of which is throughout, that the Liturgical Committee had obstinately refused all along to do what the Synod wanted them to do, and had now finally, with this Revised Liturgy of theirs, capped the climax of their disobedience, in a way which the Synod could no longer possibly endure. We have seen before how the action of one Synod after another, on to the very last one at York, had given the lie practically to this monstrous imagination. But never was this done to greater purpose than by the Eastern vote in favor of the new Liturgy at Dayton. Had the entire Eastern delegation been at hand, the vote would have been a great deal stronger. As it was, we all know in how meagre a minority it left Dr. Bomberger and his colleagues. Two of these colleagues, besides, were the delegates from the Classis of North Carolina; which has been in a state of ecclesiastical secession from the Synod, ever since the present liturgical movement commenced; and whose representatives, therefore, allowed themselves, with very bad grace certainly, to be brought North at this time, for the purpose of meddling with it in any such factious way. Aside from these ciphers, the clerical vote on that side stood next thing to nothing. And it was little, if any thing better, with the lay vote. Our Eastern Eldership, after all the attempts which had been made to alarm their fears, and set them in array against their Ministers, went almost in a body in favor of the Liturgy. Shall we hear any thing more of a want of sympathy and good understanding between the Synod and its Committee, on this subject?

What has just been said, does not mean, of course, that the Revised Liturgy has been endorsed and ratified, in form, by what was done in its favor at Dayton. The vote there, we all know, was not intended to do any thing of that sort. The time for any thing of that sort had not yet come. The vote meant simply, that the Liturgy should have fair play; that, as a work of art, it should not be subjected to the vandalism of being made so much raw material merely, for the manufacture of another work (not of art), in the hands of Messrs. Good, Rust, Bomberger & Co.; that the Eastern Synod should not be required to stultify itself, by abandoning both the work and the Committee that made it, to the tender mercies of a fanatical crusade, got up to lynch it out of existence, without judge or jury; that after having been brought, through long years of learned and laborious preparation, under the eye and ordering hand of the Synod, to the perfect working form it had now reached, it should not be kicked to the one side by the ignorant prejudice of such as knew nothing about it, but should have, at least, the opportunity of coming before the people, to be tried by them on its own merits. This is what the action, at Dayton, meant; nothing more. But this, in the circumstances, was much. Nobly has it served to redeem the honor of the Eastern Synod, and to vindicate the good name of its grossly calumniated Liturgical Committee.

So much for the historical defence of the Liturgy. How far the work itself, in the form in which it is now before the public, may prove satisfactory to the Church, remains yet to be seen. The Committee, with its friends generally, are quite willing to leave the settlement of that question where it properly belongs, with the people. They have no wish to force it into use in a single congregation. It is not felt that the honor, either of the Committee or of the Synod, depends, in the case, on what may become of the book, finally, in this way. Our appointed service is done; done faithfully, and to the best of our ability. We have got out at last, what we believe to be a good Liturgy, in good working order; and room is now made for its being put to practical experiment among our churches. If they find it to be what they want, and are willing to make use of it, either in whole or in part, it will be well. If they find it otherwise, and do not choose to adopt it, that will be all well too; nobody will have any reason to complain; the thing will have taken its right course, and come to its conclusion in a fair and right way. That is all that is wanted or wished.

Neither let it be imagined, that we object at all to having the

Liturgy subjected to examination and criticism. If it cannot bear to have its merits fairly and honestly investigated in this way, it ought not to expect favor. What its friends complain of is, not that it should be put upon trial, but that it should be attempted to put it down without trial. Not that judgment should be exercised upon its merits, but that without any regard to its merits, it should be proposed to have it condemned and set aside on other grounds altogether. The Liturgy courts enlightened criticism; it deprecates only falling into the hands of ignorant prejudice or dishonest passion.

The way is now open to pass on to the consideration of its theological character.

4

PART II.

THEOLOGICAL VINDICATION OF THE NEW LITURGY.

The discussion on the Revised Liturgy, at the meeting of the late General Synod in Dayton, brought out clearly two things. It showed that the liturgical question, as it now has place among us in the Reformed Church, is in truth a doctrinal question of the deepest significance; and it showed also that as a doctrinal question it has to do, not with one or two points of theological opinion simply, but with theology in its universal view.

This accounts for the earnestness with which the Liturgy is opposed by those who have set themselves against it. To some it has no doubt appeared strange, that the book should have become an object of such strong jealousy and dislike. For by general confession now, we are a liturgical branch of the Church; we allow the propriety of prescribed forms of worship; we hold it part of our Reformed right to use them, or not to use them, as to our congregations severally may seem best. In conformity with this freedom, we have been willing to let liturgies take their course among us heretofore, with little or no attempt at anything like ecclesiastical supervision or restraint. Our ministers might use the old Palatinate Liturgy, or some irresponsible compilation handed down from the last century, or the Mayer Liturgy, or any other Liturgy they pleased; nobody felt called upon to interfere; all were willing to let ministers and people judge for themselves what sort of service might best answer their wants. But in the case of our new Liturgy, all this tolerant indifference has suddenly come to an end. Even in its first imperfect form, as the Provisional Liturgy, the broad sanction of the Church, under which it appeared, was not sufficient to protect it from violent obloquy and assault. Pains were taken to create prejudice against it on all sides; it could not be introduced, it was said, among our people; and yet, strangely enough, its influence was deprecated with ominous apprehension, as likely to work mischief far and wide. As the Revised Liturgy, it is now relieved of its first defects, and brought into easy working form. But this has only drawn upon it more apprehensive jealousy, and more active opposition, than what it had to encounter before. Hence the onset made upon it at Dayton. That was the culmination of a movement, which looked to nothing less than the violent suppression of the new Order of Worship before it was fairly presented to the churches. The churches, it was still said, could never be brought to receive it; but it was held dangerous, now more than before, to give them the opportunity of deciding that point for themselves. Not only must the book not be formally allowed; it must be formally condemned and prohibited from use. The usual congregational liberty of the Reformed Church must here come to an end. For this Liturgy there could be no toleration. The opposition to it had grown virulent. It amounted to fanatical hatred.

To some, we say, all this may have seemed strange. But it is accounted for by the theological life of the new Order of Worship. Had the book been a mere pulpit Liturgy, a collection of dry forms for the use of the minister in the usual style of such mechanical helps, it would have called forth no such virulent opposition. But it was something altogether different from that. It carried with it the spirit and power of a true altar Liturgy; and in this character it was felt to involve, not simply a scheme of religious service, but a scheme also of religious thought and belief, materially at variance with preconceived opinion in certain quarters; the sense of which then became instinctively, where such opinion prevailed, a feeling of antagonism to the whole work. Thus at our late General Synod, the liturgical discussion proved to be, in fact, an earnest theological discussion, the interest of which extended far beyond the particular denominational occasion that gave rise to it. It was remarkable, indeed, that the opponents of the new Liturgy seemed to lay comparatively little stress on the mere ritual points, to which at other times they have taken exception. The question of responses, for example, hardly came into the argument at all. Every other consideration was for the time swallowed up by the question of doctrine. And here, again, the special was evidently ruled by the general. It was not so much dissatisfaction with single doctrinal statements here and there in the Liturgy, as hostility rather to its whole doctrinal basis, that roused and led on the war for its destruction. The Liturgy represented one system of religious thought; the opposition to it represented another; the two constitutionally different, and mutually repellent. Hence the controversy.

On the floor of the Synod, this controversy was met by the friends of the Liturgy with overwhelming success. The charges brought against it were shown to be untenable and false. Its doctrinal orthodoxy was triumphantly sustained. In the nature of the case, at the same time, this defence rebounded into the form of an attack upon the orthodoxy of the opposite side. It was shown that the offence taken with the Liturgy resulted from want of sympathy with the true idea of the Gospel, as this is owned and set forth in the forms of the Liturgy; and that the party opposing it was itself, therefore, theologically unsound, as standing in the bosom of a system which, as far as it prevails, draws after it the rationalistic subversion of the Christian faith altogether. The real character of the system in this view, it may be added, cropped out actually, from time to time, in the speeches which were made from that side of the house; in a way that served, if not actually to horrify, at least very seriously to startle, the better sensibilities of many, who had been brought up to believe different things.

What we propose now, is to bring this momentous issue between the Liturgy and its enemies into wider public view.

Vast pains have been taken all along to disseminate doubts of its orthodoxy, and to create in this way a prejudice against it in the mind of the Church. Heretofore the way has not been open properly for meeting the loose, and always more or less indefinite charge. Now, however, the time seems to have come for laying aside all silence and reserve in regard to the subject. The theological character of the Liturgy has been challenged, in a style which makes it proper and necessary to confront the challenge. Our object in this article is immediately and primarily its defence; but all such defence, as we have just seen, is necessarily at the same time a polemical assault on the system of theological thinking, from which the challenge in question proceeds. Such is the nature of the issue here joined. If the opponents of the Liturgy are sound in their theological premises, the Liturgy of course must be considered theologically unsound; but if it should appear, that it is the Liturgy in fact which rests in sound premises, then we shall know with equal certainty, that the charge of unsoundness falls upon the other side. Our vindication in one direction, becomes thus, as a matter of course, crimination in another direction. We turn upon the theological enemies of the Liturgy their own charge. In the prosecution of our argument, we shall cause it to appear that they are themselves unevangelical, just where they call in question the evangelical character of the Liturgy. We shall be under the painful necessity of showing, that by their own concession, or in the way of unavoidable inference from their premises, they stand committed to views that are heretical in the worst sense of the term.

Let it be understood, however, that this accusation is not preferred against the adversaries of the Liturgy indiscriminately. We have limited the charge purposely to its *theological* enemies; that is, to those who, consciously or unconsciously, hate and oppose the system of theological belief, in whose bosom it stands, and from whose inspiration it draws its life and power. We would fain hope, that even among these there may be some, whose minds are not closed absolutely against the truth, and who need only the help of some candid and dispassionate inquiry to be made sensible of the danger of following blindly the prejudices by which they are now led. Beyond the range of all such theological opposition, however, there is a large amount of disaffection felt toward the Liturgy at present, which rests upon other grounds altogether. It is the result of misrepresentations industriously circulated, of fears blindly awakened, of prejudices adroitly played upon by party address—all in profound ignorance, for the most part, of what the Liturgy actually is, and of what it proposes to do. With better information, much of this disaffection may be expected to disappear. The friends of the Liturgy, at all events, are very willing to have it put as widely as possible to this test. They only ask that it should be allowed to face all such popular prejudice on its own merits. Let the people have an opportunity to judge for themselves, whether it be suitable to their wants or not. We do not shrink from this tribunal, even in our present theological argument. On the contrary, we appeal to it without fear. It was said on the floor of Synod, indeed, by one who opposed the Liturgy, that its theology was of too deep a character to be intelligible to the people. As if the people, forsooth, could not find themselves properly in the Creed, the Te Deum, the Lord's Prayer, the Litany, the Ten Commandments, the Church Lessons and Collects, but only in the creations, extemporaneous or otherwise, let down upon them in the usual style from the modern pulpit. We have no such low opinion of the capacity of our laity. In the case before us, many of them at least have theological instincts, which are better and safer than all scholastic speculations; to say nothing of traditional beliefs, which no logic can set aside. To these instincts and beliefs we now make our confident appeal.

As already said, the doctrinal objections made to the Liturgy at particular points, refer themselves throughout to its general theology, the scheme or theory of Christianity, taken as a whole, in which its different parts are comprehended. A proper regard to order requires then, that we should direct our attention first to this general scheme. Only after the theology of the Liturgy in such broad view has been vindicated, will the way be open for considering briefly the errors charged upon it in special instances.

What, now, is the reigning theology of the Liturgy? It is sometimes spoken of in this country as the Mercersburg Theology. But the system is far wider in fact than any such name; and no name of this sort besides can give us any true insight into its interior character and constitution. What we need here, is not a distinctive title for the theology in question, but a distinguishing apprehension of its nature. For our present purpose it may answer to characterize it descriptively, (without pretending to exhaust the subject), under a threefold view. In the first place, it is Christological, or more properly perhaps Christocentric; in the second place, it moves in the bosom of the Apostles' Creed; in the third place, it is Objective and Historical, involving thus the idea of the Church as a perennial article of faith. These three conceptions are closely intertwined; but they admit and deserve separate consideration.

CHRISTOCENTRIC THEOLOGY.

The term is sufficiently clear. It explains itself. We mean by it, of course, that the theology before us centres in Christ. He is not simply the author of its contents: these contents gather themselves up into Him ultimately as their root. As an object of faith and knowledge, and in the only form in which it can be regarded as having reality in the world, Christianity has been brought to pass through the mystery of the Incarnation, and stands perpetually in the presence and power of that fact. All its verities, all its doctries, all its promises, all its life-giving forces, root themselves continually in the undying life of Him, who thus became man for us men and for our salvation. And such being the actual objective constitution of Christianity, it would seem to be at once plain that our apprehension of it, to be either right or safe, must move in the same order. It must plant itself boldly and broadly on the proposition, that Jesus Christ is the principle of Christianity, and that the full sense of the Gospel is to be reached only in and through the revelation which is comprehended in His glorious Person. In doing this it will become necessarily such a theology, such a way of looking at the Christian salvation, as we are now trying to describe. Learned or unlearned, it will be a theology that revolves around Christ as a centre, and is irradiated at all points by the light that flows upon it from his presence.

For the right knowledge of things everywhere, all depends on their being surveyed from the right point of view. Facts and forms are not enough; they must be apprehended in their true relations; and this requires that the beholder should occupy, in regard to them, such a centre of observation as may enable him to see them in this way. Even an outward landscape, to be seen to advantage, must be seen from the proper position. So as regards any field or range of science. The astronomy of the old world, for example, abounded in observation and study; was furnished with vast material of phenomena and facts; accomplished much in the way of scientific comparison, induction, and generalization. But it labored throughout with embarrassment and confusion, because its scheme of the heavens was projected from a wrong standpoint. It made the earth to be the centre of the system to which it belongs, and studied the motions of the heavenly bodies exclusively from this false assumption. It was geocentric, as we say, in its contemplations, and therefore every where at fault. The Copernican system, in the fulness of time, redeemed the science, and made room for its modern triumphs; not primarily by the revelation of new facts, but by finding the true centre of observation for the apprehension of old facts. It planted its scientific lever in the sun, instead of the earth, bringing its studies thus into harmony with the objective order of the world it sought to understand and expound. Astronomy, in other words, ceased to be geocentric, and became heliocentric. Hence all its later enlargement and success.

Now what this heliocentric (sun-centre) standpoint is for the right study of the heavens in the science of astronomy, we affirm the Christocentric (Christ-centre) standpoint to be, for the right study of heavenly and eternal things in the science of theology. No other standpoint can be substituted for it without boundless error and confusion. It is possible to bring in here a different centre of observation; nay, it is the natural vice of our fallen reason, that it tends continually to throw itself upon a different centre; for the full practical sense of what Christ is in this respect, belongs only to the world of faith, which as·such is at the same time the world of what transcends all natural reason. We may have a simply anthropological divinity—a mere humanitarian theology; all centering in the idea of man (anthropocentric); the earth again ruling the heavens, and the merely moral or ethical, at best, playing itself off as the divine. Or we may have, on the other hand, a simply theological divinity—a construction of theology starting from the idea of God, considered absolutely and outside of Christ (theocentric); in which the relations of God to the world, then, will become pantheistic, fantastic, visionary, and unreal; and all religion will be made to resolve itself at last into metaphysical speculations or theosophic dreams. How far these false projections of Christian doctrine, in one view antagonistic, and yet in another everlastingly intermarried, have made themselves mischievously felt in the Christian world, through all Protean forms and shapes, from their first bad birth as Ebionism and Gnosticism, down to the Socinianism, Anabaptism, and metaphysical Calvinism of the sixteenth century, and down still farther to corresponding forms of religious thought in our own time—this is not the proper place to inquire. Our object is simply to fix attention on the possibility of such wrong constructions of Christianity, for the purpose of insisting with more effect on the necessity of a construction that shall start from the right point of observation; and to make fully apparent, moreover, how much is comprehended in what we say, when we affirm that this right point of observation is the Person of our Lord Jesus Christ, and that no theology, therefore, can be either safe or sound, or truly Christian, which does not show itself to be in this view a truly Christocentric theology.

The proposition needs no proof. It is a first principle, a self-evident axiom, in Christianity. To doubt it, is to call Christ Himself into donbt. Has He not said: "I am the Light of the world"? Is it not His own voice that still rings through the ages from the isle of Patmos: "I am alpha and omega, the first and the last"? The natural world begins and ends in Him; for "all things were made by Him, and without Him was not anything made that was made" (John i. 3); and again we are told, "by Him were all things created that are in heaven, and that are in earth, visible and invisible, whether they be thrones, or dominions, or principalities, or powers; all things were created by Him, and for Him; and He is before all things, and by Him all things consist" (Col. i. 16, 17). The ethical world, the movement of humanity, the world of history as it may be called, begins and ends in Him; it is not chaotic, the sport of blind chance or iron fate; Christ is in it, causing all its powers and forces to converge throughout to what shall be found to be at last the world's last sense in the finished work of redemption. Finally, the world of revelation begins and ends in Him; it is not a number of independent utterances, properly speaking, given forth from God, but a single economy or system, through which God has made Himself known among men, with progressive manifestation, in the way, not of doctrine primarily and immediately, but of act and deed; the entire movement having its principle or root in Christ from the first, centering at last in the historical fact of the Incarnation, and running its course thence onward to the hour of His second appearing, when He shall come to be glorified in His saints, and admired in all them that believe. Jesus Christ is the alpha and omega of all these worlds (nature, history and grace), and as such the principle, centre and end, therefore, in which they all meet, and gather themselves together finally, as one (Eph. i. 10). This being so, where shall we find the key to a correct knowledge of the world, or of man, or of God, if not in that which is set before us as the first object of the Christian faith, the mysterious constitution of His blessed Person? Above all, what can we expect to know rightly in the sphere of revelation (among the facts of the Bible, and amid the "powers of the world to come" that are lodged in the Church), without the help of this key? The Old Testament throughout has no sure sense or force, except in the Christological view of its being a subordinate, relatively imperfect discipline or pedagogy, whereby the way was prepared for the coming of Christ in the flesh. It has no power to explain or interpret Christ, save only so far as it is itself made intelligible first in and through Christ. Then, as regards Christianity itself, strictly taken, what is it, we may well ask, in difference from all else pretending to call itself religion, if it be not the product and outgrowth of the new order of life, which first became actual in the world by the assumption of our human nature into union with the Divine Word (John i. 14, 17), having in this view its beginning, middle, and end in Christ, and in Christ only?

And how then, having such objective constitution, and standing thus actually and entirely in the historical being of Christ, beyond which it must necessarily resolve itself into nothing, as having no basis of faith whereon to rest; being in such sort bound to Christ, we repeat, as the alpha and omega, sum and substance of its whole existence, how possibly shall Christianity be studied and understood aright, either practically or doctrinally, either as a system of life, or as a system of theology, if it be not in the Christocentric way of which we are now speaking? To comprehend the "world which grace has made," we must take our position by faith in the great primordial centre, from which all has been evolved, and there fixing our spiritual telescope, endeavor, as best we may, to scan the wonders thus offered to our contemplation; being well assured that from any other centre, they will either not be seen at all, or else will be seen only under more or less distorted forms, and in more or less false relations and proportions. This centrality of Christ, in the Christian system, reaches forth to all parts of the system. Practically, all righteousness, all morality, all virtue, in the Christian sense, grow forth from the "law of the spirit of life in Christ Jesus." All sound Christian feeling and experience, flow from the sense of Christ formed in us as the hope of glory. And so intellectually also, Christ is our wisdom, the principle of all true Christian illumination and knowledge. Through Him only we are made to know man, his original destination, and the full extent of his fall. Through Him only, we come to have an insight into the true nature of sin, the power of the devil, the meaning of death, the idea of redemption, and the progress of the Christian salvation out to the resurrection of the last day. Through Him only, do we ever come to the true understanding of God, "in the knowledge of whom standeth our eternal life."

The theology now under consideration is decidedly of this character. It revolves around Christ. It has been strangely enough charged at times with subordinating the idea of Christ to the idea of the Church. But this is a gross mistake, if not a perverse slander. The theology in question does, indeed, lay stress on the doctrine of the Church, as stress is laid on it also in the Apostles' Creed; but only as the Church is held to be the necessary consequence of Christ (following the Creed in this also), and never as putting the Church in Christ's place. No theology in the country certainly has made more of Christ as the centre of its thinking and teaching. No theology has insisted more earnestly on the great cardinal truths of the Trinity, the Eternal Generation, the Divinity of the Son, the Incarnation, the Mediatorial Work and Reign of Christ; and no theology, it may be safely asserted, has done more, within the same time, to awaken and enforce attention to the practical significance of these truths in the American religious world.

This brings us to the consideration of what we have already named as its second distinguishing characteristic, namely; the fact, that it moves throughout in the bosom of the old Creeds, the original *regula fidei* of the Christian world.

RULED BY THE APOSTLES' CREED.

It is not necessary to waste time here on the half-learned criticisms, we hear made continually, in certain quarters, on the title and origin of this symbol. We know that it was not composed strictly by the Apostles; that it took form gradually; that there were different Creeds in the first centuries; and that among these, the formula used at Rome finally gained general credit in the fifth and sixth centuries, so as to become, for subsequent times, what is now denominated the Apostles' Creed. All this we know; but we know also, at the same time, that this final settlement upon the Roman form, involved no giving up or changing any where of a single point of faith; that the different Creeds previously, were only variations of one and the same confessional theme; that what was added to its utterance in any case, came in only as the explicit enunciation of what was included in it implicitly before; and that all in this way resolved itself into a common rule of faith, or canon of truth, which the universal Church held from the beginning as of Apostolic origin and Apostolic authority. In this character, the symbol has been received through all ages, by all branches of the Church, both Oriental and Occidental, as the primary and most fundamental expression of the Christian faith. Protestantism has claimed, from the beginning, to stand here on the same ground with Roman Catholicism. The Reformed Church, no less than the Lutheran, starts confessionally with the Apostles' Creed. Our own admirable Heidelberg Catechism, in particular, makes it, in form, the ground and rule of all it professes to teach in the way of faith.

The Apostles' Creed thus is the deepest, and for that reason most comprehensive of all Christian symbols. It lies at the foundation of all evangelical unity; it is the last basis and bond of comprehension in the conception of the Church. No sect refusing to stand on this basis, can have any right to claim footing in the Gospel, or fellowship with the Apostles.

All right theological thinking then, as well as all true evangelical believing, must start where this fundamental form of faith starts, and keep step with it at every point as far as it goes. The reason of this is plain. It lies in the constitution of the Creed; which is no summary of Christian doctrine primarily for the understanding, but the necessary form of the Gospel, as this is first apprehended by faith; a direct transcript, we may say, of what the Gospel is to the contemplation of the believer, turned wholly upon the Person of Christ. Such faith is necessarily ruled by its object; the Creed, in other words, must be Christological, must unfold itself, first of all, in the order of what are to be regarded as the fundamental facts of Christianity, growing forth from the mystery of the Incarnation. In such view, there is no room to speak of two or more different methods of faith for taking in the sense of the Gospel. As there is but one method of the objective movement of the Gospel in Christ Himself, so can there be only one method for the .apprehension of it on the part of believers. That method we have in the Apostles' Creed; and any attempt to set this aside, to substitute for it some different construction of first principles, or to subordinate its proper normative authority and signification to any later type of belief, must be looked upon at once as a serious falling away from the Gospel, and may be expected to result at last in the confusion and eclipse of faith altogether.

All this the theology before us owns and holds steadily in view. Starting in Christ, it follows the order in which the facts of religion unfold themselves with necessary connection from His Person. This order is for it not optional simply, but is felt to be inwardly bound to its own principle. It is the immanent logic of faith, determined by Him who is the central object of faith. It makes all the difference in the world in this view, whether a system of theological thought be cast in the type of doctrine that is set forth in the Creed, or constructed in some other way. To some it may seem comparatively indifferent, how the topics of religion are put together, if only the same topics nominally are made use of in the work; the form is of no account, they fancy; all depends upon the matter. But this imagination itself shows at once the wrong position of those who hold it, and is really nothing less than a vast theological blunder. The form here is in fact everything; the matter nothing, we may say, except as embraced in this form. It is a vain pretence, therefore, to say, that the authority of the Creed is sufficiently acknowledged, by allowing it to be in substance a true, though defective, representation of the Gospel, and then going on to work up the material of it into some supposed better scheme of doctrine, projected from another standpoint altogether, and moving throughout in a totally different line of thought. No confession, no catechism, no preaching, no worship, no system of divinity, carried forward in this way, can ever breathe the spirit of the Creed, or have in it the true life of the Creed; however much it may try to make the world believe that it is at the bottom in harmony with the "undoubted articles of our Christian faith," as we have them set forth in this radical symbol.

Hence it is, that where such pretended reconstructions of the material of faith prevail, the honor shown to the Creed is in fact nominal only, and theoretic at best, and never practically real. We all know how completely the symbol has fallen out of use, in all those portions of the Church, in which such reconstructed divinity has come to have the upper hand. Evidence enough, what a difference it makes, whether our religion grow forth, or not, from this "form of sound words," delivered unto us from the Apostles. The difference reaches into all spheres of practical Christianity; into family religious training; into the Sunday-school; into the work of catechetical instruction; into the character of preaching; into all sanctuary services; into all devotional offices. In the same way it reaches to every point of doctrinal Christianity. There is not a Christian dogma, that is not affected by it in the most serious manner.

The theology of the Creed does not stop short, of course, with the few, primordial articles of that first, immediate panoramic vision of faith. Within the range of this regulative scheme, it finds room for any amount of scientific study and enlargement, through the use of what matter is offered to it for this end in God's Revelation, and in the exercise of a reason that is now purified for its office by the inspiration of God's Holy Spirit; the very element, as it were, of the world of faith in which the Gospel is here felt to move. But through all such enlargement, the organization of doctrine remains rooted and grounded in the objective mystery of the new creation in Christ Jesus, as this has been first apprehended in the form of the Creed; and every doctrine is an outgrowth from this, having thus its position, complexion and quality in the system, both for faith and for knowledge, as it could not possibly have them in any other way. Every doctrine, in this way, becomes Christological, and serves to express a truth which is true only within the orbit of the Creed, and not at all on the outside of it.

It would be interesting to verify this in particular cases, by showing how the doctrine of the atonement, for example, the article of justification by faith, the idea of regeneration, the conception of sacramental grace, are found to be always something materially different in the theology of the Creed from what they are made to be in any other theology; but it would carry us too far for our present purpose, to pursue the subject in this way. We have said enough to show of what immense account the characteristic is, by which the theological system we are now defending is distinguished as being the theology of the Creed; and what a gulph of separation this necessarily involves, between it and all antagonistic theologies; which, however loud mouthed they may be in the use of cant evangelical shibboleths, stand convicted, nevertheless, of being profoundly unevangelical, just because they show themselves wanting in every sort of genuine sympathy and loyalty for the Apostles' Creed, through which the original voice of the Gospel has come sounding down upon us from the earliest times.

The theology we are defending may be said to be specially identified with the honor of the Apostles' Creed, in the religious history of this country. In our Reformed Zion, twenty-five years ago, the Creed had become almost a dead letter. It still kept its place in the Heidelberg Catechism; but that itself was in a fair way to have its life smothered out of it, by the incubus which had come to settle upon it in the form of Methodistic Puritanism; and for the fundamental significance of the gem it here held enshrined in its bosom, there appeared to be but small sense anywhere. The Creed was not heard commonly in our pulpits, and had fallen into neglect largely in our families.

Now, however, all is changed. The voice of the old symbol is once more restored. Our children are familiar with it. Along with the Lord's Prayer, it has forced itself into general liturgical use among us, even where the new Liturgy is still feared for the theological spirit that has wrought such auspicious change.

For can there be any doubt of the source from which this great change has sprung? Do we not owe it entirely to the Christological tendency, that has been at work among us for the last twenty years; which was so much assisted in its own development by the study of the Creed; and which at the same time wrought effectually to restore this to popular confidence and use?

And no one, who has observed attentively the course of things, can doubt, but that the power of this testimony has been felt, also, far beyond the narrow limits of our Reformed Church. There is a deplorable want of real sympathy still with this archetypal form of sound words, on all sides; but, a reactionary feeling has begun to set in evidently in its favor. It would be hard probably to find now, even in Puritan New England itself, any respectable so called Orthodox voice, prepared to say, as the pious "Puritan Recorder" could venture to do in 1849, that the Apostles' Creed has become, for the orthodoxy of New England, a "fossil relic of by gone ages"—a dead formulary, which "teaches in several respects anti-scriptural doctrines," so that it must be pitiful, therefore, to think of "infusing life into it, and setting it up again as a living ruler in the Church." A change, we say, has begun to come over the spirit of that dream; and our theology unquestionably has had something at least to do with bringing it about. No other theology in the country, certainly, has labored more to re-animate the symbol with its pristine life. No other has so borne it on high as the chosen banner of its faith. And we will add also in good trust, of no other is there more room to say, *In hoc signo vinces.*

5

OBJECTIVE AND HISTORICAL.

Starting in the great fact of the Incarnation, and following its movement, our theology has finally the third general character of being Objective and Historical. In other words, it is not a system simply of subjective notions, a metaphysical theory of God and religion born only of the human mind, a supposed apprehension of supernatural verities brought into the mind in the way of abstract thought; but it is the apprehension of the supernatural by faith under the form of an actual Divine manifestation in and through Christ, which, as such, rules and governs the power that perceives it, while it is felt also to be joined in its own order to the natural history of the world onward through all time. So much lies at once in the Apostles' Creed.

All revelation is primarily something that God does—an objective, supernatural manifestation, which causes His presence to be felt in the world. The right apprehension of what is thus exhibited, which can be only through the inspiration of His Spirit, becomes then the power of His word in the souls of those to whom it is addressed. Universally, it would seem, the inward illumination is bound to the outward manifestation in this way. God does not speak to the souls of men immediately and abruptly, as enthusiasts and fanatics fondly dream; that would be magic, and gives us the Pagan idea of religion, not the Christian. The order of all true supernatural teaching is, the objective first, and the subjective or experimental afterwards, as something brought to pass only by its means. Most of all, we may say, is this true of Christianity, the absolute end of all God's acts of revelation. Its whole significance is comprehended, first of all, in the Divine deed, whereby God manifested Himself in the flesh, through the mystery of the Incarnation. This objective act is itself the Gospel, in the profoundest sense of the term. In the very nature of the case, it must underlie and condition all that the Gospel can ever become for men, in the way of inward experience. True, it cannot save men without their being brought to experience its power; on which account it is, that we need to be placed in communication with it through faith; but the power that saves is not, for this reason, in our experience or faith; it is wholly in the object with which our faith is concerned. The subjective here, sundered from the objective, can give us at best only a spurious evangelicalism, which will always be found, in the end, to be more nearly allied to the flesh than to God's Spirit.

Apprehended under such objective view, the revelation which God has been pleased to make of Himself through Jesus Christ (not in the way of oracle but of act), becomes necessarily, for our faith, at the same time historical. Only so can it be felt to be real, and not simply notional and visionary. Its objectivity itself implies, that it has entered permanently into the stream of the world's life, not just as the memory of a past wonder, but as the continued working of the power it carried with it in the beginning. The Gospel is supernatural; but it is the supernatural joined in a new order of existence to the natural; and this, it can be only in the form of history. In any other form, it becomes shadowy and unreal. Sense for the objective in Christianity, leads thus universally to sense for the historical; while those who make all of subjectivity are sure to be unhistorical.

The historical character of the Gospel, objectively considered, meets us, first of all, in the Person and Work of Christ Himself, as they are exhibited to us in the Creed. Its articles are not so many theological propositions loosely thrown together, but phases that mark the progress of what may be considered the dramatic development of His Mediatorial Life, out to its last consequence in the full salvation of His people. This, of itself, however, involves then, in the next place, as we may at once see, the historical character of Christianity also, regarded as the carrying out of this mystery of godliness among men to the end of time. Not only the subjective religious experiences and opinions of men here are to be regarded as entering into the general flow of history, like their political or scientific judgments, but the objective reality, from which Christianity springs, the new order of existence which was constituted for the world by the great fact of the Incarnation, must be allowed also to be historical. Only in such view can we possibly retain our hold on the objectively supernatural, as it entered into the original constitution of the Gospel. It is not enough for this purpose, to have memories only of what was once such a real presence in the world. It lies in the very conception of the Gospel, in this objective view, that its supernatural economy should be of perennial force, that its resources and powers of salvation should be "once for all;" not in the sense of something concluded and left behind, as many seem to imagine, but in the sense of what, having once entered into the life of the world, has become so incorporated with it as to be part of its historical being to the end of time.

But this conception of a supernatural economy having place among men under an objective, historical form, an order of grace flowing from Christ, and altogether different from the order of nature, is nothing more nor less than the idea of the Holy Catholic Church as we have it in the Creed. We can see thus how it is, that this article holds the place assigned to it in that symbol. It is not there by accident or caprice. It is there as part of the faith, which is required to take in the objective, historical movement of the grace that is comprehended in our Lord Jesus Christ; and it meets us exactly at the right point, as setting forth the form and manner in which Christ, by the Holy Ghost, carries forward His work of salvation in the world. If we are to hold fast the objective, historical character of what this work was first, and still continues to be, in His own Person, it cannot be allowed to lose itself in the agency of the Spirit under a general view; it must, necessarily, involve for us the conception of a special sphere; this likewise objective and historical; within which only (and not in the world at large), the Holy Ghost of the Gospel is to be regarded as working. This is the Church. It comes in just here as a necessary postulate of the Christian faith. Standing in the bosom of the Creed, we cannot get round it. It is a mystery, like all the other articles of the symbol, which we are required to believe, because it flows with necessary derivation from the coming of Christ in the flesh. Our belief in it is not founded in our empirical knowledge of it, our having come to be sure of its ex-

OF THE NEW LITURGY.

istence and attributes in some other way. In that case it would not be faith at all in the sense of the Creed. What faith has to do with properly, here as elsewhere, is the supernatural belonging to its object; and that comes to us, not in the way of natural experience and observation, but only in the way of *a priori* challenge and demand addressed to us directly from its own sphere. We do not believe, as the old adage has it, because we understand, but we believe in order that we may understand. Where there is no faith of this sort in the Church, going before all inquiries in regard to what it is and where it is for outward view, it is not to be expected that these inquiries can be carried forward with much earnestness or effect. We may not be able to explain fully the meaning of our Saviour's descent to hades, or the time and manner of His second advent; but that is no reason why these articles should not be firm objects of our faith; we believe them, because they are felt to be involved in the objective movement of the Gospel itself in Christ's Person. And just so we believe the Church. We cannot get along without it, in our conception of the real, objective, historical working of Christ's Mediatorial Life in the world. This must, to be real at all, have a sphere of its own; which, as such, becomes, then, an order or constitution of grace, in distinction from the world in its simply natural constitution; exactly what we mean by the Church as an article of faith, back of all questions in regard to its outward organization and form. We cannot get along without it, we say, in the objective movement of the Creed. Do away with it, as modern spiritualists require, and this movement is, for our faith, brought suddenly to an end. It is either sublimated into magic, or precipitated at once into the order of mere nature.

The theology we are speaking of, then, is churchly. It believes in the Church, as we have the article in the Apostles' Creed; believes in it as a mystery, which comes in necessarily just where it stands in the Creed, as part of the ongoing movement of the general mystery of salvation, that starts in the Incarnation. It believes in an economy of grace, a sphere of supernatural powers and forces flowing from the historical fact of

Christ's birth, death, and glorification, which are themselves present in the world historically (not magically), in broad distinction from the economy of nature; and in the bosom of which only, not on the outside of it, the Gospel can be expected to work as the wisdom of God and the power of God unto salvation. So far as this goes, of course, it owns and confesses that the Church is a medium of communication between Christ and His people. They must be in the order of His grace, in the sphere where this objective working of His grace is actually going forward, and not in the order of nature, where it is not going forward at all (but where Satan reigns and has his own way), if the work of redemption and sanctification is to be carried forward in them with full effect. In this sense, most assuredly, salvation is of the Church, and not of the world; and to look for it in the world, by private spiritualistic negotiations with God, professedly and purposely pouring contempt on the idea of all church intervention, is to look for it where it is not to be found.

This, of course, means a great deal; and draws after it, in the way of necessary consequence, much that we cannot now think of noticing in detail. A churchly theology can never run in the same direction with a theology that is unchurchly; and can never breathe the same spirit. Not because it makes less of Christ, as this last is ever ready to charge; but because it makes more of Christ, and cannot consent to have Him turned into a Gnostic phantom. Not because it is less evangelical, as the unchurchly spirit, with great self-complacency, is forever prompt to assume; but because it rests in a more profound and comprehensive apprehension of the Gospel.

Such a churchly theology, we feel at once, can never be otherwise than sacramental. Where the idea of the Church has come to make itself felt in the way now described, as involving the conjunction of the supernatural and the natural continuously in one and the same abiding economy of grace, its sacraments cannot possibly be regarded as outward signs only of what they represent. They become, for faith, seals also of the actual realities themselves, which they exhibit; mysteries, in which the visible and the invisible are bound together by the power of the Holy Ghost (not physically or locally, as vain talkers will forever have it), in such sort, that the presence of the one is, in truth, the presence of the other.

In the end, also, unquestionably, the sacramental feeling here cannot fail to show itself a liturgical feeling. There is an inward connection between all the forms of religious thinking we have had thus far under consideration. They run into one another, and require one another to be in any sense, complete. A theology which is truly Christocentric, must follow the Creed, must be objective, must be historical; with this, must be churchly; and with this again, must be sacramental and liturgical. It must be liturgical, moreover, in a sense agreeing with these affinities throughout—the only sense, in fact, in which it is not absurd to talk of worship in this form. It can never be satisfied with anything less than an altar liturgy. A mere pulpit liturgy, a hand-book of forms for the exclusive use of the minister, must ever seem to it, in comparison, something very unrefreshing, not to say miserably cold and dry.

The enemies of the new Liturgy are right, then, in saying, that it is the product of the general scheme of theology we have now tried to characterize and describe, and that the spirit of this theology pervades, more or less, all its offices and forms. For this reason it is, in truth, that they dislike it, and would be glad to get it out of the way. Standing, as they do, in another order of religious thought altogether, they feel that the Liturgy is against them, and their instinct of self-preservation, as it were, impels them to seek its destruction. In this way, our liturgical controversy is, in reality, a great theological controversy; one that should be of interest to other Protestant Churches, no less than to our own. We see in it two general schemes of theology; two different versions, we may say, of the meaning of Christianity; two Gospels, in fact, arrayed against one another, with the feeling on both sides, that if one be true the other must necessarily be wrong and false. One of these schemes is the theology we have been thus far trying to describe; the other is the opposite of this, the Puritanic un-

churchly scheme, we may call it, in which the enemies of the
Liturgy now openly stand.

ANTI-LITURGICAL THEOLOGY.

And what, now, is this Puritanic scheme? It admits within
it different constructions, Calvinistic, Arminian, Methodist,
Baptistic, and so on in all manner of sect forms; but what we
are concerned with here is only its general character, the under-
lying common basis of these distinctions, as this presents itself
to our view in broad contrast with the general character of the
scheme we have just been considering. And even this general
view must be taken at present in a very cursory, wholesale way.
It will be sufficient, however, we trust, to show all unprejudiced
persons, whose image and superscription the system in question
bears, and in the service of what cause it works.

What, we ask again, is this Puritanic scheme, which finds a
"serpent" in the new Liturgy, and sees in it only a poisoned
chalice offered to the lips of the people? We will now answer.

It is a scheme, which betrays itself at once by its apostacy
from the primitive *regula fidei* of the Christian Church, the
Apostles' Creed. We know how it is ready at times, especially
in our German Churches, to squirm under this charge, and how,
like some slimy eel, it tries to slip from beneath it with every
sort of disingenuous evasion. But we mean now to hold it
tightly to the accusation; and to do this before the people (the
elders especially and laity in general of the Reformed Church),
so that all may be able to see and know just what this false
popular evangelicalism means, and in what direction it leads.
It is constitutionally and inwardly at war with the Creed. It
cannot frame its mouth to pronounce the symbol in its true
original sense; but claims the right of putting into its articles,
where it may please, a better modern sense of its own.

Hear, on this point, the "Puritan Recorder," in 1849. The
Puritans, it says, receive the Creed "in a sense consonant with
their theology," either leaving out altogether, for example, the
article of the descent to hades, or putting upon it a constrained
meaning to suit themselves. "But it is neither safe nor expe-

dient," the Recorder honestly adds, "to receive such a document in such a perverted sense; for the document once being
admitted, and its authority being made to bind the conscience,
then the way is open for those who hold the errors held by its
authors, to plead that we are bound to receive it in the sense
which its authors gave to it, and this makes it an instrument of
corrupting the faith of the Gospel." Honest confession! True
divination! The voice of the Creed allowed to proclaim itself
from week to week, without note or comment, in the churches
of New England, would, in the course of a few years, we verily
believe, sap the foundations of their existing orthodoxy, and
turn the stream of their church life into a wholly new channel.
But any such use of the Creed among them now would be cried
down as a Romanizing tendency or a hankering after ritualism;
as it would be also still, in spite of the little reactionary movement we see working here and there the other way, in all
branches of American Presbyterianism. In these ecclesiastical
regions, Puritanism has killed .the Apostles' Creed out of all
practical and theological use. It has become for them a dead
letter, in family and school, in the pulpit and in the divinity
hall. Let the thoughtful, everywhere, consider well what this
means. We speak plainly, because the fact is plain.

In our Reformed Church, especially since the theological revival we have had among us these last years, no tongue would
dare to wag itself against the Creed in the fashion of the "Puritan Recorder." With us now at least, the symbol is no dead
letter, but a living witness of Apostolical truth. So our people
are coming to regard it more and more. But the Puritanic
spirit is still among us to a certain extent; and as far as it is
so, it remains true still, in jesuitical disguise, to the outspoken
confession of the Recorder, that the Creed can be mouthed by
modern evangelicalism only in a galvanized, so-called non-
natural sense.

Were we not told as much as this, to all intents and purposes, on the floor of the late General Synod, at Dayton? Was
not the ground there taken by the enemies of the Liturgy, that
we had nothing to do with the faith of the third and fourth

centuries, the birth-period of the Creed in its full development, as we now have it; that the faith of that time is not to be considered normative or regulative, in any sense, for the faith of the modern Christian world; that the only primitive faith we are to follow, is what we can get out of the Bible directly for ourselves (every man thus following his own nose), without regard at all to any such objective form of sound words as we find employed to set forth the fundamental belief of Christendom in the first ages? This, of course, was a blow struck at *all* confessionalism; bringing down our Reformed platform, at one stroke, to a flat level with the lowest forms of sectarian subjectivity, and involving us with general confusion in the brotherhood of Anabaptists, Socinians, Quakers, Muggletonians, United Brethren, Winebrennerians, Mormons (for these, too, prate of the Bible in the same Cambyses vein), and others, out to the end of the chapter. Hence, we had, in part, a change of base; the authority of the Creed insidiously assailed from the authority of the Heidelberg Catechism; the faith of the Primitive Church required to shape itself here into conformity with what was represented to be the faith of the sixteenth century. A modern confessionalism in this way made to rule out the sense of the older confessionalism, in which, nevertheless, it professed to have its own root and ground! Did we not hear this nonsense gravely held forth at Synod? Were we not told there, that we are to take the Creed only in the sense of the fathers of the sixteenth century, and not in the sense of the fathers who first used it in the second and third centuries, if this last sense should be found not to square exactly with the sixteenth-century sense, as it was quietly granted might be the case? On the supposition, in other words, of even a casual discrepancy anywhere between the Creed and the Heidelberg Catechism, it was held that the sense of the Catechism must rule, that is, literally coerce, the sense of the Creed; in such way, that the modern symbol shall be held to be of primary normative force, and the primitive œcumenical symbol of only secondary derivative force as taken up into its bosom. How superlatively absurd! What plainer proof could we have of hostility to the Creed, than the cloven foot thus un-ceremoniously thrust upon our view? Cannot the people see it everywhere with their own eyes? The matter may be put into a nutshell. Either the Creed, in its original unsophisti-cated sense, is what the Universal Church in past ages held it to be, the one only true radix and ground type of Christian faith and doctrine; or else it is not this, but a bastard cor-ruption of the Gospel, requiring to be tinkered into new sense at least, if not new form, before it can pass muster as fairly evangelical, in the modern party sense of this much-abused term. These are the two alternatives, without the possibility of any middle ground for even a rope-dancer to stand upon. Where *they* stand, whose acrobatic performances with the sub-ject at Synod have just been noticed, needs no demonstration. They do not own the Creed, in its own proper historical sense, for the original, necessary, and radically sure norm of our Re-formed faith; but take it only, in the way the " Puritan Re-corder" took it in 1849, as being, "*most of it*, capable of a sense which harmonizes with the Scriptures," going on then to rectify it to their taste, by distilling into it their own fancies, or what they are pleased to consider the elixir of sound thinking drawn from some other quarter. That is, in plain English, the Creed is *not* for them the ultimate symbolical authority of the Reformed Church; and the fathers of the sixteenth century must be re-garded as saying what was not true, when they pretended to look upon it in that light. These modern sons of theirs know better now, and have changed all that.

But what now have our people, as a body, to say to the issue, thus fairly made up and brought before them? Will they allow their first symbol, the marrow and kernel of their confessional faith, to be ruthlessly torn from their grasp by this Puritanic enemy, which has stolen in upon us while men slept, and now threatens to rob us of all that is fairest in our theology or church life? Are we to hold on to the Apostles' Creed with good faith, taking it in its own true sense; or shall we have in place of it only a dead corpse of the Creed, eviscerated of its own true sense, and hypocritically hold this up as an argument of our fealty to the ancient symbol? Are these old primeval articles, this grand architectonic scheme of the everlasting Gospel, to be for us no longer of undoubted catholic or universal authority, as the whole is declared to be in the Heidelberg Catechism? Will the Reformed Church recognize the voice of her true teachers, in those who counsel, directly or indirectly, any such falling away from the faith of the fathers? The appeal is to the people. Let the people answer.

But we are not done yet with this anti-liturgical theology. Its opposition to the Creed shows, of course, a constitutional difference between it and the whole conception of the Gospel contained in this ancient symbol; and from what we have seen already of this, we need have no difficulty in apprehending wherein the difference consists, and to what it amounts. The difference lies just here, and we wish all to ponder and consider it well: The Gospel of the Creed is, throughout, Christological, concentrates itself in Christ, throws itself, in full, upon the Incarnation, and sees in the objective movement of this Mystery of Godliness, as St. Paul calls it, the whole process of grace and salvation on to the resurrection of the dead and the life everlasting; while this other scheme, which we now call, for distinction's sake, the Gospel of Puritanism, substitutes for all this a construction of Christianity that is purely subjective, centering in the human mind, and that gives us then notions for facts, causing metaphysical abstractions to stand for the proper objects of faith, and thus resolves all religion finally into sheer spiritualism; in which no account is made of any objective mediation of grace outside of men, but every man is supposed to come directly, face to face, with God, having, in his evangelical notions simply, whatever is necessary to give him free access to the Divine presence.

The charge of not preaching Christ, we know, is one which this theology will be ready to resent on all sides, as the last that should be seriously preferred against it. It is accustomed to please itself with the imagination of being evangelical, for the very reason that it pretends to make everything of Christ and Him crucified, and in certain of its phases at least is forever ringing changes on the themes of righteousness and free redemption through His name. Is not this the very boast of our unchurchly sects, all the land over, that *they* preach Christ, and Christianity, in opposition to such as lay stress on the idea of the Church, on the sacraments, on outward forms in any view; denouncing every intervention of this sort, as externalism, ecclesiasticism, sacerdotalism, ritualism, or something equally bad, that serves only to obscure the Saviour's glory, and to block up the way to His presence? Who in the world do preach Chris⁺, it may be asked, if it be not these sects, for whom Christ is thus, nominally, all in all?

This we understand. It is an old song; as old as the Gnostics and the Phrygian Montanists, in the days of Tertullian. But we are not to be deceived by it for a moment. Try the spirits, says St. John; do not take them at their own word; try them whether they be of God. And he gives us a simple criterion for the purpose, applicable to all times (1 John iv: 1–3). They come preaching Christ of course. How else could they claim to be Christian? But what sort of a Christ is it that they preach? Is it the historical Christ of the Incarnation. Do they confess that "Jesus Christ is come in the flesh," not in appearance only, and not for a season only, but in full reality and for all time? Or is their confession of that spiritualistic sort, that resolves His coming in the flesh into a mere speculative dream, long since sublimated in the clouds? In this last case, St. John tells us, its boasting of Christ cannot save it. It is not of God, but is the very spirit of Anti-Christ, just because it sets up a Christ which is the creature of its own subjective thinking, over against and in place of the only true objective and historical Christ of the Gospel, "who is over all, God blessed forever. Amen."

We are not to be put off here with words. Neither can we mince matters in so momentous a case. We reiterate our charge. The theology we are dragging into the light does not preach Christ, as the alpha and omega of the new creation, the beginning, middle, and end of the Gospel. It cannot stand the searching test of St. John. The Christ it talks about is not the Christ of the Incarnation, as He is made to pass before us in the sublime vision of the old Apostles' Creed; as we hear Him proclaimed (Jesus and the Resurrection and the Second Advent), by St. Peter and St. Paul, in the Acts of the Apostles; as we seem to see Him in the midst of the golden candlesticks, looking forth upon us serenely and grandly from the ecclesiastical literature of the first Christian ages. Not this, verily; as too many of us, alas, have been made painfully to feel; but another form and visage altogether; an object of thought rather than of faith, in looking to which we find that we have at last little more than our own thought to work with; and become like those that feed on wind, in trying to replenish our souls with spiritualities which our souls have themselves produced, instead of the true bread which cometh down from heaven and alone giveth life unto the world.

This is the great constitutional defect of the theology we are sitting in judgment upon; a defect which any jury of plain Christian men can understand; and it is easy to see, to what consequences, in the end, it must necessarily lead. Where the Gospel is not apprehended as the historical, enduring, objective Manifestation of God in the flesh, there can be no steady apprehension of that which constitutes the proper mystery of it in this view, namely, the union there is in it of the supernatural with the natural in an abiding, historical (not magical) form. This precisely is the true object of all evangelical faith, in the New Testament sense; the objective power of salvation, through the apprehension of which only, faith becomes justifying and saving faith. Instead of this, we shall have the supernatural resolved into a spiritualistic presence, seated in the Holy Ghost, and made to reach into the minds of men directly from heaven, in no organic conjunction whatever with the Incarnation; this being considered as, at best, the outward occasion only, and in no sense the inward medium, of the communication. In which case again, what is called justifying faith is no longer tied to the objective Gospel (without which, however, it cannot be *faith* at all), but hugs simply the Gospel of this subjective assurance a man may have of God's mercy in his own mind, becoming thus, in fact, justification by fancy or feeling. But with the real supernatural of the Gospel metamorphosed in this way into the general notion of the supernatural in a metaphysical view, the whole conception of Christianity, in fact, sinks into the order of nature. The sense of what it is as a continuous constitution of grace, the historical presence of new heavenly powers, through the Spirit in the world, is gone. As with the Gnostics of old, the spiritual has lost all concrete, objective union with the natural. The bond between them has thinned itself into airy speculation. The system has become, in one word, essentially rationalistic. The virus of unbelief is in its veins; and it has no longer power to understand or appreciate fully, at a single point, the Mystery of Godliness, as it was seen of angels, preached to the nations, and believed on in the world, at the beginning.

Hence, the trouble this unhistorical Christianity has everywhere, with whatever comes before it as an assertion of objective grace in the institutions of the Gospel. What is exhibited as thus transcending the order of life in its natural character, is set down at once for superstition. It is, of course, then, unchurchly. A Church in the sense of the Creed—the organ through which Christ works in the world (His body), the medium of His presence among men, the home of His Spirit, the sphere of His grace—is for it no object of faith whatever, but an object rather of instinctive abhorrence and scorn. The office of the ministry flows in its view, not really, but only metaphorically, from Christ's Ascension Gift (Eph. iv: 8–12). Ordination is no investiture with a supernatural commission, proceeding from the Holy Ghost. Apostolical succession, in the case, is an idle dream. Sacraments, as such, are held to be a Romanizing abomination. For the spirit in question, the sacramental in truth, wherever it comes in its way, is a very Ithuriel's spear, the bare touch of which is enough to start it into its real shape, and make it appear the low rationalistic spirit which it is in fact. Sacraments are for it signs only of grace absent, and in no proper sense seals of grace present.

That such a theology as this should have no sympathy with

the true idea of worship in its liturgical form, results, as all can see, from its very constitution; and that it should be found arrayed now against our new Liturgy, is nothing more than what was to be expected. The conflict in the case, as already said, is a conflict of theological systems; not a controversy about a few responses, and a few outward forms (as the ridiculous fuss made in certain quarters about *Ritualism* in the German Reformed Church might seem to imply), but a controversy about doctrines and articles of faith, that strikes far beyond the German Reformed Church into the life of the entire Evangelical Protestantism of this land.

So much for the subject in its general view. The two opposing schemes of divinity are before us in a contrasted form, which even plain people, it is trusted, may be able to understand; if not with full scientific insight always at every point, yet with the insight, at least, of sound theological feeling, which is something far better. It remains now to notice briefly the theological objections made to the Liturgy at certain particular points. They will be found to resolve themselves at once into the general issue, between the two systems which have been thus far compared; and with this in view, it will be very easy to see to what they amount.

PARTICULAR OBJECTIONS.

I. It has been objected at times to the *Ordination Service* (though we heard little of this at Dayton), that it makes too much of the derivation of the office of the Ministry, by historical succession from Christ, and goes too far especially in saying, as it does p. 220, that the gift and grace of the Holy Ghost are to be looked for through the laying on of hands, for the fulfilment of its heavenly commission.

But here the question at bottom is simply, whether the Church is to be regarded at all, or not, as an objective, historical, more than merely natural constitution, carrying in itself powers and functions for its own ends, which are peculiar to itself, and not to be found anywhere else. Is it after all only like a Temperance Society or a Political Party? What business has it then among the faith mysteries of the Creed?

In the view of the Liturgy, the Church is an organization, as the Creed makes it to be, which is not simply human, but is, at the same time, also, superhuman, in virtue of its organic out-flow from the fountain head of all grace and truth in the world, the union of the divine and human in the Person of our Lord and Saviour Jesus Christ, through the mystery of the Incarnation. The organization being such, must not its organs and functions be of a corresponding character? Is the Liturgy wrong in declaring the office of the ministry to be "of divine origin, and of truly supernatural character and force, flowing directly from the Lord Jesus Christ Himself, as the fruit of His resurrection and triumphant ascension into heaven?" Is not this precisely what St. Paul teaches us, in the notable fourth chapter of his Epistle to the Ephesians? May the office come to any one, then, except from Christ, and through the order He has Himself established for handing it down in the Church? "The solemnity of ordination, then, through which this transmission flows," we are justified surely in saying with the Liturgy, "is not merely an impressive ceremony, by which the right of such as are called of God to the ministry, is owned and confessed by the Church; but it is to be considered rather as their actual investiture with the very power of the office itself, the sacramental seal of their heavenly commission, and a symbolical assurance from on high, that their consecration to the service of Christ is accepted, and that the Holy Ghost will most certainly be with them in the faithful discharge of their official duties."

Do we doubt this? Does it come as a strange, mystical, dangerously hierarchical doctrine to our ears? Then must we question, to the same extent, the reality of any such order of grace in the world, as we profess to believe every time we repeat the Creed. Ordination is a mere sham, indeed, if it be not the conveyance of power and right to exercise functions appertaining to the realm or jurisdiction in which it has place, as really as the commission of the civil magistrate is for him an investiture with qualification he would not otherwise possess, to act in the name of the government he represents. The commission in either case must have quality and force answerable to the order of authority it proceeds from; and this being more than simply human and terrestrial in the case of the Gospel, it follows that the commission here must carry with it corresponding celestial character. Such being the case, it is only part of the faith which properly belongs to the transaction, when ordination is held to be the channel of supernatural official endowment for the work of the ministry; and nothing can be more proper than that the candidate, having made good confession of his general faith previously, should have the question put to him finally: "Are you truly persuaded in your heart, that you are called of God to the office of the holy ministry, and do you desire and expect to receive, through the laying on of our hands, the gift and grace of the Holy Ghost, which shall enable you to fulfil this heavenly commission and trust?"

It goes hard with the spiritualistic system, we know, to admit anything that looks to the real presence of the supernatural in this matter of fact way. The idea of grace tied to any outward occasion as such, the Holy Ghost bound to ordinances, is for it something heterogeneous with its ordinary conception of religion as an affair of purely subjective experience. It is felt to smack of mummery and superstition. Here, especially, comes in the bugbear of priestly manipulation and tactual succession, so easy to be sneered at by the frivolous. But what mummery must it not be, in fact, to go through a form of this sort, without any belief in the reality of what it pretends to be? To insist, that, while it seems to mean much, it means in truth in itself just nothing, and is only the sign of something altogether out of and beyond itself? If ordination be more than the powwowing of Pagan superstition, it *must* involve a real clothing with office in Christ's kingdom; and this can come only from Himself through the Holy Ghost. Does the candidate believe that, and look for it, in the transaction? Do those who lay hands on Him expect it, and mean it in their own minds? If not, what business have they to be mocking high heaven with their dumb show in this way?

II. *Confession and Absolution.* Exception is taken to the form in the Liturgy, by which the minister is directed, after the General Confession, to assure such as are truly penitent, that their sins are pardoned for Christ's sake (p. 10). It breathes, we are told, an odor of sacerdotalism; and serves to break the direct, immediate relation that should hold in the case between the believer and his Lord.

Now, looking at the form itself, its terms certainly would seem to be safe enough in this view even for the most fastidious Puritanic judgment. For they only say, in fact, what any one may say, and what all are bound to believe, of God's grace toward the penitent through the Gospel. "Unto as many of you, beloved brethren," the form runs, "as truly repent of your sins, and believe in the Lord Jesus Christ, with full purpose of new obedience,"—to such and no others—"I announce and declare, by the authority and in the name of Christ"—not by my own or any other authority—"that your sins are forgiven in heaven, according to His Gospel, through the perfect merit of Jesus Christ our Lord." Is there more in this at any time, than the declaration of what is at all times and in all places true? Does it imply that the minister himself pretends to forgive sins? Does it not, in the strongest manner, say just the opposite? What better is it then than spiritualistic prudery of the most captious sort, to put on a show of being scandalized with it in any such view?

But there is more in the matter than this. The offence taken is, after all, with what lies deeper than the form. It is the instinctive working as before of the unchurchly spirit, against what is felt to come in its way here as the mediation of Divine favor through the Church. God only can forgive sins, it says with the Pharisees of old; from Him only, therefore, can we have the blessing in a direct spiritual way—His spirit touching our spirit, without any intervening medium; to conceive of any such instrumentation of His grace *on the earth,* is blasphemy and superstition. In other words, this Gnostic, rationalistic spirit eschews here, as at all other points, the mystery of an organic, objective, historical connection between the Church of Christ and the Holy Ghost; and refuses to acknowledge the Holy Ghost, the Divine in Christianity, unless in the form only of an intellectual abstraction, bound to the outward organization and order of the Church in no way whatever. Of the "forgiveness of sins," in the sense of the Creed, where it is made to be a mystery for faith holding only in the bosom of the Holy Catholic Church, the spirit in question knows nothing. How should it? Have we not seen already that it is at war with the whole Creed?

The acts of the Church, we have good reason to say, in the exercise of her proper functions, and through her proper organs, are never just the same thing with what might be done by a mere civil corporation presuming to act in the same way. To think or say so, would, indeed, be to blaspheme the Gospel. As official acts, they have in their own sphere a real force, answering to the character of the sphere, and being in fact the form in which its powers reach forward to their proposed end. Who will deny this? No one, it might seem, but an infidel.

Shall we be afraid then to say, that the official act of the minister, the organ of the Church, in blessing the people, or in pronouncing to the penitent the pardon of their sins, means something more than the same declarations would mean, made by some one else in an unofficial and common way? The minister does not originate the pardon he pronounces; neither does the Church; but the voice of the Church, nevertheless, uttered by him and through him, there where he stands in the objective bosom of this grace, may be and is of immense account for bearing the sense of it with full comfort into the believer's heart. If there are any who cannot see this, sustained as it is by the known relation of thought and word universally, and by analogies to be met with everywhere in common life, they are to be pitied for the narrowness of their thinking, rather than argued with seriously in so plain a case.

III. We turn our attention next to the doctrine of the Liturgy in regard to *Baptism*. Exception is taken to it, as teaching baptismal regeneration, substituting a mechanical ceremony for the righteousness of faith, and making a mere outward form to stand for the work of the Holy Spirit. Let us see how the matter really stands.

In somewhat bewildering contrast with this, the same service, which is thus charged with making too little of the sinner's justification, has been reproached for making a great deal too much of his original guilt and condemnation. Many at least, at the Synod at Dayton, could hardly trust their ears, when they heard a Professor of Theology, in the Reformed Church, say there, openly, that he, for his part, could not go with the Liturgy, where it speaks of deliverance of our children through baptism "from the power of the Devil;" he did not believe it to be so bad with the children of Christians naturally as that; it was enough to appeal to the common sensibilities of parents (mothers in particular), to prove the contrary! This sounds strange certainly; but it needs only a little reflection to perceive, that it is, after all, only the working out at a new point of the same false spiritualism, which finds it so hard to understand or acknowledge, on the other side, the presence of any real objective grace in baptism.

The Professor of Theology referred to taught in this case, of course, blank Pelagiansism. Here precisely lay the old theological quarrel between Pelagius and St. Augustine. Pelagius, appealing to the common sensibilities of human nature, would not allow that children are born into the world under the curse of original sin, which is the power of the Devil. St. Augustine maintained the contrary, and what is especially noticeable, confounded Pelagius most of all, by appealing to infant baptism, which could have no meaning, he said, except in the light of a deliverance from the curse of sin conceived of in this real way. So, we know, the Church, also, decided against the heresiarch and his followers; and the decision has been echoed by the orthodoxy of the Christian world, from that day down to the present. We content ourselves with quoting now simply the plain words of the Heidelberg Catechism, the symbol this Professor of Theology has bound himself as with the solemnity of an oath to teach. "By the fall and disobedience of our first parents, Adam and Eve, in Paradise," the Catechism tells us, Question 7, "our nature became so corrupt, that we are all conceived and born in sin." On this then follows the question: "But are we so far depraved, that we are wholly unapt to any good (*ganz und gar untüchtig zu einigem Guten*), and prone to all evil?" to which is thundered forth, as from Mount Sinai, the soul-shaking answer: "Yes; unless we are born again by the Spirit of God." *How* this new birth by the Spirit is brought to pass, is not here of any account; what we have to do with now is simply the witness of the Catechism to the total depravity of infants. It is plain, direct, overwhelming.

And is not this what we are taught no less plainly in the New Testament? "That which is born of the flesh," our Saviour says to Nicodemus (John iii. 6.) "is flesh"—that is, mere human nature in its fallen character, which as such cannot enter the kingdom of God, but is hopelessly on the outside of that kingdom, and so under the power of the Devil; only "that which is born of the Spirit, is spirit;" and for this reason it is, that a man must be born again, "born of water and the Spirit," in order that he may have part in this salvation. But why pursue the argument in this way? Must we go about proving at length for elders and deacons, or for the people at large, in the German Reformed Church, that the Scriptures teach the doctrine of Original Sin? The very children in our Sunday-schools have a sounder theology on this subject, than the Divinity Professor, who so exposed himself in regard to it at the Synod in Dayton.

A Pelagian anthropology leads over naturally to a spiritualistic construction of the whole Christian salvation; in which, as there is no organic power of the Devil or kingdom of darkness, for men to be delivered from, so there will be no organic redemption either, no objective, historical order of grace, in the bosom and through the power of which, this salvation is to go forward; but all will be made to resolve itself into workings of God's Spirit that are of a general character, and into processes of thought and feeling, on the part of men, with no other basis than the relations of God to man in the most common, simply humanitarian view. Is there then no organic redemption needed for men, into the sphere of which they must come first of all, in order that they may have power to become personally righteous, and so be able to work out their salvation with fear and trembling, as knowing it to be God that worketh in them both to will and to do of His own good pleassure? Has the Church been wrong in believing through all ages, that "we must be delivered from the power of darkness, and translated into the kingdom of God's dear Son" (Col. i. 13), not as the end of our personal goodness and piety, but the beginning of it, and the one necessary condition first of all, without which we can make no progress in goodness or piety whatever? Has the Church been wrong in believing, that such change of state, such transplantation from the kingdom of the Devil over into the kingdom of Christ, must in the nature of the case be a Divine act; and that as such a Divine act, it must be something more than any human thought or volition simply, stimulated into action by God's Spirit? Has the Church been wrong in believing, finally, that the Sacrament of Holy Baptism, the sacrament of initiation into the Church, was instituted, not only to signify this truth in a general way, but to seal it as a present actuality for all who are willing to accept the boon thus offered to them in the transaction?

Baptismal regeneration! our evangelical spiritualists are at once ready to exclaim. But we will not allow ourselves to be put out of course in so solemn an argument, by any catchword of this sort addressed to popular prejudice. The Liturgy avoids the ambiguous phrase; and we will do so too; for the word regeneration is made to mean, sometimes one thing, and sometimes another, and it does not come in our way at all at present to discuss these meanings. We are only concerned, that no miserable logomachy of this sort shall be allowed to cheat us out of what the sacrament has been held to be in past ages; God's act, setting apart those who are the subjects of it to His service, and bringing them within the sphere of His grace in order that they may be saved. We do not ask any one to call this regeneration; it may not suit at all his sense of the term; but we do most earnestly conjure all to hold fast to the thing, call it by what term they may. The question is simply, Doth baptism in any sense save us? That is, does it put us in the way of salvation? Has it anything to do at all with our deliverance from original sin, and our being set down in the new world of righteousness and grace, which has been brought to pass, in the midst of Satan's kingdom all around it, by our Lord Jesus Christ?

For the defence of the Liturgy it will be enough to place the matter now on the lowest ground. Our spiritualists admit that God *may* make baptism the channel of His grace—may cause the thing signified to go along with the outward sign, when He is pleased to do so; only they will not have it that His grace is in any way bound to the ordinance. Will they not admit then also, that the sacrament ought to be so used as to carry with it the benefit it represents; that God designed it to be in this way more than an empty form; and that it is the duty of all, therefore, to desire and expect through it what it thus, by Divine appointment, holds out to expectation? Who will be so bold as to say, in so many words, that baptism means no deliverance whatever from the power of sin, and that it is superstition to come looking for anything of this sort from it? Why then quarrel with the Liturgy for making earnest with the objective force of the sacrament in this view?

"You present this child here," it is said, "and do seek for him deliverance from the power of the Devil, the remission of sin, and the gift of a new and spiritual life by the Holy Ghost, through the Sacrament of Baptism, which Christ hath ordained for the communication of such great grace." Is it not true, that the sacrament has been ordained for that purpose, even if this be not exclusively or necessarily bound to its administration? If not, for what other purpose under heaven was it ordained? And if for this purpose, why should those who come to the ordinance, not come seeking what it holds out in this way to the view of faith? Are they to come seeking nothing, expecting nothing, believing nothing? Or if otherwise, in the name of all common sense, tell us, O ye Gnostic dreamers, ye zealous contenders against formalities and forms, what then *are* they to seek?

The Liturgy, we allow, however, goes beyond this low view of the mere possibility of grace through the sacrament; it affirms that God, on His part, makes it to be always objectively just what it means. In other works, it teaches the reality of sacramental grace; and sees in it a birth-right title to all the blessings of the new covenant. This does not mean, that it regenerates or converts any one in the modern Methodistic sense of these terms; that it saves people by magic; or that it makes their final salvation sure in any way. Like Esau's birthright, it may be neglected, despised, parted with for a mess of pottage. But all this does not touch the question of its intrinsic value, in its own order; as being a real Divine gift and power of Sonship, nevertheless, in the family of God, for which all the treasures of the earth should be counted a poor and mean exchange.

On this subject of baptismal grace, then, we wlll enter into no compromise with the anti-liturgical theology we have now in hand. In seeking to make the Liturgy wrong, it has only shown itself wrong; and the more its errors are probed, the more are they found to be indeed, "wounds, and bruises, and putrefying sores." Starting with Pelagianism on one side, it lands us swiftly in downright Rationalism on the other. "It is impossible," says the distinguished French Reformed divine, Pressensé, in a late article, "to establish the necessity of infant baptism, except upon the ground that baptism imparts a special grace." We are most decidedly of the same opinion; and for this reason we denounce this theology as in reality, whatever it may be in profession, hostile to infant baptism, and unfriendly, therefore, to the whole idea of educational religion as this has been based upon it in the Reformed Church from the beginning. Without the conception of baptismal grace going along with the baptism of infants, there can be no room properly for confirmation; and the catechetical training which is employed to prepare the way for this, may easily come then to seem a hinderance rather than a help, to the true conversion of the young to God. Then it will be well, if baptism fall not into general contempt, and so be brought to sink finally more and more into neglect altogether. To what a pass things have already come in this respect throughout our country, by reason of the baptistic spirit which is among us, and the general theological tendency we are now considering, we will not now take time to decide. Those who have eyes to see, can see for themselves.

IV. Office for the *Holy Communion*. The central character of this service, ruling as it ought to do the whole Order of worship to which it belongs, must make it of course specially objectionable to the anti-liturgical spirit with which we are now dealing.

Particular fault has sometimes been found with the consecratory prayer in the service, as teaching a real union between Christ and the elements representing His body and blood, differing altogether from the proper Reformed doctrine on this mysterious subject. A certain Doctor of Divinity went so far at Dayton as to say, that it amounted in full to the Roman Catholic dogma of transubstantiation. But in this the Doctor of Divinity was egregiously mistaken, as in many things besides. The doctrine of the Liturgy in that prayer is not Popish, and not Lutheran, but strictly Reformed. Not to be sure Reformed in the modern Puritan sense, in which too plainly this unliturgical spirit finds its familiar home; but Reformed in the old Calvinistic sense, as this entered into the symbols of the Reformed Church generally in the sixteenth century.

It is not true that this proper Reformed doctrine made the Lord's Supper to be only a commemorative ordinance, calling to mind the fact of His death. It made it to be this; but it made it to be also the medium of a real mystical communion with this glorified life. It saw in it, not a sign only, but a sacrament; the conjunction of visible elements with the invisible represented by them, in such sort that the presence of the one could be said to involve the presence also of the other—not locally of course, but dynamically and with full virtue and effect —through the wonder-working power of the Holy Ghost. This we have abundantly shown years ago in our tract against Dr. Hodge, entitled, "The Doctrine of the Reformed Church on the Presence of Christ in the Lord's Supper;" an argument, which no one has ever yet pretended to meet, and whose historical force at least never can be overthrown; however convenient it may be for Puritanic divinity to go on repeating its traditionary song on this subject, as though history had nothing do with the matter whatever.

Now it is this old Reformed doctrine, we affirm, and no other, which is involved in the consecratory prayer of the Liturgy. Any one at all familiar with the Calvinistic terminology in regard to it, can see that it is faithfully followed at every point. It would be hard, indeed, to give the doctrine more succinctly or exactly in the same compass. God is called upon to "send down the powerful benediction of His Holy Spirit" upon the elements, "that being set apart now from a common to a sacred and mystical use, they may exhibit and represent" —these being the very terms made use of by Calvin to distinguish the Reformed doctrine from the Lutheran; may *exhibit* and *represent* "to us with true effect"—that is, not corporeally, and yet not simply in sign or shadow either, but with the energy of actual presence—"the Body and Blood of His Son, Jesus Christ; so that in the use of them"—mark again the distinction; not in the elements themselves outwardly considered, but in the use of them, that is, in the sacramental transaction, "we may be made, through the power of the Holy Ghost"—again the Calvinistic or Reformed qualification— "to partake really and truly of His blessed life, whereby only we can be saved from death, and raised to immortality at the last day."

In the face of all this, what are we to think of a Doctor of Divinity, who could stand up and say, that the Liturgy in this prayer teaches the doctrine of transubstantiation?

What are we to think of the same Doctor of Divinity, when we find him thrumming on the expression, "this memorial of the blessed sacrifice of Thy Son," in the next following prayer; as though it said *memorial sacrifice,* and meant all that is held offensive in the Roman Catholic so called sacrifice of the mass! Alas, alas, for the Liturgy, in the hands of theological criticism so utterly untheological as this!

A truce, however, to these quibbles about particular terms. The real controversy here is with the Communion service as a whole; and it turns upon the sacramental doctrine which underlies it throughout, and which in this way conditions the universal sense of the Liturgy. This anti-liturgical theology, not centering in the Incarnation, not dwelling in the bosom of the Creed, having no sense for objective historical Christianity, and no sense for the Church, can have at the same time of course no sense for the sacramental in its true form. For what is a sacrament? The visible exhibition of an invisible grace— a mystery in this view, where the visible and invisible are brought together, and held together, not simply in man's thought, but in God's power, by a bond holding beyond nature altogether in the supernatural order of grace. Does Puritanism believe this? Not at all. It will know no sacrament, save in the intelligible form of a sign, which simply represents and calls to mind what God does for men spiritually, and on the outside of the sacrament altogether. We have just seen what becomes of the Sacrament of Baptism in the hands of this spiritualistic scheme. And now it is only what might be expected, to find it bent on taking away our Lord from us after the same fashion, in the Holy Eucharist.

The Liturgy stands as a protest and defence against this sacrilege. It gives us the true Reformed view of Christ's presence in the Lord's Supper, in a form answering at the same time to the faith and worship of the Primitive Church. It teaches, that the Lord's Supper is more than an outward sign, and more than a mere calling to mind of our Saviour's death as something past and gone. It teaches, that the value of Christ's sacrifice never dies, but is perennially continued in the power of His life. It teaches, that the outward side of the sacrament is mystically bound by the Holy Ghost to its inward invisible side; not fancifully, but really and truly; so that the undying power of Christ's life and sacrifice are there, in the transaction, for all who take part in it with faith. It teaches, that it is our duty to appropriate this grace, and to bring it before God (the "memorial of the blessed sacrifice of His Son"), as the only ground of our trust and confidence in His presence. All this the Liturgy teaches. Who will say that it wrongs, in doing so, the sacramental doctrine of the Reformed Church? Are we then to have no sacraments? Must we plunge into the full abyss of Rationalism?

We now stop. Our general task is done. Enough has been said, to show how things stand between the New Liturgy and its theological opposers. We are willing to submit the case to the common intelligence of our churches. Even the West must yet come, we think, to see eye to eye here with the East. To the people at large we say: Look now on this picture, and now on that; and judge ye for your own selves, which of these theological schemes may be safest and best for the German Reformed Church to take to her bosom at the present time.

EDITORIAL INTRODUCTION TO THE LETTER TO DR. HENRY HARBAUGH

The intent of the letter addressed to Dr. Nevin by Dr. Har-
baugh is unknown. The archives of the Evangelical and Reformed
Historical Society do not have the original letter addressed to
Dr. Nevin. Nor is the letter by Dr. Nevin dated. We know that
it was written after 1860 for it was in that year that Henry
Harbaugh received the Doctor of Divinity degree from Union
College.

While a student at Marshall College and the Seminary at
Mercersburg, Henry Harbaugh (1817-1967) was greatly influenced
by John Williamson Nevin. He became an outstanding pastor at
Lancaster and Lebanon. He was also a gifted author, poet and
editor. In the fall of 1863 he was elected to the chair of
Didactic and Practical Theology at the Seminary.

He served on the Liturgical Committee which produced the
Provisional Liturgy of 1857 and the *Order of Worship*, 1866. He
was a spokesman and interpreter of Mercersburg Theology.

The letter outlines the salient thoughts of Mercersburg
as summarized by Dr. Nevin.

LETTER TO DR. HENRY HARBAUGH

Rev. Dr. Harbaugh. Please receive the foregoing sketch to
be transcribed as you propose. Your letter reached me on Mon-
day, and I had no time to attend to it before night. I have
hurried the article, to have it ready to send to you on Tuesday
morning. I have compressed it so as to keep within what I
suppose to be the bounds you mention.

Yours,

J. W. Nevin

What is called the "Mercersburg System of Theology" grew
into shape without calculation or plan. It owes its existence
properly not to any spirit of philosophical speculation as has
been sometimes imagined, but to an active interest in practical
Christianity. Questions of religious life have governed in
succession the course of its history. Still those have moved,
with more or less insight always, round a common centre; and
the system is found to be accordingly in the end sufficiently
scientific, and in full harmony with itself throughout.

Historically it may be said to have commenced with the
publication in 1843 of the *Anxious Bench* - a tract, which found
wide favor, but drew upon its author at the same time in certain quarters a perfect hurricane of reproach. Then came the
sermon on *Church Unity* preached by Dr. Nevin at the opening of
the Triennial Convention of the Reformed Dutch and German Reformed Churches held at Harrisburg in the year 1844; a discourse sanctioned by the full approbation of the worthy representatives of both Churches at the time, the positions of which,

408

however, on the subject of the Mystical Union and in opposition
to the sect system, were felt by many afterwards to involve a
dangerous *tendency*. Dr. Schaff's memorable *Principle of Protestantism* published in 1845, brought out the tendency, in the
apprehension of such persons, under still more alarming proportions. This was followed, the next year, by the *Mystical Presence*, with a translation of Dr. Ullman's most masterly tract on
The Distinctive Character of Christianity prefixed in the form
of a Preliminary Essay. The work was a vindication at large
of the old Calvinistic Doctrine of the Lord's Supper, conveying
against the general Protestantism of the present time a charge
of wholesale defection from the Protestant sacramental faith of
the sixteenth century. The tract *Antichrist* was a regular
assault upon the sect system, as being in full antagonism to
the true idea of the Church, and such a heresy as draws after
it virtually in the end a Gnostic denial of the proper mystery
of the Incarnation itself. As the occasions of Theological
discussion were multiplied, it was felt necessary to establish
a special organ for carrying it forward; the more so as it
seemed altogether impractical to gain a fair hearing in any
other quarter. Hence, the *Mercersburg Review* the pages of
which for some years form a sort of progressive picture of the
system to whose exposition and defence it has been all along
devoted. So much for the general history of the movement. We
come now to what is more important, the organization of inward
structure of the Mercersburg System regarded as a whole.

Its cardinal principle is the fact of the Incarnation.
This viewed not as a doctrine or speculation but as a real
transaction of God in the world, is regarded as being necessarily itself the essence of Christianity, the sum and substance
of the whole Christian redemption. Christ saves the world, not
ultimately by what he teaches or by what he does, but by what
he *is* in the constitution of his own person. His person in its

relations to the world carries in it the power of victory over
sin, death, and hell, the force thus of a real atonement or
reconciliation between God and man, the triumph of a glorious
resurrection from the dead, and all the consequences for faith
which are attributed to this in the grand old symbol called the
Apostles' Creed. In the most literal sense accordingly Christ
is here held to be the "way, the truth and the life," the "resurrection and the life," the principle of "life and immortality" - the "light" of the world, its "righteousness," and its
"peace." The "grace which brings salvation" in this view is of
course always a real affluence from the new order of existence,
which has been thus made to be by the exaltation of the Word
made flesh at the right hand of God. It must be supernatural
as well as natural, and the organs and agencies by which it
works must in the nature of the case carry with them objectively some thing of the same character and force. To resolve all
into the opinions and feelings of those who call themselves
believers, is to do away with the proper objects of faith altogether; for these must be apprehended as actually at hand under
a supernatural form. They are all mysteries, holding in them
objectively some measure of what belongs to the mystery of
Christ's glorification. In this way the Church is an object of
faith - the presence of a new creation in the old world of nature - the body of Christ through which as a medium and organ
he reveals himself and works till the end of time. Its ministers hold a divine power from him by apostolical succession.
Its sacraments are not signs merely, but goals of the grace
they represent. Baptism is for the remission of sins. The
Eucharist includes the real presence of Christ's whole glorified life, in a mystery, by the power of the Holy Ghost. The
idea of the Church, so sound, it is made to be in this way an
object of faith, involves necessarily the attributes which were
always ascribed to it in the beginning, unity, sanctity, cath-

olicity, and apostolicity. The spirit of sect, as it cleaves to Protestantism at the present time, is a very great evil, which is of itself sufficient to show that if Protestantism had any historical justification in the beginning, its mission thus far has been only half fulfilled, and that it can be rationally approved only as it is taken to be an interimistic preparation for some higher and better form of Christianity hereafter.

The distinguishing character of the Mercersburg Theology, in one word, is its Christological interest, its way of looking at all things through the Person of the crucified and risen Saviour. This, as the world now stands, embraces necessarily all that enters into the conception of the Church Question - the problem of problems for the Christianity of the present time. That the system has been able to solve in full the difficulties belonging to this great subject, its friends have never pretended for one moment to imagine. On the contrary, they have always confessed their sense of vast practical embarrassment confronting their views. But they have not considered this a sufficient reason for refusing to affirm what has appeared to them to be biblically or historically true, in spite of such inconvenience. Facts and principles have a right to challenge attention at times, even if no satisfactory scheme can be offered for their application. The Mercersburg Theology claims the advantage of standing here, in its main positions, on the same ground with the faith of the early Church. Its Christology is that of the ancient Creeds. It insists on casting the Christian belief of the world still in the same primitive mould; and the burden of its controversy with those who stand opposed to it is that they either ignore the Apostles' Creed altogether or else make no earnest with its proper historical sense, but vainly imagine that it may be superseded or mended by other modern forms of confession, more suited to their own unchurchly sense.

In thus agreeing with the Creed, the system of course
holds itself·to be to the same extent in full agreement with
the proper sense of the Scriptures; where in truth all stress
is laid on the Person of Christ, on his resurrection from the
dead, on his glorification at the right hand of God, on the
sending of the Holy Ghost, and on his presence and working
through all time in the Church which is his body, the fulness
of Him that filleth all in all.

                                        Dr. Nevin

To Ruthann Cochran
Installation 4/19/98
Love, Steve Wagler

PITTSBURGH ORIGINAL TEXTS & TRANSLATIONS SERIES

Remember the Mercersburgers!
This was one of 2 copies in my library — forgive
the Notes + underlines!

General Editor

Dikran Y. Hadidian

3

CATHOLIC AND REFORMED

SELECTED THEOLOGICAL WRITINGS OF JOHN WILLIAMSON NEVIN